Defaming
the Dead

Defaming the Dead

DON HERZOG

Yale UNIVERSITY PRESS

New Haven and London

Published with assistance from the foundation established in memory of Calvin Chapin of the Class of 1788, Yale College.

Yale University Press books may be purchased in quantity for educational, business, or promotional use. For information, please e-mail sales.press@yale.edu (U.S. office) or sales@yaleup.co.uk (U.K. office).

Set in Minion type by Integrated Publishing Solutions.
Printed in the United States of America.

Library of Congress Control Number: 2016947904
ISBN: 978-0-300-22154-1 (hardcover : alk. paper)

A catalogue record for this book is available from the British Library.

For the University of Michigan Law School

The just and proper jealousy with which the law protects the reputation of a living man forms a curious contrast to its impotence when the good name of a dead man is attacked. When a man dies, the law will secure that any reasonable provision which he has made for the disposal of his property is duly carried into effect and that his money shall pass to those whom he has selected as his heirs. He leaves behind him a reputation as well as an estate, but the law, so zealous in its regard for the material things, has no protection to give to that which the dead man regarded as a more precious possession than money or lands.

The dead cannot raise a libel action, and it is possible to bring grave charges against their memory without being called upon to justify these charges in a court of law or to risk penalties for slander and defamation. The possibilities of injustice are obvious.

—"LIBELLING THE DEAD," *GLASGOW HERALD* (27 JULY 1926)

Contents

Preface

Rhode Island has a curious statute. It says that if you're defamed in an obituary within three months of your death, your estate can sue. Why curious? Because as far as I know, it's the only such law in the United States. Any journalist will assure you it's axiomatic that there's no such thing as defaming the dead. Not that it's impossible to publish false statements of fact that damage their reputations: nothing easier. Rather that once you're dead, tort law will not protect your reputation. Except, in this severely limited way, in Rhode Island.

I think that's lamentable. I think we have reputational interests that survive our deaths. And I think tort law ought to protect them.

I have five aims in this book. One: I want to develop the case for tort reform. It might seem quixotic to offer any expansion of tort liability, given laments about the greedy plaintiff's bar, out-of-control damage awards, and the like. But I'm serious. I think Rhode Island shouldn't be alone. Indeed I think its statute is too narrow.

Two: I want to deepen and vindicate what's now sometimes dismissed as a quaintly old-fashioned or contemptibly obscure view of tort. I think tort is private law. Not just in the nominal sense that the typical tort suit features one private party suing another. Rather in the richer sense that tort is about private wrongs, not public interests. Tort isn't "really" about promoting efficiency or making sound social policy or anything like that. It actually is just what it looks like on its face.

Three: in a parallel register—but I'd be reluctant to say one is just the application of the other—I want to rebut the claim that finally all we care about, or should care about, are consequences. Various independent commitments often travel together under that rubric. I'll be terse here and throughout, but there is much more to moral and political theory than finding strategies to maximize good across the population or incentivize more optimal conduct. The best way to undercut the appeal of consequentialism, I suspect, isn't to offer a rival abstract view: much of what we evoke by talking about expressive dimensions or deontological side constraints is unhappily vague. It's to press its deficiencies in a concrete context—and exhibit an alternative as more promising.

Four: I want to offer an account of posthumous interests, which have seemed to some writers hard or impossible to make sense of. I take skepticism here seriously; I do my best to dramatize and support it. But I also try to show it's misguided.

Five: I want to show that we can greatly enrich our understanding of theoretical puzzles by immersing ourselves in historical cases, social practice, and legal doctrines. I have nothing against what philosophers call intuition pumps: I begin with one and recur to it repeatedly. But I worry about relying solely on extravagant examples that spin free of the nitty-gritty contours of our social lives. That's an exercise better suited to displaying the ingenuity of the author than to sharpening our grasp of the world. Then too, the conventional division in political theory between those with normative and those with historical interests is dispiriting. We can appraise historical moves as attempts to solve problems—and we can wonder if they've outlived their justifications. These aims are connected. If you like, you can think of them as five aspects of one agenda, and I won't mind if you label that agenda pragmatist. But I waste neither a moment of yours nor a syllable of mine on any metatheoretical defense of my approach.

I'm a political theorist, not a lawyer; but I've been teaching at the University of Michigan Law School for over twenty-five years now. For many years, I've taught first amendment and torts. In 2009, I taught a seminar on defamation, which got me started thinking seriously about these issues. The law school is a wonderful place: thanks to generations of my students and my colleagues for being so smart and savvy. I've quipped that I was abandoned as a foundling on the law school's steps and they took me in and raised me. I'm delighted to dedicate this book to the institution.

I presented an earlier, abbreviated, and sadly cryptic version of this argument to my colleagues at Michigan, to John Goldberg and Henry Smith's private law workshop at Harvard, and as the 2013–14 Kadish Lecture at Berkeley. I presented a relatively finished version of chapter 5 at Penn. Thanks to attentive audiences for encouraging me to persevere. That's how I chose to construe their incredulity, anyway.

Doug Dion, George Fisher, John Goldberg, Scott Hershovitz, Jill Horwitz, Webb Keane, Daryl Levinson, Peggy McCracken, Nina Mendelson, Bill Miller, Marguerite Moeller,

Julian Davis Mortenson, Sasha Natapoff, Len Niehoff, Adela Pinch, Jane Schacter, Carl Schneider, Andy Stark, and Hannah Swanson commented on earlier drafts of part or all of this work. Warm thanks for their generosity and insight.

Defaming
the Dead

I

Embezzled, Diddled, and Popped

L et's begin cheerfully: you've just died. Yes, Freud insists that "it is indeed impossible to imagine our own death; and whenever we attempt to do so we can perceive that we are in fact still present as spectators."[1] But I'll trust you to distinguish that imaginary spectator from your actual dead self.

So you're dead—and your funeral isn't going well. Sure, everything seems fine. There's an inspiring turnout: cousins have flown in, old friends scattered across the globe, too; more than a handful of colleagues from work have shown up; a smattering of neighbors sit there sternly. The décor is—well, I was going to describe the flowers, but let's say instead that the décor is whatever you think best. The minister—if that's who you'd want—celebrates your piety, your devotion to your family, your volunteer work for countless charities. But some guy

---

1. "Thoughts for the Times on War and Death," in *The Standard Edition of the Complete Psychological Works of Sigmund Freud,* ed. James Strachey, 24 vols. (London: Hogarth Press and the Institute of Psychoanalysis, 1953–74), 14:288.

in the back rolls his eyes. He leans over to the woman next to him and grumbles, "Bullshit. Try this: Embezzled money at work. Diddled children in the park. Popped kittens in the microwave for fun." Wide-eyed, she whispers, "*Really?*" "You bet," he assures her. Your family and close friends, sitting in the front, are dutifully absorbed in the ceremony, or maybe (better yet?) ignoring it, instead rapt in their emotions, in a swirl of memories, not yet fretting about their own mortality, still less jubilantly congratulating themselves on outliving you. So they don't hear this guy's lurid charge—yet.

That wide-eyed woman is talkative, despite our usual tendency to sanitize the dead. Some people caustically reject her story. Others believe it. Your family is blissfully unaware for a few weeks, but then a malicious friend insists they should know who's saying what—in grisly detail. They're horrified: the allegations are false. And factual. And defamatory. So it looks like a textbook case of slander. Indeed the claim that you committed important crimes makes this slander *per se.* That means that the common law wouldn't have required your estate to present evidence of special damages—if the law thought the dead had reputational interests. But the common law didn't. Today's law doesn't either.

I will be mining the law to probe some puzzles, but not yet. First try this: is the lurid story at your funeral an injury to you? No, not to your family, though I grant they'll suffer if the story circulates and is believed. They'll suffer emotional distress and probably more. Your daughter's fiancé may break off the engagement. (No, sorry, you may not protest that the law has abandoned amatory torts, because we're not up to the law yet.) Your son's employer might fire him. (And no, sorry, you may not protest that in a world of at-will employment this would be fine, and any suit against the slanderers on this action wouldn't get off the ground, maybe for duty reasons, maybe because the employer's act would be a superseding cause. We're not up to the law yet.) I want to know if *you* are injured.

I think you are. But some will be skeptical. "Look," says the skeptic, "I'm dead. It's over. I no longer have any interests at all, so I can't have any reputational interests. I don't have any welfare, don't enjoy any utility or preference satisfaction, don't have any plans or projects I can advance or that can be set back. So there's nothing for the concept of injury to get a grip on. I don't believe my soul is peering down—or up—wondering what happens after my funeral. When I die, I really die, all the way."

Is the skeptic indifferent to whether he's defamed at his funeral? He pauses. "Well," he ventures, "I guess I still care about how my family and friends do. My being defamed would be bad for them. So no, I'm not indifferent. I don't want it to happen."

There are subtleties here about time and knowledge worth sorting out. While alive, the skeptic disapproves the world in which he's defamed after his death, because he cringes at the thought of the suffering it will cause his loved ones. But they won't be suffering until after his death. What's it to him? Why does he care? Why *should* he care? *Après lui, le déluge:* why is caring about what happens to those still lumbering above ground any different from caring about those whose corpses are being munched by earthworms? If he's still cringing, why shouldn't he console himself that he'll never know? Is the problem just that he does know what the future holds? If he could swallow an amnesia pill and push this bit of distressing knowledge out of his head, would that solve the problem?

Consider Samuel Scheffler's striking argument that if you knew that humanity would somehow come to an end within a few generations after your death, you'd lose interest in all sorts of things you now value.[2] Nor, Scheffler holds, is this some odd or indefensible causal effect. Humanity's impending end counts as a good reason to think there's something futile about pressing on. I think Scheffler is exactly right about this. The presence of oxygen, Scheffler notes, is a causal precondition of things mattering to us, because we'd be dead without it.[3] But he doesn't suggest that there is an important respect in which oxygen matters to us more than our own survival. One might think that the future survival of humanity is in this way precisely like oxygen: "I can see that I'd lose interest in all kinds of projects without it, but I can't see why I should." We may be good at thrusting the prospect of our own deaths out of our minds—whether that thrusting is good for us is another matter—but we also know that it's a settled fact we will die. It isn't profoundly disorienting, Scheffler thinks, as it is to think of an asteroid smashing into the planet and destroying all human life, or all human beings somehow becoming infertile and the species gradually winding down. So far, one might insist, so causal. We shift into the register of reasons with the thought that the newfound sense of futility is a suitable response, on reflection, to humanity's coming doom. What's the point, you might properly think, of persisting when everything we care about will collapse? For Scheffler's view to have bite, that thought has to be distinguished from two views that flank it. One: what's the point of persisting if the universe will collapse in billions or trillions of years? Two: what's the point

2. Samuel Scheffler, *Death and the Afterlife,* ed. Niko Kolodny (Oxford: Oxford University Press, 2013).

3. Scheffler, *Death,* 26.

of persisting given that *I'm* going to die? Isn't action itself finally quixotic?

One might demur that it's odd to say that "there is an important and neglected respect in which the survival of humanity as a whole matters more to us than our own survival."[4] One might suggest that it's more apt to think of humanity's survival, for some good long while after one's own death, as a precondition of what we value, or even the very business of valuing. Scheffler doesn't mean that we are or should be more devoted to the interests of future generations than to our own. The important and neglected respect he has in mind is "that we are more dependent for our equanimity on our confidence in the survival of humanity than on our confidence in our own survival."[5] There are no guarantees here about the right reaction, and I don't think Scheffler thinks there are, either. We can imagine that it's also reasonable to doggedly continue in familiar paths—damn the future torpedoes!—and even to think that you redeem your dignity if you keep calm and carry on. Perhaps it's easier to appreciate this vantage point if we give the scenario a Bayesian tweak. Instead of stipulating that you know that humanity is coming to an end soon, suppose we say that you have some more or less well-founded probability estimate that it is. Suppose you are only 90 percent confident about the coming disaster. You assign a 10 percent likelihood to the prospect that somehow humanity will survive. You might then well think that you should carry in with your usual plans. Then play limbo with the 10 percent figure and notice that as low as you go, even to zero, it might seem reasonable to persevere.

4. Scheffler, *Death*, 83.
5. Scheffler, *Death*, 77; and see 48, 63.

Back to the subtleties about time and knowledge. Scheffler invites us to think about how we'd react to the news that humanity will soon come to an end. The scenario tracks our beliefs, not the actual state of affairs in the future. So it's worth pausing to pry apart what really is going to happen from what we believe is going to happen. I'll set aside patently unreasonable beliefs. Suppose for instance that you decide for no reason at all, or maybe on the most frivolous grounds—you've gotten excited about an opaque passage in Nostradamus—that when you would be 119 years old, the planet will explode. You will presumably lose interest in at least some pursuits that previously engaged you. If you were, say, researching pancreatic cancer, you will think, "Who gives a damn if pancreatic cancer could be cured some decades from now? No one will be around anyway." But it's easy here to say your loss of interest in your work is a mistake, pure and simple. You're properly the object of pity—or contempt.

Suppose now that you reasonably believe that humanity is coming to an end. Leading astronomers have agreed that an unpleasantly massive asteroid will collide with the earth in seventy-one years; NASA sees no way to deflect or destroy it. These predictions are wrong, but they're the best science has to offer. Scheffler-style futility kicks in anyway. You can defend it as a perfectly reasonable response: there's nothing epistemically suspect about how you adopted this belief. The omniscient observer would counsel you against it, but in his usual annoying style, he's unavailable. There's a sense in which it's a shame that you've given up, but that too trades on an epistemically unavailable or unreasonable perspective. Suppose someone accosts you: "Life is still worth living! Work is still worth doing!" She might be denying Scheffler's thesis or thinking there is dignity in carrying on as if the world weren't ending;

she might be especially stubborn at winning our game of limbo. But suppose she doesn't believe the reports about the asteroid, for epistemically indefensible reasons or no reasons at all. Given what you reasonably believe, you will properly shrug off her advice.

Suppose conversely that humanity will come to an end, but the process is opaque: a burst of previously unknown radiation which none of our devices can detect will kill all life on earth. Right up until the end, you will reasonably go about your everyday business. Again, no omniscient observer will sidle up to confide in you the real truth; again, you'd rightly dismiss jeremiads as unfounded nonsense.

Here's why I've paused to pry apart your reasonable beliefs about the future from the actual future. Abstractly, my question—is it bad to be defamed after you die?—resembles Scheffler's question. Both are attempts to elicit the intuition that your well-being can be affected by events after you die. But Scheffler's futility thesis is tracking your reasonable beliefs while you're still alive, not the actual state of affairs. Now recall the suggestion that being defamed after one's death might be bad for one's friends. Scrutinize the sentiment I inserted in the skeptic's mouth—"I guess I still care about how my family and friends do; my being defamed is going to be bad for them"— and ask the now-canonical Watergate question: what did he know and when did he know it? We might picture him as still alive, contemplating the time after he dies and knowing or reasonably believing that he'll then be defamed. Maybe he was peripherally involved in shadowy financial dealings at his firm, and though he was entirely innocent, they smell putrid, and he expects people to have a field day maliciously spinning the tale after he dies, even though they're discreetly silent while he's alive. Now we can begin to paint this picture, but I'll leave it a sketch: while alive, he is worse off, at least emotionally, because he knows or reasonably believes that his friends and family will be harmed after his death by his being defamed. He cares about them; he wants their lives to go well after he dies. Maybe the poignant thought that he'll be unhelpfully absent from the scene adds an extra layer of distress.

Such a picture would redeem the claim that it's bad for you to be defamed at your funeral. But I want to contrast Scheffler's enquiry with my own. Scheffler imagines us, here, now, knowing or anyway reasonably believing that the dooms-day scenario will come true sometime soonish. I want to ratchet up the stakes by answering the Watergate query this way: while alive, you don't know that you'll be defamed when you're dead. You don't even have any reason to believe it. So I mean to rule out the picture I just sketched.

I want to know whether you're injured when you're de-famed at your funeral *and you had no reason to think that was coming.* That's why I've positioned you as already dead, not as living and considering how you feel now about something that might happen after your death. So when I suggest that we care that being defamed at our funerals would be bad for our fam-ily and friends, I don't want to capture the thought you might have right now, reading, that you object to that future. I grant that the skeptic can identify some reason it's rational to worry about being defamed when he's dead because of how it re-dounds on his loved ones, but irrational to worry about how it redounds on himself. "*They'll* still have interests," he points out, "and I *now* care about whether they'll flourish or not, even though I won't be around to see it. Look, I don't pump up my air conditioning and shrug at global warming as something that will matter only after I'm dead. It's not only my loved ones.

I want humanity to do well. But humanity doesn't have anything at stake in whether I'm defamed. Only my loved ones do."

But again I want to rule out that thought as unresponsive. Instead, I want to ask why it should matter to you if something bad happens to people you cared about when you were alive, but it happens after you die and you had no reason to think it was coming. Imagine yourself as a hypothetical spectator at your own funeral, but not as your still living self pondering that future possibility.

So too I want to block another line of response that tries to loop back from the posthumous defamation to your welfare while still alive. The defamation at your funeral might reveal something about your life. Not the fact that you actually embezzled money or diddled children, because I'm stipulating that such charges are false. Still, that people are willing to press them, that some would believe them, might well count as evidence that you weren't as highly esteemed as you'd imagined. "I thought these people were my friends," your dead self might comment dolefully, if it could comment at all. "I thought they had a surer grasp of my character. If they could fall for these repulsive stories, what must they have actually thought of me all those years? What must they have been saying—and doing—while I was still alive?"

Does this response show that the defamation makes you worse off? That will depend on how we conceive of welfare. If, following a distinguished view in classical utilitarianism, you think welfare just consists, or bottoms out, in agreeable or desirable consciousness,[6] then you'll be inclined to think that it

6. Henry Sidgwick, *The Methods of Ethics,* 7th ed. (London: Macmillan, 1907), 396–400. Sidgwick wants to press this view about "ultimate good,"

was a good thing you spent your whole life confused in this way. You'll be inclined to think that blissful ignorance is worrisome only if it gets punctured. (Its being fragile would be worrisome *ex ante*, but irrelevant if you manage luckily to stumble through without any puncturing.) Even then, you'd want to sum the enhanced agreeable consciousness you enjoyed while suffering—enjoying—the illusion and whatever mortification surrounds its puncturing, and consider whether you'd have experienced more or less agreeable consciousness over time had you been well informed from the beginning.

But if you think welfare at least has to include considerations besides your subjective experience, you'll be inclined to reject this view. There's still room to embrace blissful ignorance. Suppose some facts are so shattering that if you ever learned them, you'd never regroup. So maybe you'd be better off if you didn't know that your friends and family thought you were a scoundrel, that your partner was cheating on you, that your best friend fathered your second child. . . . But that's different from thinking that in principle blissful ignorance is nothing to worry about, or is actually choiceworthy, or again is worrisome only if the collapse turns out to be on balance a felicific loser. Still, let's distinguish your (hypothetical dead self's) newly vivid appreciation of the facts about your life from whether you're any worse off. I agree that you've learned you weren't as well off during your life as you thought you were. In that way the defamation is newsworthy: it reveals an independent fact. But I want to know if the circulation of the charge that you

---

not welfare. In some contexts this would matter: one might think his is the best account of welfare but insist that ultimate good is something else, or anyway includes components besides welfare. I set aside these complications as irrelevant here.

embezzled, diddled, and popped actually makes you worse off—whether it *changes* the facts.

If you're still trying to reconstruct the intuition that the real injured parties are your family and friends, then that somehow transfers into an injury to you, I can make matters bleaker. Let's strip you of loved ones. You never married or had children. Your birth family is already dead. Your more distant relatives don't know you well and don't much care. If you ever had close friends, they're already dead too. I could pause to let you complain that my conscripting you in this increasingly dreary hypothetical is unfair, even repellent, but I won't: it helps isolate the question whether the defamation at your funeral—you're not such a loner than no one shows—is an injury to you, as against to those living people you actually cherish.

"Okay," concedes the skeptic, "if that's the hypo, it doesn't matter whether I'm defamed. Because I'm dead." So if it doesn't matter whether he's defamed, he's strictly speaking indifferent to whether he is, right? "Okay. Right." So if he's indifferent to whether he's defamed, he *prefers* the world in which he is defamed, as vividly as I can imagine, as long as the French fries he's going to eat two weeks from Thursday—hell, two *years* from Thursday—are marginally better than the French fries he'd otherwise get. The skeptic might respond that he's already declared his interests in the future: he doesn't crank up his air conditioning on the theory that global warming will become bothersome only after he dies. So here he might insist that he dislikes the future world in which someone says something flagrantly false. But I want to know if it's good *for him* to take the better French fries and the defamation. Does prudence or self-interest dictate that choice?

Are you wondering whether such a trivial welfare benefit would really outweigh the hideous defamations circulating after you die? But it has to if you're indifferent to the defamation. If posthumous defamation is weightless, of no moment to you, it looks like it has to be outweighed by that slight improvement in the French fries. In fact it looks like it would then be *irrational* to prefer (1) not being defamed and getting worse French fries to (2) being defamed and getting better French fries.

At the risk of impiety, let's stipulate that you don't enjoy any consciousness, agreeable or disagreeable, after you die. I renounce any appeal to religion or the afterlife, here and throughout this book. Let's stipulate too that you have no magical ability to reach back and revise the timbre of consciousness of your actual life with this unhappy new information of what others are willing to say, and apparently to believe, about you. Then if welfare is exclusively a matter of agreeable consciousness and injury is exclusively a matter of reducing welfare, being defamed at your funeral can't conceivably injure you. If welfare is more than agreeable consciousness, the stipulations don't bar the possibility that being defamed at your funeral injures you.

"What I don't know," the skeptic now announces, "doesn't hurt me." But I want to put more pressure on the thought that there's nothing wrong with blissful ignorance, because I think that that announcement is silly. (And that entails that the desirable-consciousness picture is at least suspect for apparently teetering into this view about blissful ignorance, so maybe not just suspect but silly itself.) Suppose your spouse is a cleverly programmed AI robot, not a human being, but you never find out. No problem? If we could trade in your actual spouse for a mostly identical AI robot, but one without a mildly annoying habit of your spouse—the robot doesn't leave its dirty socks on the bedroom floor—and you never found out, would you be better off? Does rationality require you to approve of that trade? You might not know you have cancer of the pancreas, but it's killing you. You might not know that your bank has filched $500,000 from your plump retirement account, but you're worse off without it, as you'll learn when you try to buy that condo on Longboat Key. Are you thinking it's hardheaded to say that you're injured only once you become aware of the problem?[7] But surely what you become aware of is that you've been injured for some time. Or suppose the cancer produces no symptoms, goes undiagnosed, and kills you while you're sleeping. You're worse off if you're raped while you're sleeping and drugged, even if you don't get pregnant, even if you don't get an STD, even if no one else ever knows about it and the rapist happens to die an hour later, even if you never know it happened: and if you're skeptical about *that* I hardly know what to say. But I'll persevere and say this: suppose the would-be rapist explains that he is thinking of raping you, and it's going to be traumatic and awful. But, he continues, all you need do is swallow this little dose of GHB, now infamous as a date-rape drug, and some Demerol, which will erase your short-term memory. He assures you that he has no STDs and he's sterile, and he promises not to tell anyone what he's done: or he shows you that he's arranged things so that he'll be shot to death as he leaves your apartment. All this, he purrs, doesn't mean only that you'll find the experience less traumatic. It doesn't merely mitigate the injury or abolish further injuries—such as emotional turmoil and mortifying publicity—that could ordinarily follow on the rape itself. It means also that you're not being injured at all. Isn't that nuts? If you're skeptical, if you're shrug-

7. I have the same sort of view as Thomas Nagel, "Death," in his *Mortal Questions* (Cambridge: Cambridge University Press, 1979), 4–5; and Joel Feinberg, *Harm to Others* (Oxford: Oxford University Press, 1984), 86–87.

ging off what you don't know as stuff that doesn't hurt you, should you be proud of yourself for being hardheaded? or should you fret that you're confused, in the clutches of high-level bromides that don't always or even often make sense? Are you tempted by the thought that the real problem here is that Demerol doesn't always induce short-term memory loss? If you're fighting the hypo with some such goofy complaint, aren't you seeking the right answer for the wrong reason?

The skeptic now tries to shift the burden of proof: "Nothing that happens after I die," he repeats, "can benefit or injure me. Death really is the end. You say offhandedly that you agree, that you're stipulating that we don't have any consciousness after we die. Are you fully serious about that? You remind me of the dead butcher in the Tibetan *Book of the Dead,* appalled to confront his judge. The poor guy can still bluster and lamely explain his many negative deeds before being condemned. Yes, he concedes, people warned him that he would 'go to the hells' for these deeds. But

> even though they advised me by saying these things, I thought, "I don't know whether I believe in the hells or not, and anyway there is no one who says they have been there, and then returned [to prove it]." So, I said to those people, "Who has gone to the hells and then returned? If the hells exist, where are they? These are just the lies of clever-talking people. Under the ground, there is just solid earth and solid rock. There are no hells. Above, there is only empty sky. There are no buddhas. So now while I'm alive, if I kill for my food, it doesn't matter. When I die, my body will be taken to the charnel ground and it will be eaten by birds and wild animals. Not

a trace will be left. My mind will vanish, so at that
time who will be left to go to the hells. HA! HA!"[8]

"You too bluster about not believing in the afterlife," he growls.
"But I think you do believe. I bet that's why you're concerned
about defaming the dead. You too think a trace will be left. For
devout Buddhists, the laugh's on the butcher, because he was
wrong. But the laugh's on you, because outside the *Book of the
Dead*, the butcher is exactly right."

If you've been chafing that so far I've been handing the
skeptic crummy lines, here I'm going to allow him to deepen
a powerful attack. He's going to remind us that folklorists, anthropologists, and historians have had a field day canvassing
the extraordinary range of cultures entertaining the beliefs that
the dead are still with us, that they must be propitiated, that
they take a pointed and sometimes malicious interest in how
we treat them. He's going to deepen the argument that I can
flatter myself all day long on how secular and modern I am,
how much I've wrested free of such beliefs, but insist that I too
am inescapably in their clutches. To be clearheaded about
death, he's going to conclude triumphantly, is to agree that
nothing that happens after you die can benefit or injure you.
To continue to rely implicitly on background beliefs you officially don't hold, let's say, is to suffer a hangover effect.

The skeptic can start with a surprisingly frequent practice
that should mystify hardheaded economists: burying wealth

---

8. *The Tibetan Book of the Dead*, trans. Gyurme Dorje, ed. Graham Coleman with Thupten Jinpa (New York: Viking Press, 2006), 323; bracketed
phrase in the translation. Such outbursts seem to be a staple of world literature: consider for instance the senator's speech in Victor Hugo, *Les misérables*,
bk. 1, chap. 8.

with cadavers. From the gold and food lavished away in Egypt's pyramids,[9] to the beads, tobacco pipes, and crockery American slaves buried with their dead,[10] people have long tried to comfort the dead or ease their transition into the afterlife or nourish them there—or to make damned sure that they stay there. In the fall of 2012, www.catacombosound.com—the website is itself now defunct—advertised a $29,000 coffin with a superb sound system and an accompanying touchscreen for the tombstone, so the living could update the music on offer. Said the Stockholm inventor, "People in Sweden are so stuck up about death—I wanted to give them something to laugh about. I was very afraid of death and I wanted to lighten it up a bit."[11] From wealth buried in deadly earnest—sorry, make that in grave earnest—sorry, anyway, wealth buried in earnest, to an odd joke. I don't know if a single such coffin was produced, let alone sold, let alone used. But you'd have to wonder about someone who bought and used one today. What could she possibly think she was up to?

More serious: take Fustel de Coulanges's stunning ac-

9. Françoise Dunand and Roger Lichtenberg, *Mummies and Death in Ancient Egypt,* trans. David Lorton (Ithaca, NY: Cornell University Press, 2006), esp. chap. 7. On the difficult Egyptian transition to the afterlife, see John H. Taylor, *Death and the Afterlife in Ancient Egypt* (Chicago: University of Chicago Press, 2001); *Journey through the Afterlife: Ancient Egyptian Book of the Dead,* ed. John H. Taylor (London: British Museum Press, 2010). On the elaborate burial mounds of some Native Americans, see A. J. Waring, Jr., and Preston Holder, "A Prehistoric Ceremonial Complex in the Southeastern United States," *American Anthropologist* (January–March 1945).

10. John Michael Vlach, *The Afro-American Tradition in Decorative Arts* (Athens: University of Georgia Press, 1990), chap. 9. Compare Roy Porter, *Flesh in the Age of Reason* (New York: W. W. Norton, 2003), 217–18.

11. Simon Tomlinson, "One Foot in the Rave: The £20,000 Hi-Fi Coffin that Plays Music on a Loop so You Can Listen to Your Favourite Tunes in the Afterlife," *Daily Mail* (14 December 2012).

count of the religious beliefs of ancient Greece and Rome and how those beliefs structured social practices.[12] There's plenty to object to in Fustel's account: his willingness to argue that Greek and Roman and for that matter Hindu sources all reveal the same thing; his insistence on religion's fundamental role, which is like vulgar Marxism in reverse; and more. But it remains a model of how to deploy literary texts to resurrect a dead social world.[13]

Fustel argues that the ancients worshipped their ancestors —each family with its own gods, traced through the male line. (This religion is older, he argues, than that of Zeus and the Olympians, but the latter never simply displaces it.) The dead had to be buried for their souls to rest. And the dead had to be nourished: libations were duly poured on the grave, food brought there too. They became gods of the family, though they could be peevish, sickening living family members and making their soil sterile if they weren't treated properly. So too the family was obliged to keep a hearth fire burning. (The Romans put out their fires every year on the first of March and promptly lit new ones.)

Fustel charts the conceptual changes enabling a city to have its own gods and hearth, the *prytaneum*. And—here's another version of the hangover effect—he notes wryly that the ancients kept stumbling through religious motions even after their belief had crumbled: "They continued to keep up this

12. Numa Denis Fustel de Coulanges, *The Ancient City: A Study on the Religion, Laws, and Institutions of Greece and Rome,* trans. Willard Small (Boston, 1874).

13. I think too in this context of M. I. Finley, *The World of Odysseus* (New York: Viking Press, 1954); and, although it makes him flinch to be in such august company, William Ian Miller, *Bloodtaking and Peacemaking: Feud, Law, and Society in Saga Iceland* (Chicago: University of Chicago Press, 1990).

fire, to have public meals, and to sing the old hymns—vain ceremonies, of which they dared not free themselves, but the sense of which no one understood." What's going on at this stage? You might imagine the locals as fully aware of the religious understanding of these practices, no longer themselves subscribing to them, but somehow feeling guilty or anxious about letting go. Or you might imagine them as mechanically showing up for the rituals, with no clue what they once transparently meant. If strategic rationality is your cup of tea, you can imagine that maybe not a single person believes in the ritual, but everyone suspects that at least some others do, so the safest bet is to play along with a straight face.

If you want to think about the staying power of rituals, or hangovers with a vengeance, consider Lawrence Durrell's reports on Corcyra in the late 1930s, that is, Greece many centuries after the world Fustel conjures up.[14] After bantering about the island's role in Homer—Odysseus visited Nausicaa there, Durrell explains to a baffled local—the presence of Judas Iscariot, and more, Durrell reports that he and his companions "attended a ceremony which furnished the seed for a whole train of arguments about pagan survivals." The count, a local notable, held "a beautiful Venetian dish, full of . . . 'pomegranate seeds, wheat, pine-nuts, almonds and raisins, all soaked in honey. Here, it really tastes rather nice. Try some.'" After a walk through the cypresses, he unlocked "what appeared to be the family vault" and the group descended three steps to some "uncouth stone tombs. . . . 'There is no need for the unearthly hush,' said the Count quietly. 'For us death is very much a part of everything. I am going to put this down here on Alecco's

---

14. Lawrence Durrell, *Prospero's Cell: A Guide to the Landscape and Manners of the Island of Corcyra* (London: Faber and Faber, 1945), 98–99.

tomb to sustain his soul. Afterwards I shall offer you some more of it at home, my dear Zarian, to sustain your body. Is that not very Greek? We never move far in our metaphysical distinctions from the body itself. There is no incongruity in the idea that what fortifies our physical bowels, will also comfort Alecco's ghostly ones. Or do you think we are guilty of faulty dissociation?'" That last question from this most urbane figure means that he knows that his audience might, to put it politely, doubt that Alecco's soul—if he has one!—needs luxurious pomegranate sustenance. The count notices Zarian examining an apparently empty tomb with a "cracked stone lid" next to it. "'Ugly things, these tombs,' says the Count. 'Like the bunkers of a merchant ship. Ah! you are looking at the empty one. It used to belong to my Uncle John, who caused us a lot of trouble. He became a vampire, and so we had him moved to the church behind the hill, where the ecclesiastical authorities could keep an eye on him. You did not know that the vampire exists?'"

Again, that last question—teasing? ironic? reproachful?— means the count knows he might be addressing skeptics, even if it ironically positions the skeptics as merely ignorant. The count's further tales of his vampire uncle trigger a lecture from Theodore, with his "vague Edwardian desire to square applied science with comparative religion. . . . The Count listens with exquisite politeness. . . . No one could guess that he has already heard it on several occasions." Zarian feverishly scribbles more illegible notes for an ethnography he'll never actually write. Durrell—his use of the passive voice leaves open just whom he has in mind—reports, "The vampire is still believed in."

By the locals? By the count? Well, the count himself might be a skeptic. He drily recalls the locals' digging up the uncle's body and plunging "a stake into his heart in the traditional fashion. I felt it was more politic to move him off the estate into the precincts of a church in order to avoid gossip." I don't know quite what the count did and didn't believe. I doubt that Durrell knew. And of course the count himself might not have known. The exchange is a nice reminder of how messily archaeological culture is, buckling and folded over, not neatly layered, so that older formations survive right next to later ones.

Ancestor worship is common. Some anthropologists have argued that, with reasonably capacious understandings of *ancestor* and *worship,* ancestor worship features in all religions, in every culture.[15] Another has warned that, at least in much of Africa, reverence is owed not strictly speaking to (deceased) ancestors but to elders, whether alive or dead; but he's noted too that the Suku of Kinshasa offer the dead (and not the living) their favorite foods, including certain mushrooms and palm wine.[16] The living can appeal to the dead for guidance and succor, and they can reproach them for not helping as they should.

Consider one last setting in which a practice lingers past the beliefs that arguably make sense of it. The Yasukuni shrine in Tokyo, next to the imperial palace's moat right in the middle of the city, memorializes Japan's war dead. Because the shrine includes war criminals from World War II, it pops up in the news now and again, for instance when then Prime Minister Junichiro Koizumi visited repeatedly. The visits irritated South Korea and helped to produce anti-Japanese riots in

15. Lyle B. Steadman, Craig T. Palmer, and Christopher F. Tilley, "The Universality of Ancestor Worship," *Ethnology* (Winter 1996).

16. Igor Kopytoff, "Ancestors as Elders in Africa," *Africa* (1 January 1971). Thanks to Webb Keane for the reference. For further complications, see James L. Brain, "Ancestors as Elders in Africa—Further Thoughts," *Africa* (3 January 1973).

China.[17] The shrine attracts some five million visitors a year.[18] But the geopolitics of modern Japan's relationship to its imperial history and World War II isn't my concern here. Dolls are. Or anyway a particular kind of doll. There's an old Buddhist tradition of using dolls to bring peace to wandering souls, to assist them in their decades of transition and absorption into Buddahood. In the early 1980s, for instance, a Mrs. Tanno in northern Japan went to consult a *kamisama* spirit medium on behalf of her distressed mother-in-law. "The medium spoke in the voice of the mother-in-law's dead son, killed as a soldier in World War II. The soldier, who had died before being married, spoke of his bitter loneliness in the void between the worlds and pleaded for his living relatives to perform a special rite for him, marrying him to a spirit in the form of a traditional bride-doll." The family did just that. A decade later, Mrs. Tanno went to see a *kamisama* medium to deal with her own distress. She learned that her daughter, who'd died as an infant, sought a bridegroom-doll, so she bought one—her budget meant it had to be cheap—and had it consecrated. Such ceremonies, not uncommon around East Asia, vary, as you

17. Norimitsu Onishi, "Japan Lodges Protest in Response to Demonstrations in China," *New York Times* (10 April 2005); Onishi, "Tokyo Protests Anti-Japan Rallies in China," *New York Times* (11 April 2005); Onishi, "Koizumi Visits War Shrine, as He Pledged," *New York Times* (17 October 2005). More recently, Prime Minister Shinzo Abe sent a shrub as a gift: Martin Fackler, "Shinzo Abe, Japanese Premier, Sends Gift to Contentious Yasukuni Shrine," *New York Times* (21 April 2015). More generally, see Ann Sherif, "Lost Men and War Criminals: Public Intellectuals at Yasukuni Shrine," in *Ruptured Histories: War, Memory, and the Post-Cold War in Asia,* ed. Sheila Miyoshi Jager and Rana Mitter (Cambridge, MA: Harvard University Press, 2007), 126–29.

18. Yuka Hayashi, "Tokyo Shrine in Limelight Again," *Wall Street Journal* (13 August 2013).

might expect. In central Japan, since the 1930s, the doll carries the spirit of Jizō, a Buddhist bodhisattva who assists lesser beings, especially children, through the stages of the soul's transmigration. In northeastern Japan, the doll carries the spirit of a living woman, usually paid for her service: the transaction triggers anxiety about whether the dead man will summon her to join him by dying. Ordinarily the dolls are rededicated every five years. After thirty years, having finished their task, they're burned or sent out to sea.[19]

So what have these dolls got to do with Yasukuni? Around the same time as Mrs. Tanno's earlier consultation, another woman, Sato Nami, sought permission to dedicate a doll to her dead son, buried at Yasukuni. The fiftieth anniversary of World War II's end saw more dolls show up; a display of the dolls in the site's museum a few years later generated more public interest. Well over a hundred dolls have shown up in Yasukuni. Now here's the puzzle: Sato Nami's relatives say she knew nothing about this Buddhist tradition, but simply thought a bride-doll would be a nice gift.[20]

We have enough examples for the skeptic to press what looks like a decisive objection. I think it's an injury to be defamed after you die, and I disclaim any belief in any kind of afterlife. So, the skeptic concludes, I am like a guy who lavishes money on a casket with a superb sound system for a cadaver I concede is deaf. I am like those ancients furtively shuffling

19. Ellen Schattschneider, "'Buy Me a Bride': Death and Exchange in Northern Japanese Bride-Doll Marriage," *American Ethnologist* (November 2001).

20. Ellen Schattschneider, "The Work of Sacrifice in the Age of Mechanical Reproduction: Bride Dolls and Ritual Appropriation at Yasukuni Shrine," in *The Culture of Japanese Fascism*, ed. Alan Tansman (Durham, NC: Duke University Press, 2009), 206–7.

around at the *prytaneum*, not believing they owe anything to any alleged ancestral gods. I am like the count, if we imagine him as ironically going through ancient motions and wasting a delicious pomegranate dish on dead family members. I am like Sato Nami, not Mrs. Tanno, wasting money on a doll. It may have made sense for people with the requisite beliefs about ancestor worship to do these sorts of things. (You could put pressure on whether it made sense for them to have the requisite beliefs. But let's concede that given those beliefs, their actions were sensible.) But once we wrest free of such beliefs, we should stop the associated conduct. And now the skeptic triumphantly brings the argument home: we should care about defaming the dead only if we imagine the dead as somehow sentient. Surrendering belief in the afterlife should then entail surrendering any and all concern about the dead's reputational interests.

Not so fast! I'll grant that concern for the dead's reputation could straightforwardly be justified by the thought that they remain conscious and concerned about such things, and could be buttressed by the further thought that they're in a position to benefit or injure us. I'll grant for the sake of argument that that is the correct explanation of how anyone ever came in the first place to worry about defaming the dead. But it doesn't follow that without such background beliefs, the belief that defamation injures the dead becomes unmotivated or irrational. It might have other justifications. Notice for instance that even if people started burying corpses to enable the dead's souls to come to rest, us boring secular humanist types might remain committed to burial not in some superstitious haze, but as a way of symbolically marking the end of a life and focusing the grieving of the living. For that matter, the count and Mrs. Nami might be able to justify their conduct and repel the claim that they are stumbling through routines that no longer make sense. But they'd have to tell some story. "Okay, but so do you, to redeem your concerns about defaming the dead." All in good time.

Notice that the skeptical view seems to furnish a wholesale line of attack or bludgeon against any and all claims about injuring the dead. It doesn't single out their reputational interests as uniquely or especially suspect. At the risk of raising the skeptic's eyebrows further, I'll blithely reveal that I think the dead, or anyway the recently dead, have all kinds of interests and claims on us. I think you owe it to your treasured colleague, not just to yourself and not just to his family, to attend his memorial service. (At memorial services, speakers regularly address the deceased. Goofy religious sentiments? But some of those speakers are emphatic unbelievers, they don't imagine that the deceased actually hear them, and they're not pandering.) I think biographers owe it to their deceased subjects, not just to their readers, to get the story right. None of this seems the least bit startling. We talk this way all the time. In "The Cornish Mystery," Hercule Poirot explains one of his odd moves: "I represent—not the law, but Mrs. Pengelley." Mrs. Pengelley is dead. Poirot blames himself—he heard her fears that her husband was trying to poison her (he wasn't, as it turns out), but arrived too late to save her. Still, he thinks, she has interests that he should vindicate.[21]

There's a depressingly familiar consequentialist strategy for reconstructing such intuitions. It offers yet another way of

21. Agatha Christie, *The Complete Hercule Poirot Short Stories,* 3 vols. (London: Folio Society, 2003), 1:343. So too in Christie's *Dumb Witness* (London: Harper Collins, 1937), Poirot pursues a charge from Emily Arundell even though she's already dead by the time he receives it.

suggesting that there's something illusory about our concern for the dead, that the real parties in interest are, as they must be, living people. Take the intuition that we owe it to the dead to respect the terms of their trusts. One might argue that we do so only in order to encourage other living people to consider making their own trusts.[22] True, that's not what we think we're up to. But in one view, whether the theory captures our self-understanding is neither here nor there. It matters only that it offers a(n allegedly hardheaded) reason justifying the same sorts of things our everyday views do.[23] I'm inclined to resist the thought that our everyday views are really deep misunderstandings. Not that there are any guarantees. We say "the sun rises" though Copernicus was right. But it's more illuminating to save the phenomena, as an Aristotelian or a pragmatist might say. So we should turn to such error theories only as a last resort.[24] We might have to do so when it comes to injuring the dead, because our everyday intuitions can seem counterintuitive, even indefensible.

How might a consequentialist reconstruct the allegedly indefensible claim that it injures the dead to defame them? What, exactly, do we gain by incentivizing people not to do that? Well, that others won't defame the dead. But why do we care? Well, because it bothers the living. But in this view, it's irrational of the living to be bothered. I suppose you could

22. Ernest Partridge, "Posthumous Interests and Posthumous Respect," *Ethics* (January 1981): 260–61.

23. Such positions can be dressed up more or less elaborately: consider John Stuart Mill, *Utilitarianism*, chap. 5; R. M. Hare, *Moral Thinking: Its Levels, Methods, and Point* (New York: Oxford University Press, 1981); and Derek Parfit, *Reasons and Persons* (Oxford: Clarendon Press, 1984), 40–43.

24. To use the felicitous language of J. L. Mackie, *Ethics: Inventing Right and Wrong* (Harmondsworth: Penguin Books, 1977).

shrug and say that it seems to be a psychic brute fact about people that they hate hearing defamatory comments about their dearly beloved. But this reconstruction is wacky. In the name of realism, it takes an everyday intuition—that it injures the dead to defame them—and urges that it's doubly confused: it injures the living, not the dead, and it shouldn't injure the living anyway. Or, again, it injures the living only if and insofar as *they* are worse off: their income goes down, say. So here the "realist" thing to say is that the living might be right to feel wounded, but they're clueless on the location of the wound. Still, the consequentialist reconstruction goes, we should have a norm against defaming the dead, in the name of not imposing a utility loss on the living. Let's just say that you have to be *quite* sophisticated to imagine that that counts as realism. But you don't have to endorse such rococo reconstructions to play skeptic. You can have the courage of your skeptical convictions and insist that we banish regard for the alleged interests of the dead.

Either way, we can crystallize the skeptical view into two theses. First is the *oblivion thesis*. Death, on this view, is the end of the person, and therefore the end of the person's welfare and interests. That leaves nothing for the concepts of wrong and harm to latch onto. Second is the *hangover thesis*. This is an explanation of why we nonetheless have intuitions that the oblivion thesis denies make any sense: it's because we continue, however embarrassedly, to cling to beliefs about the afterlife that we officially disavow.

These two theses are plausible, even powerful. But I'm convinced they're wrong.

II

Tort's Landscape

Here I sketch the terrain of tort law. I don't mean that I'll offer a hornbook or "nutshell," in the now generic name of a trademarked series of little books. (Law students use those little books, crammed with doctrine, to cram for exams.) I mean instead that I'll offer a picture of what sort of thing a tort is, how and why the law takes an interest in it, and what we can learn not from particular finicky rules, but from the basic structure of the terrain. I'll then zero in on defamation and offer an initial appraisal of what the law suggests about skepticism about defaming the dead.

Why turn to the law? Because the law embodies a normative order worth some sustained consideration, some epistemic deference too. I want to disavow the extravagant claims made in this ballpark. I'm not tempted by the thought that the law, or any other tradition, embodies a collective wisdom far more impressive than any we puny mortals can muster. (You can find a few sentences in Edmund Burke's voluminous writings treating tradition that way. They've assumed outsized importance in our grasp of his work, perhaps because so much of that work is so unsavory.)[1] Nor am I tempted by the thought that legal doctrines are somehow selected for, in even a roughly Darwinian sense, or that we should expect them to be efficient, in the Kaldor-Hicks sense of economists. (Economists say that a change is efficient if and only if the winners gain enough to compensate the losers and still remain better off. But the winners don't actually have to compensate, so this is just an elliptical way of saying, maximize [or increase, if you want to keep the focus on marginal change] something—utility, wealth, whatever—across the population. One wonders why economists don't say that straightforwardly.) Like other hand-waving about evolutionary explanation in the social sciences, painfully reminiscent of a structural functionalism long since abandoned, this move will get nowhere until and unless someone furnishes a cogent account of what the transmission and selection mechanisms are. I'm not persuaded by the accounts on offer.[2] Absent a good account, we can contemplate the eye-popping spectacle of allegedly hardheaded social scientists in-toning a secular theodicy.

But for centuries the law has had to wrestle with claims on behalf of the dead. It is one thing to puzzle over your intu-itions, and I emphatically don't say that pursuing the kind of puzzles I did in the last chapter is pointless. We can use all the leverage we can get. But you'd be forgiven for throwing up your hands and confessing that you're deeply uncertain whether defaming the dead injures them—or that even if you now have strong views, you don't trust them, because they're remote

---

1. See my *Poisoning the Minds of the Lower Orders* (Princeton, NJ: Princeton University Press, 1998).

2. In this domain, the savage skepticism of Adrian Vermeule, *Law and the Limits of Reason* (Oxford: Oxford University Press, 2009), is indispensable.

from any concrete choices you've ever had to make. Again, the law has had no such luxuries: parties file actions and the law has to respond. "But 'the law' isn't an actor. Don't be mystical." I could quibble about that, but the allegedly more concrete translation helps my argument. In the common law, many judges over many decades gnawed away at this puzzle. As we'll see, legislatures intervened, too. That's the case for sustained consideration and some epistemic deference.

Again, I don't want to lean too hard on this. One worry is about contingency, more pointedly what social scientists call path dependence. Once the common law lurches in a particular direction, *stare decisis* or deference to precedent is going to tend to refine and sharpen that approach over time, but make it harder to junk it and start afresh. Harder, not impossible: the common law sometimes narrows or even overrules bad doctrine.[3] But it is another kind of theodicy to count on its doing so—worse, to count on its having done so already. So if the common law's initial moves are mistaken, perhaps all we should expect is an increasingly polished mistake. Another worry is that our history is not a timeless present, where the law for centuries wrestles with the same problem, staggering or triangulating or marching methodically to the right answer. Our grasp of reputation, of defamation, of death, of the problems and possibilities of legal action, and apparently far-flung contextual considerations that reframe the core issues: all have shifted. (For an example of how far-flung context can matter, consider the doctrine of transubstantiation, on which during mass the host and wine literally become the body and blood of Christ. When the best reigning theories of matter describe

3. A classic modern case is Cardozo's burial of the rule of privity in *MacPherson v. Buick Motor Co.*, 217 N.Y. 382 (1916).

an unobservable substance that supports observable "accidents" or qualities, transubstantiation is straightforward: why hesitate at the claim that the substance has changed but the accidents have not? As those theories crumble, for reasons having nothing to do with Christian infighting, transubstantiation starts looking mysterious.) So it's possible that yesterday's legal solutions have outlived their usefulness or that they aren't even fully intelligible now. Since I'll be arguing that the law has gotten defaming the dead all wrong, I have no interest in dismissing such possibilities out of hand. Far from it.

Time to begin to map the terrain; first, a formal consideration. Tort is private law: in tort, someone sues someone else over an injury, seeking cash compensation or sometimes injunctive relief, that is, a court order requiring that the other party stop doing something. Criminal law, by contrast, is public law. For all the recent interest in victim impact statements, remedial justice, and the like, the law conceives of crime as an offense against the community. So ordinarily a public prosecutor brings the charges and they're filed on behalf of the state or the people. The same alleged event in the world can produce both a tort action (or actions) and a criminal prosecution (or prosecutions). So for instance the claim that O. J. Simpson murdered Nicole Brown Simpson and Ronald Lyle Goldman led to an acquittal in the criminal prosecution but to successful tort actions for wrongful death. These contradictory verdicts needn't be thought of as incoherent, as if the law decided that Simpson both was and wasn't a murderer. To prevail in a criminal prosecution, the state has to prove its case beyond a reasonable doubt. To prevail in a typical tort action, like this one, plaintiff has to show only a preponderance of evidence, or that more likely than not defendant is responsible for her injury.

Next, let's distinguish misfortunes from wrongs. Each harms the victim. But if no one has wronged the victim, if it's merely tough luck, then it's a misfortune. So it's a misfortune when you're out for a stroll on a brisk autumn day and a storm rolls in. The next thing you know, you're soaked in a frantic downpour. Running back home, you turn the corner—and you hear the crack of a gigantic old elm tree, broken by a gale of wind. A huge branch falls and knocks you to the sidewalk. Lucky, or less unlucky than you might have been, you escape with bruises and a broken shoulder.

Of course there's a straightforward sense in which a broken shoulder counts as an injury: when you're in a cast, your friend will ask how you were injured. English *injury* does double duty as both *harm* or setback of interest[4] and *wrong* or illegitimate invasion of another's interest. But as I've described matters so far, I want this on the misfortune side of the ledger. You're worse off: you're in pain; some of your treasured pursuits will be difficult or impossible for some time; you might not be able to work and so might not be paid; you'll require medical care, which might be costly. But no one has wronged you.

We could press the same point by saying no one is to blame. But someone can act wrongly without being blameworthy. *Vaughan v. Menlove*, a canonical English tort case, dramatizes the point.[5] Menlove had stacked his hay. His neighbors feared spontaneous combustion. They warned him repeatedly, but he said he'd "chance it." The hay caught fire and Vaughan's cottages were burned (along with Menlove's own barn and sta-

---

4. I follow the familiar account in Joel Feinberg, *Harm to Others: The Moral Limits of the Criminal Law* (Oxford: Oxford University Press, 1984), chap. 1.

5. Vaughan v. Menlove (1837) 132 Eng. Rep. 490 (Ct. Com. Pl.).

bles). Vaughan sued Menlove, whose lawyer suggested that Menlove, a stupid fellow, had acted to the best of his ability. It's not clear how that fits with the repeated warning, but the court ruled that even if Menlove had done the best he could, he was liable in tort. If you do the best you can, it seems hard to say you're blameworthy. (Though you could be blameworthy for getting engaged in an activity that you know or should know will make it too hard for you to care for others' interests. The drunk driver is to blame for getting behind the wheel in the first place. We don't absolve him of blame by acknowledging that given his sky-high blood alcohol level, he drove awfully well.) But what you've done can still be wrong.

Whether we put the point in terms of blame or wrong, it has both normative and causal strands. First, someone else has to have misbehaved. Not that he failed to do something admirable but not required: we're not concerned here with supererogatory action. So we might think it admirable for you to donate half your salary to poor children, but most of us don't think you're morally required to do so. Absent any such obligation, you are not to blame if those children suffer more; you haven't wronged them. The misbehavior that matters here consists in not fulfilling a duty or obligation. And then that misbehavior has to have a causal impact. If I'm driving and fiddling with my iPhone at the intersection, fail to see you walking across the street, and drift right through my stop sign into the intersection, I'm culpably careless. But if you don't know I'm coming and I don't hit you, I haven't injured you. Does it wrong someone to subject her to a risk of harm that doesn't eventuate? (You're sleeping. I decide to play Russian roulette with—on—you. I have two bullets in the six chambers of my pistol; I pull the trigger once; that chamber was empty and I leave.) I'll set aside that question, because I don't need it to get defaming the dead into sharper focus. I'll report bluntly that the basic rule of tort law is no harm, no foul; and that the law does not think exposure to a risk of harm is itself a harm.

Such complications aside, again, I want to describe the case in which the tree branch happens to break your shoulder as a misfortune, not an injury, because no one has wronged you. Contrast a case in which there's clearly a culprit. You're zipping downhill on your bicycle on a lovely spring day when the quick release on your front wheel fails. The wheel hurtles away from the bike frame, the fork slams to the ground, and your momentum hurls you over the handlebars. You crash onto the pavement and, you guessed it, break your shoulder and get a couple of bruises. There's a limit to what your helmet can do for you.

On the cursory description I've offered so far, you might well think that this too is a misfortune. But suppose I now add that your malicious neighbor slipped into your garage the night before and loosened the quick release, just enough that you'd be able to ride a few miles before it gave way. Or suppose I add that you don't trust yourself with bike maintenance, so you dutifully took your bike to the local shop for a tune-up. This is your first ride since you picked it up. The guy behind the counter assured you they'd cleaned, lubricated, adjusted, and tightened everything and the bike was ready to go. And they had—almost. But the fellow who last inspected the bike wasn't paying attention and didn't notice that the quick release was still loose.

Two broken shoulders: one a misfortune, one a wrong. The difference is not that a storm is a "natural" event, whatever that might mean, and a bicycle is an "artificial" implement. Notice that we can spin either example the other way: I'll show how to flip the case of the tree into a wrong and leave you to turn the bike crash into a misfortune. Suppose that three months ago, the city notified the elm's owner that her dying elm was a safety hazard and she had to have it taken down within a month. Suppose she ignored the notice or figured that she wouldn't bother dealing with it until next year. Now we have a blameworthy agent and an argument that you suffered an injury, not a misfortune. Yes, there still had to be a storm with a particular gale of wind, and the owner of the elm can't conceivably be responsible for that. And you had to be in just the wrong place at the wrong time, and she's not responsible for that, either. Still, had she complied with the legal requirement, you wouldn't have been injured. And the point of that legal requirement is precisely to protect the safety of people like you. (In bald outline, these are the elements of a negligence *per se* action: the unexcused violation of a statute or regulation designed to protect plaintiff against the sort of injury plaintiff suffered isn't merely evidence of a breach of duty; it settles the question.)[6]

Not that it takes breaking a law to make an act wrong. Maybe the city has no rules about old trees. Still, if it's incumbent on a homeowner periodically to inspect old trees or at least to hire an expert to inspect, the homeowner could be responsible for ignoring the hazard. It's wrong to shrug and think, "I don't care if the tree is in bad shape and might fall." But it's wrong, too, to remain ignorant—*if* it's incumbent on you to find out, or anyway to take reasonable steps to find out. The

6. Martin v. Herzog, 228 N.Y. 164 (1920), at least partly undone by the rider about an "unexcused" breach of the law. See for instance *Tedla v. Ellman*, 280 N.Y. 124 (1939) (despite statute requiring pedestrians to walk on left side of the road, permissible to be on right when traffic on left is much heavier).

eccentric homeowner who genuinely doesn't know that old trees can fall, or that branches can be dismembered in a storm, isn't callous. (Contrast the one who knows, shrugs, and decides she doesn't care.) He might well be contrite, even aghast, when his tree breaks your shoulder in a storm: "I had no idea!" he'll exclaim. But he can still be at fault, because he should have known and then he should have taken precautions.

Notice too that *you* might be wrong in not being more careful about your route home. You know that trees or branches can come crashing down in a storm: even from healthy trees. (Suppose the homeowner who failed to deal with the giant old elm argues that the storm was so severe that even a fully healthy tree would have been shattered by the storm. Would that mean she did no wrong? No, because we're not faulting her for not having a healthy tree. We're faulting her for failing to deal with her ailing tree. When you blame someone, you identify a counterfactual that she should have pursued and that would have prevented your injury. So too in negligence actions in tort, it is incumbent on plaintiff to identify defendant's breach of duty and show what better course of action would have avoided her injury. Promising tort actions founder when plaintiff botches this part of her job.) So maybe you should have avoided being under trees, or anyway big old trees. Maybe then it's your fault: maybe you injured yourself. So too even if the bike shop assures you that your bike is ready to go, maybe you're at fault for not even glancing at it yourself. Doesn't a responsible bicyclist always check her bike before she goes for a ride?

But we don't ordinarily think that only one agent can be to blame, so that if you're to blame, the bike shop must not be. You can both be at fault. And two or more other agents can be at fault when you're injured. Maybe the city is at fault for not alerting the homeowner that her elm was rotting and the homeowner is at fault for not herself figuring it out. (But a homeowner who knows the city is supposed to inspect trees might well argue that she's not obliged to pay attention, not least because the city inspector will be better at the job than she will.) We don't have a bucket theory of responsibility, on which the magnitude of the injury fixes the total quantity of wrong-doing and then we divvy up that wrongdoing among the blame-worthy parties. Put differently—Agatha Christie to the rescue again—when everyone on the Orient Express is guilty of mur-der, we don't think that each one should receive a small frac-tion of the punishment that a solo murderer should receive.

But there's an intriguing difference here between tort and crime. In the Orient Express case, everyone deserves the full punishment for murder. But in a tort case where multiple de-fendants are responsible for plaintiff's injury, the damages she can win are still fixed by her injury, so each defendant might pay less than he would if, say, he were the only defendant. (States have different and sometimes complicated rules on how to allocate fault. Those rules confusingly mix up how wrong each defendant's conduct was and how much it causally contributed to the injury. And in states with joint and several liability, any individual defendant could end up paying all the damages.) Nor do we think that agents are only either blame-worthy or not: they can be more or less to blame. Blameworthi-ness is dimensional, not binary. The same is true about wrong-ful conduct. Yes, conduct is either wrongful or not. But conduct can still be more or less wrong.

So far, these observations track everyday morality. But—no accident—they also frame the contours of tort law.[7] We can

---

7. No wonder tort scholars are mining Stephen Darwall, *The Second-Person Standpoint: Morality, Respect, and Accountability* (Cambridge, MA:

begin to get a grip on tort law with this conjecture: tort law makes injuries, but not misfortunes, legally actionable. If someone wrongs you, that is, you can sue them and seek compensation for your injuries. To stylize an intricate body of law, I'll begin with two standard routes to finding agents liable. Sometimes they intend to harm you. The neighbor who sabotages your bicycle intends that, even if he doesn't know quite how your bike will collapse or quite how you'll be harmed. (If he claims that he never intended to harm you, that it was only a prank, that he thought the wheel would come off as you started to mount the seat and that you wouldn't even fall down, things would get stickier, in part because we might not credit his testimony. As in life, so in law: often we read back from apparent action to intention.) And sometimes they are careless or, as the law puts it, negligent. The homeowner who fails to do anything about a big cracked dead elm, or who doesn't even notice it but should, is also liable. Or, as the law puts it, following everyday intuition, she's liable if it was unreasonable not to notice and remedy.

The approach is reminiscent of recent contractarian work in ethics, so it's worth flagging a problem with that work. Contrast the approaches of Thomas Scanlon and John Rawls. Scanlon "holds that thinking about right and wrong is, at the most basic level, thinking about what could be justified to others on grounds that they, if appropriately motivated, could not reasonably reject."[8] Rawls suggests that for terms of social co-

---

Harvard University Press, 2006). See Stephen Darwall and Julian Darwall, "Civil Recourse as Mutual Accountability," *Florida State University Law Review* (Fall 2011).

8. T. M. Scanlon, *What We Owe to Each Other* (Cambridge, MA: Belknap Press of Harvard University Press, 1998), 5. Contrast Scanlon's *Being Realistic about Reasons* (New York: Oxford University Press, 2014), 96: "If it would

operation "to be fair . . . citizens offering them must reasonably think that those citizens to whom such terms are offered
might also reasonably accept them."[9] There's a Goldilocks worry
about finding the right fit. Across a very wide range of pressing
issues, Scanlon's view threatens to lapse into a kind of moral
skepticism on which *no* claims of right can be justified. No
matter what your views are on abortion, affirmative action,
capital punishment, and scads of less feverish topics, can't even
a suitably motivated other person reasonably reject each and
every one of them? Isn't the problem that there are lots of reasonable alternatives? Rawls is on the other prong of the dilemma: it's way too easy to show that it's reasonable to think
others might reasonably accept one's view of the proper terms
of social cooperation. (The doubled *reasonable* makes the condition even more permissive: it's presumably possible that actually no one else could reasonably accept your view, but you
could reasonably think someone would.) The difference principle passes that test. But so does libertarianism. So do views
more egalitarian than Rawls's. (Rawls's argument for his two
principles of justice, to recur to his earlier work, is that parties
in the original position would prefer them to some familiar
alternatives. That's different from saying it would be unreasonable to choose the alternatives: and his later suggestion about
reasonableness is about real agents not behind the veil of ignorance.) If we agree that all these rival views are fair, we still
have to figure out how to choose among them.

---

be reasonable to reject any principle that would permit a certain action, then
that action would be morally wrong."

9. John Rawls, *Political Liberalism,* expanded ed. (New York: Columbia
University Press, 2005), xlii. I don't want to pursue the full contrast between
Rawls's and Scanlon's views, but note Rawls, *Liberalism,* 49–50 n. 2.

So reasonableness, at least standing alone, seems too thin or manipulable to furnish a formula for deciding what's right or fair. But it's still enough to say that it's wrong to act unreasonably, so we can more easily agree with the part of Scanlon's formulation about how to think about what's wrong. After all, it's not as if there is ordinarily only one reasonable option on the table. Then there'd be no room for the contrast I'm drawing between how we think about what's wrong and how we think about what's right or fair. But we can often agree that some courses of conduct (or inaction) are unreasonable.

So others can be liable if they act unreasonably. That's different from their taking reasonable steps and your nonetheless being harmed. Suppose the homeowner knows she isn't a tree expert, so she hires a professional who inspects the tree and assures her it's fine—but it isn't. Now the homeowner has done nothing wrong and maybe the professional hasn't, either. Maybe the tree's faults are so well hidden that even a competent professional wouldn't spot them. Or suppose that the elm was robust and healthy, but was cracked badly by lightning the day before it fell on you; the alert homeowner had noticed and already hired a tree service firm to come remove it, but they couldn't come for two weeks. You and the storm happen to show up before the tree service firm. Nothing wrong with that, though you could plausibly argue that the homeowner should have put up a neon orange warning sign when she noticed the problem, and kept it up until the tree service dealt with it. Still, the homeowner can't be to blame for the cracked branch still being there during the storm.

Recall the conjecture: tort allows you to sue others for injuring you—for their wrongful conduct when it causes you harm—but not for misfortunes. I have to consider two refinements to this way of picking out tort's territory. There's room to hedge over the first, but not the second. First: an important body of tort law holds agents legally liable when they neither intended harm nor were negligent. Under this strict liability standard, one might think, it's enough that you've caused an injury, even if you've done nothing wrong. At least as construed by American courts, *Rylands v. Fletcher*, another canonical English case, holds that if you bring large amounts of water onto your property (or do something else that qualifies as an "unnatural use") and it escapes and damages someone else's property, you'll be liable without any further showing that you were at fault.[10] It's easy to read the case as still insisting on the fault of the person who brought the water onto his land. After all, he knew he was exposing others to considerable risk, but went ahead anyway. So the fault might be located not in whatever precautions he did or didn't take to keep the water under control, but in bringing it onto his land in the first place. Yet *Rylands* specifically sets aside *vis major* (an overwhelming force of nature) or acts of God as instances where defendant would not be liable.

I don't want to quibble over *Rylands*. Arguably, modern tort law extends strict liability to settings where talk of wrongful conduct would be too attenuated. Consider manufacturing defect actions in product liability law. You buy a glass bottle of iced tea. You screw off the cap and don't notice a crack in the bottle which gashes your lip. You can sue any seller of the product, from the mom-and-pop corner store where you bought the iced tea to the company marketing the product. (Don't fret about the plight of the poor corner-store owners facing crushing liability in tort: ordinarily manufacturers' contractual terms will indemnify such actors.) The law will not let such defen-

---

10. Rylands v. Fletcher (1868) 3 L. R. H. L. 330 (Eng.).

dants urge that they're not liable by arguing that their conduct was fully reasonable. It will not let the bottler, for instance, introduce evidence that all technically available procedures for bottling plants, from how to melt and mold the glass to how to test the bottles, leave a tiny fraction of cracked ones coming off the assembly line. The law will not let the bottler argue that his bottling plant boasts the lowest rate of cracked bottles in the industry, that he liberally invests in researching even safer technology, and so on. The law will not let the corner-store owners argue that they didn't produce the bottle and couldn't have known it was defective. Or again, in many jurisdictions, if your dog, unprovoked, bites someone, you're automatically liable.[11] You may not defend by urging that you had the dog securely tied up, that you have a high fence, that you have warning signs, or by insisting on any other precautions you've taken. You might think that just as a landowner can be at fault for bringing large amounts of water on his property, just as a drunk driver can be at fault for getting behind the wheel, so too an iced-tea manufacturer can be at fault for going into the business and a dog owner can be at fault for having a dog. That would rescue the conjecture that tort is all about injury, not misfortune. But it seems contrived. There's nothing wrongful about marketing iced tea, and the bottler who has such a low rate of defective bottles coming off the line and who's working so hard to reduce that rate even further seems admirable, not blameworthy at all. You could suggest that like the landholder in *Rylands,* he's engaged in an activity that he knows or should know poses risks to others. But the easiest

---

11. See for instance *Pingaro v. Rossi,* 322 N.J. Super. 494 (App. Div. 1999), and the statute at issue, N.J. Stat. § 4:19–16; *Hill v. Sacka,* 256 Mich. App. 443 (2003), and the statute at issue, MCLS § 287.351.

way to unpack that analogy suggests that if the *Rylands* land-holder took reasonable care with his water—and reasonable care is quite a lot of care when you're dealing with something so dangerous—he wasn't blameworthy, either.

What about the wedge between wrongful conduct and blameworthy conduct that we saw in *Vaughan?* There is a sense in which it's wrong to sell someone a cracked bottle or to let your dog bite them, even if you've worked hard to avoid such bad outcomes—even if you've done far more than you're reasonably required to do, so you can't conceivably be blameworthy. Like Menlove, you're doing the best you can: but here it's not that you're a bungler, it's that anyone's best might not be good enough. You can *wrong someone else* without *doing something wrong.* The latter description is just another way of pointing to blameworthiness: if you did something wrong, we ought to be able to identify what it was, and the commendable or anyway permissible thing you should have done instead. But even when we can't do that, you can wrong someone else. You wrong someone else, again, when you sell them a cracked bottle or when your dog bites them. You do so even if you didn't do anything wrong. In this view it makes perfectly good sense to say that the fellow with the gashed lip or the bleeding leg hasn't suffered a misfortune, he's been injured. So there's no reason here to qualify the view that tort liability attaches when someone wrongs someone else.[12] Notice again that the locution "you're to blame" wobbles between "this is your fault: you wronged me" and "your conduct was blameworthy." And again, tort law tracks the former. If we embrace the sense in which it's wrong for you to sell someone a cracked bottle no matter how

---

12. Consider John C. P. Goldberg and Benjamin C. Zipursky, "Tort Law and Moral Luck," *Cornell Law Review* (September 2007).

hard you try to avoid it, we don't have to refine the conjecture and concede that these sorts of torts are misfortunes, not injuries. But if we broaden the frame—if we say, it can't be wrong to market iced tea and do your utmost to ensure that the bottles are safe; it can't be wrong to own a dog and be incredibly careful to keep it from biting people—we'll have to modify the conjecture and concede that sometimes tort law makes defendants liable for plaintiffs' misfortunes.[13]

So the first refinement to the suggestion that tort is about injury, not misfortune, would be that certain kinds of misfortune can qualify as torts. The second is that not all injuries—again understood as cases where someone is worse off because another has wronged him—are tortious. Take for instance causing someone else emotional distress. It has long been true that plaintiffs could be compensated for "pain and suffering" if those damages flowed from conduct already deemed tortious. If you batter people—if you wrongly and intentionally make harmful or offensive contact with them—you will be liable not just for their medical bills, not just for their lost wages, and so on, but also for their pain and suffering. But for a long time, tort law resolutely resisted the thought that emotional distress, standing alone, could ground a tort action. The central concern seems to have been worries about proof. So first the law decided that you could win damages for emotional distress if that distress was severe enough to produce physical symptoms. Today, most states make the intentional infliction of emotional distress (IIED) tortious—if and only if the conduct was "out-

---

13. Compare the manipulation of time frames in Mark F. Grady, "Res Ipsa Loquitur and Compliance Error," *University of Pennsylvania Law Review* (January 1994); and Gary Peller, "The Metaphysics of American Law," *California Law Review* (July 1985).

rageous" and the emotional distress is severe or unendurable. The Second Restatement, still an authority, glosses *outrageous:* "Generally, the case is one in which the recitation of the facts to an average member of the community would arouse his resentment against the actor, and lead him to exclaim, 'Outrageous!'"[14] Yes, the gloss violates your third-grade teacher's mandate that you not use a word to define that same word. But it has real content: its reference to "average member of the community" makes outrageousness a question of social fact, what the local standards are, not a normative standard allowing plaintiffs to appeal to how people should act. One wonders whether in a violently racist or homophobic community, one without reservations about such repulsive sentiments, racist and gay-bashing acts can't qualify as outrageous and so victims must be advised that IIED actions would fail.

That means that as far as accountability in tort goes, someone else is free to deliberately make you miserable as long as his conduct is not quite outrageous or your distress not quite unendurable. Surely we count that as an injury. It's blameworthy conduct; it wrongs you; it harms you. But it is not tortious. Nor is "pure economic loss" an injury that tort law protects against. Suppose your neighbor paints his house an ungodly mauve and so drives down the value of your house. Outside the law, I think we might well say he has wronged you. (Suppose he rudely refuses to consider your interests.) From the law's point of view, your house is the same as it always was. If he painted *your* house mauve, without your consent, that would be something else. In this way—and I could multiply examples—not all injuries qualify as torts.

The conjecture, again, was that tort law makes injuries,

14. *Restatement (Second) Torts,* § 46, cmt. d.

not misfortunes, legally actionable. The first refinement is the thought that some harms best seen as misfortunes might yield tort actions. The second refinement is the reminder that not all injuries are tortious. So even if we reject the first refinement, we have to agree that injury is a necessary but not sufficient condition of tort liability. Despite the two refinements, the conjecture captures a crucial feature of tort law. I can underline it by stressing a couple of formal features of the practice.[15] Only the injured party has standing in law to launch a tort action. If you were injured but don't want to sue, and I am indignant on your behalf, I can't sue. (I could file a complaint with a court claiming that someone has injured you. That complaint will be dismissed instantly.) Nor can I purchase from you the right to sue on your behalf: an economist might decry deadweight loss, but the law doesn't budge. (Your insurance contract may require you to cooperate if the insurance company decides to sue to reclaim assets they've paid you, but you have then agreed to file, and you will file in your name, even if they do all the legal work.) And you can sue only those who you can argue are responsible for your injury. Compare the familiar suggestion that the purposes of tort law are deterrence and compensation, and consider again the example of the intersection where I'm driving, fiddling with my iPhone, and drift through the stop sign without hitting you. But suppose this time you happen to stumble and break your ankle. My bad driving doesn't cause you to do that; it's sheer coincidence of timing. I can imagine a body of law that would let you sue me and win a monetary award: such legal actions would deter my

15. Here I muster the sort of observations pressed forcefully against economic analyses of tort by Jules L. Coleman, "The Structure of Tort Law," *Yale Law Journal* (May 1988).

bad driving and compensate you for your injury. But any such action would be a nonstarter in tort law, because I haven't wronged you.

These structural features underwrite the claim that tort is private law: that it's about illegitimate invasions of one person's interests by another. Some scholars have urged that really tort law is public after all: that it is or should be a body of law maximizing wealth or Kaldor-Hicks efficiency,[16] or promoting welfare and rejecting moves that would make some worse off and no one better off;[17] or a body of law, especially but not only in products liability, permitting judges to do end-runs around captured regulatory agencies and vindicate popular interests.[18] Such scholars concede that tort plaintiffs are thinking about their own interests, but, they maintain, tort is justified by the larger social ends it serves, and we should see plaintiffs as private attorneys-general. We might even see restrictive standing rules as ensuring that people who bring actions have the information and incentives to make the best case available. Even scholars agreeing that tort law is private have disagreed on how we should see it. We have the paradoxical or mischievous suggestion "that the purpose of private law is to be private law," coupled with the more helpful suggestion that tort law is about, or embodies, corrective justice.[19] We have the thesis that tort

16. Richard A. Posner, *Economic Analysis of Law,* 9th ed. (New York: Wolters Kluwer, 2014), chap. 6.

17. Louis Kaplow and Steven Shavell, *Fairness versus Welfare* (Cambridge, MA: Harvard University Press, 2002), chap. 3.

18. Thomas H. Koenig and Michael L. Rustad, *In Defense of Tort Law* (New York: New York University Press, 2001), esp. for instance 123–26, 175–76.

19. Ernest J. Weinrib, *The Idea of Private Law* (Cambridge, MA: Harvard University Press, 1995), 6.

law offers a right of redress.[20] We have the claim that tort law lets wronged parties get even.[21]

So we have two camps. One urges that tort's appearance as private law is illusory, that the real stakes are public. The other wants to vindicate that appearance. The divide here roughly parallels—and sometimes piggybacks on—disputes in ethics between consequentialists and their opponents. We've already caught glimmerings of this sort of dispute in beginning to probe the suggestion that it's not really the dead who are injured by defamation, but their aggrieved family and friends, and we want to incentivize others not to impose those injuries. Plenty of thoughtful people embrace such consequentialist stances and in turn embrace the public perspective on tort law. I find myself stubbornly opposed; I'll return to these disputes later. I turn next to laying out the basic structure of the tort of defamation.

The Tort of Defamation

The Supreme Court has changed the common law of libel, sometimes in unhappily complicated ways, because of concerns about the First Amendment.[22] If "almost everyone agrees

20. See esp. Benjamin C. Zipursky, "Civil Recourse, Not Corrective Justice," *Georgetown Law Journal* (March 2003); John C. P. Goldberg and Benjamin C. Zipursky, "Torts as Wrongs," *Texas Law Review* (April 2010).

21. Scott Hershovitz, "Corrective Justice for Civil Recourse Theorists," *Florida State University Law Review* (2011); for a shift in his view, see his "Tort as a Substitute for Revenge," in *Philosophical Foundations of the Law of Torts,* ed. John Oberdiek (Oxford: Oxford University Press, 2014).

22. I have in mind the law flowing out of *New York Times Co. v. Sullivan,* 376 U.S. 254 (1964). Here's one strand of that law. *Gertz v. Robert Welch,* 418 U.S. 323, 349 (1974), holds that "the States may not permit recovery of presumed or punitive damages, at least when liability is not based on a showing

that defamation law, to put it simply, is a mess,"[23] I'm inclined
to say it's the Court's fault, not the common law's. Happily we
can leave these issues aside. If you want to sue someone for
defaming you, you ordinarily have to argue that he published
a false and defamatory statement of fact about you. He needn't
have intended to injure you. Nor need he have known that
the statement is false. Put as skeletally as possible, those are
the constituent elements of the tort. As you'd expect, there
are intriguing disputes about the boundaries of every one of
those elements. The allegation that you embezzled, diddled,
and popped would unequivocally count as defamation—if you
were still alive.

Before I canvass the elements, consider a threshold puzzle. I've insisted that torts are wrongs. But surely sometimes it's
not wrong to publish a false defamatory statement of fact about
someone. Journalists sometimes enjoy what the law calls a

---

of knowledge of falsity or reckless disregard for the truth." "Reckless disregard" sounds like a legal term of art for heightened negligence, but here it
means subjective doubt or disbelief in what's being reported. Likewise, *New
York Times's* "actual malice" sounds like a legal term of art for bad motive,
but it means "reckless disregard" in the sense just defined or actual knowledge of falsity. See *St. Amant v. Thompson,* 390 U.S. 727 (1968). The language
of *Gertz* is clarified or modified by *Dun & Bradstreet v. Greenmoss Builders,*
472 U.S. 749, 761 (1985): "In light of the reduced constitutional value of
speech involving no matters of public concern, we hold that the state interest
adequately supports awards of presumed and punitive damages—even absent a showing of 'actual malice.'"

For the contemporary state of play in state law on what showings plain-
tiffs do and don't have to make, see Robert D. Sack, *Sack on Defamation:
Libel, Slander, and Related Problems,* 4th ed., 2 vols. (New York: Practising
Law Institute, 2014), §§ 2:4.17, 2:8.3.

23. Dan B. Dobbs and Ellen M. Bublick, *Cases and Materials on Advanced
Torts: Economic and Dignitary Torts* (St. Paul, MN: Thomson/West, 2006),
174.

qualified privilege to do that, say in offering good-faith coverage of criminal charges that turn out to be false. So too lawyers during a trial enjoy what the law calls an absolute privilege—it serves as an ironclad defense regardless of their motives—to defame witnesses. (Picture the sneering lawyer impeaching the witness's credibility: "But you have your own history of having embezzled, diddled, and popped, don't you?" The law wants to secure clients' right to a vigorous defense. No, the law doesn't think flinging such charges maliciously or gratuitously is choiceworthy. It thinks that attempting to police a more refined line by allowing tort actions even in flagrantly abusive cases would chill vigorous advocacy we want to protect.) In such cases, defamation is not a wrong—and then it gives rise to no liability in tort. Or consider the tort of battery. We usually define its elements as intentionally making harmful or offensive contact with another. But sometimes such contact is perfectly permissible. The linebacker can smash into the opposing team's player and bruise him, even break a bone. Here the law says the players have consented to such contact by playing the game, so it isn't wrongful: and then once again, it gives rise to no liability in tort. There are interesting disputes about the scope of consent: the players surely consent to more than the official rules permit, but not anything and everything: if a linebacker pulls out a pistol and shoots another player, he will surely be liable. It matters, too, whether plaintiff has the burden of showing that he never consented to the contact in question or whether defendant can try to show consent as what the law calls an affirmative defense. Such considerations are often crucial in litigation. But at the end of the day, regardless of the practical urgencies of who has to show what, if the conduct isn't wrong, it won't qualify as tortious.

So back to the elements of defamation. *Publication* means

passing on the charge to at least one third party. If someone
confronts you in private and explodes, "you've embezzled,
diddled, and popped!" there's no publication. If the publication is oral, we call the defamation slander; if it's written, we
call it libel. (Increasingly the law treats broadcasts of various
kinds as libel: so the underlying issue may be the relative per-
manence of the publication, not literally whether it is words on
a page or spoken words.) Common law used to hedge about
truthful defamatory claims.[24] A standard formulation was that
it was permissible to publish such claims only "with good motives and for justifiable ends." State statutes, even constitutions,
are still heavily peppered with that language.[25] But it's likely
unenforceable, surely so when the claim is on a matter of public interest, probably across the board.[26] Today American law
is adamant that the statement has to be false. If you did in fact
embezzle money from your employer, it is not defamatory to
publish that fact. (States have varied on whether plaintiff has
the burden of showing the statement was false or whether defendant has the burden of showing that it was true.) Republication is tortious, too. Ordinarily we sharply distinguish asserting something from reporting that it has been asserted.
("Matt hates you" is different from "Rebecca says that Matt
hates you.") Tort law deliberately smudges that distinction, lest

24. Roy Robert Ray, "Truth: A Defense to Libel," *Minnesota Law Review*
(December 1931), remains helpful.

25. For instance, Illinois Const., Art. I, § 4; MCLS Const. Art. I, § 19;
Miss. Const. Ann. Art. 3, § 13; Ne. Const. Art. I, § 5; W. Va. Const. Art. III,
§ 8.

26. No wonder the *Restatement (Second) Torts*, § 558, takes falsehood as
a constitutive element of the tort and emphasizes (§ 581A) that truth is a
complete defense. The first *Restatement (Torts)*, §§ 558, 582 already did the
same. See *Sack on Defamation*, § 3:3.2.

defamers have a foolproof recipe for defaming and getting away with it: they could always say, "I've heard people say he's embezzled, diddled, and popped," and then shrug off a defamation suit by insisting they were reporting, not asserting.

The statement has to be defamatory: it has to tend to lower your reputation in at least some reputable segment of the community. It might not if your reputation is so very bad—or so very good—that the charge won't make a difference. Similarly, it might not if the putative defamer has no credibility. If everyone knows that when he's plastered, the town drunk spouts malicious fantasies, *his* drunken claim that you've embezzled, diddled, and popped won't qualify, either. Nor do disreputable communities count. His fellow criminals will think worse of Johnny the Thug if a rival sneers that Johnny is such a wimp that he has never murdered anyone. That will injure Johnny: it will deprive him of his livelihood and it will lead his peers to hold him in contempt. But the law will not allow Johnny to vindicate this reputational interest. Most people might not care about or even understand the claim that Dr. Zimmerman can't figure out when to do a ventriculostomy instead of a vertebrectomy, so they won't think worse of her. But her fellow neurosurgeons will, so tort law will let her press a defamation charge on that basis. In cases of defamation *per se,* the law assumes without further evidence that the plaintiff has suffered reputational harm: the classic ones are violation of a serious criminal statute (*embezzled* and *diddled* surely qualify; *popped* might); incompetence in one's profession (Zimmerman would seize on this); and having a loathsome disease or—in the case of a woman—lacking sexual chastity. That last has morphed in modern law into serious sexual misconduct, by men or women alike.

Why doesn't the law require evidence of injury in some

cases? One view: the law doesn't want to waste time hearing the evidence, since we're confident that such charges do harm plaintiff's reputation. Another view: the law itself condemns publishing these particular false claims about others. In all other putative defamation cases, the law is agnostic: it hands off to whatever community is at stake the question of whether the claim does reputational harm. In these latter settings, at least, plaintiff will seek to provide evidence of actual injury.

The statement has to concern a matter of fact, not opinion. "Ezra stole $50,000 from his law firm" is unequivocally a factual claim. "Fred is a fucking asshole" is unequivocally a matter of opinion.[27] But it can be defamatory to imply a factual claim: "I don't get it. Cora must still have tons of debt from college and law school, and she can't be making serious money as a public defender. But she eats out at fancy French restaurants all the time and is off for a lavish vacation in the Swiss Alps. Oh, and people have been muttering about $500,000 mysteriously missing from a government grant in her office." These issues were in play when William F. Buckley, Jr., sued Franklin Littell for libel. Littell had described Buckley as a fellow traveler of fascists and intimated that he smeared and libeled others in *National Review*: "Like Westbrook Pegler, who lied day after day in his column about Quentin Reynolds and goaded him into a lawsuit, Buckley could be taken to court by any one of several people who had enough money to hire competent legal counsel and nothing else to do."[28] Buckley won nominal compensatory damages of $1, because the court

27. See the hilarious list of examples from actual cases in *Sack on Defamation*, § 2:4.7.
28. Franklin H. Littell, *Wild Tongues: A Handbook of Social Pathology* ([New York]: Macmillan, 1969), 51.

doubted his reputation had suffered, but also $7,500 in punitive damages.[29] (Today this judgment might be unconstitutional, because the Supreme Court has ruled that it probably violates due process when punitive awards exceed some unspecified multiple of compensatory damages.)[30] On appeal, despite vigorous argument by Buckley, the court decided that the claim that someone is a fascist was, at least in this context, a matter of opinion. It left standing the finding of libel for the claim that Buckley was himself a libelous journalist, but reduced the punitive damages award to $1,000.[31]

Finally, the defamatory charge has to refer to you, or, in the law's stilted cadences, it has to be "of and concerning" you. That was one problem Kimerli Jayne Pring faced when she sued over a *Penthouse* short story about a Miss Wyoming named Charlene, a baton twirler whose oral sex made men levitate— a stunt she performed onstage during the competition, to the audience's applause. Pring was the actual Miss Wyoming that

---

29. Buckley v. Littell, 394 F. Supp. 918 (S.D.N.Y. 1975).

30. BMW of N. Am. v. Gore, 517 U.S. 559 (1996).

31. Buckley v. Littell, 539 F.2d 882 (2d Cir. 1976). Painter James McNeill Whistler won nominal damages of one farthing after John Ruskin published these words: "I have seen, and heard, much of Cockney impudence before now, but never expected to hear a coxcomb ask two hundred guineas for flinging a pot of paint in the public's face." For a loving reconstruction of the 1878 case, see Linda Merrill, *A Pot of Paint: Aesthetics on Trial in Whistler v Ruskin* (Washington, DC: Smithsonian Institution Press in collaboration with The Freer Gallery of Art, 1992). The defense focused on whether Ruskin had "criticized the plaintiff's productions in a fair, honest, and moderate spirit," or "whether Mr. Ruskin's criticism is a fair criticism, and whether it oversteps the reasonable bounds of moderation," and conceded that he "did subject [Whistler's work] to a severe and slashing criticism—or, if you choose, to ridicule and contempt" (162–63). The salient question here is about the boundaries of the privilege of fair comment, which goes to the question of whether Ruskin's publication was wrongful.

year and she was a baton twirler. The jury found that the story did refer to her and awarded her $26.5m.[32] The judge reduced that award to $14m. An appeals court overturned it on the grounds that the story pressed no factual claims: "It is impossible to believe that anyone could understand that levitation could be accomplished by oral sex before a national television audience or anywhere else. The incidents charged were impossible. The setting was impossible."[33] Not to put too fine a point on it, this is dumb. The appeals court can say this if and only if they think no reasonable jury could find a factual claim here. But surely a reasonable jury conversant with fiction—and hyperbole—could find claims that Pring used a sensational skill at oral sex to advance in the competition.

The law distinguishes compensatory and punitive (or exemplary) damages. The former compensate plaintiff for his injuries. We can break down this category into pecuniary and nonpecuniary damages. The former, easily calculated, compensate for cash losses: the cost of medical care, lost wages, and so on. The latter require an impressionistic judgment: how much money should be awarded for, say, this much pain and suffer-

32. Douglas C. McGill, "Writer's Plight: A Libel Suit," *New York Times* (19 July 1981). For a detailed rendition, see Gerry Spence, *Trial by Fire: The True Story of a Woman's Ordeal at the Hands of the Law* (New York: William Morrow, 1986). Compare *Yecker v. State*, 142 Tex. Crim. 358 (1941) (campaign flier reproducing the criminal record of a man who happened to have the same name as defendant's opponent in the race).

33. Pring v. Penthouse International, Ltd., 695 F.2d 438, 443 (10th Cir. 1982). The lower court opinion, *Pring v. Penthouse International, Ltd.*, 7 Med. L. Rptr. 1101 (D. Wyo. Jan 7, 1981), ruled that Pring was not a public figure and denied Penthouse's motion for summary judgment on the grounds that the question of whether the story was "of and concerning" her had to go to a jury.

ing? Punitive damages are awarded only if, to put it roughly, plaintiff can show that defendant acted maliciously or recklessly. The law does not fuss terribly over the present value of money or the tax implications of damages awards; nor, usually, over the chunk of plaintiff's award that her attorney will take. There are tantalizing disputes about how best to understand both sorts of damages, but with due melancholy I pass them by as irrelevant to my quest here.

Wrongful publication of a false defamatory statement of fact about you: these are the core classic elements of the tort of defamation. I should add that not only does the law face endless problems about how to draw the boundaries around each element, but also it occasionally departs from them. Take the case brought by Crawford Burton, a steeplechaser, after two photographs of him appeared in an advertisement for Camel cigarettes with the accompanying captions, "WHEN YOU FEEL 'ALL IN'—" and "GET A LIFT WITH A CAMEL!" One photograph caught his saddle and girth at just the right angle to suggest he had a preposterously large penis.[34] The inimitable Judge Learned Hand ruled that Burton could make out a case for libel even though he couldn't plausibly point to any defamatory statement of fact:

> We dismiss at once so much of the complaint as alleged that the advertisement might be read to say that the plaintiff was deformed, or that he had indecently exposed himself, or was making obscene

34. The advertisement is splendidly reproduced at www.deceptology .com/2011/11/grotesque-monstrous-and-obscene-well.html (last visited 1 June 2016).

jokes by means of the legends. Nobody could be fatuous enough to believe any of these things; everybody would at once see that it was the camera, and the camera alone, that had made the unfortunate mistake. If the advertisement is a libel, it is such in spite of the fact that it asserts nothing whatever about the plaintiff, even by the remotest implications.[35]

Still, Hand argued, Burton's reputation had been damaged. He'd been exposed to ridicule and contempt. Or so a jury could reasonably find. On one view, Hand offers a deeper account of defamation, one casting the traditional constituent elements as only the most obvious way in which one can be defamed. On another view, the now canonical elements of the tort I've presented crystallized as rigid requirements only more recently, so Hand's view was sensible enough when he offered it. On yet another view, Hand rejects the thought that the criteria for defamation will take the form of necessary and sufficient conditions. He argues instead that it's a family-resemblance concept, that what happened to the steeplechaser is close enough to ordinary defamation that it should qualify. The language of Hand's opinion tilts toward the first interpretation, but we might still endorse the last—not least because there are plenty of ways of subjecting someone to ridicule and contempt that don't begin to qualify as defamation at law. Take saddling someone with a ludicrous or degrading nickname.[36] Take com-

---

35. Burton v. Crowell Pub. Co., 82 F.2d 154 (2d Cir. 1936).

36. Consider the court's treatment of an inaccurate use of the nickname "Wicked Wayne" in *Tartaglia v. Townsend,* 19 Mass. App. Ct. 693 (1985). A nickname that itself embeds an allegedly defamatory claim is another mat-

ically mimicking someone's eccentric gait.[37] Then again, we might decide that despite his stature, Hand blew it and the ordinary requirements—defendant wrongly published a false defamatory statement of fact—should be seen as constitutive of the tort.

One can profitably put pressure on any and every dimension of this tort. For instance, we might wonder what various strands are woven together in the concept of reputation.[38] But my strategy here is to put pressure on just one feature of the tort: the thought that it offers no protection for the reputational interests of the dead.

Law's Skepticism and Ours

For indeed, overwhelmingly—I'll provide detail in chapter 4— modern American tort law rejects the claim that defaming the dead is a legal injury. But there are two crucial features of the law's stance.

One: you could insist that the dead can't experience hurt

---

ter: thus the treatment of "la vieja," ordinarily "the old woman," to intimate that a man is gay in *Garcia v. MAC Equip., Inc.*, 2011 U.S. Dist. LEXIS 104502 (S.D. Tex. Sept. 15, 2011).

37. Such mimicking is alleged in *Jones v. Johnson & Wales Univ.*, 2010 U.S. Dist. LEXIS 102040 (D.R.I. Aug. 20, 2010), with multiple causes of action all dismissed on summary judgment: tellingly the court does not think the mimicking is any part of the defamation claim.

38. Indispensable here are Robert C. Post, "The Social Foundations of Defamation Law: Reputation and the Constitution," *California Law Review* (May 1986); and Lawrence McNamara, *Reputation and Defamation* (Oxford: Oxford University Press, 2007). There are closely connected issues in James Q. Whitman, "The Two Western Cultures of Privacy: Dignity versus Liberty," *Yale Law Journal* (April 2004).

feelings, so they can't be injured by defamation. But hurt feelings, or in legalese pain and suffering, aren't an element of the tort. Yes, plaintiffs who are defamed can recover damages for their pain and suffering. And I don't doubt that it's excruciating to know that others believe something defamatory about you. Again, one reason the law sometimes doesn't require any proof of pain and suffering might be that one would more or less automatically expect it to follow from defamation. But a plaintiff who doesn't allege any pain and suffering can win a defamation action. He can testify that he never fretted, that he had dry contempt for others' believing the defamation—but he can still adduce ways in which he's worse off. "The claim that I embezzled, diddled, and popped didn't bother me, but it got me fired": that might reduce his monetary award and the jury might find it baffling; but if defendant argues that it means plaintiff wasn't defamed or can't recover, the judge will reject that argument out of hand.

Two: you could return to the oblivion thesis and insist that once you're dead, you have no interests at all. In this view, there's nothing special about defaming the dead. You'd expect to have no posthumous interests that tort law could vindicate if you think there are no posthumous interests, period. But the law does recognize some posthumous interests.

Let's start here: a legally valid will enables you to dispose of your property after you die. Well, not quite: you won't be around to do that. More precisely, a legally valid will enables you, while you're still alive, to decide how your property will be distributed once you're dead. Your will may be challenged: people you've given short shrift can argue that you weren't competent to make a will—you were delusional or drunk or coerced or unduly influenced, say—or that your will has been forged or that they have a later valid will, which would take precedence.[39] But if the will is valid, the law will ensure that the will's executor respect your intentions, however extraordinary.

The straightforward interpretation of this practice relies on what we say and think all the time: we owe it to the dead to respect their wishes. Shrugging at the will and deciding we know better what to do with the property would seem downright contemptuous. As usual, a consequentialist can reconstruct these intuitions. The real parties in interest, he'd argue, are the beneficiaries of the will. They're alive, thank you very much, and they have an interest in the will being enforced. But why prefer their interests to the interests of those cut out of the will? And why insist on their interests when they're pets? Leona Helmsley left her Maltese, Trouble, a cool $12m in a trust: because of the sort of trust it was, a court was able to knock it down to $2m on the ground that Trouble couldn't conceivably live long enough to need more even to be supported palatially.[40] But no court would rule that because it's perverse to leave a fortune to a pet, Helmsley's will should be flouted. No court would decide to assign those millions to increase social welfare, say by giving them to an inner-city hospital. That maneuver is plain out of bounds.[41]

---

39. Kaprelian v. Kerri Barsamian Harstad, 2010 Cal. App. Unpub. LEXIS 10065 (Dec. 20, 2010) (delusional); In re Estate of Willer, 225 Iowa 606 (1938) (drunk); Matter of Aoki, 99 A.D.3d 253 (N.Y. App. Div. 2012) (coercion or undue influence); Daroff Estate, 1964 Pa. Dist. & Cnty. Dec. LEXIS 317 (Pa. C.P., Orphans' Ct. Div. 1964) (upholding trial verdict rejecting deceased's brother's accusations that deceased's girlfriend murdered him and forged his will). On missing later wills, compare *Sanderson v. Norcross*, 242 Mass. 43 (1922) and *In re Williams' Will*, 121 Misc. 243 (N.Y. Sur. Ct. 1923).

40. Jeffrey Toobin, "Rich Bitch: The Legal Battle over Trust Funds for Pets," *New Yorker* (29 September 2008).

41. On deference to testator's intent, see esp. *Smithsonian Institution v. Meech*, 169 U.S. 398 (1898).

Trouble (the dog) looks like trouble for a consequential-ist. How might he counter? Consider three possibilities. First, he could adopt a modified error theory: we serve the interests of the living by cultivating excessive regard for testamentary intentions, enforcing them even in cases where no living persons are served. By being overinclusive in this way, we strengthen living people's security that we will adhere to the terms of their wills. Second, he could adopt a rule-consequentialist move: it's efficient, or optimal in whatever sense you like, to enforce valid wills across the board, because the error and transaction costs of trying to figure out which individual wills aren't optimal are too high. The error costs would be those of refusing to enforce wills that actually do serve efficiency (but not enforcing wills that shouldn't be enforced, because we're comparing case-by-case appraisal to a blanket policy of enforcing all valid wills). The transaction costs would be the judicial and other resources consumed in appraising the consequences of particular wills. This second move must be contrived if optimality means anything like maximizing utility. Plenty of wills are made by wealthy people passing their wealth on to their children. Is there a plausible story about how they serve some optimal end? Isn't it suspicious how diminishing marginal utility plays Cheshire Cat in these discussions, appearing and disappearing unpredictably? Third, he might argue that by letting people write enforceable wills, the law saves them from having to distribute their property while they're still alive, which could corrupt their relationships with friends, loved ones, charitable agencies, and so on. Sure: but wills also let people jerk around potential beneficiaries by dangling alluring rewards or nasty denials. It's hard to see why the allegedly sophisticated consequentialist stance is more appealing than sticking with the everyday intuition that we owe it to Helmsley to enforce her will.

The consequentialist stance is badly engineered: it has too many rickety moving parts. Yes, I'm ruefully aware that a consequentialist can now go meta and argue that our everyday intuitions, nonconsequentialist as they seem, are properly kitted out for the mentally feeble beings that we are, and were we sufficiently brainy we would embrace his more elaborate reconstructions without hesitation.

Still, when we enforce a will we are respecting the intentions once entertained by a living agent. Defaming the dead is different: it's contrived to say that living agents intend not to be defamed after their deaths, because you can't have intentions about what independent agents do. However we describe the difference, my next examples of the law's regard for the dead can't be set aside as easily.

Take the confidentiality of privileged attorney-client communications. (Those communications are privileged when they are offered to the lawyer in his capacity as a lawyer, not say as a personal aside, and only when offered in private or only in the presence of the lawyer's associates and agents: a secretary, say. Note the contrast: demeaning statements of fact qualify as defamation if and only if published to third parties; communications don't qualify for the privilege if they are published to third parties.) A grand jury wanted to know what Vince Foster had to say to his lawyer nine days before he committed suicide. But the relevant federal rule of evidence instructs courts to "look to the principles of the common law as they may be interpreted by the courts of the United States in the light of reason and experience,"[42] and the Supreme Court easily found that Foster's communications were still properly confidential. Again I think the straightforward interpretation is that we owe

42. USCS Fed. Rules Evid. R. 501.

it to Foster to respect confidentiality here, even though he's dead. Again there are consequentialist reconstructions and indeed the Court offered some: "Without assurance of the privilege's posthumous application, the client may very well not have made disclosures to his attorney at all, so the loss of evidence is more apparent than real. In the case at hand, it seems quite plausible that Foster, perhaps already contemplating suicide, may not have sought legal advice from Hamilton if he had not been assured the conversation was privileged."[43] But even the dissenters conceded "that a deceased client may retain a personal, reputational, and economic interest in confidentiality."[44] In some jurisdictions, the living lawyer does not merely have the right to maintain the confidentiality of privileged communications. He has a duty to do so. As an Illinois court put it, citing state statutes, "It is therefore immaterial that the attorney, called as a witness, is willing to disclose them and as the privilege applies to the communication it is immaterial whether the client is or is not a party to the action in which the questions arise. . . . This protection, given by the law to communications made during the relationship of attorney and client, is perpetual and does not cease by the death of the client."[45]

So too for other privileged communications. In a California case, worries about the validity of a will were not enough to override the confidentiality of the deceased's communications with his doctor. In a 1962 will, Alice Marie White bequeathed her son Albert a trust and provided that Stanford

43. Swidler & Berlin v. United States, 524 U.S. 399, 409 (1998).
44. *Swidler & Berlin* at 412 (O'Connor, J., dissenting).
45. In re Estate of Busse, 332 Ill. App. 258, 266 (1947) (citing, at the ellipses, 28 R. C. L. 548, § 138 and 28 R. C. L. 570, § 160).

University would inherit any remaining assets at Albert's death. But then in 1985 the public administrator found Alice's 1981 will in her safe-deposit box. This one left everything to Albert outright. Seeking to challenge the validity of this later will, Stanford wanted to press the theory that it was merely a gesture to persuade the then mentally disabled Albert that he was securely provided for. So they tried to subpoena Albert's medical records. The court refused. California law provided that holders of such privileges—from confidential communications between attorneys and clients, doctors and patients, penitents and clergy members, and more—were free to insist on them or waive them. Albert was now dead; his estate's administrator held the privilege and wished to enforce it. No more had to be said.[46]

You might well wonder why the legislature would adopt such a rule. Once again, there's a consequentialist reconstruction. (There always is, isn't there?) The court put it this way: "The possibility of posthumous exposure of sensitive, highly personal, and sometimes embarrassing information about one's physical or mental condition, information which often involves surviving family members or other individuals with whom the patient has had contacts, would hinder the free communication between patient and professional which the privilege is designed to encourage."[47] The merits of that reconstruction aside, the administrator has fiduciary obligations to represent

46. Rittenhouse v. Superior Court, 235 Cal. App. 3d 1584 (1991). For the substantive guarantee, see Cal. Evid. Code § 912. Compare the treatment of attorney/client privilege in *In re Layman's Will*, 40 Minn. 371 (1889). For more on medical privacy after death, see Daniel Sperling, *Posthumous Interests: Legal and Ethical Perspectives* (Cambridge: Cambridge University Press, 2008), chap. 5.

47. *Rittenhouse* at 1590.

the interests of the deceased, not to do whatever he takes to be socially optimal or economically efficient, not to think about whether he imagines Stanford is a deserving beneficiary, not anything remotely like that. Similarly, had Stanford showed up in the internecine court proceedings over Leona Helmsley's will and urged that they were more deserving than Trouble, the court wouldn't have given them the time of day.

Legislation sometimes secures posthumous interests. Take Washington state's statute on the right of publicity, securing "a property right in the use of his or her name, voice, signature, photograph, or likeness. . . . The property right does not expire upon the death of the individual or personality, regardless of whether the law of the domicile, residence, or citizenship of the individual or personality at the time of death or otherwise recognizes a similar or identical property right."[48] Litigation over the exclusive right to commercially exploit Jimi Hendrix's likeness and name produced a flurry of constitutional challenges to this provision. They failed.[49] You might think the real beneficiaries of the rule are the living inheritors of Hendrix's intellectual property rights, but not all such legislation can be disposed of so readily.

So consider a quirky complication in U.S. copyright law. We tend to think of the "moral rights of the artist" as a European obsession. But visual artists now enjoy a right—the qualifications needn't concern us—"to prevent any intentional distortion, mutilation, or other modification of that work which would be prejudicial to his or her honor or reputation, and any intentional distortion, mutilation, or modification of that work

---

48. Rev. Code Wash. (ARCW) § 63.60.010.
49. Experience Hendrix L.L.C. v. Hendrixlicensing.com Ltd, 762 F.3d 829 (9th Cir. 2014).

is a violation of that right . . . and to prevent any destruction of a work of recognized stature, and any intentional or grossly negligent destruction of that work is a violation of that right."[50] The visual artist continues to enjoy these rights even when someone else owns the work of art. And visual artists who created their art before 1990, when this legislation took effect, and still owned it then enjoy that right for decades after they die.[51]

Here's another bit of intellectual property law. Under the Lanham Act, as a general matter trademarks shall issue on application—but not for "matter which may disparage . . . persons, living or dead . . . or bring them into contempt, or disrepute."[52] What's the point of this restriction? Surely one plausible view—I don't insist that it stands alone—is that it invades the rights of the dead to use them for marketing in such derogatory ways. Denial of a trademark is far removed from liability in tort. But here the law does seem solicitous of the dead's reputational interests.

Sometimes the law protects posthumous rights even when the legislature hasn't explicitly addressed the matter. Take the Freedom of Information Act (FOIA), honeycombed with exemptions designed to protect individual privacy. Does the provision exempting information that "could reasonably be expected to constitute an unwarranted invasion of personal privacy" extend to protecting the privacy of the dead?[53] One court ruled it does: "the death of the subject of personal information does diminish to some extent the privacy interest in

50. 17 USCS § 106A(a)(3).
51. 17 USCS § 106A(d)(2), incorporating by reference 17 USCS §§ 302–3. Thanks to Jessica Litman for pointing me to *Experience Hendrix* and for guiding me through the complexities of this statute.
52. 15 USCS § 1052(a).
53. 5 USCS § 552(b)(7)(c).

that information, though it by no means extinguishes that interest; one's own and one's relations' interests in privacy ordinarily extend beyond one's death."[54] The Supreme Court, considering the same provision in a challenge to a denial of a FOIA request for the death-scene photos of Vince Foster, relied on the thought that publicizing the photos would invade the privacy of Foster's surviving family members.[55] But that was precisely the rationale urged by Foster's family and by the solicitor general in their briefs and there was no reason for the Court to take up Foster's own interests *sua sponte*, or on its own accord.[56]

These features of law are so deeply entrenched that it's easy to ignore them. On the view that dead people still have interests that the law should respect, they are crystal clear and make perfect sense. Those denying that view can offer elliptical reconstructions or argue that the law is wrong. But the law is utterly solicitous of your testamentary intentions, however eccentric; and the law will enforce the confidentiality of your privileged communications after your death; and the law will extend some statutory protections to cover the dead, even absent any pressing evidence that the bare language of the statute requires doing so or that the legislature intended that result.

54. Schrecker v. United States DOJ, 254 F.3d 162, 166 (D.C. Cir. 2001). This continues to be binding law in the circuit: see *Plunkett v. DOJ*, 924 F. Supp. 2d 289 (D.D.C. 2013).

55. Nat'l Archives & Records Admin. v. Favish, 541 U.S. 157 (2004). Likewise, on a parallel FOIA exemption, see *Badhwar v. United States Dep't of Air Force*, 829 F.2d 182 (D.C. Cir. 1987). Contrast the reliance on *Restatement (Second) of Torts*, § 652I, in *Mineer v. Williams*, 82 F. Supp. 2d 702 (E.D. Ky. 2000) (denying the possibility of tort liability for invading the privacy of a dead person).

56. 2003 U.S. S. Ct. Briefs LEXIS 808; 2003 U.S. S. Ct. Briefs LEXIS 816.

Recall what I dubbed the oblivion thesis, one powerfully seductive attack on worries about defaming the dead. Recall the appeal of the dead butcher's haunting refrain: "When I die, my body will be taken to the charnel ground and it will be eaten by birds and wild animals. Not a trace will be left. My mind will vanish, so at that time who will be left to go to the hells. HA! HA!" Our skeptic bravely sides with the butcher and taunts us for implicitly relying on belief in the afterlife, just the sort of belief the Tibetan *Book of the Dead* enlists to show that the joke's on the butcher. And again I want to argue that the oblivion thesis is false—and I want to deny that doing so requires any such reliance on the afterlife.

For now, I want to emphasize this. Rejecting a privacy claim brought on behalf of a dead woman, another New York court said bluntly, "Death deprives us of all rights, in the legal sense of that term."[57] As a matter of positive law, that was wrong when the court said it. It remains wrong today. Because the law won't entertain tort claims for defaming the dead, I can't enlist the law as support for my view. But neither can fans of the oblivion thesis.

57. Schuyler v. Curtis, 147 N.Y. 434, 447 (1895).

III

Speak No Evil

This obituary went viral:

> Marianne Theresa Johnson-Reddick born Jan
> 4, 1935 and died alone on [August] 30, 2013. She is
> survived by her 6 of 8 children whom she spent her
> lifetime torturing in every way possible. While she
> neglected and abused her small children, she re-
> fused to allow anyone else to care or show compas-
> sion towards them. When they became adults she
> stalked and tortured anyone they dared to love. Ev-
> eryone she met, adult or child was tortured by her
> cruelty and exposure to violence, criminal activity,
> vulgarity, and hatred of the gentle or kind human
> spirit.
>
> On behalf of her children whom she so abra-
> sively exposed to her evil and violent life, we cele-
> brate her passing from this earth and hope she lives
> in the after-life reliving each gesture of violence,
> cruelty, and shame that she delivered on her chil-

dren. Her surviving children will now live the rest of their lives with the peace of knowing their nightmare finally has some form of closure.

Most of us have found peace in helping those who have been exposed to child abuse and hope this message of her final passing can revive our message that abusing children is unforgiveable, shameless, and should not be tolerated in a "humane society." Our greatest wish now, is to stimulate a national movement that mandates a purposeful and dedicated war against child abuse in the United States of America.[1]

Months later, the obituary's author outed herself online. One of Johnson-Reddick's daughters, she furnished wrenching detail of child abuse and responded to the charge that it was outrageous to craft such an obituary:

How could anyone write a scathing and public obituary showing such disdain for a parent? For me, it was a natural "normal" process for ending and celebrating the death of someone who camouflaged themselves as a mother.

There are no words or expressions to adequately describe the sense of freedom I felt upon a phone call from my brother singing "Ding Dong, the witch is dead."

1. *Reno Gazette-Journal* (10 September 2013). Reprinted with permission of Katherine Reddick, Ph.D. Organizational Consultant, specializing in reforming America's foster care system.

The resoundingly positive online comments included this gem: "I applaud you. Congratulations on the loss of your mother."[2] Whether or not the daughter acted wrongly in publishing this obituary, it isn't innocuous. It wouldn't have gone viral—globally—if it hadn't so blatantly transgressed our deep sense that you should speak no ill of the dead. That norm is so powerful that even Richard Nixon benefited from it. Yes, Tricky Dick—I came of political age despising him, way before Watergate, so I recycled the name for the ludicrous orange vinyl clown my small daughters used as a bath toy; they relished the vaguely obscene noise it made when they squeezed it, and I figured political socialization can't start too early— died and suddenly was no longer the guy you wouldn't buy a used car from.[3] Instead he was instantly reincarnated as a sage statesman. Even the *New York Times,* not renowned for its devotion to Nixon or the GOP, ran an obituary that pivoted from acknowledging Watergate to intoning, "Yet Mr. Nixon, surely one of the half-dozen pivotal figures of American politics in the quarter-century that followed World War II, wrought foreign policy accomplishments of historic proportions that had proved beyond the reach of his Democratic foes."[4]

2. Katherine Reddick, "I Wrote the 'Scathing Obituary' about My Mother, and Here's Why I Did It and Have No Regrets," www.xojane.com/it-happened -to-me/scathing-obituary-katherine-reddick (18 February 2014) (last visited 10 June 2014), footnotes removed. See too Siobhan McAndrew, "Brutal Obituary Reveals Lives of Neglect, Abuse: Daughter, Son Didn't Expect Mother's Obit to Go Viral," *Reno Gazette-Journal* (11 September 2013).

3. "The Salesman"—of caskets, not cars—in Herbert Block, *The Herblock Gallery* (New York: Simon & Schuster, 1968), 171–72, reprinted in Block, *Herblock Special Report* (New York: W. W. Norton, 1974), 68–71, ought to be better known.

4. R. W. Apple, Jr., "The 37th President; Richard Nixon, 81, Dies; A Master of Politics Undone by Watergate," *New York Times* (23 April 1994).

So even if it can be overridden, there seems to be some serious commitment to the view that we ought not speak ill of the dead. Our skeptic might be impatient. "Johnson-Reddick is dead," he'll say. "She's in no position to be wronged. Make the obituary as flagrantly false as you like. Make the daughter's motivations as wretched as you like. It makes no difference. Johnson-Reddick is beyond harm, beyond wrong. I grant," he continues, "that the prohibition on speaking ill of the dead goes back a very long way. Indeed an early statement comes from Chilon of Sparta, from the sixth century B.C.[5] But you've rightly credited me with commitments to the oblivion thesis and the hangover thesis. Recall Fustel's account and you'll see why people thought they shouldn't speak ill of the dead. It's prudent to refrain if you imagine their spirits are alert, powerful, vengeful. But once you surrender that picture, you ought to realize that the dead are well and truly gone. They're in no position to suffer distress, let alone to take vengeance on us: who will be left to go to the hells? ha! ha! Johnson-Reddick cannot reach out from beyond the grave and punish her daughter for her audacity. So there is no reason to hesitate at speaking ill of the dead. Not that a weighty presumption against doing that could in principle be overridden, as many thought was true in the case of the daughter's obituary for her mother. Rather that there's no apparent justification for having any such presumption in the first place. Or anyway, that presumption would have to depend on the claims of the living, because they're the only critters with any claims at all."

The skeptic is right about one thing: cultural disapproval of speaking ill of the dead, even skittishness about it, is long-

<hr />

5. Diogenes Laertius, *Lives of Eminent Philosophers*, trans. R. D. Hicks, 2 vols. (Cambridge, MA: Harvard University Press, 1950), 1:70.

standing. It's undeniable that we think it's ordinarily an awful thing to do, at least about those who've died recently, at least by those who knew them, or to people who knew them or in settings where those people will learn about it. Talk of cross-cultural universals is notoriously tricky, but I also think it un-deniable that some such sentiment is utterly common across centuries and continents. I turn now to canvassing some his-torical sources: like law, they offer an opportunity to go beyond intuition; and like law, they're worthy of some epistemic defer-ence. Here I briefly sample some discussions from early mod-ern England. I don't imagine that any such snapshots could begin to furnish a properly historical account. But I do want to invoke some argumentative maneuvers available in the set-ting shaping the common law. Then I'll probe one nineteenth-century American controversy in depth.

Some Views from Early Modern England

Earnest moralists and churchmen in England loved to recur to the Latin maxim *de mortuis nil nisi bonum*: of the dead, noth-ing unless good; or, for its actual force, speak no ill of the dead. The injunction to speak no ill of the dead even made it into a children's primer with the monarch's stamp of approval.[6] Ad-dressing Parliament and Queen Elizabeth on the nefarious role of the deceased Philip II of Spain in the Anglo-Spanish War, the Lord Keeper quoted *de mortuis* and then underlined it with hyperbole: "I would be loth to speak of the dead, much more

---

6. *The New Universal Primer, or, An Easy Book, Suited to the Tender Ca-pacities of Children: Authorised by His Majesty King GEORGE* (Derby, [1790?]), 50. See too John Tapner, *The School-Master's Repository; or, Youth's Moral Preceptor* (London, [1761]), 29.

to slander the dead."[7] Remember, some urged, that Solon in his wisdom had made *de mortuis* a law for Athens. Plutarch reports Solon's justification: "It is pious to think the deceased sacred, and just, not to meddle with those that are gone, and politic, to prevent the perpetuity of discord."[8] The discord might be among the living, divided by their disputes about the dead. Or it might also be visited on us by the resentful dead. This is an ancient belief, but it surfaces later than you might expect. One (fictionalized) 1691 source observes, "*Plato's Ring* had this *Motto* on it, *It is easier to provoke the Dead, than to pacifie them, when once provok'd*. Intimating thereby, That the *Souls* of the *Departed*, are sensible of the Injuries that are done them by the *Living*."[9] Again I disclaim any reliance on the claim that the dead are aware of and interested in what the living say. So again if it turns out that's the only way to make sense of worries about defaming the dead, we should—I should—stop worrying.

One divine likened those bashing a dead prelate to hissing adders and "*Cannibals* . . . delight[ing] to feed on dead mans flesh, by tearing of their Fame."[10] The parallel to cannibalism isn't unique. One 1611 writer sighed, "Mee thinks, that Calumny should ende with the carkasse of her subiect, and not

7. Sir Simonds D'Ewes, *The Journals of All the Parliaments during the Reign of Queen Elizabeth, Both of the House of Lords and the House of Commons*, rev. Paul Bowes (London, 1682), 599–600.

8. *Plutarch's Lives*, trans. Bernadotte Perrin, 10 vols. (London: William Heinemann; Cambridge, MA: Harvard University Press, 1914), 1:461.

9. [Mahmut] to Dgnet Oglou, 20th of the 1st moon of the year 1649, in [Giovanni Paolo Marana], *The Third Volume of Letters Writ by a Turkish Spy, Who Lived Five and Forty Years, Undiscover'd, at Paris* (London, 1691), 356.

10. Isaac Basire, *The Dead Mans Real Speech: A Funeral Sermon Preached on Hebr. Xi. 4* (London, 1673), 32–33. See more generally William Davy, *A System of Divinity, in a Course of Sermons*, 26 vols. (Lustleigh, [1798–]1807), 8:275–76.

haunt the graue till the last bone be consumed."[11] (Would our skeptic say that shrinking from cannibalism is itself indefensible? "It's protein, and it's just a cadaver, not a person. Probably it's an environmental winner to eat corpses: Greenpeace ought to get over their irrational disgust and start lobbying. I guess you'd want to know about mercury and saturated fat, bacteria too; but that's to serve your welfare, not the dead person's." I'll turn to corpse desecration in chapter 5.) It's worth mentioning a cultural setting the early modern English were less fond of: according to one hadith, the Prophet reproved two men for commenting nastily on a man stoned to death for adultery. As they passed a dead donkey, the Prophet invited them to partake of its flesh. They were stunned—until the Prophet explained that their dishonoring the dead man was worse than eating the carcass.[12]

Just how is speaking ill of the dead like cannibalism? We might say that each practice treats the dead unacceptably, but that wouldn't provide much leverage. That is, it wouldn't follow that cannibalism is objectionable for the same reasons that speaking ill of the dead is. But maybe it's just that each is an invasion of a feature closely associated with persons: bodies in one case, reputations in the other. If you think it's wrong to invade such features when persons are alive, you might think it remains wrong when they're dead. It remains open whether worrying about such invasions after the person's death is irrational, even contemptible, or perfectly sensible.

11. [Anthony Stafford], *Staffords Niobe: or His Age of Teares* (London, 1611), 137.

12. Imam Abu Dawud As-Sijistani, *Sunan Abu Dawud: The Third Correct Tradition of the Prophetic Sunna*, trans. Mohammad Mahdi al-Sharif, 5 vols. (Lebanon: Dar Al-Kotob Al-ilmiyah, 2008), 5:50, an extension of Quran 49:12.

Some indicted the cowardice of defaming the dead: "It is not less cowardly to speak ill of the Dead, than it would be to kill an Enemy incapable of making his own Defence."[13] Others seem to have found a violation of gallantry: "Amongst generous Spirits, it is accounted base to be valiant amongst them that cannot resist, or to hurt the name and reputation of the dead."[14]

The dead can't defend themselves. These authors appeal to that ineluctable fact to support a principle sounding in fair play: one ought to attack only those capable of self-defense; criticizing the dead is then like taking candy from a baby. (Compare two nearby principles: "Pick on someone your own size"; and "If you have something to say about me, say it to my face.") The same ineluctable fact could be spun epistemically: we're less likely to learn what can be said in the dead's defense. After all, the living might well know exculpatory things about themselves that others don't know. And they might well have a keener incentive to defend themselves. These reasons offer the outlines of a defense of the view that we should speak no ill of the dead. But the stricture against speaking ill of the dead doesn't seem to extend to criticizing the comatose or far-off people who speak foreign languages. So this justification is overinclusive as against the norm we're trying to understand.

13. [Jean Baptiste Morvan, Abbé de Bellegarde], *Reflexions upon Ridicule*, 3rd ed., 2 vols. (London, 1717), 1:143. See too [Adam Petrie], *Rules of Good Deportment, or of Good Breeding, for the Use of Youth* (Edinburgh, 1720), 58; *A Collection of Select Aphorisms and Maxims* (Dublin, 1722), 8; Charles Palmer, *A Collection of Select Aphorisms and Maxims* (London, 1748), 14; Chilo the Lacedemonian, in Erasmus, *The Apopthegms of the Ancients*, 2 vols. (London, 1753), 1:77; *The Instructor: or, The Art of Living Well* (London, 1754), 146.

14. John Guillim, *A Display of Heraldry* (London, 1679), 165. See too John Spencer, *Kaina Kai Palia: Things New and Old* (London, 1658), 206.

Most early modern English opponents of *de mortuis* do not endorse the oblivion thesis. They do not say that the dead have no claims on us. Instead they argue that the norm may be properly overridden, just as many thought Johnson-Reddick's daughter was justified in publishing her blistering obituary. Or they argue that *de mortuis* chips away too broadly at frank discussion of the dead, some of which would be salutary. One pamphleteer assaulting the recently executed Charles I spat out, "I am not ignorant what senslesse maxims and ridiculous principles have gotten credit in the World (as undoubted Oracles indisputably to be obeyed) as that *de mortuis nil nisi bona,* but by no means to tread on the sacred Urne of Princes, though living never so vicious and exorbitant, as if death had bequeathed unto them a supersedeas for the covering over their faults and licencious reignes, and to close them up in the Coffin of Oblivion."[15] (A contemporary defined *supersedeas:* "In our common Law it signifieth a commandement sent by writing, forbidding an officer from the doing of that, which otherwise he might and ought to doe.")[16] Jonathan Swift fumed, "These excellent Casuists know just *Latin* enough, to have heard a most foolish Precept, that *de mortuis nil nisi bonum,* so that if *Socrates,* and *Anytus* his Accuser, had happened to die together, the Charity of Survivers must either have obliged them

15. *The Life and Reigne of King Charls, or the Pseudo Martyr Discovered* (London, 1651), preface, sig. A4 recto. The piece is sometimes attributed to John Milton, but that seems wrong. There's no mention of it in *Complete Prose Works of John Milton,* ed. Don M. Wolfe et al., 8 vols. (New Haven: Yale University Press, 1953–82).

16. I. B., *An English Expositor: Teaching the Interpretation of the Hardest Words Used in Our Language* (London, 1641), s.v. *supersedeas.* Note Hobbes's characteristic worry about fragmented authority: Tho[mas] Hobbes, *De Corpore Politico: or, The Elements of Law, Moral & Politick* (London, 1652), 153.

to hold their Peace, or to fix the same Character on both."[17]
The thought is that we have pressing interests in sharpening
our moral appraisals, and it would make us less intelligent to
declare the dead off limits. Given one strand of the complicated gender history of free speech, on which public reason
invigorates manly citizens and humble deference effeminates
subjects, Dr. Johnson may have been agreeing when he scoffed
that *de mortuis* "appeared to me to favour more of female
weakness than of manly reason."[18]

These writers rallied to underline the public benefits of
speaking ill of the dead when the ill is deserved; that is, when
the charges are truthful; that is, when it would not today qualify at tort law as defamation even were the subjects alive. That
stance might explain this apparent irony: "I am not fond of libelling the dead," one writer assured his readers before pum-
meling one of English legal history's most deserving targets,
Judge Jeffreys of the infamous bloody assizes.[19] Nothing libelous about rehearsing the actual record of Jeffries's scandalous
abuses. So—I want to emphasize this point—it's a mistake to
imagine that *de mortuis* underwrites the case for making it a

---

17. *An Answer to a Paper Called a Memorial* (Dublin, 1728), in *The Prose
Works of Jonathan Swift*, ed. Herbert Davis, 14 vols. (Oxford: Basil Blackwell,
1939–68), 12:24–25. See too Swift's *An Examination of Certain Abuses, Cor-
ruptions, and Enormities in the City of Dublin* (Dublin, 1732), in *Prose Works*,
12:226–27.

18. "Young," in Samuel Johnson, *The Lives of the Most Eminent English
Poets, with Critical Observations on Their Works*, ed. Roger Lonsdale, 4 vols.
(Oxford: Clarendon Press, 2006), 4:149.

19. [Philip Withers], *Alfred's Appeal: Containing His Address to the Court
of King's Bench, on the Subject of the Marriage of Mary Anne Fitzherbert, and
Her Intrigue with Count Bellois* (London, 1789), 52. Compare *Reveries of the
Heart; during a Tour through Part of England and France*, 2 vols. (London,
1781), 2:186–87.

tort to defame the dead. It's a mistake to imagine that the critics I've quoted expose that case as silly. To the contrary! So far as they're complaining that *de mortuis* is overinclusive, their views explain why tort law shouldn't make it actionable to offer truthful criticism of the dead. But truth is not defamatory anyway, whether the target of the attack is alive or dead. Indeed, early modern English critics' emphasis on the social value of criticizing dead public figures, especially political and legal authorities, anticipates crucial strands of today's First Amendment law, though obviously they couldn't know that.

More generally, *de mortuis* was pernicious nonsense that would make it impossible to write history, impossible to inspire readers to be moral:

> They say, *De Mortuis nil nisi Bonum,*
> Thieves and Murderers never stone 'um.
> Do all mischief live or dead,
> Expect not to be punished,
> Nor so much as mentioned.
> Why then should Vertue be rewarded,
> If Vice must not be regarded?
> These are simple, silly Themes,
> The Offspring of idle Dreams.
>
> Burn all Histories to Ashes,
> Call *Plutarch, Tacitus* and *Livy,* Flashes.
> For daring to record the Doom
> Of Tyrants, in *Greece* or *Rome.*[20]

---

20. R[obert] D[ixon], *Canidia, or The Witches: A Rhapsody* (London, 1683), 168. See too [John Carrington], *The Lancashire Levite Rebuk'd: or, A Farther Vindication of the Dissenters from Popery, Superstition, Ignorance, and Knavery* (London, 1698), preface; [Benjamin] Victor, *The History of the*

Even one churchman, Abraham Markland, agreed that one ought to speak evil of those who really deserved it: "As it is no Injury to the Dead, it is a Justice we owe to the Living; the greatest Kindness and Charity; and may serve to discourage and deter them from following such wicked Examples."[21]

Appeals to *de mortuis* exasperated even whimsical Laurence Sterne. In *Tristram Shandy* he had taken a nasty swipe at the weirdly named—but, as always with Sterne, think about puns and lascivious associations, and, um, make it a short *u*—Kunastrokius.[22] Contemporaries figured out that this clown was the late Dr. Richard Mead. One of Sterne's correspondents reproached him by reciting *de mortuis*. He'd "waited four days to cool myself," responded Sterne, "before I would set pen to paper to answer you." Then he let fly this zinger: "I can find nothing in it, or make more sense of it, than a nonsensical lullaby of some nurse, put into Latin by some pedant, to be chanted by some hypocrite to the end of the world, for the consolation of departing lechers."[23]

Theatres of London and Dublin, from the Year 1730 to the Present Time, 2 vols. (London, 1761), 1:36–37; Richard Saumarez, *A New System of Physiology*, 2nd ed., 2 vols. (London, 1799), 1:87 n. Contrast *A Modest Vindication of Oliver Cromwell from the Unjust Accusations of Lieutenant-General Ludlow in His Memoirs* (London, 1698), 76.

21. Abraham Markland, *Sermons Preach'd at the Cathedral-Church of Winchester*, 2 vols. (London, 1729), 2:120–21.

22. *Tristram Shandy*, vol. 1, chap. 7, from the narrator's ruminations on hobby horses, with an unmistakable intimation of oral sex, if not oral-on-anal bestiality: "Did not Dr. Kunastrokius, that great man, at his leisure hours, take the greatest delight imaginable in combing of asses' tails, and plucking the dead hairs out with his teeth, though he had tweezers always in his pocket?"

23. Laurence Sterne to Dr. ******, 30 January 1760, in *The Florida Edition of the Works of Laurence Sterne*, ed. Melvyn New et al., 8 vols. (Gainesville: University Presses of Florida, 1978–2008), 7:114. For a different rendition of

Notice another motif in these last few sources: prospective thieves, murderers, tyrants, and lechers can be deterred if they believe *de mortuis* will not protect their reputations once they're dead. Not only will free discussion of the dead's vices sharpen our moral understanding; it also will lead people to behave better. The invocation of deterrence means we will behave better, not just because of our sharpened understanding, but because we ourselves don't want to be castigated once we're dead. Here again the living's concern for their postmortem reputations is a prop in the argument that—the paradox is only apparent—it's okay, all things considered, to criticize the dead.

Is it irrational of the living to care about their postmortem reputations? True, we joke about posterity: "What's posterity ever done for me?" True, we can imagine the cunning rogue whose plans depend on not getting caught only as long as he's alive. He might deride the thought that his schemes would count as failures if they were detected only after his death. "By then," he might say, "I'll have pocketed and enjoyed my ill-gotten gains, and never been punished." But many of us do want to be thought well of by posterity, if we're remembered at all. Or at least we want to be thought of justly. We want not to be credited with misdeeds we're not actually guilty of. In short, we want not to be defamed after we're dead. If you're skeptical, you could shrug this off as a brute psychological fact and say we might as well capitalize on it to promote the interests of the living. You could then redouble the attack on *de mortuis:* it's only an obstacle to deterring bad actions.

Mead's sexual predilections, see *Florida Edition,* 3:57–58. A critic of *Tristram Shandy,* for reasons that escape me, presented himself as Kunastrokius's son: *Explanatory Remarks upon The Life and Opinions of Tristram Shandy: Wherein, the Morals and Politics of This Piece Are Clearly Laid Open, by Jeremiah Kunastrokius, M.D.* (London, 1760), 5.

Writers today may not tip their hats to, or scoff at, *de mortuis,* but it's not hard to find them flouting its putative wisdom. Here's Terry Eagleton taking deadly aim at two famous writers, living son and dead father. He starts with a quotation:

> "They're gaining on us demographically at a huge rate. A quarter of humanity now and by 2025 they'll be a third. Italy's down to 1.1 child per woman. We're just going to be outnumbered.... There's a definite urge—don't you have it?—to say, 'The Muslim community will have to suffer until it gets its house in order.' What sort of suffering? Not letting them travel. Deportation—further down the road. Curtailing of freedoms. Strip-searching people who look like they're from the Middle East or from Pakistan ... Discriminatory stuff, until it hurts the whole community and they start getting tough with their children." ...

Not the ramblings of a British National Party thug, but the reflections of the novelist Martin Amis, leading luminary of the English metropolitan literary world. There might, perhaps, be a genetic excuse for this squalid mixture of bile and hysteria: Amis's father Kingsley, after all, was a racist, anti-Semitic boor, a drink-sodden, self-hating reviler of women, gays, and liberals, and Amis *fils* has clearly learnt more from him than how to turn a shapely phrase.[24]

---

24. "Introduction to the 2007 Edition," in Terry Eagleton, *Ideology: An Introduction* (London: Verso, 2007), x. For the quotation, see www.ginny dougary.co.uk/the-voice-of-experience (last visited 12 December 2015).

It's easy to fret that tort liability would deprive us of the pleasures—not all of them ignoble—of reading this sort of thing. We could bicker over whether Eagleton's claims about Kingsley Amis are fact or opinion, for instance, or (transplanting the matter from the U.K. to the U.S.) whether an action brought on behalf of Kingsley would founder on his being a public figure. But rules and remedies are not yet the point. We're still trying to sort out whether it makes any sense to think there's a presumptive injury here, even if we finally decide that offsetting considerations suggest that tort liability must be carefully refined—or precluded outright. Look how easily Abraham Markland could concede that "it is no Injury to the Dead" to assail their reputations. You could interpret him as endorsing the global thesis that there's nothing for the concept of wrongful injury to get a grip on. But again the context of his remark is crucial: he's considering truthful reports of the dead's misdeeds. So perhaps he's saying only that they have no cause for complaint if their deeds are reported accurately.

Still, I grant that Markland might champion the oblivion thesis. But recall that that thesis, whatever its merits, is an awfully awkward explanation for tort law's refusal to recognize defaming the dead as a cause of action, because the law readily protects other posthumous interests. So too, *de mortuis* wouldn't ground a defense of tort liability for defaming the dead, because the maxim is crudely wholesale. It covers evil spoken of the dead whether it's true or false. But it's a constitutive element of the tort of defamation that the charge be false. You can recur to earlier strands in the common law, where even true defamatory claims could be tortious unless they were published for good ends, say to warn innocent third parties against dealing with a scoundrel. But *de mortuis* is even broader than that. It is an apparently absolute proscription. The oblivion thesis and *de mortuis* pair off nicely as rivals, then. But the law is drawing more fine-grained distinctions than either rival view suggests.

You might think that we don't need an argument for the oblivion thesis, that it's obviously true. So consider this darkly hilarious epitaph:

Sacred to the Memory of the wanton and libidinous
E—S—V—G—,
Whose Life as variegated as the pantomimical Garb;
The Colours of which may each of them be considered
emblematic of her numerous destinies.
The Sable, the Gloom of a Prison, which she but too
often inhabited;
The Azure, that Calmness of Fortune, she seldom was
acquainted with,
And the OR, that Honor, Happiness, and Affluence which
was
no sooner in her Grasp than discarded from Self-vanity,
Profligacy, and Inconsiderateness.
But to mark what she has been, and to ascertain what she
should
have been, cannot but be affecting and deviating from
that humane, tho' unwise Injunction,

DE MORTUIS NIL NISI BONUM.

Of Ability, she was an uncommon Owner:
Of Fortune, 'till she abused the fickle Goddess, she never
knew the want;
And in her Matrimonial Connection, she might have been
peculiarly happy, had she not forfeited the Affections
of a deserving Husband, the Friendship of

her Relations, and the Esteem of
her Friends, by
Infamy unparalleled;
Prostitution unrestrained,
Extravagance unbounded:
and Perfidy unmerited.
In the 39th Year of her Age, she departed this Life, friendless,
worn out by Debauchery and Want.[25]

These charges could help motivate the living to steer
clear of lurid vices ("I don't want *that* on my gravestone!"), just
as inscriptions touting the virtues of the dead could help motivate the living to pursue virtue themselves. But suppose that
E.S.V.G. didn't deserve a word of this, that it's malicious fabri-
cation from start to finish. Let's return to the core puzzle: was
she injured by it? (Suppose her enemies don't taunt her with
the language before she dies.) Suppose someone erects a headstone or a monument with a similar tale about you after you
die. Are you indifferent to that prospect? Or is the only reason
you care that your family and friends would find it upsetting?

But now I want to tighten the screws because I'm convinced that that move sidesteps the issue. What would your
family and friends be upset about? Presumably they think that
you've been wronged. The loving family member who's actually thinking, "Oh hell, dear departed's reputation matters only
if and insofar as it affects *my* life," is self-absorbed. To put it
mildly. If you think the defamatory epitaph is wrong only insofar as it harms or offends the survivors, and they think the

---

25. [Herbert Croft], *The Wreck of Westminster Abbey, Being a Selection
from the Monumental Records of the Most Conspicuous Personages*, 6th ed.
(London, [1788]), 34–35.

injury is to the deceased, we're going around in a perverse circle. Sure, you could resolve the paradox by insisting that it's irrational for *anyone* to care about such matters. But what makes you so confident about that? I see the appeal of an error theory that impeaches our beliefs about our interests after we die, even if I'm not inclined to subscribe to it: there are abundant puzzles and anyway it's hard to be confident in our intuitions. But I balk when it seems that that same error theory dictates that the everyday reactions of grieving survivors are simply misconceived. Imagine confronting E.S.V.G.'s indignant and sobbing daughter. "Not a word of it is true!" she gasps. "You have nothing to worry about," you purr soothingly. "It's no injury to your mother. After all, she's dead." Surely the daughter will glare at you as if you're a blithering idiot. Want to persist and explain to her that she's confused? If she's more belligerent and threatens to defame your recently deceased mother to dramatize what's at stake, do you want to shrug and say, "Be my guest"? If you shrink from that, do you want to defend the view that shrinking is irrational?

Let's return briefly to the Johnson-Reddick obituary and canvass the interests of the living that might underlie a commitment to *de mortuis*. Living onlookers might have some interest in knowing the truth about Johnson-Reddick. So *they* would be ill-served if the obituary were false, and it might then matter that Johnson-Reddick is in no position to respond to it. But if it's true and they have reason to care, they're better off for its publication. (But maybe they don't or shouldn't want only to believe what happens to be true. Maybe they do or should want their belief to be justified, and so maybe they too will or should worry about charging someone who can't respond. Or maybe they are people who don't want their longstanding affection for Johnson-Reddick exploded by this news: after all, we have interests in emotional well-being and serenity, not just in maximizing how many true beliefs we hold. This last suggests that it's overstated to cast truth as the sole regulative ideal of belief formation.) And the obituary makes an explicit appeal to the public interest in understanding that child abuse is an outrage and in acting accordingly. That broader public, too, might be benefited, not least the children whose abuse would be averted by greater efforts, though—the epistemic point again—it would be bad for the cause if it turned out the ghastly charges in the obituary were false, because others would suggest that we are suffering a case of moral panic about child abuse and we should realize that the phenomenon is overblown. Consider the flap surrounding the revelation that Cambodian activist Somaly Mam had invented her tale of being sold into sex slavery as an orphan.[26]

But does it make sense to say that Johnson-Reddick herself could be wronged by the publication of this obituary? Were she alive and were the charges false, surely the publication would be wrong. Tort law would recognize this as a straightforward case of libel. Trickier: suppose Johnson-Reddick were alive but the charges were true: could she be wronged by their publication? Or could she have a right that others not publish true but damaging information about her? What if they'd voluntarily agreed not to? What if their sole purpose in doing so was to cause her distress? Would that last go only to assessing their motivation but not to whether the publication itself was right or wrong? Whatever your inclination about those ques-

26. Thomas Fuller, "Cambodian Activist's Fall Exposes Broad Deception," *New York Times* (14 June 2014) ("A government study conducted five years ago found that 77 percent of children living in Cambodia's orphanages had at least one [living] parent").

tions, we needn't resolve them to get a clearer grasp of the legal issues surrounding defaming the dead, because—the point bears repetition—as a matter of law truthful claims cannot qualify as the tort of defamation.

Can the Dead Defame the Dead?

I turn now to a more extended example. First I lay out the source materials, in a roughly chronological narrative. Then I explore some queries about them.

Margaret Fuller drowned on 19 July 1850, some fifty yards offshore, with onlookers making no rescue effort as the boat went down. She was returning from Italy with her husband, Count Ossoli (though some scowled that they were only lovers), and their child; Ossoli and the child drowned too. Today she's known mostly by feminists with historical interests, for her *Woman in the Nineteenth Century*—you might know Edgar Allan Poe's apocryphal gibe, that humanity is divided into "men, women, and Margaret Fuller"—and by those interested in American transcendentalism.[27] Fuller was prom-

---

27. For a curious defense, insisting that Fuller was "large-breasted," that "the strand of tawny blond hair that survives negates all claims that it was stringy and lusterless," and that Europeans found her "graceful and charming," see Joseph Jay Deiss, "Humanity, Said Edgar Allan Poe, Is Divided into Men, Women, and Margaret Fuller," *American Heritage* (August 1972). You can't make this stuff up. Deiss's concession—"True, she was nearsighted and squinted disconcertingly"—is more of the same. The wording attributed to Poe, deployed endlessly since then, is from Perry Miller, *The Transcendentalists: An Anthology* (Cambridge, MA: Harvard University Press, 1950), 467; it's also in *Margaret Fuller: American Romantic; A Selection from Her Writings and Correspondence,* ed. Perry Miller (Garden City, NY: Anchor Books, 1963), 192. Miller offers no citation and I've found no earlier instance of the language, though I blanch at the thought that Miller, a superb scholar, in-

inent enough in those circles for Emerson to prevail on Thoreau to descend on the accident site and recover what he could. Thoreau was joined by other transcendentalists.[28] Fuller and Nathaniel Hawthorne knew one another well: she was a regular visitor at Brook Farm, site of a utopian experiment where Hawthorne lived and worked—and which he put to work in writing *The Blithedale Romance,* whose Zenobia is surely modeled on Fuller. There are notorious difficulties linking biography to art, but it's been plausibly argued that Fuller resurfaces elsewhere in Hawthorne's fiction, too.[29]

Nathaniel Hawthorne died on 19 May 1864: he'd had a stomachache. He left behind not just classics of American literature, but hundreds of unpublished journal pages.

Hawthorne's wife Sophia published material from his journals, but omitted inflammatory passages. Hawthorne's son Julian exhibited no such restraint. *Nathaniel Hawthorne and His Wife,* which Julian published in 1884, ignited a firestorm over the inclusion of an excerpt from Nathaniel's Roman jour-

vented it. Thanks to Eliza Richards for pointing me to Poe's response to Fuller's *Woman in the Nineteenth Century:* "Miss Fuller has erred, too, through her own excessive objectiveness. She judges *woman* by the heart and intellect of Miss Fuller, but there are not more than one or two dozen Miss Fullers on the whole face of the earth." See "The Literati of New York City—No. IV," *Godey's Lady's Book* (August 1846), reprinted in Edgar Allan Poe, *Essays and Reviews* (New York: Library of America, 1984), 1173.

28. Ralph Waldo Emerson to Marcus Spring, 23 July 1850, in *The Letters of Ralph Waldo Emerson,* ed. Ralph L. Rusk and Eleanor M. Tilton, 8 vols. (New York: Columbia University Press, 1939–91), 8:254; also in *The Selected Letters of Ralph Waldo Emerson,* ed. Joel Myerson (New York: Columbia University Press, 1997), 358; Henry David Thoreau to Ralph Waldo Emerson, 25 July 1850, in *The Correspondence of Henry David Thoreau,* ed. Walter Hardin and Carl Bode (New York: New York University Press, 1958), 262–63.

29. Thomas R. Mitchell, *Hawthorne's Fuller Mystery* (Amherst: University of Massachusetts Press, 1998).

nal that mused on Fuller and her relationship with Count Ossoli. It was, declared one contemporary, "the great literary
sensation of the season."[30] Nathaniel begins by recording the
judgment of sculptor Joseph Mozier, an apparently knowledgeable friend with whom Fuller had stayed a while in Italy.
Ossoli's family was poor and disreputable. Ossoli, thought
Mozier, worked as a servant or kept someone's apartment. He
"was the handsomest man that Mr. Mozier ever saw, but entirely ignorant, even of his own language; scarcely able to read
at all; destitute of manners,—in short, half an idiot, and without any pretension to be a gentleman." Margaret had asked
Mozier to teach Ossoli sculpture, but after four months' work
Ossoli crafted a foot with the big toe on the wrong side.

Then Nathaniel shifts into his own voice. Ossoli, he
muses,

> could not possibly have had the least appreciation
> of Margaret; and the wonder is, what attraction she
> found in this boor, this man without the intellec-
> tual spark,—she that had always shown such a cruel
> and bitter scorn of intellectual deficiency. As from
> her towards him, I do not understand what feeling
> there could have been; . . . as from him towards her
> I can understand as little, for she had not the charm
> of womanhood. But she was a person anxious to
> try all things, and fill up her experience in all direc-
> tions; she had a strong and coarse nature, which she
> had done her utmost to refine, with infinite pains;
> but of course it could only be superficially changed.

30. Caroline Healey Dall, "The Hawthorne Book Censured," *Republican*
(15 December 1884).

The solution of the riddle lies in this direction; nor does one's conscience revolt at the idea of thus solving it; for (at least, this is my own experience) Margaret has not left in the hearts and minds of those who knew her any deep witness of her integrity and purity. She was a great humbug,—of course, with much talent and much moral reality, or else she could never have been so great a humbug. But she had stuck herself full of borrowed qualities, which she chose to provide herself with, but which had no root in her.

Emerson and others had soaring hopes for Fuller's manuscript on the 1848 revolutions in the Italian states, one item Thoreau hoped to retrieve. But Hawthorne jeered that there never had been such a work. Mozier had assured him that Fuller "had quite lost all power of literary production" before leaving Rome, and that the alleged manuscript "never had existence." And then this:

Thus there appears to have been a total collapse in poor Margaret, morally and intellectually; and, tragic as her catastrophe was, Providence was, after all, kind in putting her and her clownish husband and their child on board that fated ship. There never was such a tragedy as her whole story,—the sadder and sterner, because so much of the ridiculous was mixed up with it, and because she could bear anything better than to be ridiculous. It was such an awful joke, that she should have resolved— in all sincerity, no doubt—to make herself the greatest, wisest, best woman of the age. And to that end she set to work on her strong, heavy, unpliable, and, in many respects, defective and evil nature, and adorned it with a mosaic of admirable qualities, such as she chose to possess; putting in here a splendid talent and there a moral excellence, and polishing each separate piece, and the whole together, till it seemed to shine afar and dazzle all who saw it. She took credit to herself for having been her own Redeemer, if not her own Creator;[31] and, indeed, she was far more a work of art than any of Mozier's statues. But she was not working on an inanimate substance, like marble or clay; there was something within her that she could not possibly come at, to re-create or refine it; and, by and by, this rude old potency bestirred itself, and undid all her labor in the twinkling of an eye. On the whole, I do not know but I like her the better for it; because she proved herself a very woman after all, and fell as the weakest of her sisters might.[32]

A Providence that mercifully kills a woman trying to escape femininity: I scarcely know what to say. Nasty stuff, though the original, even nastier than Julian's transcription, isn't vague about whom Ossoli might have been a servant or kept an apartment for. It says it was Fuller. And Nathaniel refers to Ossoli not as a "man without the intellectual spark," but as a "hymen"

31. Fuller did resolve to be "my own priest, pupil, parent, child, husband, and wife": Megan Marshall, *Margaret Fuller: A New American Life* (Boston: Houghton Mifflin Harcourt, 2013), 182–83.

32. Julian Hawthorne, *Nathaniel Hawthorne and His Wife: A Biography*, 2 vols. (Boston, 1884), 1:259–62.

without it.[33] So much for whatever claim to masculinity Ossoli's splendid good looks gave him.

Julian's publication gave rise to *de mortuis* sentiments we've already seen. "We object to this whole business of laying bare the unpleasant things that have been said of people, and by people, after they are dead and gone," demurred the *Literary World*. Fuller and Nathaniel could no longer speak for themselves.[34] "A sad depreciation of poor Margaret Fuller, and a terrible pulling down of Ossoli," lamented the *Evening Star*.[35] But the *New York Times* saluted Julian's two volumes: "All Hawthorne admirers . . . will read the work with profound satisfaction and uninterrupted pleasure." The review quoted much of the passage on Fuller, admitting it was the sort of thing "likely to create discussion." But the reviewer embraced the passage. "Hawthorne, we may be sure, never wrote these lines for publication. But how worthy of his powers of insight they were!"[36]

Others recoiled. Christopher Cranch, another transcendentalist, denounced the passage as "an abominable libel of Hawthorne upon Margaret Fuller Ossoli and her husband," "a gross & extreme libel." This doesn't make sense as a narrow or technical legal judgment, at least by our lights. Recall the elements of defamation: wrongful publication of a false and defamatory statement of fact. Here we have publication. But

---

33. Nathaniel Hawthorne, *The French and Italian Notebooks*, ed. Thomas Woodson, in *The Centenary Edition of the Works of Nathaniel Hawthorne*, ed. William Charvat et al., 23 vols. ([Columbus]: Ohio State University Press, 1962–97), 14:155 [3 April 1858].

34. "The Hawthorne-Fuller Case," *Literary World* (10 January 1885).

35. "Tipping over an Idol," *Evening Star* (23 December 1884).

36. "Hawthorne," *New York Times* (23 November 1884). For more approval, see "A New View of Margaret Fuller," *Little Falls Transcript* (19 December 1884).

do we have any false defamatory statements of fact? That Ossoli was a stupid boor, Margaret a charmless humbug with a defective and evil nature: all of this, as far as tort law goes, is simply unactionable as opinion. So no judge would permit a jury to bring in a finding of libel on those charges. That Fuller never wrote her projected history is a factual claim and might well be false, but it's hard to see how it's defamatory: hard, that is, to see why it would tend to damage her reputation in the eyes of any respectable segment of the community. Emerson and others would be disappointed if they came to believe the charge was true. But it's hard to see why they would be indignant or contemptuous. (Hard, not impossible. Suppose for instance that Fuller frequently boasted about the manuscript, which did indeed exist and was indeed wonderful, but because of the publication of this passage others came to believe she was a phony who'd never written it.)

I doubt that Cranch meant to press a strictly legal judgment. Law aside, we find it easy to say that Hawthorne smeared Fuller's reputation. (It is then an interesting question why tort law singles out one way of damaging another's reputation—by publishing a false defamatory statement of fact—as actionable.) That depends in part on Hawthorne's magisterial standing. To have an authoritative figure prescribe that you think ill of another, even absent any reason at all, can damage that other's reputation. The libel "might defeat itself," mused Cranch, "but many persons might still be influenced by it, coming from a writer of Nathaniel Hawthorne's fame."[37]

---

37. C. P. Cranch to Thomas Wentworth Higginson, 2 December 1884, in Margaret Fuller Papers, Folder 7, Ms. Am. 1450 Collection, Rare Books and Manuscripts, Boston Public Library. Cranch presses similar formulations in "Hawthorne and Margaret Fuller," *Boston Evening Transcript* (9 January 1885).

Identifying herself as "a friend both of Margaret Fuller Ossoli and of Nathaniel and Sophia Hawthorne," Sarah F. Clarke averred, "The mischief done to Mme. Ossoli's reputation cannot be very great, since there are many of her intimate friends still living who would not recognize her in the coarsely drawn and distorted portrait of this private journal." In a nice swipe, she credited Sophia Hawthorne with the delicacy and wisdom not to publish journal passages "not characteristic of his genius or his normal temper. The son, it seems, has not shown the qualities that distinguished his mother in performing this task."[38] And a contributor to the *Woman's Journal* impeached Nathaniel's assessment by reflecting on "Wedded Isolation," suggesting that Nathaniel and Sophia's absorption in their marriage explained their pinched judgments of others.[39]

Julian wasn't budging. Rebutting Clarke, he managed to reproduce the offending passage in full. "I foresaw, of course, that [publication] would create a fluttering in the dove cotes of Margaret's surviving friends, and of the later disciples." But his hands were tied: "I did not consider myself justified thereby in omitting so sound and searching a bit of analysis. Hawthorne knew Margaret thoroughly, and he has told the exact truth about her." (Julian was four years old when Fuller died, but this was indeed his view too.)[40] The public had an interest in reach-

---

38. Sarah F. Clarke, "Margaret Fuller Ossoli and Hawthorne," *Boston Evening Transcript* (12 December 1884).

39. T.W.H., "Wedded Isolation," *Woman's Journal* (20 December 1884).

40. Julian Hawthorne and Leonard Lemmon, *American Literature: An Elementary Text-Book for Use in High Schools and Academies* (Boston, 1891), 150–53; for a riposte blasting the "mean sarcasm and personal spite" of that entry, C.W., "A Book Unfit for Schools," *Boston Evening Transcript* (13 August 1891).

ing a proper estimation, and any independent interest in emotional serenity wouldn't be severely threatened: "The majority of readers will, I think, not be inconsolable that poor Margaret Fuller has at last taken her place with the numberless other dismal frauds who fill the limbo of human pretension and failure."[41] He wasn't acting, then, solely as someone duty-bound to see his father's papers published; he was doing his bit to deflate an overblown reputation. Two weeks later, Julian returned to the battleground. Remarking that his father had always been credited with deep insight into human nature, he acerbically demanded an explanation for the turnabout denunciation of Nathaniel's portrait of Margaret and archly quoted Virgil: "Tantaene animis caelestibus irae?" ("Is there so much anger in the minds of the gods?")[42]

Cranch pounced on this argument. There were already four or five biographies of Fuller, some by friends, all of them judicious and disinterested. "And the testimony of her biographers is borne out in the love and admiration of large numbers of the best men and women who knew her, and can never forget her. But if all these persons were mistaken in their estimate of her—which of course they were if what is called Hawthorne's 'analysis' of her character has any truth—then either they were the most gullible of mortals, or she the most artful." Did it make sense to prefer a private judgment Nathaniel had scrib-

41. Julian Hawthorne, "Hawthorne and Margaret Fuller," *Boston Evening Transcript* (2 January 1885).

42. "Mr. Julian Hawthorne Rejoins," *Boston Evening Transcript* (16 January 1885). Thanks to Bruce Frier for help deciphering the blotchy typography and for translating the Latin (*Aeneid* 1:11). Fitzgerald has "Can anger / Black as this prey on the minds of heaven?" Virgil, *The Aeneid,* trans. Robert Fitzgerald (New York: Random House, 1983), 3.

bled "many years after her death"?[43] Perhaps to inoculate himself and his readers against such broadsides, Julian had already
sniffed, "As for Mr. C. P. Cranch, I remember him . . . as an
amiable and inoffensive gentleman, with an entertaining talent for ventriloquism."[44]

Likewise, Sophia Hawthorne's sister blamed Julian for
publishing "jotted down impressions" that didn't reflect Nathaniel's considered views. "Yes, I know that paragraph about
Margaret Fuller in Julian Hawthorne's 'Life.' Of course Hawthorne wrote it, but he never meant it in the world." Nathaniel,
she recalled, had urged her, "'Never print anything you have
written until you have read it over in many moods of mind.'"[45]
The *Evening News* thought it ridiculous to imagine that Julian
wanted to assist the public in coming to sound judgments.
They charged that he wanted only "to keep himself before the
people. . . . He continues the Margaret Fuller controversy, and
it's nuts and raisins to him, because it keeps him 'up.'" Abruptly
addressing Julian, the paper sneered, "Margaret, why, boy, she'd
more sense in her little finger than you'll ever acquire, and d'ye
mind, sonny, she could write English, and that's more than
you've been able to do yet."[46]

Yet another commentator invoked legal language: in publishing the journal excerpt, Julian Hawthorne had adminis-

43. Christopher P. Cranch, in "Hawthorne and Pharisaism," *Boston Evening Transcript* (10 February 1885). Compare "The Hawthornes," *American*
(16 May 1885).

44. "Mr. Julian Hawthorne Rejoins."

45. Minna Caroline Smith, "Elizabeth Peabody: Reminiscences and Interests of Her Active Life," *Boston Daily Advertiser* (25 August 1887), reprinted with incidental variations in *London American Register* (15 October
1887).

46. *Evening News* (28 January 1885), 2.

tered "bitter, uncalled-for blows, resurrected from the dead
to slander the dead, by the bad judgment of the living."[47] We
might then begin a more sustained appraisal by asking: Did
Julian injure members of the public, in particular fans of Fuller?
Did he injure himself? Did he injure Nathaniel? Did he injure
Fuller?

"Biographers have not often the will, even if the power,
to inflict such wounds as the friends and relatives of Margaret
Fuller Ossoli have received" at Julian's hands, began one sustained essay.[48] So what are those wounds? Not the pain of being
reminded that treasured Margaret is dead: I suppose that affectionate and respectful references to Margaret wouldn't trigger any such pain. Is it the pain of knowing that someone else,
even a celebrated someone else, at least sometimes thought
poorly of Margaret? Surely one could love Margaret without
insisting that others love her. (I love my wife and children, but
I don't mind that you don't. I wouldn't mind even if you knew
them. Likewise with literary figures: I adore Donald Barthelme's
work, but it's fine with me if you don't.) Is it the pain in thinking that Nathaniel and those rallying to his view think that the
affection of friends and relatives is misplaced? Is it wondering
if it is in fact misplaced? But what kind of friend and relative is
even tempted by epistemic deference to such a journal entry?
Or, as I suspect, does the wound depend on the thought that
Margaret has been injured? If that thought is confused or false,
if the wound is an unreasonable or indefensible brute fact about
people, we might still have reason to embrace some version of
de mortuis. Like it or not, we'd say, speaking ill of the dead

47. W. C. Burrage, in "Hawthorne and Pharisaism."
48. Frederick T. Fuller, "Hawthorne and Margaret Fuller Ossoli," *Literary
World* (10 January 1885); small capitals removed.

seems to upset their friends and relatives: go figure. If, however, we can vindicate the claim that Margaret was injured, this injury to her friends and family will in turn seem perfectly straightforward.

What about other kinds of injuries—or benefits—to a broader public? The same essayist closed by declaring that Nathaniel's "words, I am confident, cannot really harm her." Like Markland's "no injury to the dead," this might seem to evoke the oblivion thesis, but again I think it doesn't. The publication of Nathaniel's journal entry could direct public attention to Fuller's work and life. Some might "study and know her better, learning to hate and shun her faults as she did, and catching, as so many of her own generation have already done, the inspiration of her noble purpose." (Suppose a living person were defamed and the public interest in sorting out the claim ended up benefiting her. Would that mean that the defamation was not an injury? No: a wrong that also benefits you is still a wrong. The surgeon who removes a dangerous tumor without your consent is still liable, though you probably wouldn't sue him.) Another writer agreed that Fuller's reputation would be unharmed. "In so far as the mental status of Margaret Fuller is concerned, no harm has, of course, been done." Yet again, that might sound like the oblivion thesis, partly because "mental status" is cryptic at best. But the author went on to explain that only "shallow, superficial and impulsive" individuals would let their allegiance to Fuller crumble. The same author fretted about "the unignorable emphasis it places upon a certain tendency in the popular mind," a passion for "post-mortem mutilation," for seizing on some "single detail" and trashing a fine reputation.[49] This re-

49. C. A. Ralph, "With Regard to Margaret Fuller," *Boston Evening Transcript* (15 January 1885).

sentment, or, better, this Nietzschean *ressentiment*, was deplorable. Julian himself adduced another kind of benefit to the public. Fuller, he insisted, was exemplary of a "large and still surviving class, the existence of which is deleterious to civilization and discreditable to human nature": namely, holier-than-thou pharisees.[50] Puncturing her vices could lead to moral reform: this is just an instance of the broader thesis that *de mortuis* makes us morally stupid.

Did Julian injure himself? That he'd exhibited "injudicious frankness" and "bad taste" were some of the milder formulations on offer.[51] The *Atlantic* credited Julian with "the most utter and heroic disregard of the sensibilities of any living person."[52] Here too we have a brute fact: that some thought worse of Julian. That's enough to make him worse off, assuming he has any reason to care about his own reputation. But—I don't mean to be finicky—it doesn't follow that he has wronged himself. Just as one might not act wrongly and still make others worse off (your car hits a child who darts out so quickly that no one could have stopped in time), so too you might not wrong yourself and still be worse off. Suppose the concept of injury here tracks wrong, not harm. If you think Julian acted rightly in publishing, you might think he didn't injure himself. But even then you might think that it can be wrong to act when you know or should know others will think worse of you. It would depend on such considerations as what the stakes were to you and how reasonable, even if finally unfounded, others'

50. Julian Hawthorne, "Mr. Hawthorne and His Critics," *Boston Evening Transcript* (5 February 1885).

51. T.W.H., "Wedded Isolation"; *Appletons' Annual Cyclopaedia and Register of Important Events of the Year 1884*, n.s. (New York, 1885), 9:439.

52. *Atlantic Monthly* (February 1885), 262.

disapproval was. Then again, there is an apparently powerful objection to the claim that he wronged himself: he acted voluntarily, so he consented: *volenti non fit injuria*. However we sort out such difficulties, the question of Julian injuring himself too is parasitic, at least largely, on the question of whether others were injured.

Did Julian injure Nathaniel? Not by design: but you can injure others unintentionally, even with the best of intentions. Suppose Nathaniel's reputation suffered: readers had thought of him as a sage and good man, but he turned out, in the privacy of his study, to be mean-spirited. (You can injure someone by publicizing an embarrassing or discreditable true fact about him, even if it wouldn't qualify as the tort of defamation.) We're back to the core puzzle: is that an injury to Nathaniel, or once dead is he beyond injury?

So too for the question whether Julian injured Margaret Fuller. Let's suppose he made at least some think significantly worse of her. Does that make her worse off? If so, is it a wrong or illegitimate way of making her worse off? The language we've seen—Julian's publication "cannot really harm her" and "no harm . . . has been done" to her "mental status"—goes only to her reputation. We still talk idiomatically about harming or benefiting someone's reputation, not just harming or benefiting persons. And it would be captious to deny that your reputation survives you. But the skeptic can drive a wedge right there: Yes, he can concede, Julian may have harmed Nathaniel's reputation, and likely he did harm Margaret's reputation. But that doesn't entail that he harmed Nathaniel or Margaret, because neither one is around to be harmed any more. The dead person has no interest in his or her ongoing reputation. —Maybe.

I'll add one question: did Nathaniel injure Margaret? It

might in the first place be wrong to inscribe, even in a private notebook, such a harsh portrait of someone you've at least sometimes had warm dealings with. But it's hard to see how it harms her. If you believe nothing is wrong unless it harms others or unreasonably risks harming them, this will of course undo the claim that it might be wrong. Compare: you delight in pricking a voodoo doll of your best friend or your romantic partner. You know that voodoo dolls have no causal efficacy whatever. Does that make it okay? Suppose you say, "Well, it has one effect: it relieves my aggression. In fact this way I can treat that person better in the real world." Does that make the voodoo routine choiceworthy? Or try something discomfiting: Someone you know well fantasizes raping you. His actual behavior is always exquisitely correct. Surely it would be creepy to learn about the fantasy. Only because you'd worry he might act on it?[53]

Suppose Nathaniel somehow knows the journal entry will be published when he's dead but when Fuller is still alive. Or suppose he believes it likely will. True, he never instructed Julian or anyone else to start publishing his papers, but he is after all a celebrated author whose posthumous publications the public will devour. It's enough that he has set in motion a train of events that he knows or should know would injure Fuller, even if the injury occurs after his death. (Compare: you secretly lace your neighbor's Tylenol with potassium cyanide. You die before he takes a couple of pills, collapses, and dies. It would be nuts to deny that you're responsible on the ground that you don't exist anymore.)

So Nathaniel can't be off the hook just because he was

53. See generally Adela Pinch, *Thinking about Other People in Nineteenth-Century British Writing* (Cambridge: Cambridge University Press, 2010).

dead at the time Julian published the offending excerpt. But he could be lucky because Margaret was dead, too. (Your neighbor happens to die before ever opening that bottle of Tylenol. His daughter throws it out.) Unless Margaret is harmed by this publication, much talk of wrong and injury threaten to unravel. It might seem Nathaniel didn't act wrongly in writing the journal entry, because it never harmed her; that Julian didn't act wrongly, for the same reason; and that even her friends and families have only rationally indefensible distress to adduce. Not all the apparent problems in play depend on the claim Margaret was harmed: recall the fears about norms of public discussion, or more generally how *de mortuis* would prevent our sharpening our moral judgments, deprive us of some incentive to act well, and get in the way of writing history and the like. Still, I think the dominant intuition motivating the claim that Julian acted wrongly in publishing this excerpt is the thought that he harmed Margaret. Even though she was dead: indeed, partly *because* she was dead and couldn't even defend herself.

Our skeptic, then, has to believe that the brouhaha surrounding Julian's publication of Nathaniel's journal excerpt was largely irrational. More important, our skeptic has to believe that the very consideration motivating much of the anguish— that Nathaniel and Margaret were dead—is precisely the consideration explaining why the anguish was misplaced. Again, that doesn't mean the skeptical position is wrong. But it underlines how boldly revisionist it is—not only against our intuitions, but also against our considered actions.

IV

Legal Dilemmas

Back to where we started: you've just died. At your funeral, someone fumes, "Embezzled money at work. Diddled children in the park. Popped kittens in the microwave for fun." The story takes off—but this time I'll imagine that you're concerned. You know that even though you're dead, a lawyer can make sure your will is enforced; even though you're dead, a lawyer can protect your privacy. The law manifestly doesn't adopt the oblivion thesis, whatever skeptics may think. You know too that we generally shrink from speaking ill of the dead. Surely, you think, a lawyer can vindicate your reputation by filing a lawsuit. After all, defamation is a tort.

But in fact the law doesn't think there's a viable cause of action here—or at least modern American law doesn't. You're dead, and that makes all the difference. Here I offer a sketch of how the law adopted this position, or, put differently, of the intractable dilemmas faced by a litigant who wants to sue over defaming the dead. Remember that I think the considered judgments of the law are entitled to some epistemic deference: many thoughtful people have wrestled with these issues for centuries. Judges, in particular, have had to consider careful arguments presented by parties wishing to vindicate such reputational interests and parties wishing to deny them. But remember too that I reject the stronger claims sometimes made here: that the law outstrips our puny intelligence or that it magically selects for efficient or otherwise optimal outcomes. As it happens, I'll need the space between those two kinds of views, because again, I think it's illuminating to puzzle over the law, but the law has got this one dead wrong.

Right or wrong, the law is adamant. A Virginia court in 1987 was loftily dismissive: "The tort of defamation protects a person's interest in his good name, reputation, and standing in the community. An individual, it is said, has a basic right to personal security that includes his uninterrupted entitlement to enjoyment of his reputation. . . . The right is especially personal to the person defamed. It has never been designed to safeguard the memory of a deceased person against remarks made subsequent to his death which might conflict with the manner in which the decedent's family and friends wish him to be remembered."[1] A Massachusetts court in 1974 was more concise: "One who defames the memory of the dead is not liable civilly to the estate of the decedent or his relatives."[2] That echoes the firm language of the Second Restatement: "One who publishes defamatory matter concerning a deceased person is not liable either to the estate of the person or to his descendants or relatives."[3] Or take this blunt announcement from a Louisiana court in 1992: "Once a person is dead, there is no

1. Smith v. Dameron, 12 Va. Cir. 105, 107 (1987).
2. Casamasina v. Worcester Tel. & Gazette, Inc., 2 Mass. App. Ct. 801, 802 (1974).
3. *Restatement (Second) of Torts*, § 560.

extant reputation to injure or for the law to protect."[4] That's silly. Quick: can you remember a single dead person? And no, there is no implicit syntax in the concept of reputation that makes it unidiomatic to apply to dead people. Hitler still has a dreadful reputation. But the peremptory dismissal underlines the antipathy of modern American law to the thought that defaming the dead might be legally actionable.

Was it always so? Not quite. Let's reach back to Elizabethan England.

The Case of the Mischievous Squib, Crime, and Tort

Archbishop John Whitgift, infamously remembered by Macaulay as "a narrow-minded, mean, and tyrannical priest, who gained power by servility and adulation, and employed it in persecuting both those who agreed with Calvin about church-government, and those who differed from Calvin touching the doctrine of Reprobation,"[5] earned the enmity of Puritans even in his death. The early modern English had the quaint habit of attaching elegies to hearses. But when Whitgift was buried in 1605, some rogue slapped onto his hearse "The Lamentation of Dickie for the Death of His Brother Jockie." Dickie was Richard Bancroft, Whitgift's successor; Jockie was Whitgift. The lines are crummy poetry, but as you'll know if you have any sense

4. Gugliuzza v. KCMC, 606 So.2d 790, 791 (La. 1992); see too *Perez v. McCormick & Co.,* 693 So.2d 294 (La. 1997).

5. "Francis Bacon," *Edinburgh Review* (July 1837): 12, reprinted with incidental variations in Thomas Babington Macaulay, *Critical and Historical Essays, Contributed to the Edinburgh Review,* 5th ed., 3 vols. (London, 1848), 2:296.

for the venomous combat between Puritans and the Church
of England, they're explosive anyway. Here are some:

> Popishe Ambition[,] vaine superstition,
> coulured conformity[,] canckared envye,
> Cunninge hipocrisie[,] feigned simplicity,
> masked ympiety, servile flatterye,
> Goe all daunce about his hearse,
> & for his dirge chant this verse
> Our great patron is dead and gone,
> & Jhockey hath left dumb dickey alone.[6]

It took the government a while to sort out what was going on,
but almost a year later Privy Council pounced on a copy of the
lines in the possession of one Puritan, who promptly fingered
another: Lewis Pickering, a teenaged student at Cambridge University who presumably was not delighted to find himself hauled
before Star Chamber by as formidable a prosecutor as Coke.[7]

So what was Pickering's offense? Recall today's elements
of defamation: wrongful publication of a false defamatory
statement of fact. By our lights, it's hard to find an actionable
statement of fact either made in or implied by the verse. But
Coke's report of Star Chamber's opinion—much of which I
suppose is Coke's own opinion—included the brisk passing
comment, "It is not material whether the Libel be true." Perhaps then the constitutive elements of libel have changed; in-

---

6. BL Add. MS 38139, fol. 58r. I've followed the meticulous account in
Alastair Bellany, "A Poem on the Archbishop's Hearse: Puritanism, Libel, and
Sedition after the Hampton Court Conference," *Journal of British Studies*
(April 1995).

7. Charles Henry Cooper and Thompson Cooper, *Athenae Cantabrigienses*, 3 vols. (Cambridge, 1858–1913), 2:446.

deed, some of the opinion's passing comments or dicta look like a sketch of a general theory of libel, whether "against a private man, or against a Magistrate or publick person."[8] But I think the underlying offense here is *scandalum magnatum*, not only because Coke's report opens with the claim that the verse "scandalized and traduced" both churchmen. Longstanding statutes singled out "great men" and peers for special legal protection.[9] The legal offense of *scandalum magnatum* included libel and more: so for instance in 1672 one Staniel was found

8. De Libellis Famosis (1606) 77 Eng. Rep. 250 (Star Chamber). For helpful context, see Lawrence McNamara, *Reputation and Defamation* (Oxford: Oxford University Press, 2007), 86–89.

9. For the statutory background, see 3 Edward I c. 34 (1275) (providing in part, "None shall report slanderous News, whereby Discord may arise"); for penalty provisions for "telling slanderous Lyes of the Great Men of the Realm," see 2 Richard II Stat 1, c. 5 (1378) and 12 Richard II c. 11 (1388). For a dictionary gloss the year after these Star Chamber proceedings, see John Cowell, *The Interpreter: or Book Containing the Signification of Words: Wherein Is Set Forth the True Meaning of All, or the Most Part of Such Words and Termes, as Are Mentioned in the Law VVriters, or Statutes of This Victorious and Renowned Kingdom, Requiring Any Exposition or Interpretation* (London, 1607), s.v. *scandalum magnatum*: "*Scandalum Magnatum*, is the especiall name of a wrong done to any high personage of the land, as Prelates, Dukes, Earles, Barons, and other Nobles: and also of the Chanceler, treasurer, clerk of the priuy seale, steward of the kings house, Iustice, of the one bench or of the other, & other great officers of the realm, by false news: or horrible & false messages, whereby debates and discords betwixt them and the commons, or any scandall to their persons might arise." For overviews, see W[illiam] Sheppard, *Action upon the Case for Slander* (London, 1662), chap. 4 (suggesting that to qualify the charges must be "false" or "false and horrible"); Thomas Starkie, *A Treatise on the Law of Slander, Libel, Scandalum Magnatum, and False Rumours; Including the Rules Which Regulate Intellectual Communications Affecting the Characters of Individual and the Interests of the Public* (London, 1813), chap. 6; John C. Lassiter, "Defamation of Peers: The Rise and Decline of the Action for *Scandalum Magnatum*, 1497–1773," *American Journal of Legal History* (1978).

liable for saying, "The Earl of Pembroke is of so little esteem in the country, that no man of reputation hath any esteem for him; he is a pitiful fellow, and no man will take his word for two-pence; and no man of reputation values him more than I value the dirt under my feet."[10] No false statement of fact here, either; only opinion; but still an offense. So a treatise on Star Chamber principally written in 1621 devoted a chapter to "Libelling, and Scandalous Words against Nobles" and glossed *libel* as including, among other offenses, "scoffing at the person of another in rhyme or prose, or . . . personating him, thereby to make him ridiculous; or . . . setting up horns at his gate . . . or publish[ing] disgraceful or false speeches against any eminent man or public officer." (The horns would mean he was a cuckold.) The author doubted that the dead archbishop could have made out a common law tort action against Pickering, but said Pickering still had offered a "scornful libel" and added that because it was written, questions of its truth were irrelevant.[11] And a 1647 commentator on the law of slander underlined the inequality: a man of "quality and reputation" could win £100 in damages with no evidence of any actual injury, but "an Action doth not lie for words betwixt common persons, but in case where they are touched in life or Member, or much in reputation."[12] No wonder that the same year the audacious

10. Earl of Pembroke v. Staniel (1672) 89 Eng. Rep. 38 (Common Bench). I owe the reference to Lassiter, "Defamation," 225.

11. William Hudson, *A Treatise of the Court of Star Chamber*, in *Collectanea Juridica: Consisting of Tracts Relative to the Law and Constitution of England*, 2 vols. (London, 1791–92), 2:100–104. For the dating of the treatise, *DNB* s.v. Hudson, William (c. 1577–1635).

12. Jo[hn] March, *Actions for Slaunder, or, A Methodicall Collection under Certain Grounds and Heads, of What Words Are Actionable in the Law, and What Not?* (London, 1647), 5–6, 136.

Puritan Pickering was hauled before Star Chamber, the king's chaplain intoned, "it is not now the fashion to set out sin in his colours, nor strike at impietie in the highest: thats *Scandalum Magnatum,* rude and barbarous, fitter for the forge; then the Princes pallace."[13] (One wonders at intimating to the royal family that they might be sinful, but it would be rude to point it out.)

One of Pickering's defenses was that his verses, however construed, couldn't qualify as libel: "beinge of a deade man he tooke it no offence."[14] To say that Whitgift took no offense is not yet to say he wasn't injured.[15] Again, in the garden-variety

---

13. W[illiam] S[mith], *The Black-Smith: A Sermon Preached at White-Hall* (London, 1606), 32. The sermon is a commentary on 1 Samuel 13:19.

14. *Les Reportes del Cases in Camera Stellata 1593 to 1609: from the Original Ms. of John Hawarde,* ed. William Paley Baildon (privately printed, 1894), 223. There too is a variant of the offending verse. A sharply different version is recorded in Sir Peter Manwood of Kent's papers, BL MS Harley 6383, fol. 71r:

> The lamentation of Dicky for ye death of Jocky.
> The Prelates Pope: the Canonists hope:
> the Papists broker: ye Atheists cloker:
> dumm dogs pastor: non residents champion:
> a slanderer of reformers: a punnisher of new pastors:
> cankered envy: masked impiety:
> cullored conformity: cunning hippocrisy:
> papisticall ambition: vaine superstition:
> a Lattin Doctor: a commons Proctor.
> The ould virgins spectacles.
> Our ould pastor is dead and gone
> and Jocky hath lefte dumb Dicky alone.

The variations suggest folk circulation of the libel.

15. Though early modern *offense* can bear the sense of *injury* as well as dismay or annoyance: see *OED* s.v. *offence* sb., 4a.

defamation case, plaintiff need not produce any evidence that he was offended, in the sense of bothered or dismayed, by the publication, even if one should expect such testimony as a persuasive appeal for damages. Regardless, Coke's report of the proceedings shows that Star Chamber was unmoved by this gambit. Death shall not bar actions, they held, whether the ostensible victims are private figures or officeholders: "Although the private man or Magistrate be dead at the time of the making of the Libel, yet it is punishable for in the one Case it stirreth up others of the same family, blood, or society to revenge, and to breach the peace and in the other the Libeller doth traduce and slander the State and government, which dieth not."[16] So Pickering was convicted and sentenced: a whopping fine of £1,000; a year in jail; and stints in the pillory in London, Croydon, and Northampton, with his ears to be nailed to the pillory if he didn't confess. Ah, the ingenuities littering the history of punishment: ear mutilation was a persistent tactic against Puritans and other offenders. William Prynne lost his ears to the pillory in 1634. When the authorities sent him back to the pillory in 1637, they ordered that the remaining stumps of his ears be cut off.[17] Earlier English law dictated cutting out the tongue of one who addressed insulting words to another.[18]

---

16. *De Libellis Famosis.*

17. I'd love to regale you further, but it would take me too far afield: see *A Briefe Relation of Certaine Speciall and Most Materiall Passages, and Speeches in the Starre-Chamber Occasioned and Delivered the 14th Day of Iune, 1637: at the Censure of Those Three Famous and Worthy Gentlemen, Dr. Bastwicke, Mr. Burton, and Mr. Prynne* ([Leiden], 1638), 3–17.

18. 3 Edgar, 4 (c. 946-c. 961); 2 Canute, 16 (c. 1027-c. 1034). Compare Grágás Ib 183, in *Laws of Early Iceland: Grágás. The Codex Regius of Grágás with Material from other Manuscripts,* trans. Andrew Dennis, Peter Foote, and Richard Perkins, 2 vols. (Winnipeg: University of Manitoba Press, 1980–2000), 2:198: "The penalty is full outlawry if a man composes [verses] on

No wonder Coke's report appeals to the interests of the living community: this is a criminal prosecution. The law has long conceived of crime as an injury to the public. But we needn't wring our hands over whether there are or should be victimless crimes to see the force of Star Chamber's shrugging off Whitgift's being dead. The squib was a potent swipe at the Church of England. In a society where many believed, as Hobbes put it, that "in the well governing of opinions consisteth the well governing of men's actions in order to their peace and concord,"[19] with a state all too aware of its limited capacity and a church extensively caught up in governing, the mischievous squib menaced public order. So the criminal law acted. True, an eighteenth-century commentator recalling Pickering's libel was unruffled, even amused: "A primate in modern times," he suggested, "would probably have only laughed at it, or invited the author to dinner"; he added that there was "something very quaint" in the thought that a libel on a dead magistrate is a reflection on the government, which never dies.[20] But there was nothing even vaguely irrational or paranoid about the Star Chamber proceedings against Pickering.

Recalling the affair some years later, Coke said, "the Slander of a dead Man is punishable in this Court, as *Lewis Pickering* is able to tell you, whom I caused here to be censured for a Slander against an Archbishop that is dead; for Justice lives, though the Party be dead; and such Slanders do wrong the

---

someone who was Christian and is dead, or if he recites any poetry that was composed to blemish or mock someone who is dead. Procedure in such a case is the same as in a killing case." Thanks to Bill Miller for the reference.

19. Thomas Hobbes, *Leviathan*, chap. 18.

20. Daines Barrington, *Observations on the More Ancient Statutes from Magna Charta to the Twenty-First of James I. Cap XXVII.*, 3rd ed. (London, 1769), 82–83.

living Posterity and Alliance of the Man deceased."[21] In the
dock this time was a Mr. Wraynham, for denouncing Francis
Bacon's flagrantly unjust role, as he saw it, in complicated proceedings about damages owed Wraynham by one Fisher. This
was some years before Bacon's spectacular fall from political
grace on charges of corruption, with possible charges of sod-
omy lurking in the background. Contemporary English law
did think truth an affirmative defense to the claim of tort.[22]
Even if criminal law recognized no such defense then, the en-
comium to Bacon underlines the wrongfulness of Wraynham's
charge to a legal order horrified by pointed criticism of the
authorities. Coke's appeal to the wrong done to the dead man's
living descendants might offer a picture of a tort action they
could bring in their own name. But it might only return us to
the specter of breach of the peace and private revenge, considerations offered to explain the public interest in criminal
prosecution. Coke also remarks of defamation, "I will not omit
a dead Man; for, tho' spoken of him, it is a living Fault."[23] This
statement too is suggestive but ambiguous, because Coke might

21. *A Vindication of the Lord Chancellor Bacon, from the Aspersion of Injustice, Cast upon Him by Mr. Wraynham* (London, 1725), 34.

22. William Holdsworth, *A History of English Law*, 2nd ed., 12 vols. (London: Methuen, 1937), 5:207. This remains true, with the burden on the defense to show the truth of their charges: see 15 and 16 Geo. 6 and 1 Eliz. 2,
c. 66 (1952). For a drily amusing variant wrestling with what a jury must
have thought about the substantial truth of some charges, see *Grobbelaar v.
News Group Newspapers Ltd*, [2002] UKHL 40 (24 October 2002), reinstat-
ing judgment against the newspaper for alleging that a soccer star took
money to fix games, but knocking down the jury's initial award of £85,000 to
£1. The law lords later ordered Grobbelaar to pay two thirds—more than
£1m—of the newspaper's attorney's fees: Clare Dyer and Vivek Chaudhary,
"Ex-Soccer Star Faces Ruin after £1m Libel Case Bill," *Guardian* (27 November 2002).

23. *Vindication*, 33.

still be thinking of the scandal—and political damage—to the living community. But he might be affirming that one wrongs a man, here and now, by defaming him: that his being dead is irrelevant.

So the case of the mischievous squib might look like a successful tort action for defaming the dead. But it's a criminal action. No wonder a dispute surfaces on whether Whitgift was harmed, because that's the sort of thing that straightforwardly makes for a criminal offense. But no wonder either that it finally doesn't matter. I'm reluctant to lean hard on any of the passing language here: I don't know if these players had a considered view on whether libeling the dead harms them. Then again, Whitgift's 1699 biographer declares that Pickering and others "sought by an infamous Libel to stain the glory of his ever honourable Name" and rejoices in the "honourable Sentence" meted out by Star Chamber.[24] The biographer, at least, doesn't seem to be thinking of any public stakes.

There's no reason to imagine that our own ready distinction between tort and crime was always in place. Apparently—the sources are perilously thin and I'm not competent to assess them—if we reach back as far as twelfth-century England, we find that private actors could routinely bring criminal prosecutions, not because of occasional *qui tam* proceedings enabled by statute. Or, better, we find that tort and crime were, from our anachronistic point of view, blurred into a picture of "undifferentiated wrong."[25] Victims could themselves carry out

24. George Paule, *The Life of John Whitgift* (London, 1699), 122.
25. For this picture, see Paul R. Hyams, *Rancor & Reconciliation in Medieval England* (Ithaca, NY: Cornell University Press, 2003), chaps. 3–4; see also John Hudson, *The Formation of the English Common Law: Law and Society in England from the Norman Conquest to Magna Carta* (London: Longman, 1996), chap. 3; Patrick Wormald, *The Making of English Law: King Alfred to*

punishment for crime.[26] Convictions for wrongs could lead
to both punishment and orders of compensation. As Plucknett
puts it, "The modern distinction between crime and tort is
therefore one of those classifications which it is futile to press
upon mediaeval law."[27] We may well hear lingering echoes of
this earlier approach in the Star Chamber proceedings against
Pickering. We will hear further distant echoes resounding centuries after the law has differentiated between tort and crime
not only in theory but also in practice: in the rules of standing,
in procedure, in the burden of proof, and more.

Criminal libel proceedings didn't die with Star Chamber.
In 1716, legal commentator William Hawkins offered a gloss
on libel which would frequently be echoed and, as we'll see,
make its way into American law: "a Libel in a strict Sense is
taken for a malicious Defamation, expressed either in Printing
or Writing, and tending either to blacken the Memory of one
who is dead, or the Reputation of one who is alive, and to expose him to publick Hatred, Contempt or Ridicule." Libels, he
continued, are actionable because they disturb the peace "by
provoking the Parties injured, and their Friends and Families
to Acts of Revenge, which it would be impossible to restrain by
the severest Laws, were there no Redress from Publick Justice
for Injuries of this kind."[28] There's no equivocation here in urging that the dead, too, can be libeled.

---

the Twelfth Century (Oxford: Blackwell, 1999), 143–61. Consider the rough
parallel of when the king is entitled to wergild in the law of Æthelred:
Wormald, Making, 324–25.

26. Hudson, Formation, 159–60.

27. Theodore F. T. Plucknett, A Concise History of the Common Law, 5th
ed. (Boston: Little, Brown, 1956), 422.

28. William Hawkins, A Treatise of the Pleas of the Crown, 2 vols. (London, 1716–21), 1:193 (chap. 73). An 1884 Queen's Bench opinion, R. v.

The year 1790 saw criminal charges that *The World* had defamed the Earl of Cowper just a couple of months after he'd died in Florence.[29] The offending publication scornfully indicted the earl's dissipated life abroad. It revealed, for instance, that decades before, the earl was unmoved by news of his father's death—or, better, moved in being happy to inherit money: "He had debased his mind out of all emotions that can honour human nature, to the enervating depravities of Italy! . . . he put on mourning—he changed the Coronet on his coach, and he went, as usual, to Mad. CORCI and the Opera."[30] The earl's family already had prosecuted author and printer alike. (We find

---

Labouchere [1884] All E. R. 959 (QB), skeptical about even criminal libel actions when the alleged victim is dead, cites Hawkins as an authority for its skepticism. The language it quotes—"the court will not grant this extraordinary remedy . . . "—appears in the 1795 edition: William Hawkins, *A Treatise of the Pleas of the Crown*, rev. Thomas Leach, 7th ed., 4 vols. (London, 1795), 2:128–29 (chap. 73), reproduced in Thomas Edlyne Tomlins, *The Law-Dictionary, Explaining the Rise, Progress, and Present State of the British Law*, 4th ed. with additions by Thomas Colpitts Granger, 2 vols. (London, 1835), s.v. Libel, III. For transcript material from the case, with discussion of a planned duel, see "The Lawson-Labouchere Libel Case," *Glasgow Herald* (19, 22, 23, 24, 25 March 1881); see too *Reports of Cases in Criminal Law Argued and Determined in All the Courts of England*, ed. Edward Cox et al., 31 vols. (London, 1846–1941), 15:415–30.

29. *DNB* s.v. *Topham, Edward*.

30. *The World* (17 February 1790), also in *The English Chronicle, and Universal Evening Post* (16–18 February 1790). This must be the action that Charles Pigott is referring to in his infamous *The Jockey Club: or A Sketch of the Manners of the Age*, pt. 1, 11th ed. (London, 1792), 165: "An action was brought by a MR. COWPER, for *something* written (for nobody could understand what it was perfectly) about LORD COWPER who was dead." I don't know why Pigott thought the substance of the alleged libel was doubtful. For some of the Cowper family tree, see "Genealogical and Historical Memoir of the Right Hon. Leopold-Louis-Francis Cowper," in *The European Magazine and London Review* (October 1812), 340–44.

private prosecutions not just in the remote mists of twelfth-century England, but straight through 1879.[31] In fact, they're still possible today.) This time, they were going after the publisher. Formidable advocate Thomas Erskine insisted on the wrongfulness of defaming a man "incapable of protecting his own reputation":[32] though it might seem finicky, we should distinguish the nastiness of beating up on someone helpless from the question of whether Cowper was in fact injured by any such beating. Meanwhile the defense attorney argued that the publisher couldn't be liable unless it could be "proved that he knew of the insertion." It's unclear whether scienter here attaches to the content of the story or the further knowledge the story is defamatory, but let that go. The defense also argued "that the charge could not be a libel, as it defamed no person *living*."[33] Yet the jury found the publisher guilty.[34]

On appeal, the court of King's Bench discarded the indictment, but not on the ground that the dead have no reputational interests. Instead, the court pressed a point we've seen from critics of *de mortuis:* "to say, in general, that the conduct of a dead person can at no time be canvassed; to hold that, even after ages are passed, the conduct of bad men cannot be contrasted with the good, would be to exclude the must [*sic*]

31. The Prosecution of Offences Act, 42 & 43 Vict. c. 22 (1879), established the office of Director of Public Prosecutions.

32. I assume this is Thomas, who did sometimes appear as prosecutor. See his own reflections on prosecuting Thomas Williams, the bookseller of Paine's *Age of Reason,* in *Mr. Erskine's Speech on the Trial of Thomas Williams* ([London? 1797]), 3.

33. *The Annual Register, or A View of the History, Politics, and Literature, for the Year 1790,* 2nd ed. (London, 1802), 211–12.

34. *London Chronicle* (1 July 1790).

useful part of history." So authors would have a privilege if they pressed their claims against the dead "fairly and honestly." But publication, "whether soon or late after the death of the party, if it be done with a malevolent purpose, to vilify the memory of the deceased, and with a view to injure his posterity . . . then it is done with a design to break the peace, and then it becomes illegal." Since the indictment here made no such allegation, it was defective.[35] When Star Chamber convicted Pickering in the case of the mischievous squib, they were willing to assume that his publication would stir up social disorder. But almost two centuries later King's Bench avers that that determination has to go to a jury. And this is also a year before Fox's Libel Act, a great victory for Whigs and radicals, mandates that in libel actions the judge may not consign the jury to finding only the fact of publication. He must also assign to them the question of whether the publication is defamatory.[36]

Apparently it runs in the family. On 4 February 1799, the *Times* ran the following paragraph:

> A Noble Earl, not many months come into the possession of his inheritance, and who was lately in treaty for a considerable estate in Hertfordshire, has within a very few days lost upwards of SEVENTY THOUSAND POUNDS to a Noble Duke, well known on the turf. His despair of mind in having been so much the dupe had nigh led to the most fatal consequences. We leave it to the feelings of the Noble

35. R. v. Topham (1791) 100 Eng. Rep. 931 (KB).
36. 32 Geo. III c. 60 (1792).

Winner to justify this desperate gambling. We understand the whole sum was paid at the instant,
having been the accumulations of his minority.[37]

The paragraph referred to the new Earl of Cowper, son of the
man smeared with charges of his dissipated life in Italy. The
new earl was thirteen years old when his father died. He recently had reached the age of majority and taken control of
the family's considerable assets. On 14 February, the *Times*
solemnly reported that the earl had died two days earlier—
not, apparently, in consternation over their libel, but from a
ruptured blood vessel in his lungs. The doctors blamed his
refusal to be bled in response to an earlier accident horseback
riding: he'd never recovered his health.[38]

Once again another Cowper pursued criminal charges
against the publisher of the newspaper. A family member who
managed the earl's estate testified that the earl "certainly was
not addicted to the vice of gambling. From what knowledge he
had of him, remarkably the contrary. He believed his Lordship
disliked play very much, and he had often heard him express
his disapprobation of it." Had the earl lost and paid £70,000, he
added, he surely would have known about it. Why have any
confidence that such a blatantly false libel was "of and concerning" the earl in the first place? Because of the bit about his
negotiating for an estate in Hertfordshire: it had belonged to
one Paul Benfield, and Cowper had indeed been trying to get
it. Then too, Cowper had come into possession of his inheri-

37. *Times* (4 February 1799).
38. *Times* (14 February 1799). The story got the fourth earl's name wrong:
this was George Augustus Clavering Cowper, not George Nassau Clavering
Cowper, who was the third earl.

tance the previous August. Those facts were enough to fix the reference. But "the offensive part was absolutely false."

This time, Erskine appeared in his more usual role, defending the press. John Walter, publisher of the *Times*, "was living in the country, and knew nothing about the publication of this paragraph till afterwards, when he was extremely sorry for it." Erskine was willing to concede that Walter could be civilly liable, that is liable in tort, simply for owning a paper that published such a paragraph. (This would depend on the doctrine of *respondeat superior*, on which the master is liable for the deeds of his servant, unless the servant is, as the law puts it, on a frolic, that is, far outside the scope of what he's entrusted to do.) But, he argued, Walter couldn't be criminally responsible, because "no man ought to be convicted of a crime without a wicked intention": this is the doctrine of *mens rea*. The rumor was circulating widely before the paper published it. A family friend promptly protested and demanded a retraction. After expressing concern about his proposed language backfiring, the paper had retracted the defamatory charge just two days after publishing it: "We are extremely sorry, through the medium of our Paper, to have given currency to a report which has for some days prevailed, respecting a Noble Earl who was stated to have been reduced to a state of despair, in consequence of having lost a large sum of money at play, as we have the most unquestionable authority for stating that it is totally without foundation."[39] Summing up, Lord Kenyon instructed the jury that Erskine's appeal to *mens rea* didn't correctly state the law: as if "a book may be sold by a man's wife, by his children, or by his servants, and however libelous it may be, he is not answerable, if he keeps out of the way and does not

39. *Times* (6 February 1799).

know it." The consequences would be dire. "If this were to be considered as law, the lowest and meanest of the people might be found ready to engage in such business. . . . Is this to be the situation of the public?" The jury found Walter guilty.[40]

The situation of the public: it sounds like an unvarnished consequentialist appeal. On this reading, the court is thinking, sure, it's unfair to John Walter to punish him for the publication of this paragraph when he had nothing to do with it. (Poor Walter already had served time for criminal libel—for inserting paragraphs the government was paying him to publish.)[41] But if the law fails to extend criminal liability here, scoundrels will publish and wriggle free. (Not until 1843, by statute, did English law hold that mere ownership wasn't enough to make a publisher criminally liable.)[42] In the face of that discouraging prospect, fairness be damned. But the situation of the public also sounds in concern about a social world in which reverence or at least due respect for nobility will be corroded by caustic accounts of what outrageous gamblers and spendthrifts they are. In an aristocratic society, that could well seem a harm to the community. The perpetrators, however broadly conceived, should then be criminally liable, at least when the story is false, as it was here.

Consider one last English criminal case from 1887, *R. v. Ensar and Carr*, "an alleged libel on the memory of Mr. John Batchelor, to whom a statue had been erected by the Liberals of Cardiff."[43] Scorning Batchelor as "a political agitator and an

40. Ironically perhaps, this relatively detailed account of the trial is from *Times* (3 July 1799). For the brief formal opinion, see *R. v. Walter* (1799) 170 Eng. Rep. 524 (KB).

41. *DNB* s.v. Walter, John (1739?–1812).

42. 6 & 7 Vict. c. 96, s. 7 (1843).

43. *Birmingham Daily Post* (11 February 1887). For Batchelor's role in the

associate of, and sympathizer with, the Chartists," that working-class movement finally crushed in 1848, Carr had suggested that Batchelor had "left his country for his country's good."[44] The prosecution was based on the theory that this amounted to an accusation that Batchelor had been transported: that is, sent to Australia for his crimes. The court directed an acquittal "on the ground that an action for libeling a dead man would not lie unless it was published with the intention of vilifying his posterity. The dead had no rights and suffered no wrongs."[45] That last is overstated: again, the law does not adopt the oblivion thesis. That aside, it sounds much like the rationale that King's Bench adopted in deciding the indictment for libeling the third Earl of Cowper was defective.

On this side of the Atlantic, in 1808 a Massachusetts judge adopted Hawkins's gloss—"A libel is a malicious publication, expressed either in printing or writing, or by signs and pictures, tending either to blacken the memory of one dead, or the reputation of one who is alive, and expose him to public hatred, contempt, or ridicule"—without attribution.[46] The bit about the dead was pure dictum, but other Massachusetts courts applauded it: "To the correctness of this definition no objection can now be urged."[47] Other dicta emphasized the link between defaming the dead and public violence: "A libel

---

Chartist movement, see R. P. Hastings, *Chartism in the North Riding of Yorkshire and South Durham, 1838–1848* (Heslington: University of York, Borthwick Institute of Historical Research, 2004), 7–12. The case seems to be reported only in the newspapers.

44. *Western Mail* (14 February 1887).

45. *Birmingham Daily Post* (11 February 1887).

46. Commonwealth v. William Clap, 4 Mass. 163 (1808).

47. Clark v. Binney, 19 Mass. 113, 115 (1824). See too *Commonwealth v. Origen Batchelder,* Thach. Crim. Cas. 191 (Boston Mun. Ct. 1829).

even of a *deceased person* is an offence against the public, because it may stir up the passions of the living and produce acts
of revenge."[48]

One New Jersey defendant tried to quash an indictment
for libeling the dead by urging that there was no evidence that
he sought to bring the family into disrepute "and induce them
to break the peace." Citing *R. v. Topham* and other cases, he
insisted that absent such evidence, a criminal libel action was
a nonstarter: "The authorities are all one way and cannot be
disregarded." "If the doctrine contended for is true," protested
the state, "then a dead man who leaves no descendants or relatives can be libeled with impunity." If you shrink at its being
open hunting season on such dead people—and if you're
thinking tortishly, not criminally, let's leave aside for now who
might have standing to assert their interests or fob it off on the
estate—perhaps you do think the injury is indeed to the dead
person. (But you might demur that it's unseemly without fix-
ing on that picture of injury.) The court ruled "that the tendency to induce violence must exist equally, whether the libel
be upon the dead or upon the living; *subject to one proviso*,
however, and that is, that the person deceased shall have lived
so recently that his cotemporaries and intimate associates shall
be the persons exposed to the temptation to do violence." So
the indictment had to state, and the prosecution had to show,
only that the defamed wasn't long dead and that he'd left such
"cotemporaries."[49] This move probably keeps us firmly on the
terrain of worrying that libeling the dead is a crime, not a tort.
If one's reputational interests linger only as long and precisely

48. Commonwealth v. Taylor, 5 Binn. 277 (Pa. 1811).
49. State v. Herrick (Passaic Cty. N.J. Quarter Sessions 1881), 3 *Crim. L.
Mag.* 174 (1882).

insofar as one has contemporaries willing to avenge one, all the heavy lifting seems to be done by the threat of violence. But perhaps the New Jersey court would have admitted that it's possible a contemporary, young at the defamed's death, would still be willing to take vengeance because of a defamation decades later, but not recognize any legal action, on the grounds that a necessary condition of the action is that the dead still have reputational interests and that those interests erode over time.

Hawkins's gloss on libel also made it into a Washington state statute. The state high court considered an appeal of a conviction for libeling George Washington in a newspaper—in 1916. Once again the defendant appealed to *R. v. Topham*, insisting that the court take judicial notice of the fact that George Washington and all his contemporaries were dead and so as a matter of law his story couldn't be libelous. He added that his speech was anyway protected by the First Amendment. The court was unmoved: "We are quite unable to appreciate an argument which suggests that any one has a constitutional right to maliciously defame the memory of a deceased person, though such person's memory lives only in history, any more than to maliciously defame a living person." The Supreme Court hadn't yet incorporated the First Amendment against the states. (A passing riddle about the theory of incorporation: if the work was done by the due process clause of the Fourteenth Amendment, why didn't the Supreme Court notice until the 1920s?) Nor was there any reason to construe the statute as having any such time limit. So the court didn't flinch in affirming the conviction.[50] Suppose the defamed hadn't been the fa-

---

50. State v. Haffer, 94 Wash. 136 (1916). *Barnum v. State*, 92 Wis. 586 (1896) upholds a criminal libel conviction against a procedural challenge; the case is misreported in "Can Libel the Dead," *Penny Press* (10 March 1896).

ther of our country. Would a prosecutor have taken any interest? Would a jury have cared? Would the state high court have
applied the same rule? Doesn't this look just like *scandalum
magnatum?*

It's droll to find such horror at criticism of political authorities in republican America. This case is not alone: an Ohio
newspaper waxed apoplectic over a proposed nasty epitaph for
James Buchanan,[51] and a New York City newspaper seethed in
fury at an attack on the late James Garfield.[52] But First Amendment law has flipped *scandalum magnatum* on its head. Today it
is harder, not easier, for public figures to win libel suits.[53] So too

---

For a 1940 criminal libel conviction against the editor of the *Daily Worker,*
see "Hathaway, Editor of Daily Worker, Guilty with Publishing Company in
Liggett Libel," *New York Times* (4 May 1940). The widow also won a civil
action: for brief procedural notations, see *Liggett v. Daily Worker,* 255 A.D.
793 (N.Y. App. Div. 1938) and *Liggett v. Comprodaily Pub. Co.,* 256 A.D.
1005 (N.Y. App. Div. 1939).

51. "Defaming the Dead: A Base and Heartless Attack on Mr. Buchanan,"
Newark Advocate (5 June 1868).

52. "Slandering the Dead," *Frank Leslie's Illustrated Newspaper* (15 April
1882). Compare *Defaming the Dead: Work of Cooper's Smut Machine; An
Attack on the Memory of a Beloved Divine That Will Be Vigorously Resented*
(n.p., [1882]), assailing an attack on Democratic candidate for governor of
Pennsylvania Robert E. Pattison's dead father.

53. This is the central thrust of *New York Times* v. *Sullivan,* 376 U.S. 254
(1964). Justice Brennan tried to persuade the Court to extend the standard
to any discussion of public interest, regardless of the status of the parties
involved. Compare *Time, Inc. v. Hill,* 385 U.S. 374 (1967) (majority embracing that view) with *Rosenbloom v. Metromedia,* 403 U.S. 29 (1971) (plurality
of three for that view) and *Gertz v. Robert Welch,* 418 U.S. 323 (1974) (majority of five against that view). Contrast *Snyder v. Phelps,* 562 U.S. 443 (2011)
(overturning an intentional infliction of emotional distress award against
Westboro Baptist Church where "Westboro addressed matters of public im-
port on public property, in a peaceful manner, in full compliance with the
guidance of local officials," 1220, even though neither Albert Snyder nor his
dead son, target of the church's protest, was a public figure). *Hustler Magazine*

Justice Jackson's comment, the deepest claim in all First Amendment law—"Authority here is to be controlled by public opinion, not public opinion by authority"[54]—inverts Hobbes's claim. The cases I've canvassed so far are criminal prosecutions. So again the law's interests in these matters are public, not private: the injuries that count are to society, not to the defamed parties. No wonder that from the case of the mischievous squib on, courts returned to the worry that loyal family members will avenge themselves or that expressions of contempt for the constituted authorities are an acid bath corroding social order. No wonder courts were brusque with defendants who urged that their ostensible victims weren't injured because they're dead. No need for them to figure out how or whether it's sensible to say a defamed dead man has been injured. They weren't worried about that. They were worried about the interests of the living.

Such criminal prosecutions are brought today even in the West. German law states, "Whoever defames the memory of a deceased person shall be liable to imprisonment of not more than two years or a fine."[55] Swiss law too makes defaming the dead a crime—but not if the target has been dead for more

---

v. Falwell, 485 U.S. 46 (1988) had extended the New York Times standard to intentional infliction of emotional distress. There Falwell was a public figure. Snyder treats the First Amendment as an absolute bar, Hustler as ratcheting up in various ways what a plaintiff would have to show to prevail.

54. West Virginia State Bd. of Ed. v. Barnette, 319 U.S. 624, 641 (1943).

55. Straftgesetzbuch [STBG] [Penal Code], § 189 (Ger.), translation at www.gesetze-im-internet.de/englisch_stgb/englisch_stgb.html#StGBengl _000P189 (last visited 23 November 2014). Holocaust denier Gerald Fredrick Töben is sometimes described as having been convicted for defaming the dead, but apparently he was prosecuted under § 130: see Emma Alberici, "Alleged Australian Holocaust Denier Arrested," ABC Transcripts (Australia) (2 October 2008).

than thirty years.[56] There's evidence that contrary to mythology, criminal libel actions survive in these United States, even if they don't produce published opinions. One author found sixty-one actions in Wisconsin between 1991 and 2007. One, for instance, was brought after a University of Wisconsin at Eau Claire teaching assistant broke up with her boyfriend. He circulated a letter to the faculty of her department falsely accusing her of sleeping with one of her students. He pleaded guilty and got two years probation.[57] Then again a series of state courts have ruled the relevant statutes unconstitutional.[58] But

56. Schweizerisches Strafgesetzbuch [STGB], Code Penal Suisse [CP], Codice Pénale Svizzero [CP] [Criminal Code] Dec. 21, 1937, SR 311.0, Art. 175 (Switz.), translation at www.admin.ch/opc/en/classified-compilation/19370083/index.html (last visited 12 December 2015).

57. David Pritchard, "Rethinking Criminal Libel: An Empirical Study," *Communication Law and Policy* (Summer 2009).

58. Compare *Commonwealth v. Armao*, 286 A.2d 626 (Pa. 1972); *Weston v. State*, 258 Ark. 707 (1975); *Eberle v. Municipal Court*, 55 Cal. App. 3d 423 (1976); *Gottschalk v. State*, 575 P.2d 289 (Alaska 1978) (striking down criminal defamation statute as "unconstitutionally vague, and therefore overbroad," at 290: this is a sadly common mistake about the relationship between vagueness and overbreadth in First Amendment law); *People v. Ryan*, 806 P.2d 935, 941 (Colo. 1991) ("The statute remains valid to the extent that it penalizes libelous attacks under the facts of this case, where one private person has disparaged the reputation of another private individual"); *State v. Powell*, 114 N.M. 395 (N.M. Ct. App. 1992) (where trial court struck down statute on its face, repeating the essentials of such an analysis but ruling only that the law failed here on an as-applied basis); *State v. Helfrich*, 277 Mont. 452 (1996) (considering criminal prohibition of stalking brought to bear against posting of perhaps truthful fliers); *Ivey v. State*, 821 So.2d 937 (Ala. 2001); *I.M.L. v. State*, 2002 UT 110 (2002) (accepting overbreadth challenge brought by student prosecuted for posting online defamatory claims about other students, teachers, and the principal); *Parmelee v. O'Neel*, 145 Wn. App. 223 (2008), *rev'd on other grounds and remanded*, 168 Wn.2d 515 (2010).

as far as I can tell, we no longer criminally prosecute defaming the dead.

Tort's Doctrinal Dilemma: The First Prong

So there's an ample history of criminal prosecutions for defaming the dead. Some of those actions at least flirt with the thought that the dead themselves suffer an injury: but again there's no reason for the criminal law to work out a considered view on that. And again, modern American courts are adamant that a tort action for defaming the dead is simply a nonstarter. Why? I'll show that tort law has left would-be litigants with an apparently insoluble dilemma—or, if you like, facing a pincer attack. On one side, the law denies that the action can be brought in the name of the dead person. On the other, if living relatives bring the action, the law denies that they been injured, so they don't have standing to pursue the matter.

I begin with the first prong of the dilemma, which goes back far enough in the common law to have an imposing Latin name: *actio personalis moritur cum persona,* or a personal action dies with the person. (The standard contrast category to *personal* is *real,* referring to one kind of property claim.) To realize its force, notice that the law has to take a stand not only on whether it's a tort to defame an already dead person, but on what we now call the right of survival. Suppose you're defamed while alive and you file a lawsuit, but you die before there's a final judgment. May your estate continue to press the claim and collect damages if you win? Or should the action be dismissed when you die? *Actio personalis* is the longstanding rule of the common law, set down in Latin by Coke in 1612, and it means that there is no right of survival: the action dies when you do.[59] It will follow *a fortiori* that "embezzled, diddled, and popped" won't give rise to a legal action, because you're dead when that outrageous charge is "published" or circulated.

Learned commentators have been stern, even relentless, in denouncing the maxim. Holdsworth suggested that Coke just plain made it up, and added, "the maxim when it first appeared in its modern shape was both untrue and misleading."[60] My wonderful colleague Brian Simpson found the Latin tag in 1479, 1496, and 1521, so he discarded the claim that Coke, that "old rogue," was to blame; but Simpson thought it noteworthy that the Latin tag then disappeared until 1612, and he drily described its murky contrast between real and personal actions as "peculiarly unfortunate": "most of the maxims of the common law," he added, "are not distinguished by their profundity."[61] Pollock described it as a "barbarous rule."[62] Pluck-

---

59. Pinchon's Case (1612) 77 Eng. Rep. 859 (KB).

60. William Holdsworth, *A History of English Law,* 5th ed., 16 vols. (London: Methuen, 1942), 3:576. Note too H. Goudy, "Two Ancient Brocards," in *Essays in Legal History: Read before the International Congress of Historical Studies Held in London in 1913,* ed. Paul Vinogradoff (London: Oxford University Press, 1913), 226: "Perhaps Coke himself invented it."

61. A. W. Brian Simpson, *A History of the Common Law of Contract: The Rise of the Action of Assumpsit* (Oxford: Oxford University Press, 1975), 562–65. Percy H. Winfield, "Death as Affecting Liability in Tort," *Columbia Law Review* (March 1929): 344, beat Simpson to the punch in refuting Holdsworth; I should note that Winfield is skeptical that *actio personalis* ever made much difference. For a typically unhelpful attempt to gloss the sense of *personal* at issue here, see Edward Leigh, *A Philologicall Commentary: or, An Illustration of the Most Obvious and Useful Words in the Law,* 2nd ed. (London, 1658), 5–6.

62. Frederick Pollock, *The Law of Tort* (New York, 1895), 40–41. For apt arguments for why defamation actions should survive, see Note [Luke De-Grand], "Challenging the Exclusion of Libel and Slander from Survival Statutes," *University of Illinois Law Review* (January 1984); Note [Florence Frances

nett denied that it ever correctly stated the law.[63] No reason to think that just because it's stated in Latin and has an imposing history, it makes any sense.

But I think that modern academic skepticism is best understood, because most plausible, if directed at the hazy question of what makes a legal action personal, not at the thought that in the early common law, personal legal claims, however conceived, extinguished when the parties did. So a 1658 commentator remarks that *actio personalis* applies not generally but only in "cases where the wrong did principally and immediately rest upon a mans person, as if one scandalize or beat another."[64] The language implicitly acknowledges that there's uncertainty or confusion about what makes a legal action personal, but it also takes scandalizing—the word is common enough in contemporary English, but in this context I think it again summons up not just *scandalum magnatum* but defamation more generally[65]—as a paradigm case of a personal legal claim.

I'm skipping over the jurisdictional history that for centuries assigned defamation actions to England's ecclesiastical courts, also over what those courts made of the conceptual contours of the offense and the remedies on offer.[66] But a 1678

Cameron], "Defamation Survivability and the Demise of the Antiquated 'Actio Personalis' Doctrine," *Columbia Law Review* (December 1985).

63. Theodore F. T. Plucknett, *A Concise History of the Common Law,* 5th ed. (Boston: Little, Brown, 1956), 376.

64. Leigh, *Philologicall Commentary,* 6.

65. *OED* s.v. *scandalize,* v. 1, s. 3: "To utter false or malicious reports of (a person's) conduct; to slander, to charge slanderously."

66. See esp. R. H. Helmholz, *The Canon Law and Ecclesiastical Jurisdiction from 597 to the 1640s* (Oxford: Oxford University Press, 2004), chap. 11. For a 1645 presentment in ecclesiastical court for slandering a man's dead

commentator on that body of law, John Godolphin, considers
a question posed "rather by the Casuists than Canonists," that
is, by theorists and not church lawyers: "Whether satisfaction
for the dammage done by *Defamation*, be to be made to the
Heirs of the *Defamed*, in case he died before such dammages
were recovered by him?" The casuists "agree the rule of law"
(that *actio personalis* is a correct statement of positive law? that
it is the desirable rule?), but deny it applies in the defamation
action, because they deny that reputational interests are personal in the relevant sense. If you set another's house on fire,
they point out, and die before the victim can recover, your
heirs will be held liable. The property interest isn't personal.
Surely, the casuists urge, "A mans Good Name and Reputation
is far more precious than his habitation: he that consumes that
Good Name and Credit without cause, shall refund the dammage out of his Estate, and death it self (before satisfaction
made) shall not excuse his Heirs." Godolphin is unmoved: "But
when all is said (for some will superabound in their own Judgments) the said Rule of Law must stand void of all Exceptions,
and hold good and applicable to the Premises, That *Actio Personalis moritur cum persona.*"[67] The point about exceptions isn't
quite right, because the issue is whether defamation properly
falls in the domain controlled by *actio personalis*. The suggestion that it's not is compatible with believing that in its domain, *actio personalis* is absolute. But Godolphin's discussion
makes clear that at least here the worry is about what legal

---

mother by calling him "sonn of a whore," see www.isle-of-man.com/manx
notebook/famhist/wills/1645_mc.htm (last visited 24 November 2014).
    67. John Godolphin, *Repertorium Canonicum: or, An Abridgment of the
Ecclesiastical Laws of This Realm, Consistent with the Temporal* (London,
1678), 63–64.

actions are personal, not about whether personal actions die with the death of the parties.[68] However we construe modern historians' hesitation about how accurately *actio personalis* stated the common law, I've been unable to find a single tort case brought by an estate in reaction to the defamation of a dead person. As far as our core problem goes, then, *actio personalis* seems to have correctly stated the law. What sense does—or did—it make? Notice, as you may already have, that it meant that a legal action would die upon the death of plaintiff—*or defendant*.[69] (Without mentioning the Latin tag, a King's Bench opinion from the late sixteenth century notes that defendant's death is ordinarily a reason not to award plaintiff what the jury had decided on.)[70] What might justify such a curious rule? Why should a living plaintiff be told, "You're no longer entitled to

68. For further discussion of the scope of *actio personalis* putting pressure on what *personal* means, see esp. William Leonard, *The Fourth Part of the Reports of Several Cases of Law* (London, 1687), 44–46. See too [Thomas Wentworth], *The Office and Dutie of Execvtors* (London, 1641), 156; William Sheppard, *The Tovch-Stone of Common Assurances* (London, 1648), 481.

69. So W[illiam] N[oy], *A Treatise of the Principall Grounds and Maximes of the Laws of This Kingdom* (London, 1641), 6, glossing *actio personalis*: "As if batterie be done to a man, if he that did the batterie, or the other die, the Action is gone." Winfield, "Death," led me to Noy. See too John Godolphin, *The Orphans Legacy: or, A Testamentary Abridgment* (London, 1674), 129; William Blackstone, *Commentaries on the Laws of England*, 4 vols. (Oxford: Clarendon Press, 1765–69), 3:302; Edward Vaughan Williams et al., *A Treatise on the Law of Executors and Administrators*, 10th ed., 2 vols. (London, 1905), 1:606; William L. Prosser, *Handbook of the Law of Torts*, 2nd ed. (St. Paul, MN: West Publishing, 1955), 706. Those fond of the dubious glories of law-French should also consult John Latch, *Plusieurs Tres-Bons Cases, Come ils etoyent adjugees es trois premiers ans du Raign du feu Roy Charles le Premier en La Court de Bank le Roy* (London, 1661), 167.

70. *Select Cases on Defamation to 1600*, ed. R. H. Helmholz (London: Selden Society, 1985), 83.

relief, because the party who injured you is now dead"? Consider three possibilities.

One: it's unfair, one might think, for defendant's heirs to have to cough up assets to remedy a wrong they never committed. Likewise, it might seem unfair for plaintiff's heirs to profit from an injury to plaintiff. The law would no longer be rectifying a wrong between two parties, in this view. It would just be grabbing assets from heirs who never committed a wrong, awarding them to heirs who never suffered one. But this justification is an optical illusion. When defendant's heir complains, "hey, *I* never committed this wrong," he's implicitly imagining that the assets in question are his property. But if defendant did commit a tort against plaintiff, defendant himself no longer had full rights to the assets in question. He had possessor rights. The plaintiff suing him could not seize the property before winning a final judgment. Nor would the plaintiff have the right to decide which assets the defendant should liquidate or deliver in order to satisfy the judgment. But the defendant had no right to bequeath the full value of his assets to the heir. So the heir is in no position to complain that *his* property is being taken: some of it wasn't rightfully his in the first place. Likewise, in reverse, for the thought that plaintiff's heirs are enjoying some undeserved windfall.

Two: a partly anachronistic way to grasp the period of "undifferentiated wrong" is to see tort actions as piggybacking on criminal prosecutions. A criminal suspect's death meant the end of the crown's interest in prosecuting, so there was nothing left for a tort action to piggyback on. Whatever one makes of this conjecture, notice that it won't explain the further curious feature that the *victim's* death also eliminates the tort action. So it's at best a partial account of *actio personalis*. And whatever justificatory force it may have had is now long dead.

Today, of course, just as tort has properly declared independence from contract,[71] so too it is independent from criminal law.

Three: I think there's a much more plausible theory to explain why *actio personalis* extended to the death of defendant: it depends on a conception of tort as a substitute for private violence, coupled with doubts about the likelihood of family feuds. The worry—that in the absence of a legal remedy, private actors will take matters into their own hands—has surfaced repeatedly in this chapter. It shows up later than you might imagine: an 1872 court upholding a punitive damages award for spitting in someone else's face wrote, "The act in question was one of the greatest indignity, highly provocative of retaliation by force, and the law, as far as it may, should afford substantial protection against such outrages, in the way of liberal damages, that the public tranquillity may be preserved by saving the necessity of resort to personal violence as the only means of redress."[72] I'll cheerfully concede that worries about private violence once justified the extension of tort liability. But it can't, for us, count as a justification of tort law: not wholesale, as to why we should have such a practice; and not retail, as to why *actio personalis* or any other particular doctrine ought to be the rule. To be cheekily polemical about it: wanna defend the thesis that quadriplegics ought to be disqualified from tort actions?

Three purported justifications, none of them any good. It's hard to see any other justification for *actio personalis*. As one modern court put it, "It would be anomalous to breathe

---

71. Once again I'm thinking of Cardozo's overthrowing the rule of privity in *MacPherson v. Buick Motor Co.*, 217 N.Y. 382 (1916).

72. Alcorn v. Mitchell, 63 Ill. 553, 554 (1872).

life into this maxim, since all agree it had no foundation in principle."[73] As recently as 1983, a federal district court firmly brushed it aside.[74] *Time* and *Life* magazines linked Kenneth MacDonald to the FBI's Abscam investigation. He sued for defamation but died before the matter was resolved. All parties first agreed to let his estate continue the action, but then defendants demanded summary judgment on the ground that his cause of action died when he did. The court declared,

> if the plaintiff had a valid cause of action here, there is no just reason why it should not survive his death. To say that a man's defamed reputation dies with him is to ignore the realities of life and the bleak legacy which he leaves behind.
>
> There is no valid reason which should deny the family of Kenneth MacDonald the right to clear his name and seek compensation for its destruction. Why should a claim for a damaged leg survive one's death, where a claim for a damaged name does not. After death, the leg cannot be healed, but the reputation can.

Or more pointedly: "The cases which have held that a defamation claim does not survive death rest on some contrived fiction or technical label." The contrived fiction or technical label must be *actio personalis*. The court also enlisted New Jersey law, governing this diversity action, and Prosser's *Torts,* pre-

---

73. Canino v. New York News, Inc., 96 N.J. 189, 191 (1984) (affirming the survival of a libel action after death of the defamed plaintiff).
74. MacDonald v. Time, Inc., 554 F. Supp. 1053 (D.N.J. 1983).

dicting the extension of survival in tort actions.[75] But the central thrust of its rationale is normative. Once you wrest free of the hypnotic effect of *actio personalis*'s Latin and historical pedigree, you can see that it's as peremptory as *de mortuis*. Whatever its merits, though, *actio personalis* explains why legislatures had to intervene to create, say, a tort action for wrongful death—and, perhaps, why the law has conceptualized the injury as one to survivors, not to the dead party.[76] And it explains the crafting of statutes about the right of survival. Even today, some states' survival statutes lop off defamation and insist that your estate cannot continue to pursue an action if you die after the alleged injury and after suing, but before a trial comes to completion.[77] So too modern British law pro-

---

75. Prosser, *Handbook,* 709.

76. Sean Hannon Williams, "Lost Life and Lost Projects," *Indiana Law Journal* (Fall 2012).

77. See for instance Illinois 755 ILCS 5/27-6; Indiana IC 34-9-3-1; Kansas K.S.A. § 60-1802; Kentucky KRS chap. 411.140; Missouri R.S. Mo. § 537.030; Ohio ORC Ann. § 2311.21. Some states allow defamation actions to survive the plaintiff's death: see for instance Michigan MCL § 600.2921; New Jersey N.J. Stat. § 2A:15-3; Pennsylvania 42 Pa.C.S. § 8302; Texas Tex. Civ. Prac. & Rem. Code § 71.021. Pennsylvania used to refuse to recognize a right of survival in defamation cases, but the state high court rejected that restriction on an equal protection challenge: see *Moyer v. Phillips,* 462 Pa. 395 (1975). Contrast *Innes v. Howell Corp.,* 76 F.3d 702 (6th Cir. 1996), rejecting an equal protection challenge to the Kansas statute on the hyperdeferential view that the legislature could have been worried about free speech, even if there's no evidence that they were. Even in toothless gummy slobbering rational-basis review, the kind (in)famously deployed in *Williamson v. Lee Optical,* 348 U.S. 483 (1955), how could a quite general objection to libel law serve as a rationale for distinguishing survival actions? Why are they any more problematic for free speech than other defamation actions?

Hatchard v. Mège (1887) 18 L. R. Q. B. 771 (Eng.), doesn't allow a libel action to go forward after death of plaintiff, but allows on the same back-

vides that all tort claims shall survive the death of plaintiff
or defendant—except defamation actions.[78] Fans of incentive
effects will notice that given the arthritic pace at which the
typical civil suit lumbers through our courts, it's open hunting
season on the reputations of the sick and elderly in such jurisdictions. It would make a nice radio spot. "Feeling malicious?
Check the yellow pages and find an assisted living facility near
you. Act now!"

For centuries, then, *actio personalis* meant that a defamation action would die the moment either party did. The law's
adamant stance against survival meant, *a fortiori*, that it was
a simple nonstarter to sue on behalf of parties defamed after
their deaths. No wonder I've found no such actions from the
heyday of *actio personalis*. That's the first prong of the dilemma
facing would-be litigants.

Tort's Doctrinal Dilemma: The Second Prong

Recall a thought we've seen repeatedly, from imagining your
funeral to Star Chamber's judgment and more. Set aside our
central question, whether it's bad for you to be defamed after
you die. Isn't it bad for your loved ones? They're still alive, so
actio personalis won't bar them from suing. Here's the second

---

ground facts slander on title—the estate's property interests in the alcohol
dealership are at issue. In the name of free speech, *Re X (a minor) (wardship:
restriction on publication)* [1974] 2 W.L.R. 335 (Eng.), rejects a plea from a
mother and stepfather to block the impending publication of a book retail-
ing their teenaged daughter's father's disgusting sexual predilections. The
dead father was Peter Duval Smith and the book appeared as Richard West,
Victory in Vietnam (London: Private Eye, 1974).

78. 24 & 25 Geo. 5 c. 41 (1934).

prong of the dilemma. Right, *actio personalis* won't stop them—but the *Palsgraf* principle will.[79] The principle is very deep in tort law and reminds us how much that law really is private law. We can put the principle this way: a wrong to one party that causes a harm to a second is not a tort against the second.

The *Palsgraf* principle is named after *Palsgraf v. Long Island Railroad Co.*, probably the single most exemplary modern torts case. Waiting for a train to Rockaway Beach, Helen Palsgraf stood on the platform. Some distance away, the "guards" (conductors, I suppose) fumbled a bit in helping a passenger board another train. The passenger held an unmarked parcel. The conductors' jostling made the parcel drop. It contained fireworks; the impact set them off; the blast made a scale looming over Palsgraf fall; the scale injured her. So Palsgraf sued the railroad.

This is a negligence action, so canonically it has four elements. Palsgraf had to show that the railroad (1) owed her a duty of care, that it (2) breached that duty, and that that breach (3) caused her (4) injury. The usual duty for common carriers such as the railroad was one of utmost care. But New York did not extend that heightened duty to maintaining "platforms, halls, stairways and the like,"[80] or even to the employees' conduct.[81] The duty extended only to the condition of the equipment and the road bed. Still, Palsgraf could argue that the conductors were careless, that they didn't conduct themselves

79. I adopt the coinage "*Palsgraf* principle" from John C. P. Goldberg and Robert H. Sitkoff, "Torts and Estates: Remedying Wrongful Interference with Inheritance," *Stanford Law Review* (February 2013): 380–82.

80. Kelly v. Manhattan Railway Co., 112 N.Y. 443, 450 (1889).

81. Stierle v. Union R. Co., 156 N.Y. 70 (1898).

with reasonable care, and that their jostling the package caused her injury.[82] So check off the four elements: there was a duty of care, it was breached, and that did cause her injury. No surprise that she won at trial. No surprise that the first court to hear the railroad's appeal upheld that verdict.

But New York's highest court overturned the judgment. The majority opinion is unfortunately written in the curious idiolect I sometimes call Cardozo-speak. But here's the crux. Judge Cardozo insists that plaintiff "sues in her own right for a wrong personal to her, and not as the vicarious beneficiary of a breach of duty to another."[83] The crucial fact for Cardozo is that the parcel of explosives was unmarked. So reasonably careful conductors worry only that if they make it fall, it will break. (Or perhaps that it will bruise or break someone's foot.) They have no reason to worry about the welfare of Mrs. Palsgraf. And—more Cardozo-speak—"the risk reasonably to be perceived defines the duty to be obeyed."[84] Perhaps then the railroad owes Palsgraf no duty of care *in dealing with the passenger with the parcel.* Better, perhaps, to say that nothing the conductors are doing implicates that duty; or, better yet, that as a matter of law they didn't breach it. ("As a matter of law"

---

82. Apparently her lawyer's initial complaint identified the railroad's breach as permitting passengers to bring fireworks and other flammable materials onto the platform. That invites: well, how could the railroad stop them? By announcing a policy? Suppose passengers ignore the policy. It would still be possible to argue that it was the railroad's fault. It seems the trial judge agreed that the railroad had no duty to search every passenger or examine all parcels, but his instructions to the jury are what transformed the breach question into the conductors' jostling the package. See William H. Manz, *The Palsgraf Case: Courts, Law, and Society in 1920s New York* (Newark, NJ: LexisNexis, 2005), 30, 49.

83. Palsgraf v. Long Island Railroad Co., 248 N.Y. 339, 342 (1928).

84. *Palsgraf,* 248 N.Y. at 344.

means the judge should so rule, because no reasonable jury could find otherwise, given these facts.) So Cardozo also says, "The conduct of the defendant's guard, if a wrong in its relation to the holder of the package, was not a wrong in its relation to the plaintiff, standing far away."[85] So here's the *Palsgraf* principle: if anyone was wronged here, it was the man with the parcel. The guards' wronging him happened to harm Mrs. Palsgraf. But that doesn't mean they wronged Mrs. Palsgraf. And if they didn't wrong her, she can't conceivably prevail in a tort action. Cardozo is not thinking that if he were on the jury, he wouldn't find the railroad liable. He is saying it was a legal error to let the jury finding stand.

The *Palsgraf* principle suggests there's something invidiously loose or sloppy in thinking that negligence law incentivizes the optimal level of care. The law could easily hold the railroad responsible for Palsgraf's injuries. It could say more generally that when your carelessness harms others, you're ordinarily liable, whether you've wronged them or not. I suppose that in principle that legal rule would incentivize marginally more care—assuming that people somehow know what the law says (another familiar hand-waving gesture from these discussions). I can't imagine why that extra quota of care would be too much or inefficient or anything like that. If I had to take a stab at the relevant empirical considerations, I'd guess that the *Palsgraf* principle means tort law is incentivizing not quite enough care. *Stab* and *guess* underline another objection. Neither judges nor juries are in an epistemic position to have a clue as to what rule would incentivize optimal care. Indeed the rules of evidence make many of the relevant considerations

85. *Palsgraf,* 248 N.Y. at 341.

inadmissible.[86] Actual tort law is ill designed to serve public values.

Regardless, when the defamed dead's survivors bring tort actions in their own names, they run headlong into the *Palsgraf* principle. These plaintiffs seem to be arguing that a wrong to the deceased has harmed them. So they don't prevail. A Mr.

---

86. Consider competing interpretations of the "Hand rule," laid down in Learned Hand's opinion in *United States v. Carroll Towing Co.*, 159 F.2d 169, 173 (2d Cir. 1947): "If the probability [of injury] be called *P;* the injury, *L;* and the burden [of taking precautions], *B;* liability depends upon whether *B* is less than *L* multiplied by *P:* i.e., whether *B* [is] less than *PL.*" Changing the variable names and oddly recasting the inequality as an equation, Hand cautioned against taking the formula literally in *Moisan v. Loftus*, 178 F.2d 148, 149 (2d Cir. 1949):

> It is indeed possible to state an equation for negligence in the form, C equals P times D, in which the C is the care required to avoid risk, D, the possible injuries, and P, the probability that the injuries will occur, if the requisite care is not taken. But of these factors care is the only one ever susceptible of quantitative estimate, and often that is not. The injuries are always a variable within limits, which do not admit of even approximate ascertainment; and, although probability might theoretically be estimated, if any statistics were available, they never are; and, besides, probability varies with the severity of the injuries. It follows that all such attempts are illusory; and, if serviceable at all, are so only to center attention upon which one of the factors may be determinative in any given situation.

I'd add the obvious worries about incommensurability: it isn't brave, it's foolhardy, to insist that everything can be collapsed into dollars, let alone utils. Throwing caution to the winds is Judge Richard Posner in *McCarty v. Pheasant Run, Inc.*, 826 F.2d 1554, 1557 (7th Cir. 1987): "For many years to come juries may be forced to make rough judgments of reasonableness, intuiting rather than measuring the factors in the Hand Formula." One wonders what will change.

Wellman sued the New York *Evening Sun* for an 1890 story alleging that his wife had been unfaithful and had died getting an abortion. Wellman complained that his practice as a lawyer had suffered, as had his reputation. The court dismissed the complaint. "No cause of action is stated in favor of the plaintiff. The injurious publication solely affects the deceased lady, and is a personal wrong which died with her."[87] The dismissal mixes *actio personalis* and the *Palsgraf* principle: she's no longer in any position to complain of an injury and he can't complain that an injury to her that causes harm to him is a tort against him. It's actually the *a fortiori* extension of *actio personalis:* the wrong didn't die with her; it postdated her decease. But the court clearly thinks that Wellman wasn't wronged, even if he's worse off as the result of some wrong to his wife.

So too for the woman who sued a doctor after her daughter, Clara Nelson, died. She alleged not just malpractice, but also that the doctor repeated "a false, untrue, and malicious charge that the said Clara had been pregnant, and had had a miscarriage." And she won $5,000. On appeal the court fretted about that second cause of action. "The action is for damages suffered by a living person from maligning the memory of a deceased relative. No authority for the maintenance of such an action is to be found." That didn't imply that the action couldn't be sustained, the court conceded, but it surely counted against it. "It would seem plain that the imputation on the character of the daughter did not necessarily or naturally affect the reputation or character of the plaintiff. And, as it is only injury to reputation which gives a right of action, it is apparent that the

87. Wellman v. Sun Printing & Publishing Ass'n, 66 Hun. 331 (N.Y. Sup. Ct. 1892).

present action in this respect cannot be maintained."[88] Likewise for the widow who claimed that she'd been defamed by a newspaper story alleging that her husband committed suicide in accordance with a deal with his business associates (!).[89] The court balked. "The general rule is that a libel upon the memory of a deceased person that does not directly cast any personal reflection upon his relatives does not give them any right of action, although they may have thereby suffered mental anguish or sustained an impairment of their social standing among a considerable class of respectable people of the community in which they live by the disclosure that they were related to the deceased."[90]

Hawkins's bit on blackening the reputation of the dead also pops up in a Missouri statute still on the books in 1967:

> Libel defined.—A libel is the malicious defamation of a person made public by any printing, writing, sign, picture, representation or effigy tending to provoke him to wrath or expose him to public hatred, contempt or ridicule, or to deprive him of the benefits of public confidence and social intercourse, or any malicious defamation made public as aforesaid, designed to blacken and vilify the memory of one who is dead, and tending to scandalize or provoke his surviving relatives and friends.[91]

---

88. Sorenson v. Balaban, 4 N.Y. Ann. Cas. 7 (1896). See too *Bradt v. New Nonpareil Co.,* 108 Iowa 449 (1899).

89. The story, from the *Boston Advertiser* (23 February 1941), is reproduced in full (twice, no less) in Plaintiff's Declaration at 1–5, 6–10, Hughes v. New England Newspaper Publ'g Co., 312 Mass. 178 (1942) (No. 372059).

90. *Hughes,* 312 Mass. at 179.

91. § 559.410, R.S. Mo. 1959, V.A.M.S.

Could that statutory language help a plaintiff trying to overcome the *Palsgraf* principle? Violette Bello sued Random House for publishing *Harlow: An Intimate Biography.* She was the widow of Marino Bello, Jean Harlow's stepfather, who plays no savory role in that book. (In one juicy vignette, Bello has Harlow stage a phony suicide attempt after he sneers at her, "You want to be crucified for a little Jew?")[92] "The petition charged that defendants maliciously published false, defamatory and libelous printed matter concerning Marino Bello which blacken and vilify the memory of the deceased Marino Bello and scandalize or provoke his surviving relatives and friends ... and that plaintiff as his widow is scandalized, provoked and libeled by reason of the publication of the book." The parties disputed whether connected abatement statutes applied and whether California law governed. Talk of provocation once again summons up the concerns of the criminal law. But the state high court found another reason to endorse the lower court's dismissing the action. Violette herself hadn't been defamed. She wasn't even mentioned in the book.

But what of the plain language of the statute? Why couldn't Violette sue, as she did, in part on behalf of her deceased husband? The court insisted that the statute "was not intended to modify the common law by creating an entirely new cause of action for the recovery by surviving relatives and friends of damages for the defamation of a dead person." Had the legislature intended any such departure, they would have specified who had the right to bring such actions and how any damages should be distributed.[93] So Violette couldn't assert

---

92. Irving Shulman, *Harlow: An Intimate Biography* (New York: Bernard Geis Associates, 1964), 156.
93. So too *Renfro Drug Co. v. Lawson*, 138 Tex. 434, 442 (1942).

Marino's interests. Nor could she assert her own: "No action lies by a third person for a libel directed at another." The statute's definition of libel applied to both civil and criminal actions. The court didn't even pause to explain that perhaps the bit about provoking survivors might apply only to criminal prosecutions. They just ignored it.[94]

An Oklahoma court found another way to sidestep the same statutory borrowing from Hawkins. The state first defined civil libel in 1890, they explained, and that definition said nothing about the dead. Yes, in 1890 they also codified the now familiar language—"blacken or vilify the memory of one who is dead, and tending to scandalize or provoke his surviving relatives or friends"—but that was explicitly about *criminal* libel. In 1895, the legislature "slightly altered" the definition of criminal libel. In 1910, a Code Commission doing some Benthamite cleanup adopted the 1895 definition for both criminal and civil libel: "The definitions formerly carried in 'Crimes and Punishments,' having been amended in 1895, are used, as being the latest expression of the legislature on the subject, those contained in the old chapter on 'Persons' having been adopted in 1890." So yes, as a matter of black-letter law plaintiff's claim in 1984 looked plausible. But brushing aside the language as mere drafting confusion, the court didn't hesitate to appeal to the authority of the First and Second Restatements to rule out tort actions for defaming the dead.[95]

A Texas court took an equally dim view of a defamation action brought by Clyde Barrow's living siblings. "Appellants allege that the movie, 'Bonnie and Clyde,' depicted Clyde Bar-

94. Bello v. Random House, Inc., 422 S.W.2d 339 (Mo. 1967).
95. Drake v. Park Newspapers of Northeastern Oklahoma, Inc., 683 P.2d 1347 (Okla. 1984), bracketed insertion deleted.

row as a sodomist and homosexual engaging in criminal acts of armed bank robbery, murder and resisting arrest." They too could point to a state statute with the same language from Hawkins about blackening the memory of the dead.[96] They too asserted both Clyde's interests and their own: "Plaintiffs . . . are persons who are so intimately connected with the memory of their brother and his reputation, that the defamation of CLYDE BARROW is at the [same] time a defamation of him and in particular of the Plaintiffs who so closely identified with their brother." This court also denied that Hawkins's gloss offered any basis to assert Clyde's interests. And it easily appealed to the *Palsgraf* principle to toss out the siblings' assertion of their own interests: "It is now a settled law that in order for one to maintain an action for defamation, he must be the particular person with reference to whom the defamatory statements were made. . . . Appellants admit that they were never named, referred to or identified, either directly or indirectly, in the movie, 'Bonnie and Clyde.'"[97]

Jack Rose's widow and children sued after a newspaper wrongly identified the dead man as "Baldy Jack Rose," a confessed murderer fretting about gang vengeance. A New York court swatted away the claim. The surviving family members had asserted only their own interests. "Defendant does not deny that the publication complained of was a libel on the memory

96. Still the law in the state, now codified as Tex. Civ. Prac. & Rem. Code § 73.001. See too O.C.G.A. § 16–11–40; Idaho Code § 18–4801; Nev. Rev. Stat. Ann. § 200.510; N.D. Cent. Code, § 12.1–15–01; Utah Code Ann. § 45–2–2. Colorado recently repealed a criminal libel statute with Hawkins's gloss: 2012 Colo. SB 102.

97. Keys v. Interstate Circuit, Inc., 468 S.W.2d 485 (Tex. Civ. App. 1971). See too *Skrocki v. Stahl*, 14 Cal. App. 1 (1910); *Saucer v. Giroux*, 54 Cal. App. 732 (1921); *Flynn v. Higham*, 149 Cal. App. 3d 677 (1983).

of the deceased Jack Rose. Plaintiffs make no claim of any right to recover for that wrong. They stand upon the position that the publication—while it did not affect their reputations in respect of any matter of morals—tended to subject them in their own persons to contumely and indignity and was, therefore, a libel upon them." The court acknowledged precedent showing that you could be libeled if someone asserted a living family member was a criminal. "In this State, however, it has long been accepted law that a libel or slander upon the memory of a deceased person which makes no direct reflection upon his relatives gives them no cause of action for defamation." This time a dissent urged that the story should be actionable for exposing widow and children to "ridicule and contempt."[98] (Recall *Burton*, where Learned Hand thought it defamatory to publish a picture suggesting a man had an implausibly large penis.) But it was a dissent.

Back to *Palsgraf*—the case, not the principle. It wouldn't be an exemplary case were the dissent simply stupid. Judge Andrews's dissent is best known for shrugging aside Cardozo's central question—to whom did the railroad owe a duty as they assisted the man with the parcel?—by insisting we owe a duty of reasonable care to the world at large, and arguing instead that the case is about proximate cause: that when you act carelessly, you set in motion an indefinitely long stream of events, some of which may be injuries, and at some point the law draws an arbitrary line and says you are no longer responsible. This bit *is* simply stupid: it is hard to know why anyone, let alone a judge on an appeals court, who must offer reasoned justifications for his opinions, would be cheerful at the thought

---

98. Rose v. Daily Mirror, 284 N.Y. 335 (1940). See too *Kelly v. Johnson Publishing Co.*, 160 Cal. App. 2d 718 (1958).

that a central feature of tort law is arbitrary. I'm not making this up. "Because of convenience, of public policy, of a rough sense of justice, the law arbitrarily declines to trace a series of events beyond a certain point. This is not logic. It is practical politics." "It is all a question of expediency. There are no fixed rules to govern our judgment." "This is rather rhetoric than law. There is in truth little to guide us other than common sense." "We draw an uncertain and wavering line, but draw it we must as best we can."[99]

Andrews is on firmer ground when he suggests that the law has manipulated the question of to whom duties of care are owed. "We now permit children to recover for the negligent killing of the father. It was never prevented on the theory that no duty was owing to them. A husband may be compensated for the loss of his wife's services. To say that the wrongdoer was negligent as to the husband as well as to the wife is merely an attempt to fit facts to theory."[100] The latter refers to loss of consortium. The early cases are caught up in coverture, the legal theory holding that when she marries, a woman's legal personality disappears into that of her husband.[101] Consortium claims were routinely added to lawsuits over criminal conversation (adultery) or alienation of affection, causes of action eliminated by legislatures in the early twentieth century.

But consortium, suitably revamped, is alive and well in tort law. Earlier than you might imagine, the law makes the

---

99. *Palsgraf,* 248 N.Y. at 352 et seq.

100. *Palsgraf* at 349–50.

101. See for instance *Bigaouette v. Paulet,* 134 Mass. 123 (1883) (male employee may pursue loss of consortium against his boss on the allegation that his boss raped the employee's pregnant wife, and indeed it makes no difference whether it was rape or consensual sex).

rights of husband and wife fully equal.[102] It's enough to show loss or impairment of the enjoyment of one's spouse's society or companionship. The loss of further "services," whether sexual or housecleaning or whatever else, can lead to an award of greater damages, but isn't any essential part of the tort. Not any injury to one's spouse will generate a plausible consortium claim.[103] In that way the *Palsgraf* principle still has gravitational force.

More generally, it's worse than facile to suggest that the duty prong of a negligence action collapses into foreseeability. That third parties are harmed by torts is just business as usual. It's foreseeable that if a car hits you and breaks your hip, your family will be worse off, your fellow employees will be worse off, and so on. That doesn't begin to give them a tort action. So too it's worse than facile to adopt Prosser's easy cynicism, on which duty is "the sum total of those considerations of policy which lead the law to say that the particular plaintiff is entitled to protection."[104] The appeal here is to replace an allegedly mysterious enquiry into private interests with some kind of consequentialist judgment. At the very least, we should instantly agree that much that sensibly qualifies as policy must be off limits. In the typical tort case, no one cares whether a ruling for plaintiff would advance the interests of the Republican Party or increase GDP or anything like that. When Paula Jones

---

102. See for instance *Bennett v. Bennett*, 116 N.Y. 584 (1889), surveying decisions from various jurisdictions and affirming the right of women to bring such actions: "The actual injury to the wife from the loss of consortium, which is the basis of the action, is the same as the actual injury to the husband from that cause. His right to the conjugal society of his wife is no greater than her right to the conjugal society of her husband" (590).

103. See for instance *Maloy v. Foster*, 169 Misc. 964 (N.Y. Sup. Ct. 1938).

104. Prosser, *Handbook*, 326.

sues President Bill Clinton for intentional infliction of emotional distress, no one tiptoes toward the thought that the merits of his political agenda are even vaguely relevant to the legal merits.[105] And it is an odd kind of sophistication to insist that those political considerations really drive the outcome. "But isn't the fate of Clinton's agenda far more important?" I guess. But that public interest doesn't register in tort. Gestures toward public values in this domain are mind-numbing, not incisive. So too the vocabulary of preference and utility is too flaccid to carve the terrain. Conservatives and feminists alike might be delighted for Clinton to lose: so what? Nor does the law weigh Clinton's psychic payoff in exposing himself and propositioning Jones, maybe adding a Bayesian forecast of his pleasure at any ensuing sex, against the dismay she feels.[106] Even harm or setback of interests won't do the trick. The central organizing category of the terrain is wrong. As a classic case remarks, a child who kicks another in the classroom is liable for battery. The same kick administered on the playground wouldn't be tortious, because the "implied license" of the playground means that that conduct wouldn't be wrongful there.[107]

Now consider a consortium action flowing out of an alleged underlying libel, though with no dead parties to be found. In the early twentieth century, newspapers across the country assiduously reported on the doings of Mrs. Everett Garrison of Newark, New Jersey. "One of the most attractive and prominent social leaders in Newark and north Jersey society," she

105. Jones v. Clinton, 974 F. Supp. 712 (E.D. Ark. 1997).
106. Contrast Richard A. Posner, *Sex and Reason* (Cambridge, MA: Harvard University Press, 1992), 386–87.
107. Vosburg v. Putney, 80 Wis. 523, 527 (1891).

disappeared sometime around 1903—just a few days after one Elliot A. Archer, a family and business friend of the Garrisons, abandoned his wife and two young children and fled: he must have known a local bank was about to discover some tens of thousands of dollars in forged receipts. Everett moved to Manhattan, wouldn't talk about his wife, and tried to make a new life for himself. In 1908 Mrs. Garrison turned up in Seattle, a leading socialite there too, ostensibly married to Archer, now going by the name Archie Carter. A New Jersey detective, sent to arrest Archer for those forgeries, identified her. (Washington's governor refused to extradite Archer to New Jersey. Mrs. Garrison-cum-Carter had led his inaugural ball with him.) In "another amazing tangle," she sued Archer for divorce while her original and therefore real husband, Garrison, was suing her for divorce and, apparently, Archer's original and real wife was suing him for divorce. Friends of Mrs. Garrison-cum-Carter hoped that when the dust settled, she would happily marry Archer for real.[108]

108. "Held for Theft in East," *Oregonian* (20 November 1908); "Seattle Man Is Charged with Forgery," *Seattle Star* (21 November 1908); "Alleged Forger Held," *New-York Daily Tribune* (22 November 1908); "$70,000 Forger Arrested after Six-Year Chase," *St. Louis Post-Dispatch* (22 November 1908); "Caught after Four Years," *Washington Post* (22 November 1908); "Held for Big Forgeries" and "Jersey Fugitive Found," *Washington Times* (22 November 1908); "Fugitive Archer Caught," *New York Times* (22 November 1908); "The Northwest," *Pullman Herald* (27 November 1908); "News of a Week in Itemized Form," *Cleveland Gazette* (28 November 1908); "Will Fight Extradition," *Salt Lake Tribune* (4 December 1908); "Governor Protects Reformed Fugitive," *New York Times* (5 December 1908); "Governor Mead Refuses to Honor Requisition," *San Jose Mercury News* (5 December 1908); "Fort Protests Requisition Refusal," *New-York Tribune* (6 December 1908); "Refused Requisition," *Bennington Evening Banner* (8 December 1908); "Mead's Hot Retort," *Daily Picayune* (27 December 1908); "Gov. Mead Caustic to Gov. Fort," *New-York Daily Tribune* (27 December 1908); "Didn't Get Gov. Mead's

Now peruse this paragraph from a detailed story in New York's *Sun:* "At the time of Archer's disappearance Mrs. George E. Garrison of 426 Summer Avenue also disappeared. Later she wrote to her husband from Denver that she had been deserted and begged forgiveness. Garrison sent her money and she returned to the East. She disappeared a second time and later was heard from as being with Archer on the Pacific coast."[109] George E. Garrison sued the publisher.[110] Now he claimed that he had been libeled and that had suffered loss of consortium: his wife, living with him, was distraught as a result of this publication. Had the wandering Mrs. Garrison once again reunited with her husband in Manhattan? Was the story "of and concerning" Everett Garrison? Did he prefer the name of his middle initial to the dread George? (But then why not G. Everett Garrison?) Well, no. The published story was substantially true about Mrs. Everett Garrison, who lived in Newark on 436 Summer Avenue. It was just false as to Mrs. George E. Garrison, who lived in Newark on 426 Summer Avenue. (I don't know if the Garrisons were related.)

Garrison's first attempt to sue misfired on the procedural ground that he had run together claims that he should have kept separate: that he was libeled and that his wife was

---

Letter," *Sun* (28 December 1908); "Eloping Newark Wife Led Ball with Governor Mead," *Philadelphia Inquirer* (29 December 1908); "Jersey Eloper Queen in West," *Trenton Evening Times* (29 December 1908); "Divorce to Save Jersey Elopers," *Trenton Evening Times* (15 January 1909); "Still after Archer," *Salt Lake Tribune* (22 January 1909); "Another Try for Forger," *Spokane Press* (22 January 1909).

109. "Archer Caught in Seattle," *Sun* (22 November 1908); see too "Fugitive Archer Caught," *New York Times* (22 November 1908).

110. For the identification of this publisher with the *Sun*, see *Sun Printing & Publishing Ass'n v. Charles William Edwards*, 194 U.S. 377 (1904).

libeled.[111] So he amended his complaint. The publisher filed a demurrer to both claims: that meant they argued that even if Garrison could show that all his factual allegations were true, he wasn't entitled to relief. The court sustained the demurrer on the claim that George had been libeled. "The husband's forgiveness of an unfaithful wife and extending to her his aid and protection are acts of courage and manliness which will not be considered by right thinking men and women as holding him up to public scorn, contempt or infamy." No doubt, though, that the wife could win a libel *per se* action on these facts. And the "inability of the wife to perform her household duties and the loss of her society" counted as a wrong to her husband: the wrong of loss of consortium.[112]

So the law permits George Garrison to argue that by libeling his wife, the *Sun* wronged him. It does not rule out the claim as a violation of the *Palsgraf* principle: it does not object that Garrison is trying to marry a wrong to his wife with a resulting harm to himself. The law's willingness to indulge this consortium action means that Andrews is onto something in his quarrel with Cardozo in *Palsgraf*. Nor did Cardozo have any worries about consortium: he joined an opinion affirming that wives had the same rights as husbands under this cause of action.[113]

The Garrison case emphatically does not entail that de-

111. Garrison v. Sun Printing & Publishing Ass'n, 144 A.D. 428 (N.Y. App. Div. 1911).

112. Garrison v. Sun Printing & Publishing Ass'n, 74 Misc. 622 (N.Y. Sup. Ct. 1911), *aff'd by* Garrison v. Sun Printing & Publishing Ass'n, 150 A.D. 689 (N.Y. App. Div. 1911) (the husband may recover for his wife's physical illness if that illness followed on mental anguish from being libeled); *aff'd by* Garrison v. Sun Printing & Publishing Ass'n, 207 N.Y. 1 (1912).

113. Oppenheim v. Kridel, 236 N.Y. 156 (1923).

scendants can win actions for libeling the dead. As we've seen, they lose them. It mattered to the New York courts wrestling with this claim that Mrs. Garrison was still alive and could win a libel suit in her own name—as indeed she did.[114] But the law could make a further move. It could say that libeling the dead wrongs, say, survivors in the immediate family—wrongs them, and not just harms them or makes them worse off.

It's tempting to think that any such possibility is shut off by the doctrine's "of and concerning" requirement: that to qualify as defamation, the statement must refer to plaintiff.[115] But it's possible that by publishing a defamation "of and concerning" one party, a defamer wrongs another. Compare a gruesome example: by tying a mother to her chair and making her watch him rape her daughter, the rapist simultaneously batters the daughter and commits intentional infliction of emotional distress against the mother. In that case it's merely contingent that the sort of harm suffered by the mother isn't the same as that suffered by the daughter. So survivors of a defamed dead loved one could even claim that they have suffered reputational harm. (If someone says your deceased spouse was a crook, people might well think you must have known what was going on.) And then the law could say that it's neither here nor there whether defaming a dead person wrongs that person. It could

114. Mrs. Garrison's $100 award survived a procedural snafu: Garrison v. Sun Printing & Publishing Ass'n, 164 A.D. 737 (N.Y. App. Div. 1914); Garrison v. Sun Printing & Publishing Ass'n, 222 N.Y. 691 (1918).

115. Here I depart from a passing suggestion in an important article: Benjamin C. Zipursky, "Rights, Wrongs, and Recourse in the Law of Torts," *Vanderbilt Law Review* (January 1990). Zipursky suggests (17–18) that the "of and concerning" requirement fixes the question of who's wronged by defamation. And he wants to enlist that as further evidence of tort law's deep commitment to the *Palsgraf* principle.

even cling to the commitment that dead people cannot be wronged. But it could still say that a defamation of and concerning a dead person wrongs the survivors. Yes, they'd have to show that it really was a libel: that it was wrongful publication of a false defamatory factual claim. And they could happily agree that it referred to, that it was "of and concerning," the dead person. But they wouldn't argue that it wronged the dead. They'd argue that it wronged them. Then the *Palsgraf* principle wouldn't block their lawsuits. Nor would they have to worry about any lingering remnants of *actio personalis:* they'd still be alive.[116]

Too contrived or perilous a way to navigate the prongs of tort's dilemma? Consider one last case where a state legislature adopting Hawkins's gloss apparently had made it actionable "to expose the memory of one deceased to hatred, contempt or ridicule."[117] After Sammie Gugliuzza was murdered, his widow

116. William Gladstone's sons adopted another strategy to respond to the published claim that the dead prime minister's habit was "in public to speak the language of the highest and strictest principle, and in private to pursue and possess every sort of woman" (Peter Wright, *Portraits and Criticisms* [London: Eveleigh Nash & Grayson, 1925], 152). They sent Wright a letter saying, "Your garbage about Mr. Gladstone in 'Portraits and Criticisms' has come to our knowledge. You are a liar. Because you slander a dead man you are a coward. And because you think the public will accept inventions from such as you, you are a fool" (*The Argus* [12 September 1925]). And they got London's prestigious Bath Club to expel Wright. Wright sued for libel and lost; the jury noted, "We are unanimously of the opinion that the evidence which has been placed before us has completely vindicated the high moral character of the late Mr. William Ewart Gladstone." See "Lily Langtry Named in Gladstone Case," *New York Times* (28 January 1927); "Gladstone Cleared: Son Wins Libel Suit," *New York Times* (4 February 1927).

117. For yet more evidence of the legal circulation and variation of Hawkins's account, see *Judicial and Statutory Definitions of Words and Phrases,* 8 vols. (St. Paul, MN: West Publishing, 1904–5), s.v. *Libel,* 6:4116–20.

and son watched a television announcer intone, "There is another possible motive for the death of Sammie Gugliuzza which officers are not talking about. It is rumored on the streets that Gugliuzza had gambling debts and ties to organized crime and that his murder is some sort of a pay-back." So they sued for defamation. The trial court dismissed the action. But the Louisiana Court of Appeal argued that as a civilian court— remember here the unique influence of the *Code Napoléon*—it wasn't nearly as bound by common-law precedent as other states. The court accepted a version of *actio personalis:* "The deceased person simply suffers no damage and is unable to exercise any right of action for defamation of his memory. This concept is consistent with what actions are 'personal' and abate on death." But the broadcaster owed a duty of care to the dead man's widow and son "not to defame the memory they hold of the decedent." Yes, "defame the memory" is contrived. One defames a person, not a memory. But I suppose the court wanted an account of why Gugliuzza's immediate family could sue, but not, say, an old friend or a concerned citizen. Still, the widow and son could sue in their own names: they could argue the broadcast wronged them.[118] They'd still have to show that the broadcast claim was a false, defamatory statement of fact, but their action wouldn't be parasitic on an actual or imagined tort claim brought by Sammie's estate.

Let's call this the *Gugliuzza* solution. It makes defaming the dead actionable in tort by conceiving of it as a wrong to survivors in the immediate family.[119] It respects both *actio per-*

118. Gugliuzza v. KCMC, Inc., 593 So.2d 845 (La. App. 1992).

119. Compare *Case of Putistin v. Ukraine,* Application No. 16882/03 (ECHR 21 Feb. 2014), http://hudoc.echr.coe.int/eng?i=001-128204 (last visited 10 November 2015), affirming a cause of action under Article 8 of the

sonalis (these plaintiffs are alive) and the *Palsgraf* principle (they claim a wrong to themselves). So it neatly navigates what other litigants found an insoluble dilemma.

But this ruling didn't stand on appeal. Like the other state courts I've canvassed, Louisiana's Supreme Court denied Hawkins's gloss created a cause of action in tort. After all, they noted, it was in the criminal code.[120] I'm no expert in Louisiana law, but that sounds right. Still the 1992 appeals court opinion demonstrates that tort's dilemma isn't insoluble. Yet it's not the solution I'm looking for and it's worth underlining why not.

An action along the lines of *Gugliuzza,* before the state supreme court pulled the plug on it, would incentivize potential defamers to shut up. It would compensate family members for their distress and other injuries. And it would require showing that the deceased had been defamed. But it wouldn't vindicate the intuition that the dead target of the libel was wronged: that would be neither here nor there. It would count only as a clumsy way to come close.

That might seem arid, pettifogging, even risible. But the stakes are real: should the survivors' injuries qualify for damages? It's one thing to grant them standing to pursue the injury against Sammie—more on that later. It's another to say they may pursue their own injuries, not any ostensible injuries suffered by Sammie. It's cavalier to shrug off the difference between these two legal actions as of mere distributive interest

---

Convention, safeguarding privacy, when the son of a football player complained about a newspaper story claiming his dead father had collaborated with the Gestapo.

120. Gugliuzza v. KCMC, Inc., 606 So.2d 790 (La. 1992). See La. R.S. 14:47.

and insist that what finally matters is promoting social welfare or Kaldor-Hicks efficiency.

Coda

Let's review: here's the chapter by buzzword. *Scandalum magnatum:* the law once took an interest in defaming the dead, when they were great men, anyway. But that was criminal law, not tort law. So the injury that counted was that to the public. Archbishop Whitgift might die, but the Church of England and the realm lived forever. I don't want to resurrect *scandalum magnatum*—American First Amendment law rightly rejects it—but I'm not interested in making it a crime to defame the dead. I'm defending a remedy in tort.

Actio personalis cum moritur: a personal action dies with the death of the person. In the common law, a defamation lawsuit would terminate when either plaintiff or defendant died. So *a fortiori,* it wasn't a tort to defame the dead. *Palsgraf* principle: a wrong to one party that harms but does not wrong a second isn't a tort against the second. No wonder actions brought by aggrieved descendants of dead ones who've been libeled founder. We could treat the survivors as the wronged parties: then the *Palsgraf* principle would pose no obstacle. Doing so would in some sense hold defamers accountable and in some sense offer compensation. Close enough, perhaps, if you think tort law is all about deterrence and compensation. But not close enough, if like me you think it matters enormously that a tort plaintiff says, and must say, to a defendant, "you wronged me": and if in turn you want to redeem the intuition that it wrongs the dead to defame them. Or even if you're paying attention to just which injuries should be compensated.

These two obstacles have explanatory, not justificatory,

force. They provide an account of why libeling the dead is a nonstarter in modern tort law. But they don't give us good reason to embrace that fact. *Actio personalis* depends most plausibly on the thought that tort prevents private violence. But we may rightly seek to hold people accountable for their wrongs without beginning to believe that if we don't, feuds will erupt. And the *Palsgraf* principle is compatible too with thinking that defaming the dead wrongs them. It is far-fetched, remember, to muster the oblivion thesis and urge that there are no posthumous legal interests, period. *That* position is far more revisionist, far more radical, against current law than any cause of action I'm recommending here would be.

V

Corpse Desecration

I'm now ready to argue that defaming the dead ought to be a tort and to offer a more direct rebuttal of the skeptic's case. But first I want to take a detour—I hope it's illuminating—and try out an abbreviated version of the analysis so far, this time on corpse desecration. Forget the afterlife: does it injure you if your corpse is badly treated after your death?

A Skeptical Dialogue

You can decide if you want to play skeptic or interlocutor, but here's the script I'd supply.

So you still think that nothing that happens after you die makes any difference to you?

—Yes, that's right. I'm dead. It's over. Ha ha and all that.

Traditional funerals are pricey. The federal government offers a helpful checklist[1] of stuff your family will have to shell out for—casket, burial vault, visitation services, funeral ser-

---

1. See www.consumer.ftc.gov/articles/0301-funeral-costs-and-pricing-checklist (last visited 29 September 2014).

vices, graveside ceremonies, hearse, gravestone, and so on. Add flowers, food for the grieving, and the like. We're talking thousands of dollars. Suppose your family balks. Someone offers his pickup truck to drive your corpse eight miles outside city limits and dump it some yards off the road. Probably a crime, but unlikely to be detected. To make sure your corpse can't be identified, the driver will first hack it up and pour acid on your face. None of this is bad for you?

—No. How could it be?

You're not appalled to learn that your family would do that to you?

—It's not me, you know. It's the body I used to occupy. When I was alive. I'm dead; I am no more. So they're not treating *me* any way at all. The only point to a traditional funeral is that it's good for the grieving. If they prefer dumping my body, more power to them: whatever gets them through the day. They still have interests; I don't. This isn't a novel thought. Here's an English surgeon applauding cremation in 1873: "I assume that there is no point of view to be regarded as specially belonging to the deceased person, and that no one believes that the dead has any interest in the matter."[2]

Well, it's one thing to deny that a dead man has a point of view, another to deny he has interests. But all in good time. For now: you're not appalled to learn that your family would do that to your corpse?

—Slow to catch on, eh? Why should I be appalled? Would you be appalled if your family used a color poster of you as a target for darts?

---

2. Sir Henry Thompson, *Cremation: The Treatment of the Body after Death*, 3rd ed. (London, 1884), 5. For the dating of the initial publication, *Cremation*, 14.

Probably, depending on what else you tell me, but I'll ask the questions here, thank you very much. Once again, let's set your family and loved ones aside: in the kinship and social circles you cherish, you're the last to die. Some public authority would ordinarily bury your body, cheaply but with dignity. But tax-cutting savagery has set in and instead the government wants to heave your corpse onto the municipal dump. Vultures will eat some of it, feral dogs some more; some will rot; and so on. Not a problem?

—I don't see what you hope to gain by varying the example. I'll just keep saying, "I'm dead, it's over, I have no interests, I have no welfare, nothing that happens can matter to me." I can play your dubious parlor game too. I don't care if they run my corpse through the mulcher and use the chunks to fertilize the garden. I don't care if they do it while guffawing about my allergies or hatred of worms. I don't care if they mock my religious commitments by sticking a ham and cheese sandwich in my mouth.

Your mouth?

—My corpse's mouth. Whatever.

I thought you don't exist. How can you have a mouth or a corpse?

—Oh, don't seize on the curiosities of syntax.

You know that if you committed suicide in *ancien régime* France, the government could have your corpse dragged through the streets and then unceremoniously dumped in the trash, right?[3]

---

3. Ordonnance criminelle du mois d'août 1670, titre xxii. For a general survey and analysis of older European practices, see Lieven Vandekerckhove, *On Punishment: The Confrontation of Suicide in Old-Europe* (Leuven: Universitaire Pers Leuven, 2000).

—No, I didn't, but so what?

You agree that people care about what happens to their corpses.

—Some people do. I don't.

You think the people who care are confused?

—Yup.

What makes you so confident?

—I still subscribe to the oblivion thesis: nothing that happens after you die can have any impact on your interests, your welfare, the quality of your life, or any such notion. *Nothing*. If nothing can, then nothing that happens to your corpse can: that's a trivial lemma.

—And I still subscribe to the hangover thesis. I think people care because they inherit or illicitly rely on beliefs about the afterlife. You officially renounce any such beliefs, but I don't see what else you can adduce. In many cultures, people believe they have to bury your body, or do whatever the locals count as suitable, for your soul to come to rest. Achilles ties Hector's corpse to his cart and then drags it face down in the dust. The brutality doesn't only upset Hector's parents; it's also a problem for Hector: remember that in a dream Patroklos tells Achilles that until he's buried properly, he won't be able to cross into Hades.[4] In 447, Valentinian III promulgated a decree against violating tombs and profaning cadavers: "the souls love the abode of the bodies which they have left, and for some kind of mysterious reason, they rejoice in the honor of their tomb."[5] I

---

4. *Iliad*, bks. 22–24.

5. Éric Rebillard, *The Care of the Dead in Late Antiquity*, trans. Elizabeth Trapnell Rawlings and Jeanine Routier-Pucci (Ithaca, NY: Cornell University Press, 2009), 66. Consider the "Edict of an Emperor on the Violation of Sepulchres," probably from Augustus, imposing capital punishment for removing bodies: "It is my pleasure that graves and tombs which anyone has

find that bit about "some kind of mysterious reason" ironically amusing: if it's hard to figure out why even souls should care about their corpses, isn't it going to be downright impossible to figure out why anyone who doesn't believe in souls would? —Then there's the darkly hilarious belief that God won't be able to resurrect you unless your corpse's physical integrity is maintained. (One wonders about those pesky earthworms.) Take this Lombardy epitaph, likely some fifteen hundred years old: "I beg you, Christians all and my guardian, most favored Julian, [to make sure that] no one ever violate this tomb, so that it be preserved until the end of the world so that I may come back to life without impediment when He comes who will judge the living and the dead."[6] In the early nineteenth century, England's anatomists needed more cadavers for medical education. The demand produced not just grave robberies but murders.[7] Jeremy Bentham got his parliamentary acolytes to pass a measure flipping the default rule against dissection, so that the state could hand over your cadaver to the anatomists unless it could be shown that you had objected (with two witnesses) or that surviving relatives did.[8] The authorities proved suitably aggressive in applying this rule against those who died

---

prepared as a pious service for forebears, children, or members of his household are to remain forever unmolested" (Allan Chester Johnson et al., *Ancient Roman Statutes,* ed. Clyde Pharr [Austin, TX: University of Texas Press, 1961], 133). For discussion, Rebillard, *Care,* 59–61.

6. Rebillard, *Care,* 74–75; Rebillard's brackets. Philippe Ariès, *The Hour of Our Death,* trans. Helen Weaver (New York: Alfred A. Knopf, 1981), 32, notices the same epitaph.

7. Lisa Rosner, *The Anatomy Murders: Being the True and Spectacular History of Edinburgh's Burke and Hare and of the Man of Science Who Abetted Them in the Commission of Their Most Heinous Crimes* (Philadelphia: University of Pennsylvania Press, 2010).

8. 2 & 3 Will. IV c. 75, s. 7 (1832).

in workhouses,[9] now thrust into the ignoble position formerly occupied by murderers.[10] Horror at being on the dole may well have something to do with this fate—and, though it's hard to be sure, with the accompanying worry that being hacked up might deprive you of an afterlife. At least one writer in the *London Medical Gazette* felt compelled to deny that last.[11]

—Now I don't believe any of this, so I don't think it mat-

9. See generally Ruth Richardson's wonderful *Death, Dissection, and the Destitute*, 2nd ed. (Chicago: University of Chicago Press, 2000).

10. 25 Geo. II c. 37, s. 2 (1752), reiterated by 9 Geo. IV c. 31, s. 4 (1828), repealed by 2 & 3 Will. IV c. 75, s. 16 (1832). For denunciation of the new rule before its formal adoption, see for instance *John Bull* (24 May 1829). And see the wonderfully snotty suggestion in the *Age* (13 April 1828): "We propose that 'every member of the House of Commons should, after death, be given to the surgeons for dissection.' This would ensure an ample supply, and as the great majority of these gentlemen are of no manner of use to the public during their lives, it would be only fair that they should be turned to good account after death." For concern about the transition from criminals to the poor, see for instance *The Journal of Sir Walter Scott*, ed. W. E. K. Anderson (Oxford: Clarendon Press, 1972), 505–6 (16 January 1829); Walter Scott to Maria Edgeworth, 4 February 1829, in *The Letters of Sir Walter Scott*, ed. H. J. C. Grierson, 12 vols. (London: Constable, 1932–37), 11:125–26.

11. "Dissection Viewed with Reference to the Resurrection," *London Medical Gazette* (25 February 1832). I owe the reference to Richardson, *Death*, 273. For a scattering of early modern English writers trying to figure out how resurrection worked, see R[ichard] O[verton], *Mans Mortallitie* (Amsterdam, 1643); *The Prerogative of Man* (London, 1645); Humphrey Hody, *The Resurrection of the (Same) Body Asserted* (London, 1694); Winch Holdsworth, *A Defence of the Doctrine of the Resurrection of the Same Body* (London, 1727); A[nthony] Fleury, *A Short Essay on the General Resurrection: Wherein It Is Proved, that We Shall Rise with the Same Bodies We Now Have* (Dublin, 1752); The Author of Simple Truth, *The Spiritual Body: Being an Humble Attempt to Remove the Absurdity from the Doctrine of the Resurrection* (London, 1789); Rev. Edward Barry, M.D., *Theological, Philosophical, and Moral Essays*, 2nd ed. (London, [1797?]), 262–65; and, for professed ignorance awaiting ecstasy, see the inimitable John Dunton, *Upon This Moment Depends Eternity* (London, 1723), 48. Much of the later debate spins

ters what happens to my corpse. You say that you don't believe in the afterlife either, or at least that you're not relying on any such belief. So why do you care what happens to your corpse? Again, I think you're suffering from a hangover of these quaint beliefs. Time to get with the program! In 1830, denouncing "the filthy, disgusting, and unnatural traffic in dead bodies," the *Lancet* acknowledged the poor's "abhorrence of dissection."[12] By 1906, the journal was pushing back against that abhorrence: "probably many of the waverers could be easily persuaded to give their consent if a little pressure were brought to bear upon them."[13] And in 2003, the *Journal of Medical Ethics* ran an editorial insisting that "it is immoral to require consent for cadaver organ donation": "The body should be regarded as on loan to the individual from the biomass."[14]

In the United States, grave robberies for anatomists fell disproportionately on the poor and on blacks.[15] That doesn't bother you?

---

off from the discussion in John Locke's *Essay Concerning Human Understanding*, bk. 2, chap. 27.

12. *Lancet* (10 April 1830). I owe the reference to Richardson, *Death*, 75.

13. *Lancet* (13 January 1906).

14. H. E. Emson, "It Is Immoral to Require Consent for Cadaver Organ Donation," *Journal of Medical Ethics* (June 2003). The same author offers a priceless bit of empiricism: "At death the soul departs from the body—I have watched this occur."

15. Edward C. Halperin, "The Poor, the Black, and the Marginalized as the Source of Cadavers in United States Anatomical Education," *Clinical Anatomy* (July 2007). For American disputes on the practice, see Michael Sappol, *A Traffic of Dead Bodies: Anatomy and Embodied Social Identity in Nineteenth-Century America* (Princeton, NJ: Princeton University Press, 2002), chap. 4. More generally see John Harley Warner and James M. Edmonson, *Dissection: Photographs of a Rite of Passage in American Medicine, 1880–1930* (New York: Blast Books, 2009).

—Why should it? Genuinely bad things happen to poor people and black people. That isn't one of them.

"Soylent Green is people!" Not horrifying?

—Well, I can think that it doesn't matter what becomes of corpses without wanting to eat them. But I'll bite: it seems like a great way to save money wasted on funerals, a sensible use of protein. The government could ensure public health standards. With a suitable nudge or three, a little pressure brought to bear, survivors could learn to bask in the socially valuable work their deceased loved ones were doing. You want affordable housing? Raze those cemeteries, excavate the bodies—or not—and start building.

Insert deep sigh here. Well, one last example. You're six months pregnant when you're murdered. At the county coroner's office, an employee high on alcohol and cocaine has sex with your cadav—

—That's sick. That's really disgusting. You sit around and make up stuff like that?

Some Snippets of Culture

Corpses matter. In every culture I know of, the treatment of a corpse is important. The shrinking from corpse desecration, indeed the alacrity with which we summon up the category *desecration,* underline the point. (Our skeptic may object that *desecration* reveals that we still imagine the corpse as sacred, strictly speaking. But surely *desecration* can mean treating something of great value as if it weren't valuable, or had much lesser value. People who worry about flag desecration needn't be idolaters.) Sure, there's plenty of variation on what counts as an appropriate way to dispose of a corpse: some approve of cremation, some don't. We Americans assume that burial is forever. But today in China, you can rent a burial plot for a renewable term of fifty to seventy years;[16] in Germany, you ordinarily rent a plot for some twenty or thirty years, and states vary on whether the lease is renewable;[17] in Greece, you get a plot for just three years.[18] So what counts as appropriate or respectful is a matter of social convention, and no doubt those conventions are shaped at least in part by economic considerations: consider the trend toward cremation where land is scarce.[19] But that too is consistent with the baldly, boldly universalist claim that every culture thinks the treatment of a corpse is important. No culture seems to adopt the skeptic's view.

That doesn't mean the skeptic is wrong. I have the same stance about widespread cultural convictions that I have about the common law: they're worth some epistemic deference, in the sense of taking them seriously and wondering what reasons might be—and have been—adduced on their behalf. But again I'd reject any claim of the form that they must be right or are automatically more credible than any critical insights we can bring to bear once we have taken them seriously.

Humphrey Gilbert subdued a 1569 rebellion in Munster, Ireland. Here's one of his tactics, as described by a contemporary defender:

---

16. "Leased Graveyards Last 50–70 Years," *Shenzhen Daily* (6 April 2011).

17. See http://berlin.angloinfo.com/information/healthcare/death-dying (last visited 15 October 2014).

18. Alex Mar, "Rent-a-Grave," www.slate.com/articles/life/faithbased/ 2011/02/rentagrave.html (last visited 15 October 2014). For the emergence of burial in perpetuity in France, see Ariès, *Hour,* 517–18. On the transition from churchyards to cemeteries, see esp. Thomas Laqueur, *The Work of the Dead: A Cultural History of Mortal Remains* (Princeton, NJ: Princeton University Press, 2015), chaps. 4–5.

19. For instance, see Nicholas Iovino, "Ashes to Ashes: Cremation Is on the Rise," *Malden Observer* (13 September 2013).

His maner was that the heddes of all those (of what
sort soeuer thei were) whiche were killed in the daie,
should bee cutte of from their bodies, and brought
to the place where he incamped at night: and should
there bee laied on the ground, by eche side of the
waie leadyng into his owne Tente: so that none
could come into his Tente for any cause, but com-
monly he muste passe through a lane of heddes,
whiche he vsed *ad terrorem,* the dedde feelyng
nothyng the more paines thereby: and yet did it
bryng greate terrour to the people, when thei sawe
the heddes of their dedde fathers, brothers, children, kinsfolke, and freendes, lye on the grounde
before their faces, as thei came to speake with the
saied Collonell. Whiche course of gouernemente
maie by some bee thought to cruell, in excuse
whereof it is to bee aunswered. That he did but then
beginne that order with theim, whiche thei had in
effecte euer tofore vsed toward the Englishe. And
further he was out of doubte, that the dedde felte
no paines by cuttyng of their heddes.[20]

20. [Thomas Churchyard], *A General Rehearsall of Warres, Called Church-
yardes Choise* (London, 1579), n.p. (the nearest preceding subheading is
"The order and course of his gouernement"). I owe the reference to Kenneth
R. Andrews, *Trade, Plunder, and Settlement: Maritime Enterprise and the
Genesis of the British Empire, 1480–1630* (Cambridge: Cambridge University
Press, 1984), 184–85.
    Compare *Peter Oliver's Origin & Progress of the American Revolution: A
Tory View,* ed. Douglass Adair and John A. Schutz (Stanford, CA: Stanford
University Press, 1967), 132, repelling revolutionary complaints about Indian
"savages": "As to taking the Scalp off a dead Man, it will not give any great
Pain; & this is the Trophy of their Victory, which they return Home with as

The applause here is tempered: they started it, and anyway corpses feel no pain, a point worth edgily repeating. The author knows that at least some contemporary readers will shrink in revulsion—and indignation.

Now consider a Goya engraving from the early nineteenth century, part of his astonishing *Disasters of War* series. The immediate context is the Peninsular Wars, with France's brutal assertion of control over Spain. The engraving's title, *Grande hazaña! con muertos!* most easily translates as "Great Deeds! with [the] Dead!" (see fig. 1), though usually *con* is rendered as "against" instead of "with," which reshapes the caption's meaning. The tone of searing irony resounds through the series of engravings: "This Is What You Were Born for," announces one engraving of a man vomiting over a bunch of corpses strewn on the ground; "This Is Bad" is the laconic comment on French soldiers stabbing a monk in the back; "This Is Worse," reports an engraving of a naked armless corpse stuck in a tree, a corpse far more vividly detailed than the French soldiers behind it.

These dead soldiers weren't left sprawling on the ground. Some French soldier had to work to truss and display them on the tree—and not just to strip their corpses but also to hack them apart and slash off their genitals. No dignified or respectful burial here: but not I think disinterested cruelty, some atavism, as some would have it, an eruption of thoughtless savagery as the thin veneer of civilization peels away in the heat of battle; rather a calculated strategic gesture to sap Spanish morale. (That it's calculated is wholly compatible with the possibil-

---

their Voucher; & as to any Damage it may do to a dead Person, it is of no more Consequence than taking off the Shirt of his Garment."

Fig. 1. Francisco Goya, *Grande hazaña! con muertos!* from *Los desastres de la guerra* (1810–15). Museo Nacional del Prado, Madrid. Photo: akg-images.

ity that the French soldiers were furious as they hacked away, also with the possibility that some military superior did the calculating and they were merely following orders.)

The engraving is cringeworthy. You can't see the face of the corpse with his head bent forward, but you sure can see the others, rendered carefully enough to make them specific individuals. There's a shrewd comment on what Goya is up to, or at least how we react, from British artists Dinos and Jake Chapman: "Goya's *Great Deeds Against The Dead* represent, as we see it, a Humanist crucifixion. 'Humanist' because the body is elaborated as flesh, as matter. No longer the religious body, no longer redeemed by God. Goya introduces finality—the absolute terror of material termination."[21] If that's right, the skeptic is wrong to imagine that the horror of treating corpses this way depends, however furtively or illicitly, on religious conviction. Instead it underlines a horror for which we can find no solace. The Chapman brothers offered their own rendition of this Goya engraving, a rendition whose three-dimensional realism makes it downright pornographic. The genital areas are daubed in bright red paint as though the nauseating knife work were done just before the viewer enters the scene. The Chapmans have what I'd call an antihumanist agenda of their own, merrily shocking the audience with renditions of children with penises for noses, splayed vaginas, extra body parts, and the like: "We would like to rub salt into your inferiority complex, smash your ego in the face, gouge your swollen eyes from their sullen peep-holes and piss in the empty orifices, but we'll settle for a few *aesthetic* shlock tactics."[22] Antihumanism, if that's what it is, might supply its own dubious consolation for the fragility of our bodies and the horror of carving up corpses and stashing them in trees. But at that point, we're far from Goya.

Not far at all is a 1901 cartoon by Jean Veber called *Le verger du Roi Éduoard* (King Edward's Orchard), as unsettling as the Goya, as propaganda if not as art (see fig. 2). The context is the Second Boer War, honorably installed in the pantheon of military conflict for Britain's use of concentration camps, where

21. "Revelations: A Conversation between Robert Rosenblum and Dinos & Jake Chapman," in *Unholy Libel: Six Feet Under*, ed. Jake Chapman and Mollie Dent-Brocklehurst (New York: Gagosian Gallery, 1997), 150.

22. Jake Chapman, "Unholy Libel (Six Feet Under): Pleasurable Disgust in the Theatre of Abhorrence; Spastic Thought, Terminal Tics and Hyperbolic Ambivalence," in *Unholy Libel*, 6–7. The color plates in the back of this volume include their version of the Goya and a sampling of these other images; or you can cruise http://jakeanddinoschapman.com.

Fig. 2. Jean Veber, *Le verger du Roi Éduoard,* from the satirical magazine *L'assiette au beurre* (28 September 1901). Courtesy of University of Michigan Library (Special Collections Library).

tens of thousands died.[23] Veber's caption points to the contemporary allegation that Lord Kitchener had issued an order to take no prisoners, but to hang everyone captured. Irish MP John Dillon demanded a parliamentary investigation. He acknowledged that the evidence was hazy and that Kitchener had denied the claim. But he also quoted Kitchener: "He desired to give them every chance to surrender voluntarily and finish the war by the most humane means possible. If the conciliatory method he was now adopting failed, he had other

23. Denis Judd and Keith Surridge, *The Boer War* (London: John Murray, 2002), 194–96; for a more defensive account, Philip Magnus, *Kitchener: Portrait of an Imperialist* (London: John Murray, 1958), 178–81.

means which he would be obliged to exercise."[24] The British government took the matter seriously enough to prosecute— no, not Kitchener: rather a South African newspaper editor for criminal and seditious libel for pressing the same charge against Kitchener. The prosecutor contacted Kitchener, who again denied it: "We treat enemies who have surrendered with every consideration."[25] (But did British troops let them surrender?)

Veber, though, presents the allegation as hard fact, indeed as a quotation from an official report that Kitchener sent to the war office. The caption invites the viewer to see the cartoon in the first instance as an indictment of killing people who should have been taken prisoner. One man has struggled enough to untie his hands: that unobtrusive reminder of a death struggle is perhaps a protest that he should be dead at all.

But there's more. Six men strung up on the same scaffold: these faces too are well defined enough to be those of real individuals, but the sheer efficiency of their execution is dehumanizing. Who builds a gallows big enough to hold so many bodies at once? So what's the builder thinking? The corpses bear more than a passing resemblance to carcasses for sale at a butcher's. And why are they barefoot? Maybe because the British forces want their boots or maybe to prevent their spastic kicks from injuring anyone. But I don't think it's contrived to detect something prehensile or maybe pawlike about their toes and feet, another way of registering the horror of treating individuals with such contempt, as if they were mere animals being slaugh-

24. *Parliamentary Debates*, 4th ser., vol. 89, col. 1249. See too for instance Rebecca Harding Davis, "Lord Kitchener's Methods," *Independent* (7 February 1901).

25. "For Libel on Kitchener: Cape Town Editor Put under Arrest on a Charge of Sedition," *Washington Post* (8 February 1901).

tered. We are tiptoeing, maybe sprinting, toward the repulsion at mass graves, about which I'll say more in a bit. The shadowy soldiers are generic, abstract, a clump. There's a trick with perspective: the soldiers manage to be less distinct than the corpses they're in front of. Smaller, too, as if their diminutive size revealed their moral inferiority. Only a fuzzy corporate blob, suggests the cartoon, could perform such an atrocity. These dead men, vividly individual, deserve better than twisting in the wind. So Veber is protesting the treatment of their corpses, too.

Must our skeptic insist that we are confused in shrinking from these images? No. Consider Ronald Dworkin's distinction between derivative and detached conceptions of the value of human life.[26] Quickly, so roughly: The derivative conception says that life is valuable as a condition of someone's pursuing his interests. The detached conception says that life is intrinsically valuable, not as an enabling condition to the pursuit of some further end. Now these are conceptions of what makes *life* valuable, and we're wondering about the treatment of corpses. But it's easy to extend Dworkin's distinction. A corpse has derivative value only if or insofar as its dignified treatment, say, is a condition of realizing—its interests? No: more plausibly, the interests of the person whose corpse it is. A corpse has detached value insofar as it is intrinsically wrong to mistreat it, because, say, doing so expresses contempt for human life.

Our skeptic will put pressure on the derivative conception, because he believes that once you're dead, you have no interests at all. And I suppose he will deny that a corpse is the kind of thing that can have interests: it has no plans or projects

26. Ronald Dworkin, *Life's Dominion: An Argument about Abortion, Euthanasia, and Individual Freedom* (New York: Alfred A. Knopf, 1993), 11–14.

to advance, so no particular interests; no general conditions it needs to secure to be in a position to adopt and pursue plans and projects, so no general interests. (On this much, I agree with the skeptic.) But there's no reason our skeptic has to deny or even doubt that mangling a corpse or displaying it limbless on a tree with its genitals hacked away expresses contempt for human life as such. And that means that the skeptic can scold me for pretending to exploit a mismatch between his skepticism and the universality of cultural regard for corpses.

At least at first pass, the distinction between derivative and detached conceptions maps neatly onto the distinction between tort law and criminal law. Recall that tort law is private law: it allows injured parties to sue their putative wrongdoers. But criminal law is public law: crimes ordinarily have victims, but we conceive of crime as an offense against the people or the state, so prosecutions ordinarily are mounted by a public official and brought in the name of the people or the state. No surprise that state after state makes it a felony to mistreat a corpse. Here for instance is Arkansas's statute:

> (a) A person commits abuse of a corpse if, except as authorized by law, he or she knowingly:
> (1) Disinters, removes, dissects, or mutilates a corpse; or
> (2)
>> (A) Physically mistreats or conceals a corpse in a manner offensive to a person of reasonable sensibilities. . . .
>> (C)
>>> (i) As used in this section, "in a manner offensive to a person of reasonable sensibili-

ties" means in a manner that is outside the
normal practices of handling or disposing
of a corpse.

(ii) "In a manner offensive to a person
of reasonable sensibilities" includes without
limitation the dismembering, submerging,
or burning of a corpse.[27]

In 1994, a bleeding Kimberly Ann Dougan drove not to the
hospital, but to a highway outside town, where she deposited
her stillborn baby's body in a dumpster. This earned her six
years in prison and a $10,000 fine.[28] The whole sorry debacle
can be understood without venturing any tendentious suggestions about a stillborn infant's interests in its proper burial. In
2011, the legislature amended the statute, raising the offense
from a class D to a class C felony: this increases the potential
punishment. So this is no dead-letter law, but a matter of on-

27. A.C.A. § 5-60-101 (2014). See *Model Penal Code* § 250.10.
28. Dougan v. State, 322 Ark. 384 (1995). Compare people pitching in to
provide a respectful burial for a murdered baby: Casey Sumner, "Burial Rite
Slated for Baby Left in Freezer," *Blade* (3 July 2012). Michael Rosen, *Dignity:
Its History and Meaning* (Cambridge, MA: Harvard University Press, 2012),
131–42, agrees that corpse desecration is wrong, but not as a gesture of contempt to the person whose corpse it was. After all, he rightly notes, we worry
about desecrating the corpses even of early fetuses. Those who deny those
fetuses are persons worry too. But we needn't have a unified explanation for
our sentiments about corpse desecration. Riddles about Rosen's appeal to
duty aside, it seems fine to urge that corpse desecration is always an affront
to humanity and also ordinarily an affront to the person whose corpse it is.
Compare Pepys's lament over the cruelty of not promptly burying those
struck down by the plague: *The Diary of Samuel Pepys: A New and Complete
Transcription*, ed. Robert Latham and William Matthews, 11 vols. (London:
Bell, 1970–83), 6:201 (22 August 1665), 6:212 (4 September 1665).

going legislative concern. Mutilating a corpse also can qualify as an aggravated circumstance in homicide and so justify enhancing the punishment.[29]

Our skeptic might diagnose our shrinking from the Goya and Veber illustrations as arising from the same detached considerations that motor these strands of criminal law. The worry, he could say, is the affront to the value of human life. The butchery defiles or desecrates humanity, as if we were nothing but lower animals. (Even most patrons of animal rights, alert to "speciesism," can agree that humans are valuable in ways lower animals aren't.) To underline the point, he can emphasize we don't need any actual human beings in the background to understand the shrinking. Ever flatfooted, I've treated the Goya and Veber illustrations as records of actual horrors visited on actual corpses. But we'd be horrified even if Goya and Veber invented these displays. We'd be horrified by chainsaw massacre movies even if we understood they were done with clever digital wizardry, no actual actors or actresses anywhere in sight. So the skeptic can urge that our shrinking from what is done to these corpses makes perfectly good sense *if* it hangs on a detached conception. That's compatible with his conviction that imagining injury to those corpses or to the persons whose bodies they once were, and so relying on the derivative conception, is nonsensical.

Probably, too, the skeptic can fend off objections raised by considering the extraordinary care taken with corpses in some religious traditions. Take the practice of *tahara*, performed in Orthodox Judaism by members of a *chevra kadisha*, who themselves have to be pure. I'll be terse with the painstak-

29. For instance, *State v. Bearup*, 221 Ariz. 163 (2009).

ing ritual's details.[30] The *chevra kadisha* bathe the corpse and dress it in plain white clothes. Addressing the dead person by name, the *chevra kadisha* ask forgiveness for any disrespect they've shown and place the body in a coffin. The ritual does not secure a happy afterlife for the dead person: the afterlife in any case is not prominent in Judaism. But the skeptic can pounce on the religious trappings of the ceremony and insist that it must be wrapped up with divine commandment. That's compatible with their believing they do it for the person who died, but the skeptic can still protest that this practice can't count as evidence against his hardnosed view.

But what about time-honored military practices of taking significant risks to retrieve the fallen? In Mogadishu in 1993, American troops kept trying to retrieve a helicopter pilot's body—they knew he was dead—even as they came under sustained fire. "Are they going to be able to get the body out of there?" demanded a general. "I need an honest, no shit, for-real assessment." They needed twenty minutes more, the troops replied. "We will stay the course until they are finished," he decided.[31] In 2008, Israel traded five militants, one a convicted murderer, and the remains of some two hundred militants for the dead bodies of two Israeli soldiers.[32] We struggle not only to reclaim corpses on the battlefield, but to find, identify, and respectfully bury corpses from wars that are years or even decades old.[33]

30. For more, see Rochel U. Berman, *Dignity beyond Death: The Jewish Preparation for Burial* (Jerusalem: Urim Publications, 2005).

31. Mark Bowden, *Black Hawk Down: A Story of Modern War* (New York: Atlantic Monthly Press, 1999), 285.

32. Ayat Basma and Avida Landau, "Hezbollah Delivers Remains of Two Israeli Soldiers," *Reuters* (16 July 2008).

33. See generally Michael Sledge, *Soldier Dead: How We Recover, Identify,*

And what about the exquisite care the U.S. military takes in repairing the corpses of dead soldiers? This too happens on an industrial scale, with numbers illustrating the grisly ramifications of being on a more or less permanent war footing: over sixty mortuary workers working in a building of seventy-two thousand square feet. But once cargo jets bring back the corpses, every step is suffused with respect for these dead individuals. White-gloved men in uniform transfer the incoming coffins to white vans, which bring them back to the mortuary. Watch your tax dollars at work: morticians embalm the body, wash it, shampoo the hair, wire together broken bones, repair damaged tissue with stitches and suitably colored wax, even try to get the facial wrinkles right: "'It has to look normal, like someone who is sleeping,' said Petty Officer First Class Jennifer Howell, a Navy liaison with a mortician's license." Not a single loose thread on the uniforms they'll be dressed in and every medal accurate, even if the coffin will remain resolutely shut in the funeral ceremony.[34]

Some of what these military morticians say is puzzling.

Bury, and Honor Our Military Fallen (New York: Columbia University Press, 2005). On the heroic efforts to identify and respectfully bury the Union dead in the Civil War, see Drew Gilpin Faust, _This Republic of Suffering: Death and the American Civil War_ (New York: Alfred A. Knopf, 2008), chap. 7: the War Department spent over $4m (236). On the use of embalming for shipping bodies back north, Faust, _Republic_, 92–98. The practice already inspired grumbling worries about ripoffs: for their full and hilarious flowering, see Jessica Mitford, _The American Way of Death_ (New York: Simon and Schuster, 1963), esp. chap. 6.

34. James Dao, "Last Inspection: Precise Ritual of Dressing Nation's War Dead," _New York Times_ (25 May 2013). Sutures aren't mentioned in the print story, but are in the accompanying online audio snippet from William Zwicharowski, mortuary branch chief: www.nytimes.com/2013/05/26/us/intricate-rituals-for-fallen-americans-troops.html (last visited 8 December 2014).

One suggests that it's important to make the bodies look realistic to make the surviving family members stop fantasizing that their soldier isn't this dead one; another muses that he does this work for himself. Perhaps they're abashed by knowing what a skeptic would say, so they don't say what seems straightforwardly true: they work on behalf of dead soldiers, not as an anonymous or collective group, but for each and every one of them. It would be different to occasionally select a corpse at random and put it through this laborious process, just as the Tomb of the Unknown Soldier expresses something very different from the grave of any named soldier. That the military does this unhesitatingly when no one will ever see the restored corpse—that, as I suppose, they do it when no close family members survive—means it can't be done solely as a consoling gesture to the living, either. This, thinks the military, is something we owe to the dead. As an official in charge of supplying the uniforms says, "'That's our job. . . . We'll do everything we can to help honor any service member who gives the ultimate sacrifice for their country.'"[35]

Not only the military thinks this way. On Facebook, someone posted the lead photo with the *New York Times* article reporting this practice. It shows a sergeant tending to the uniform for Captain Aaron R. Blanchard, thirty-two years old, killed a few days after arriving in Afghanistan; there's no corpse or body part anywhere in the photo, so it can't be exercising a kind of repellent fascination. That Facebook post went viral, or close enough: 192,221 "shares"; 281,324 "likes"; and 24,210 comments, with stinging denunciations of a woman who ex-

---

35. Beth Reece, "Uniforms for the Fallen," www.dla.mil/Loglines/Pages/LoglinesJA2011Story09.aspx (last visited 13 October 2014).

pressed skepticism among the most liked ones.[36] Some of the comments offer generic patriotism or support of the military. But some of the most liked ones focus precisely on the gesture of respect to individual dead soldiers. Here's Kelsey Taylor: "Seeing my husbands casket arrive in Dover, watching him get received by a group of white gloves, carried (marched rather) to a van, then driven off only to see him 3–4 days later in a funeral home, dressed in a way that only he could dress himself. . . . I can't thank these men enough. They showed the utmost respect to my husband. Someone they don't even know." And here's Kathy Klumfoot Jacobson: "Thank God there are still men and women in our country who value and honor the people who serve and die in our country's defense. I am moved to tears with respect for the people who do this every day as an act of love and honor to fallen fellow soldiers. Your acts of kindness are not in vain, nor unnoticed." Finally, here's Barbara Cothran: "The respect is over the top. But think this guy gave his life for his country. He should get this kind of respect!!" It would be captious for the skeptic to seize on Jacobson's "Thank God" as a sign of the sort of religious background commitment I've forsworn in suggesting it's bad for you if your corpse is desecrated. But the skeptic might well pause when he notices how many of us fiercely disagree and how we invest actual resources, not least emotionally excruciating work, in doing what we can to restore these dead soldiers' corpses. We don't adopt or even entertain the allegedly realistic view that once someone's dead, he is no more and so has no interests, no claims on the living. We say instead that it is wonderful to pay him respect. And we say it effortlessly, as if it's obvious. What

---

36. See www.facebook.com/SheepDogIA/photos/a.120546321315282
.8152.118696028166978/621789111190998 (last visited 10 October 2014).

makes the skeptic want to roll his eyes or chortle? What makes him so confident that we're wrong?

Or consider the mortician, forensic pathologist, and trusty hands-on secretary confronted with "bits and pieces of people" after a German bomb killed around twenty in the Blitz. It was a "hideous human jigsaw puzzle," but they got to work and managed to sort out all but a few stray pieces into individual corpses. "The job, beastly as it was, simply had to be done." What was the necessity? Not, it seems, any legal requirement: rather the respect owed to these particular dead individuals.[37]

Likewise for the repulsion summoned up by mass graves. Let's switch our focus from war to Catherine Corless's explosive allegation: that it seemed that at least 796 children who'd died in a home for unmarried mothers run by an order of nuns in Tuam, County Galway, Ireland had been buried in a mass grave—apparently in an abandoned septic tank.[38] The septic tank is more gruesome yet, at least if it's wrong to treat corpses like shit. Corless denied ever saying they were "dumped" in a septic tank. Church apologists seized on that concession to suggest she'd never made a claim about a septic tank, either.[39]

37. Molly Lefebure, *Murder on the Home Front* (New York: Grand Central Publishing, 2013), 171.

38. Alison O'Reilly, "A Mass Grave of 800 Babies," *Irish Mail on Sunday* (25 May 2014). For the septic tank, Catherine Corless, "The Home," *Journal of Old Tuam Society* (2012): 81, following up stories about "a sort of crypt" with "small skulls": "By placing a tracing of the 2007 map on top of the 1905 map, it is quite evident that this tank is right in the middle of the graveyard."

39. The two charges are conflated in Rosita Boland, "Tuam Mother and Baby Home: The Problem with the Septic Tank Story," *Irish Times* (7 June 2014). Corless explicitly mentions the septic tank in the accompanying online video: see www.irishtimes.com/news/social-affairs/tuam-mother-and-baby-home-the-trouble-with-the-septic-tank-story-1.1823393 (last visited

Corless found the children's names in the birth and death registers, but not in any burial records. The sister of one of those children is waiting for a response from the attorney general. Records show that her brother, who died as a baby, "was emaciated with a voracious appetite." She thinks he died of neglect and not of measles, as his death certificate reports while branding him "a congenital idiot." So she wants the grave excavated, DNA used to identify her brother's corpse, and, if possible, the true cause of death identified. Now consider this: "'I want justice and I want closure for my brother and my mother, who didn't get it when they were alive,'" she also says.[40]

I don't know if she's a devout Catholic or if her brand of Catholicism would include the claim that her dead brother and mother are peering down from their perch in the afterlife, unable to rest without justice being done to them. Even on that

---

13 October 2014). Contrast too Eamonn Fingleton, "Why That Story about Irish Babies 'Dumped in a Septic Tank' Is a Hoax," *Forbes* (9 June 2014), with Amelia Gentleman, "The Mother behind the Galway Children's Mass Grave Story: 'I Want to Know Who's Down There,'" *Guardian* (13 June 2014).

On the use of common graves for paupers and the desire of family members to secure them individual burial in England around 1900, see Julie-Marie Strange, *Death, Grief, and Poverty in Britain, 1870–1914* (Cambridge: Cambridge University Press, 2005), 138–48. Close to one million are buried in New York City's Potter Field on Hart Island, but for well over a century every body has gotten its own casket: Corey Kilgannon, "Visiting the Island of the Dead," *New York Times* (15 November 2013). See too one soldier's flinching at the 1815 mass burial of two hundred of the British war dead in New Orleans: "A more appalling spectacle cannot well be conceived than this common grave, the bodies hurled in as fast as we could bring them" (*The Autobiography of Sir Harry Smith, 1787–1819*, ed. G. C. Moore Smith [London: John Murray, 1910], 241). Compare Nina Bernstein, "Bodies Given to N.Y.U. Ended Up in Mass Graves, Despite Donors' Wishes," *New York Times* (27 May 2016).

40. Alison O'Reilly, "'Excavate Mass Grave to Find My Brother,'" *Irish Mail on Sunday* (28 September 2014).

view, we can turn the skeptic's deriding that "mysterious reason" that souls have for caring about their corpses against him: just why would a dead soul care about the disposal of its corpse? The traditional Catholic answer can't be that resurrection requires the corpse's physical integrity: not because even burial in a septic tank doesn't interfere with that, but because the church fathers considered the matter in their usual meticulous way and decided that God can reassemble the particles of your body, however widely scattered they are. (Yes, they fretted too about the same particles appearing in different bodies, not least because of cannibalism.) Indeed in the early church some saints' corpses were deliberately divided so they could be buried in different locations and attract more prayers.[41]

Once again we see the role of convention and context: dividing a saint's corpse is a mark of respect, even adoration. So too is festooning the remains in jewelry: gaudy, even garish, for some of us today, but a profound honor in the eyes of contemporary believers.[42] The family members in saga Iceland who brandished severed heads and other bloody relics of the deceased to goad others into revenging them weren't dishon-

41. Caroline Walker Bynum, *The Resurrection of the Body in Western Christianity, 200–1336* (New York: Columbia University Press, 1995); Elizabeth A. R. Brown, "Death and the Human Body in the Later Middle Ages: The Legislation of Boniface VIII on the Division of the Corpse," *Viator* (1981). For the role of ghosts in popular Christian culture in the Middle Ages, see Jean-Claude Schmitt, *Ghosts in the Middle Ages: The Living and the Dead in Medieval Society,* trans. Teresa Lavender Fagan (Chicago: University of Chicago Press, 1998).

42. See the astonishing photographs in Paul Koudounaris, *Heavenly Bodies: Cult Treasures & Spectacular Saints from the Catacombs* (New York: Thames & Hudson, 2013). A sampling is online at http://hyperallergic.com/83446/medieval-bling-skeletons-encrusted-in-jewels-and-gold/ (last visited 27 January 2015).

oring the dead: quite the contrary.[43] So too for those in today's China who publicly display corpses to protest wrongful deaths.[44] Jeremy Bentham suggested that corpse displays could be endlessly intructive.[45] The Soviet Union and its satellites knew that, too; so did Hugo Chávez, though his teary rhapsodies over Simón Bolívar's bones hurtle us into bathos.[46] Even cannibalism can be a gesture of respect.[47] Ordinarily, though, severed, decorated, and jumbled remains are a sign of contempt. Likewise for corpses left unburied.

So there's a general response to mass graves: as far as we can, we delicately excavate, sort out individual bodies, identify them, and accord them dignified burial. It's possible, if tricky, to thread the needle here and argue that jumbling different individual corpses together is an affront not to those particular

43. William Ian Miller, "Choosing the Avenger: Some Aspects of the Bloodfeud in Medieval Iceland and England," *Law and History Review* (1983).

44. Yaqiu Wang, "Invasion of the Body Snatchers: Why Aggrieved Chinese Citizens and Chinese Police Are Fighting over Corpses," *ChinaFile* (6 May 2015). Thanks to Mary Gallagher for the reference—and for reporting this: "A researcher on petitioning told me about meeting a woman who carried her son's head around in a bag while she went from office to office in Beijing trying to get a just decision on the cause of death."

45. See *Auto-Icon; or, Farther Uses of the Dead to the Living* (not published, 1842?), in *Bentham's Auto-Icon and Related Writings*, ed. James E. Crimmins (Bristol: Thoemmes Press, 2002). Compare William Godwin, *Essay on Sepulchres: or, A Proposal for Erecting Some Memorial of the Illustrious Dead in All Ages on the Spot Where Their Remains Have Been Interred* (London, 1809).

46. Katherine Verdery, *The Political Lives of Dead Bodies: Reburial and Postsocialist Change* (New York: Columbia University Press, 1999); "Bolívar Exhumed," *Economist* (22 July 2010).

47. Jerome T. Whitfield, Wandagi H. Pako, John Collinge, and Michael P. Alpers, "Mortuary Rites of the South Fore and Kuru," *Philosophical Transactions of the Royal Society B* (2008). Thanks to Scott Hershovitz for the reference.

individuals, but to the detached value of human life: imagine learning that the Tomb of the Unknown Soldier had the body parts of two or three different soldiers. I don't deny that regard for the detached value of human life helps motor widespread horror at mass graves, that it is one reason people do the gory work of patiently disaggregating the corpses and, as far as they can, according each one a respectful burial. But here's the clincher against the view that it's *only* a matter of detached value, that we don't believe there is any wrong to the individuals consigned to mass graves: over and over in these cases, family members come forward to claim their own loved one's corpse. If mass graves were an affront only to the detached value of human life, you wouldn't expect that. No, don't say it's just an efficient scheme to divide the labor.

Many years after genocidal attacks in Srebrenica, the authorities removed bodies from a mass grave, identified them, and put them in labeled coffins: "There were 500-plus coffins and large groups of family members. The people walk around and look for their loved ones. There is a name on the coffin. They are looking for their relatives, so there are lots of people coming and going between the coffins looking for their loved ones. Once they find them, they stop there and pray and touch the coffin and spend time with it."[48] Or again: during the potato famine, many ailing Irish immigrants deboarding at Ellis Island were quarantined. The thousands who died were buried

---

48. Kathy Ryan, "Under Cover: Paolo Pellegrin on Photographing Srebrenica, 20 Years after the Genocide," *The 6th Floor: Eavesdropping on the Times Magazine* (30 May 2014), at http://6thfloor.blogs.nytimes.com/2014/05/30/under-cover-paolo-pellegrin-on-photographing-srebrenica-20-years-after-the-genocide (last visited 14 October 2014).

unceremoniously, "three and four deep," behind the hospital. Then this, from coverage of a more respectful burial ceremony of the remains, carried out over 150 years later: "Jack King, 71, who said he believed that two of his ancestors were quarantined after arriving from Ireland, will participate in the ceremony on Sunday. 'I'm probably one of the proudest Irishmen that you could find, to know that relatives had gone through this and I have an opportunity to put them to rest,' he said. 'This puts a final end to their sorrows.'"[49] Or again: in 1948, federal authorities chartered a jet to deport Mexican farmworkers, some undocumented, some outstaying their work permits.[50] The plane crashed. "The bodies of the four crew members were shipped to family members, but the remains of the 28 Mexicans were buried in a mass grave." Woody Guthrie's "Plane Wreck at Los Gatos" limns the indignity: "You won't have your names when you ride the big airplane / All they will call you will be 'deportees.'" Decades later, a son and grandson of Mexican farmworkers spent two years identifying those twenty-eight by name. More than six hundred assembled for a memorial service and the unveiling of a new headstone naming every one of them. Then this:

> Caritina Paredes Murillo was 11 when news
> of her father's death in a plane wreck reached her
> family in Guanajuato State in central Mexico. For
> days, everyone in her house wept. But after 65

49. Edna Ishayik, "Refugees of Irish Famine to Get a Proper Burial," *New York Times* (25 April 2014).

50. "32 Killed in Crash of Charter Plane," *New York Times* (29 January 1948).

years, her memories of her father feel more like impressions now: the way he left for long stretches to work, and the sound of his voice singing ballads to her mother when he returned home.

"In my heart I feel happy and sad at the same time," said Ms. Paredes, 77, who traveled from Mexico to attend the ceremony. "It feels like they were all buried for the first time today."[51]

Again, I don't doubt that these stories also show regard for the detached conception of human life. Jack King didn't instigate the reburial of those Irish remains. But he's not there to vindicate the value of human life as such. He wants to put his relatives to rest. Yes, his reference to ending their sorrows may well indicate he's convinced he can resolve their unhappiness in the afterlife. But what about Caritina Paredes Murillo? She too didn't instigate the reburial of her father and others. But this old woman comes from Mexico to Fresno for what seems to her a first burial, the first time her father's remains have been treated with the dignity she thinks they deserve: not as a symbol of human life, not even as a representative of Mexican migrant labor, but as her father. The man who struggled to name the twenty-eight migrant laborers in a mass grave may have thought simply that all human corpses deserve names. His lineage, though, suggests he is acting on a broader notion than kinship, but one pointing to the same direction: that he owes this effort to Mexican migrant workers, but not finally as a category: rather to these particular workers, for their individual sakes.

51. Malia Wollan, "65 Years Later, a Memorial Gives Names to Crash Victims," *New York Times* (3 September 2013).

What's Law Got to Do with It?

Now I want to consider how the law has responded to complaints about disturbing and desecrating corpses. Remember that corpse desecration is a crime, but that's public law. The question is whether an affront to an individual corpse might register as a tort, or more generally in private law. Who would be claiming an injury? And just what would that injury be?

There can be no property in a corpse: that principle is deep in the common law, or at least it comes to seem that way.[52] Coke's *Institutes* declares, "The buriall of the Cadaver (that is, *caro data vermibus*) is *nullius in bonis*, and belongs to Ecclesiasticall cognisance, but as to the monument, action is given (as hath been said) to the Common law by defacing thereof."[53] Corpses may be given over to the worms, as the Latin parenthesis has it, but Coke seems really to be saying that despite the ordinary jurisdiction of the church courts in such matters, the common law still has a role to play in actions about the monument. Perhaps Blackstone offers better support for the traditional reading. His startling example underlines the point. Even if we don't know who owns some property, he reports, the law will permit criminal prosecution. "This is the case of

---

52. For a first-rate review and apt skepticism about how some of the canonical sources have been enlisted, see Daniel Sperling, *Posthumous Interests: Legal and Ethical Perspectives* (Cambridge: Cambridge University Press, 2008), chap. 3. More generally, see the breathless treatment in Percival E. Jackson, *The Law of Cadavers and of Burial and Burial Places*, 2nd ed. (New York: Prentice-Hall, 1950), chap. 2. For the suggestion that a corpse that's been worked on—embalmed, say, or mummified—and attained some monetary value does qualify as property, see *Doodeward v. Spence*, 6 C.L.R. 406 (Australia 1908).

53. Edw[ard] Coke, *The Third Part of the Institutes of the Laws of England* (London, 1648), 203.

stealing a shroud out of a grave; which is the property of those, whoever they were, that buried the deceased: but stealing the corpse itself, which has no owner, (though a matter of great indecency) is no felony, unless some of the gravecloths be stolen with it."[54] Whatever its actual background in jurisdiction, the denial of property in a corpse hardens over time. "Our law recognises no property in a corpse," bluntly declared the Court of King's Bench in 1857.[55] "A dead body by law belongs to no one," as one late-nineteenth-century compendium of English law put it.[56]

But this denial came under pressure. One man sued when the town selectmen decided to close a cemetery and transfer the buried bodies to a new one: he didn't want his loved ones' remains disturbed. The court scrutinized his claim: what rights could he be claiming? He didn't own the soil they were buried in; he could plead no breach of contract. "But while [the corpse] is not property in the ordinary sense of the term, it is regarded as property so far as to entitle the relatives to legal protection from unnecessary disturbance and wanton violation or invasion of its place of burial."[57] So this man stated a plausible legal

54. William Blackstone, *Commentaries on the Laws of England,* 4 vols. (Oxford, 1765–69), 4:236; see also 2:429. See *Guthrie v. Weaver,* 1 Mo. App. 136, 141 (1876) (echoing Blackstone, but denying property even in the shroud). See too *Meagher v. Driscoll,* 99 Mass. 281 (1868); *Bonham v. Loeb,* 107 Ala. 604 (1894) (suit alleging plowing and tilling over the bodies of plaintiff's relatives fails for lack of a sound property claim); *Bessemer Land & Improv. Co. v. Jenkins,* 111 Ala. 135 (1895). For an opinion tripping up on the question whether a corpse has property rights, see *Lawson v. State,* 68 Ga. App. 830 (1943), *overruled by McKee v. State,* 200 Ga. 563 (1946).

55. R. v. Sharpe (1857) 169 Eng. Rep. 1959 (KB).

56. Ephraim A. Jacob, *An Analytical Digest of the Law and Practice of the Courts . . . of England,* 11 vols. (New York, 1879–86), 3:4386.

57. Page v. Symonds, 63 N.H. 17, 20 (1883).

claim, even if he wouldn't prevail: there was nothing unnecessary or wanton about the selectmen's action. It was regulation in the public interest, the sort of thing nineteenth-century American courts effortlessly upheld against claims of private right.[58]

In another case, a widow and her children wanted to move her husband's body to a nearby cemetery, but the husband's siblings opposed the move. "There is not a property right to a dead body in a commercial sense," agreed the court, "but there is a right to bury it which the courts of law will recognize and protect."[59] So too another court agreed there is no property in a corpse, but promptly added that there is "quasi property," with rights and obligations for disposing of it enforceable in equity.[60] More recently, Tri-State Crematories didn't cremate some bodies. Instead they left them jumbled on their property and returned concrete dust to the grieving relatives: or so a class action suit maintained. The court had no worries about the legal basis for the action: "Georgia recognizes a quasi property right in the deceased body of a relative, belonging to

58. William J. Novak, *The People's Welfare: Law and Regulation in Nineteenth-Century America* (Chapel Hill: University of North Carolina Press, 1996). See too *Kincaid's Appeal,* 66 Pa. 411, 424 (1870); *Sohier v. Trinity Church,* 109 Mass. 1, 21–22 (1871).

59. Neighbors v. Neighbors, 112 Ky. 161, 163 (Ky. Ct. App. 1901). Compare *In re Ackermann,* 124 A.D. 684 (N.Y. App. Div. 1908); *Wynkoop v. Wynkoop,* 42 Pa. 293 (1861); *Weld v. Walker,* 130 Mass. 422 (1881) (affirming a husband's right to move his wife's remains when he pleaded that he had succumbed to her sisters' pleas while under great emotional strain).

60. Pierce v. Proprietors of Swan Point Cemetery, 10 R.I. 227 (1872). Compare *Beatty v. Kurtz,* 27 U.S. 566, 584–85 (1829). For many more such opinions, see Jackson, *Law of Cadavers,* 133 n. 57. On the law's invoking quasi property in this setting and elsewhere, see Shyamkrishna Balganesh, "Quasi-Property: Like, but Not Quite Property," *University of Pennsylvania Law Review* (June 2012).

the husband or wife, and, if neither, to the next of kin."[61] In the exasperated words of an old and frequently cited case, "this whole subject is only obscured and confused by discussing the question whether a corpse is property in the ordinary commercial sense," because some have rights to control and bury the body.[62]

Not property in a commercial sense—you can't buy or sell a corpse—but property, or quasi property, in other senses: you may have the right to control the disposition of a corpse and others may be obliged not to interfere. These courts, most of them writing decades before, adopt the view we associate with the legal realists of the early twentieth century, now canonically casting the right to property as a bundle of sticks, which the owner may hold more or fewer of, and not a unitary right.[63] I think the insight is a lot older. It's common to use Blackstone as the foil:[64] "There is nothing which so generally strikes the imagination, and engages the affections of mankind as the right of property; or that sole and despotic dominion which one man claims and exercises over the external things of the world, in total exclusion of the right of any other individual in the universe."[65] But Blackstone presents sole and despotic dominion as a popular—and, as he goes on to say, unconsidered—view. His ensuing hundreds of pages, catalog-

---

61. In re Tri-State Crematory Litig., 215 F.R.D. 660, 697 (N.D. Ga. 2003).

62. Larson v. Chase, 47 Minn. 307, 310 (1891).

63. Key pieces include John R. Commons, *The Distribution of Wealth* (New York, 1893), 70, 92; Robert L. Hale, "Rate Making and the Revision of the Property Concept," *Columbia Law Review* (March 1922); Morris R. Cohen, "Property and Sovereignty," *Cornell Law Review* (December 1927).

64. For instance, in Felix S. Cohen's characteristically hilarious "Dialogue on Private Property," *Rutgers Law Review* (Winter 1954): 362.

65. Blackstone, *Commentaries*, 2:2.

ing all kinds of restrictions on property, deftly undo this popular fantasy.

So too whether a corpse counts as property will depend
on what sort of legal claim is being pressed. When a young
adult died without indicating how to dispose of his body, his
divorced parents agreed on cremation. But they couldn't agree
on where the ashes should rest. The father petitioned probate
court to treat the ashes as property and partition them equally.
That court refused; citing Blackstone and King's Bench as authorities, an appeals court agreed.[66] One woman filed a replevin
action to get her brother's corpse back from the undertakers,
who were holding onto it because she hadn't paid the bill. The
court dismissed the claim: because corpses aren't property, it
didn't make sense to invoke a legal remedy for reclaiming
personal property.[67] The Fifth and Fourteenth Amendments
provide that neither the federal nor state governments may deprive any person of life, liberty, or property without due process of law. For purposes of that guarantee, ruled one court, a
corpse won't qualify as property either.[68]

Property in some senses, not others, for some legal purposes, not others; or quasi property, coupled with the relatively
freewheeling approach to decision making that lawyers shelve
under the name equity jurisdiction: this is one basic recipe allowing courts to respond to claims that something has gone
badly amiss in the treatment of a corpse. As an 1852 opinion
put it, "It cannot be that it is necessary to produce formal proof
of authority from a mother to a son to do all that was necessary

66. Wilson v. Wilson, 138 So.3d 1176 (Fla. Dist. Ct. App. 2014).
67. Keyes v. Konkel, 119 Mich. 550 (1899). So too *Lascurain v. City of
Newark,* 349 N.J. Super. 251, 267–71 (2002).
68. Albrecht v. Treon, 118 Ohio St. 3d 348 (2008).

and proper for the burial of her deceased son in the family tomb. The law will imply a license from the nature and exigencies of the case, the relation of the parties, and the well-established usages of a civilized and christian community."[69] Here too the skeptic might pounce on the passing appeal to Christianity, but I think he won't be able to show that such sentiments must depend on religious conviction.

I want next to consider two sorts of cases: first, corpses damaged in transit; second, autopsies gone awry. Remember, the skeptic's commitment to the oblivion thesis means that he will insist that nothing I shall report here could count as an injury to a dead person. His commitment to the hangover thesis means that he will insist that any intuitions to the contrary must depend on continuing to cling to older religious commitments. As we'll see, the doctrinal structure of these complaints is slippery: interference with a quasi-property interest in exercising the right to bury a loved one, or—not formally available until the 1970s or so—the negligent infliction of emotional distress, or something more or less unstated. The Second Restatement sets out a special tort of corpse desecration: "One who intentionally, recklessly or negligently removes, withholds, mutilates or operates upon the body of a dead person or prevents its proper interment or cremation is subject to liability to a member of the family of the deceased who is entitled to the disposition of the body."[70] The reporters promptly explain that at bottom are claims about interference with quasi property or the infliction of emotional distress, whether negligent or intentional. On any of these frames, the injury is to the sur-

69. Lakin v. Ames, 64 Mass. 198, 221 (1852). More pointedly, *Osteen v. Southern R. Co.,* 101 S.C. 532, 543 (1915).
70. *Restatement (Second) of Torts,* § 868.

vivors, not the dead person. I'll be putting pressure on that thought. Regardless, that it's hard to say precisely what the legal complaint is does not mean the law thinks nothing wrong is going on. Quite the contrary.

One caution: I draw freely on cases from different jurisdictions over many decades. I claim neither that the law has shifted nor that it hasn't: there just aren't enough cases to be confident. It's enough for my purposes to highlight the problems that tort law has responded to.

Misdelivery by Train

Your loved one dies hundreds of miles from home. You want to bury the corpse in the local cemetery, so you hire a railroad company to bring it back. They botch the job.

Or they manage to transform a living person into mangled body parts strewn far and wide. In 1905, a man boarded a Southern Railway train in Statesville, North Carolina. The train was bound for Carrabis, some twenty miles away; he intended to get off along the way to spend the night with his aunt. He never arrived. The *Charlotte Daily Observer* reported the tragedy: Bert Kyles, around twenty-six years old, "was killed last night by east-bound passenger train No. 12 at Barber's Junction. Just how the accident occurred has not been learned."[71]

His widow, Hattie, sued the railroad company. He happened to be their employee, though that wasn't an issue. Nor did Hattie allege that the railroad had caused his death. She sought to recover for the treatment of his corpse, but the trial court "nonsuited" her: they ruled that even if she could show the facts she alleged, nothing in the law would entitle her to

71. "Killed by a Train," *Charlotte Daily Observer* (21 January 1905).

recover. She appealed that judgment and the Supreme Court of North Carolina overruled the trial court. Lest you fear I'd be brazenly overstating the facts, I'll quote the court's dispassionate report:

> The body was found on the defendant's track—head, pool of blood, hair, eyeballs, etc., near the 4-mile post from Salisbury; arms and legs 75 yards farther in direction of Salisbury, and the body 250 or 275 yards from head in the same direction; hair, blood, and parts of body along track, inside and outside of the rails, for some distance; and evidence that body was dragged and knocked from one side of the track to the other; hair on angle bars or nuts where the rails are joined. The body was stripped of its head, legs and arms and all clothing; overcoat found near the place, torn and cut; a piece of it was found one mile east of the body, and a pocket west of Statesville, 27 miles therefrom, in a different direction. The drawers were picked up on the track one-fourth of a mile west from body. Between 9 o'clock on the evening of the 19th and 6 o'clock on the afternoon of the 20th the body and its fragments lay strewn up and down the track between the rails and were run over by every passing train. During this time fifteen or more trains passed over the defendant's track—six or more during the night and six or more during the day—after the defendant's agent discovered the body, and one train was seen to strike the body as it lay upon the track. The watch that the deceased wore was mashed, and the hands pointed

to 7 1/2 minutes to 9 o'clock. Train No. 12 passed the four-mile post going towards Salisbury and the scene of the killing about this time, with a full headlight. The track was straight for one mile each way and no object was discovered upon the track, as the engineer swore. Train No. 35, from Salisbury, passed No. 12 near that city, and passed the four-mile post a few minutes thereafter. This last train evidently struck the deceased first. That the body was further mutilated is shown by the fact that the headless body was 250 or more yards east of the four-mile post; the drawers were found 1 1/4 miles west; a part of the overcoat a mile east; pocket of overcoat 27 miles west; arms 75 yards east and on north side of track; legs still further east and on the south side of track; head near the four-mile post, and hair all along down the track on angle bars; trunk all rolled up in cinders and dirt, and mangled and mutilated beyond recognition. A dozen or more trains passed over the body, as already stated, and one was seen to strike it. This evidence of all these things can hardly be reconciled with the theory that *only one train struck the deceased.*

The evidence indicates rather that the body was struck after death by different trains going east and west, and that it and parts thereof were thrown hither and thither, backwards and forwards, by the passing trains going in opposite directions. This was an infringement upon the legal right of the plaintiff to have the body for burial in the condition in which it was when life became extinct.

The court scoffed at one defense the railroad offered:

> It is no answer to such negligence or indifference
> to say that the defendant did not remove the body
> from the track because the section master was wait-
> ing for the coroner. Humanity and decency required
> that the body and its scattered members should
> be reverently picked up, laid off the track in some
> nearby spot and sheltered by a covering from the
> sun and flies and dust and irreverent eyes, and pro-
> tected from the dogs by some better agency than,
> according to the testimony, the volunteer aid of
> small boys attracted thither by curiosity, but who
> showed more respect for humanity than those who
> represented this defendant. On this condition of af-
> fairs being reported to the proper official, he should
> have seen that such steps were promptly taken as
> were required by decency and the respect shown in
> all civilized communities to the dead. It could in
> nowise aid the investigation of the coroner to ex-
> pose the headless body on the track beneath the
> passing trains, becoming begrimed with cinders
> and dust beyond recognition, nor was there excuse
> for leaving the other portions of the body uncol-
> lected and scattered up and down the track, and for
> days even after a part of the body was sent home.
> Besides, there was negligence in keeping the body
> for eleven hours waiting for a coroner, when Salis-
> bury was only four miles distant.

The court's judgment didn't mean that Hattie Kyles won her
lawsuit. It meant only that the lower court was wrong to say that

these facts wouldn't amount to a tort against her. "While the common law does not recognize dead bodies as property, the courts of America and other Christian and civilized countries have held that they are *quasi* property and that any mutilation thereof is actionable."[72] The railroad could still argue that these factual claims were wrong or misleadingly incomplete. But Hattie Kyles finally won a judgment of $1,000.[73]

There are dispiritingly many published opinions about trains and damaged corpses. They must represent a proper subset of actual fiascos with trains and corpses: surely some cases settled outside court and others went to trial but weren't appealed, which ordinarily would produce no published opinion. I want to highlight the puzzles arising when the law tries to identify what is wrong with desecrating a corpse—and to whom the wrong is done. So I'll select this way: if you had a corpse to transport in the early twentieth century, it looks like you didn't want to hire the Louisville & Nashville Railroad Company.

The Hull family was in Asheville when Mrs. Hull died. Mr. Hull bought three train tickets—for the corpse, himself, and their child—to go as far as Nashville. There he needed to pick up new tickets and transfer to get home to Slaughtersville, Kentucky. Anxious, Hull telegraphed ahead for the tickets to be ready, but the agent shooed him to the back of the line. He finally got his tickets and promptly alerted the baggage master to the need to transfer the corpse. The baggage master reassured him and Hull took his seat. Seeing luggage being brought aboard, but not the coffin, he appealed to the conductor. The conductor went to check; two minutes later the train pulled

72. Kyles v. Southern R. Co., 147 N.C. 394 (1908).
73. "Budget from Statesville," *Charlotte Daily Observer* (3 June 1908).

out and the conductor told Hull his wife's remains were on the wrong train. "Hull said: 'How did this happen? This is an awful thing.' He said: 'I don't know. It is a terrible blunder. It is an inexcusable mistake.'" People had turned out for the funeral, but it had to be postponed. Everything was ready to go the next day, but it rained and attendance was bad.

Hull sued the railroad, apparently on a breach of contract theory, and won $1,640 in damages. Urging that there is no property in a corpse and that pain and suffering damages aren't available for breach of contract, the railroad appealed the judgment. The appeals court remanded for a new trial—they thought $1,640 unreasonably high and they found some of Hull's lawyer's statements to the jury prejudicial. But the court shredded the railroad's claims about property and damages. Imagine, the court remarked, that the railroad had *lost* the corpse. Would there really be no recovery? Ordinarily, breach of contract would not yield damage awards for emotional harm,[74] but that rule didn't apply here. (Today we'd say that that rule does not apply to contracts with "elements of personality," an opaque suggestion raising the same difficulties as construing *actio personalis*.)[75] "The tenderest feelings of the human heart cluster about the remains of the dead. The duty of Christian burial is one which loving hands perform as a privilege. An indignity or wrong to a corpse is resented more

---

74. Consider *Louisville & N. R. Co. v. Clark*, 205 Ala. 152 (1920) (no emotional damages available when woman, relying on negligently maintained railroad clock, fails to get back on board the train carrying her son's corpse).

75. Consider for instance *Valentine v. General Am. Credit*, 420 Mich. 256 (1984); thanks to Bruce Frier for the reference. More generally see *Restatement (Second) of Contracts*, § 353; thanks to Veronica Aoki Santarosa for the reference.

quickly than a wrong to the living, and, if mental suffering may be recovered for in the one case, it is hard to see why it may not be recovered for in the other."[76]

Penina Wilson hired Louisville & Nashville Railroad to get her husband Hamp's remains from Atlanta to Warrington, over one hundred miles. Over her protest, the train company left the corpse out in the rain for several hours when it was transferred. Penina sought not just $75 for damages to the coffin and shroud—remember Blackstone—but $2,000 for "great humiliation and shame and mental suffering." The appeals court made short work of the railroad company's plea that a corpse is not property: "It certainly can not be said by the defendant company that a corpse is sufficiently property for a railroad company to receive and accept pay for its transportation, but is not sufficiently property to authorize a recovery for a breach of duty arising therefrom, or to prevent any duty from arising under such circumstances." The court didn't quite commit to the claim that Penina ought to be able to win emotional damages, but it did suggest that her action was more promising than one for emotional damages with no underlying physical harm: "Here the action is for a tort, and there is an allegation of actual pecuniary damage to the coffin and shroud, and of injury to the body."[77]

That suggestion is utterly familiar when tort law is grap-

---

76. Louisville & N. R. Co. v. Hull, 113 Ky. 561 (Ky. Ct. App. 1902). See too *Louisville & N. R. Co. v. Bishop,* 17 Ala. App. 320 (1919) (overturning on technical grounds a judgment of $833 for bungling a transfer and delaying the shipment of a corpse); *Chicago, B. & Q. R. Co. v. Hoeffner,* 44 Ill. App. 137 (1892) (upholding damages award for delayed shipment of a corpse); *Alabama C., G. & A. R.R. v. Brady,* 160 Ala. 615 (1909) (affirming that in principle emotional damages are available for delayed shipment of a corpse).

77. Louisville & N. R. Co. v. Wilson, 123 Ga. 62 (1905).

pling with emotional damages. Probably the underlying worry is epistemic: in the absence of any physical harm, why should we trust the plaintiff's claim that she is emotionally worse off? No wonder then that another plaintiff didn't recover on the allegation that a train—relax, from a different company—had struck the wagon conveying his dead infant to the funeral and the infant had landed on the ground. Here the record showed no mutilation or other damage to the corpse.[78] But it didn't seem to take much physical damage. Biscomb Hall was charged with getting the body of his seven-year-old sister home for burial. This time the railroad—yes, Louisville & Nashville again—negligently dropped the casket on the ground. Biscomb himself, with the help of other passengers, placed it on the train. What damage did the body suffer? "He describes it as being all spotted, and states that it had been disarranged in the casket." That was enough to win $500 damages: the appeals court deemed the award large, but not unreasonably so.[79] These

78. Hockenhammer v. Lexington & E. Ry. Co., 74 S.W. 222 (Ky. Ct. App. 1903).

79. Louisville & N. R. Co. v. Hall, 219 Ky. 528 (Ky. Ct. App. 1927). Contrast *Long v. Chicago, R. I. & P. R. Co.,* 15 Okla. 512, 520 (1905) (because there is no property in a corpse, "Where a corpse is mutilated before or after the burial, in such a way as to render necessary the expenditure of extra money or labor in caring for it, or where injury is done to the coffin or clothes, the actual damages sustained may be recovered, and this rule was applied in the case at bar; but after carefully considering all of the authorities at our command, we are firmly convinced that no recovery can be had for mental pain and anguish caused by the negligent mutilation of such body"), with *St. Louis S. R. Co. v. White,* 192 Ark. 350 (1936) (railroad can be liable for negligently running over and mutilating corpse on tracks even when they did not put it there; far from being valueless, the corpse "had the right of sepulture, conferred by the simplest and earliest practices of civilized peoples," 352). *Long* is described as "practically without any support in the decisions of recent years," in *Wilson v. St. Louis & S. F. R. Co.,* 160 Mo. App. 649,

two Kentucky cases might of course be distinguished in other
ways, but they show what's odd about the thought that emotional damages without underlying physical harm are especially difficult.[80]

Autopsies Gone Awry

Sometimes there are pressing reasons to perform an autopsy.
The police need to know how someone was killed. Family
members hope to gain knowledge that will assist their own
medical care. But autopsy is already teetering dangerously close
to corpse desecration. All it takes is one false step.

One man sued when a coroner and undertaker plucked
his son's body from the coffin and dissected it against his will.
Worse, perhaps, "the brain, liver and spleen were removed, and
in the presence of friends and relatives were conveyed to and
thrown into a privy or water-closet." The coroner argued that
he had a statutory right to perform the autopsy because the
cause of death was unclear; he added for good measure that
there is no property in a corpse. That was good enough for
him to win on a general demurrer: once again, a trial court
found that even if the father could establish the facts he alleged, he wasn't entitled to legal relief. But the appeals court
overturned that verdict. Maybe the coroner had the right to
perform an autopsy, though it sounded like he hadn't followed

657 (1912) (collecting cases and affirming damages for emotional suffering
when railroad kept dumping baggage on coffin, damaging coffin and cadaver alike, despite the husband's protests).

80. See too *Gostkowski v. Roman Catholic Church of Sacred Hearts of Jesus
& Mary*, 262 N.Y. 320 (1933) (emotional damages available to widower
when priest moves buried widow to a new plot and is verbally "harsh" in
explaining why).

mandated procedures for establishing that right and claiming the body. Still, nothing could excuse his dumping the body parts in the privy. "Such conduct violates every instinct of propriety, and could not fail to outrage the feelings of the kindred of the deceased." The law would properly recognize that as an injury.[81]

Let's continue with our usual transgressor, the Louisville & Nashville Railroad Co. After a train crash, the company sent a surgeon to attend to the badly injured engineer. The surgeon cared for him for thirty-six hours. Then the engineer died and the surgeon moved his body to an undertaker's. Without the family's consent, the surgeon then performed a splendidly brutal autopsy, "sawing said dead body from the top of the breast bone clear down nearly to the pelvic bone," removing the internal organs, then restoring them. The widow didn't see what had happened until the remains showed up for burial. She sued to recover for her "intense mental pain and anguish." I don't know what cause of action she alleged, but the court ruled that the railroad wasn't liable for the surgeon's conduct. (As the court could have said, the question was one of vicarious liability under the doctrine of *respondeat superior.* Here the doctor was on a frolic, not a detour: his conduct, even if tortious, was far enough away from what the railroad company hired him to do that they couldn't be liable for it.) Yet the

---

81. Palenzke v. Bruning, 98 Ill. App. 644 (1901). So too *Hassard v. Lehane,* 143 A.D. 424 (N.Y. App. Div. 1911); *Alderman v. Ford,* 146 Kan. 698 (1937); *Liberty Mut. Ins. Co. v. Lipscomb,* 56 Ga. App. 15 (1937); *Janicki v. Hosp. of St. Raphael,* 46 Conn. Supp. 204 (Conn. Super. Ct. 1999). Consider *Sudduth v. Travelers' Ins. Co.,* 106 F. 822 (C.C.D. Ky. 1901) (refusing to construe an insurance contract clause granting the company the right to "examine the person or body" as including autopsy or dissection); *Travelers Ins. Co. v. Welch,* 82 F.2d 799 (5th Cir. 1936) (on "examine the person," same result).

court ruled that the surgeon could be found liable on these discouraging facts.[82]

In September 1977, Edward Cramer robbed the Sidetrack Bar in a tiny town in Michigan's Upper Peninsula and kidnapped twenty-one-year-old waitress Laura Lee Allinger. She was found beaten and strangled in a field; Cramer was convicted of murder. Doubtless her murder was the worst blow her parents suffered—but not the only blow. In November 1977, the Allingers showed up in district court for Cramer's preliminary examination. There they found their daughter's hands in a plastic bag. When they'd buried her, they had had no idea that her hands had been removed. So they sued the funeral director and the medical examiner. I'll ignore the action against the director, which sounds in breach of contract.[83] The suit against the examiner alleged that learning about the amputated hands had caused them to "suffer outrage, shock, grief, humiliation and extreme and persistent mental anguish and emotional distress," also that they had "become physically and morbidly depressed and distracted from the enjoyments and activities of life that was their custom and nature prior to the discovery."[84] You might dourly suspect that their

82. Louisville & N. R. Co. v. Blackmon, 3 Ga. App. 80 (1907). See too *Doxtator v. Chicago & W. M. R. Co.*, 120 Mich. 596 (1899) (railroad not responsible when hospital burns amputated limbs of fatally injured switchman). *Deeg v. Detroit*, 345 Mich. 371 (1956), denies a right of survival on widow's lawsuit for wrongful autopsy of her husband.

83. Contrast *Ginsberg v. Manchester Mem. Hosp.*, 2010 Conn. Super. LEXIS 268 (Feb. 2, 2010) (negligent infliction of emotional distress claim available when funeral home negligently gashes forehead, bruises eyes, and breaks nose of corpse).

84. "Convicted in U.P. Murder Case," *Daily Globe* (22 June 1978); "Removal of Hands Shocks U.P. Couple," *Ironwood Daily Globe* (18 April 1983). Cramer's appeal failed: see *People v. Cramer*, 97 Mich. App. 148 (1980). The

depression was caused by the murder, not the amputation. But the Allingers could try to show that they were doing better before the preliminary examination than after—and that it wasn't the reminder that Laura was dead that so upset them. The trial court dismissed this complaint. The emotional distress claim, it thought, foundered on the problem that the Allingers' distress was triggered months after the autopsy.

The appeals court rejected this analysis. That rule, they said, applied when parents complain that a wrong to their children has caused them distress. But here the wrong was in the first instance to the living Allinger parents, not their dead daughter, so there was no reason to worry about the elapsed time. Yet the appeals court found another reason to dismiss the tort claims against the medical examiner: he enjoyed statutory immunity. He hadn't removed the hands for fun. He believed they were needed for evidence in the case: under the statute, that relieved him of the duty to get the parents' consent.[85] The grant of immunity safeguards the state's pressing interest in investigating and prosecuting crime. The case then underlines the point with which I started this section: what

---

newspaper stories call the victim Allinger-Gardner and Gardner; the legal proceedings call her Allinger. She was estranged from her husband and living at home with her parents. "Seek Dismissal of Amputation Suits," *Daily Globe* (31 January 1979), says the parents were notified of the impending exhibit of the hands; it also says that Cramer stabbed Allinger and hit her with a tire wrench during an argument at the bar.

85. Allinger v. Kell, 102 Mich. App. 798 (1981). The case reports that the examiner also removed her hair: I don't know why. The opinion is blurry on whether his belief had to be reasonable. "Removal of Hands" reports that the parents argued that he could have obtained fingerprints and blood samples without removing the hands. But a reasonableness standard, more searching on its face than the blunt factual question of whether the coroner actually believed it, is still highly deferential.

might otherwise qualify as the grievous wrong of corpse desecration isn't wrongful in the law's eyes if it serves some pressing public interest. Not, I add, that the Allingers needed to find
that consoling. That public claims can override private ones
does not mean that private ones are weightless or illusory.

One last instance of autopsy gone awry. Seventeen-year-
old Jesse Shipley was killed in a car accident. His father consented to the autopsy, but asked the medical examiner to make
the body "'nice and clean because I wanted the boy to look
good for his funeral and stuff.'" The examiner returned the
body without the brain and without telling the Shipleys that he
had held onto it: curious, since he'd already decided Jesse had
died from a broken skull and brain hemorrhaging. Later, students from Jesse's high school touring the mortuary noticed a
striking specimen among the jars: a brain labeled "Jesse Shipley." Word wound its way to his sister, a student at the same
school, and that's how his parents learned what happened. The
relevant New York statute specifically provided for the return
of body parts.[86] The Shipleys won $1m at trial; on appeal a
court found this unreasonably high and knocked it down to
$600,000, which as usual the Shipleys could accept or appeal.
They appealed—and eventually lost. The court of appeals
ruled that the medical examiner was free to retain a body part
and not inform the family.[87] If you're thinking something
flukey must have happened, I regret to report that the New
York City medical examiner's office retained over ninety-two

---

86. NY CLS Pub. Health § 4215.
87. Shipley v. City of New York, 2009 N.Y. Misc. LEXIS 6586 (N.Y. Sup.
Ct. Mar. 4, 2009); Shipley v. City of New York, 80 A.D.3d 171 (N.Y. App. Div.
2010); Shipley v. City of New York, 34 Misc. 3d 1239(A) (N.Y. Sup. Ct. 2012);
Shipley v. City of New York, 2013 N.Y. LEXIS 3314 (Dec. 12, 2013); Shipley
v. City of New York, 25 N.Y.3d 645 (2015).

hundred brains—some claim it was for pathologists to practice on, though the immense number suggests crazed bureau-
cratic routine.[88]

Claims of infliction of emotional distress, whether intentional or negligent, are notoriously hard to prevail on. That so
many of these litigants prevail is evidence of just how seriously
the law takes corpse desecration. The same extends to what we
might think of as adjacent issues of mistreating corpses. In
2009, a Connecticut funeral home accidentally swapped two
bodies. So instead of preparing the body of ninety-five-year-
old Aurelie Germaine Tuccillo for a Catholic burial, they cre-
mated it. What to do? Why, dress the other body in Aurelie's
clothing and try to pass it off on the Tuccillo family. When the
family protested at the wake that it didn't look like their dear
Aurelie, the funeral home director assured them that it was:
embalming, he said, can change the appearance of a corpse. A
court had no problems finding that these allegations made for
a good claim of negligent infliction of emotional distress.[89] But
not any tampering will be tortious. When an Ohio funeral
home switched two bodies on display for the grieving families
but righted the problem an hour later, an appeals court ruled
that it was a legal error for the trial court to permit a jury to
find negligent infliction of emotional distress. Not that it wasn't
upsetting: the bereaved widower "was throwing chairs around

88. John Clarke, "Medical Examiner's Office Refuses to Release More
Than 9,000 Brains Belonging to New Yorkers so They Can Use Them for
'Experiments and Practice,'" *Mail Online* (29 October 2012). For more such
cases, see Wendy Gillis, "Ontario Pathology Service Facing Deadline to
Match Autopsy Organs to Families," *Toronto Star* (23 October 2014).

89. Tuccillo v. Buckmiller Bros. Funeral Homes, Inc., 2013 Conn. Super.
LEXIS 323 (Feb. 13, 2013).

the funeral home."[90] Rather that the conduct wasn't outrageous enough, the distress not severe enough, to qualify for this cause of action in tort.

Taking Stock

Recall the dilemma faced by those wishing to bring legal complaints about defaming the dead. They were stuck between *actio personalis* (the blanket denial that the dead have legal interests) and the *Palsgraf* principle (to win in tort, you have to show that you've been wronged, not that you've been harmed by a wrong to someone else). The way to slip through the prongs of the dilemma was what I dubbed the *Gugliuzza* solution, after the case where it was approved: the living family members could argue, "when you defamed our dead loved one, you wronged us." But defamation law overwhelmingly rejects the *Gugliuzza* solution: indeed, in *Gugliuzza* itself, the solution was rejected on appeal. Defamation, the law is convinced, is a wrong to the person defamed, not to family members harmed as a result.

But the abstract structure of the *Gugliuzza* solution reigns triumphant in cases about corpse desecration. The law doesn't even pause at the thought that corpse desecration wrongs living family members, at least those closest to the deceased. So

90. Audia v. Rossi Bros. Funeral Home, Inc., 140 Ohio App. 3d 589, 591 (2000). For another case of swapped corpses yielding damages, this time without any added duplicity but after the corpses had been prepared for burial in the wrong religious traditions, see *Lott v. State,* 32 Misc. 2d 296 (N.Y. Ct. Cl. 1962). I owe this last citation to Norman L. Cantor, *After We Die: The Life and Times of the Human Cadaver* (Washington, DC: Georgetown University Press, 2010), 255–56.

these actions are brought, not by the estates of the deceased, but by living family members. Those living members have nothing to fear from *actio personalis* or its living remnants in law. And their complaints comport with the *Palsgraf* principle. So they win over and over. That's why it's hard to find any tort cases about defaming the dead—people learn not to bring such unpromising charges—and those few cases are failures to boot, but it's easy to find winning tort cases about corpse desecration. I want to explore just a few more, with an eye to the following question.

Your loved one dies and her corpse is desecrated. (You may be as detailed and gruesome about that as you like.) You find this intensely distressing. But what does that distress hang on? I suspect it's the thought that your loved one has been wronged. That wouldn't eliminate the possibility that you've been wronged, too. Remember that some injuries to your spouse will simultaneously enable you to file an action for loss of consortium: those injuries then count as wrongs to each of you. But if you don't think your loved one has been wronged, what exactly are you so distressed about? Not that she's dead: she is, but we're trying to grasp the additional distress you suffer from corpse desecration.

Two more cases will help dramatize the question. If you didn't want your corpse on the Louisville & Nashville Railroad, you sure don't want it deposited in the Hamilton County, Ohio, coroner's office. In January 2001, over three hundred photographs surfaced of dead bodies in the morgue, "bodies in unnatural 'artistic' poses, often employing props for effect." For instance, "Christina Folchi, who was photographed with sheet music placed on her body and a snail near her groin area as well as other items pressed into her hand and mouth." The coroner had given a photographer free rein to enter the morgue:

he wanted to produce an art book. (You could get in with the onerous security code *7. Morgue employees had no guidance on who should be coming and going.)[91] In August 2014, the same morgue was back in the news for just-discovered events from the 1980s. Kenneth Douglas, an attendant there, liked to have sex with the corpses. How many corpses? "It could have been a hundred," he offered. "I would do crack and go in and I would drink and go in."[92] The victims included Charlene Appling. My imagination is not as depraved as the skeptic feared: she was six months pregnant and Douglas had his way with her the day she was strangled.[93]

I probably shouldn't help myself to the view that Appling was the victim. Her father is party to the suit against Douglas and the county: so at law he will argue that *he* was the victim. That is, he will argue that in penetrating his daughter, Douglas wronged him. That seems decidedly odd. Or ponder the words of the judge sentencing the photographer to two and a half years in prison for gross abuse of a corpse and excoriating those photographs: "'They're not art,' he said. 'They're sick, they're disgusting, they're disrespectful and really the worst invasion of privacy.'" Whose privacy? Folchi's survivors? Really? Isn't it an invasion of Christina Folchi's privacy? (Recall the court rul-

91. Chesher v. Neyer, 477 F.3d 784 (6th Cir. 2007).

92. Print descriptions vary. I'm quoting Douglas from the bits of his deposition aired on television news: see the video at www.wcpo.com/news/local-news/court-oks-trial-in-hamilton-county-corpse-abuse-lawsuit (last visited 23 October 2014).

93. Greg Noble, "Kenneth Douglas: Sex-with-Corpses Lawsuit against Hamilton County Can Go to Trial, Court Rules," *Associated Press* (19 August 2014); Esther Tanquintic-Misa, "Sex with the Dead: Ohio Man Admits Doing It with 100 Corpses," *International Business Times Australia* (19 August 2014); Range v. Douglas, 763 F.3d 573 (6th Cir. 2014).

ings that FOIA requests may be denied if they would invade a dead person's privacy.) As quoted at that sentencing, her father's language was garbled, whether in the saying or the reporting I don't know, but still moving: "I'd like to know what a symbolic object would be taking a picture of my daughter's pubic hair."[94]

You might think these cases are evidence for an inverted *Palsgraf* principle: a harm to one party can count as a wrong to someone else. So: by harming my daughter in this way, you wronged me. That way of putting it would depend on thinking that it's possible to harm a dead person. But then why isn't it also possible to wrong her? Ordinarily of course it is wrong to harm others. In some settings, the law tracks everyday moral intuitions by labeling some conduct that does indeed set back others' interests as privileged. If your employer fires you because someone better suited to the job waltzes in, your interests have been set back. But (in a world of at-will employment) neither your employer nor the new employee has acted wrongly. It's hard to see any parallel to such settings here. So if it harms Folchi to rape her cadaver, why doesn't it wrong her? It would be eccentric, to put it mildly, to think: "Okay, so dead people have enough moral standing that you can harm them, but not enough that you can wrong them in so doing."

If you configure the tort here as a wrongful invasion of a quasi-property right, it more straightforwardly qualifies as a wrong to the next of kin: "I had a right to bury a corpse that hadn't been mistreated." But notice what *mistreated* already summons up. If you think of it as negligent infliction of emo-

94. Quoted in Maria Rogers, "Death of Innocence," *City Beat* (18 April 2002).

tional distress, it sounds awfully like the cases in which a parent watches his or her child being struck by a driver.[95] All those cases depend crucially on the undeniable premise that a grievous tort has been committed against the child: the law's puzzle was whether that act would also qualify as a tort against the parent. The next of kin's tort claim for corpse desecration also seems to hang on the thought that they've become aware of a grievous injury to someone else: not, again, to the corpse; rather to the person whose corpse it is. The law then seems convinced that there is more than what the skeptic is willing to concede, our regard for the detached value of human life. The law is convinced, just as we are—recall for instance the military's painstaking efforts to repair the corpses of dead soldiers—that corpse desecration wrongs dead individuals.

If the survivor's actions here depend on the thought that the dead person has been wronged, how might we apprehend that wrong? Let's consider one last case, curiously straddling corpse desecration and defaming the dead.

In 1956, Louie Elmer Gillikin died when a truck hit his car. The truck driver was an agent of the coroner, who soon popped up at the scene. "He refused to permit a highway patrolman or the sheriff's department of Carteret County to take charge of and assume responsibility for the investigation. He refused to hold an inquest." Gillikin's father thought he would have had a promising wrongful death action, but claimed that the coroner conspired with a patrolman, a photographer, and insurance company agents to make it look like his son was at

---

95. The classic line of cases is *Waube v. Warrington,* 216 Wis. 603 (1934); *Amaya v. Home Ice, Fuel & Supply Co.,* 59 Cal. 2d 295 (1963); *Dillon v. Legg,* 68 Cal. 2d 728 (1968); *Thing v. La Chusa,* 48 Cal. 3d 644 (1989).

fault. He alleged that they had coerced his son's passenger into giving false testimony. But—this is our concern—he also claimed that the coroner

> covertly and with malicious intent did secure a beer can and a 7-Up bottle and placed them in a prominent position in the car and directed a commercial photographer, who had been called to the scene of the accident, to make faked-up and trumped-up pictures to not only defame and degrade the good name and reputation of Louie Elmer Gillikin but directed the taking of pictures for the wicked and wrongful purpose of framing and shaping testimony, evidence and facts to fit in with his own selfish interests and in order that he might prevail in any litigation to be brought.[96]

These explosive allegations produced a flurry of lawsuits and counterclaims. Gillikin's father did press a claim that the photograph had defamed his dead son. But the court balked for a reason that won't surprise you: Louie Gillikin was dead. The common law was clear: any defamation claim was then going nowhere fast. If the legislature wanted to change the law, they could. But they hadn't.[97]

Seeing your dead son presented as a drunk when he wasn't one is surely distressing, over and above the fact of his death and the belief that the coroner is going to dastardly lengths to blame him for the accident and thus let others es-

96. Gillikin v. Springle, 254 N.C. 240 (1961).
97. Gillikin v. Bell, 254 N.C. 244 (1961).

cape legal liability. Let's assume the father's allegations are true. Then the photograph makes a false, defamatory statement of fact. (The law doesn't pause in thinking photos can make factual claims. That ad suggesting that the horseback rider had a giant penis just happened not to press a factual claim.) That's a dignitary harm: it lowers Louie's standing in the community. It's okay to drive, okay to drink, and decidedly not okay to do both at once: in North Carolina in 1961, a respectable part of the community can think that.

Our cases of corpse desecration, too, present dignitary harms, or so I want to suggest. It's insulting to let train after train run over a corpse. It's contemptuous to put a kid's brain in a jar and stick it on a shelf. It's lamentably easy to slide into imagining the nub of dignitary harm is the hurt feelings of the victim or target, and then to pounce on the reminder that dead people don't have hurt feelings. But dignitary harms are public, objective, sociological. A diminution of your reputation doesn't happen in your head, though you might well feel bad about it. It happens in how others discuss you, in how they think of you, in how they treat you.

Compare California's provision in the code governing funeral directors and embalmers: "Using profane, indecent, or obscene language in the course of the preparation for burial, removal, or other disposition of, or during the funeral service for, human remains, or within the immediate hearing of the family or relatives of a deceased, whose remains have not yet been interred or otherwise disposed of constitutes a ground for disciplinary action."[98] This law prohibits undignified lan-

---

98. Cal. Bus. & Prof. Code § 7700. See too Nebraska Admin. Code Title 172, 67–011.04(3); MCLS § 339.1810(e).

guage around a corpse. The presence of a family member is not a required element of the offense; nor, indeed, is the presence of anyone else. Surely the worry is the insult to the dead person. There's no way to discard this law as a bit of curious rent-seeking or regulatory capture. It's the opposite: it burdens the funeral industry.

When Kenneth Douglas has sex with Charlene Appling's corpse, you can insist the corpse is indeed worse for wear: if being spotted and jostled around in a coffin qualifies, why not having semen in your vagina? But what about propping up Christina Folchi's corpse to take an offensive photograph? There's no permanent effect on the corpse, but it's still tortious as well as a crime. Back to quasi-property: conversion of property is also a tort. The core of the tort is asserting control over someone else's property: using it in unauthorized ways as if it's your own, or exceeding your authorized use of it. Nothing in that tort requires that you damage the property. Suppose you've given me your apartment key so that if you lock yourself out, you can knock on my door. Then knowing that you're out of town for three weeks, I move in. I'm liable for conversion of property even if I do a meticulous job cleaning up and you can't show the place is any worse for wear.[99] So too a company that "despite adamant protests by the property owners" drove over their snowy land to deliver a mobile home was liable for trespass to the tune of $1 compensatory damages and $100,000 punitive damages, a verdict finally upheld despite

99. Compare for instance *State v. McKinnon*, 21 Ohio Dec. 346 (Ohio C.P. 1911) (tortious of state treasurer to withdraw money from treasury and use it to earn interest himself even if he returns the money to the treasury). *State v. McKinnon*, 1912 Ohio Misc. LEXIS 172 (Ohio Cir. Ct. 1912) extends liability to the bondholders.

the Supreme Court's worry about the ratio between those two kinds of damages and the due process clause.[100] No matter that the property was none the worse for wear.

So what's wrong with posing Christina Folchi's corpse and taking that photo? Whatever the law says to award relief, I don't think the injury is properly understood as infringing in some significant way on her father's property right in her body. Yes, he'd never consent to that use of the body. But that's because it's not just disgusting, but insulting to her. I think the injury is the affront to her. Her being dead doesn't preclude her body's being used in such a demeaning way; it makes it possible, as if she were alive and drugged into a stupor. That's the core of the injury, I think, whatever doctrinal hoops the law requires parties to jump through.

It matters that the law does not talk this way and indeed sometimes explicitly denies it. "Who has been hurt?" demanded one court in a case where a murdered body was left on the train tracks and negligently run over. "The man was dead when he was put there; he has suffered no pain, no mental anxiety, no doctor's bill, no loss of time; there is nothing on which to assess damages." Nor could the administrator of his estate claim anything. "What can he do with a dead, buried, and decomposing body? Literally nothing, the worms are rioting in the corpse before the administrator has the right to possess the estate."[101] The skeptic might grin triumphantly: and I concede that in this way my account is revisionist as against the law. But I do think it's hard to unpack the injury to the survivors

---

100. Jacque v. Steenberg Homes, 209 Wis. 2d 605 (1997); BMW of N. Am. v. Gore, 517 U.S. 559 (1996).

101. Griffith v. Charlotte, C. & A. R.R. Co., 23 S.C. 25 (1885).

without invoking the claim that corpse desecration is an injury to their dead loved one.

In that way, corpse desecration and defamation are very close. Here's a conjecture: both at bottom are dignitary claims. No wonder some critics likened speaking ill of the dead to cannibalism. The law smiles on lawsuits brought to protest corpse desecration. It frowns on lawsuits brought to protest defaming the dead. Here as always, you can find some way to distinguish the two issues. (All lawyers have to be expert at two maneuvers: these two things look different, but they're really the same; these two things look the same, but they're really different.) But how compelling would that distinction be?

I presume our skeptic will want to resolve the apparent inconsistency not by extending tort liability for defaming the dead but by eliminating it for corpse desecration. What reason do we have to take the opposite approach and make it tortious to defame the dead?

VI

"This Will Always Be There"

W e don't believe that the dead have no interests, no claims on us, no standing. (These are not three ways of saying the same thing, but we needn't pause over the distinctions.) We pay more than lip service to the thought that we should speak no ill of them. We respect their wishes about how to handle their corpses. I could add that we respect their wishes for how to be posed at their funerals: on a motorcycle, in a boxing ring, relaxing with a beer and a cigarette.[1] Even when advised they're under no legal obligation, surviving family members sometimes pay the debts of their loved ones.[2]

Nor does the law does believe the dead have no interests, no claims, no standing. It is routine for estates—the collection of legal interests and obligations, centered on property, broadly understood—to show up in litigation. The law takes the fidu-

---

1. Campbell Robertson and Frances Robles, "Rite of the Sitting Dead: Funeral Poses Mimic Life," *New York Times* (21 June 2013).

2. David Streitfeld, "You're Dead? That Won't Stop the Debt Collector," *New York Times* (3 March 2009).

ciary obligation of the executor—the obligation to represent the interests of the estate—very seriously. In 2014 an Iowa court decided it was an abuse of discretion (a hard standard to meet) for a trial court *not* to remove an executrix on a record showing self-dealing in arranging the sale of the estate's farm.[3] That fiduciary obligation runs not only to the living beneficiaries of the estate, but also to respecting the wishes of the dead.[4] And when there's a will, so the law doesn't turn to the default rules for intestates, the beneficiaries are the beneficiaries precisely because the dead so designated them. "Despicable," sniffed one court at the self-dealing of one executor;[5] "contemptible," sniffed another;[6] "outrageous," sniffed a third, upholding a \$1.5m judgment.[7] After you die, the law will respect not just the terms of your will, but also in some settings your privacy, and more. The criminal law will take an interest in anyone desecrating your corpse, and your close survivors will win a tort action against any such miscreant.

So we don't accept the oblivion thesis and neither does the law. Does our skeptic insist that we and the law are horribly confused? Let's distinguish soft and hard versions of skepticism. On both versions, the skeptic will hold that what we and the law think and say is in fact confused. But the soft version defangs the apparent force of that skepticism: here the skeptic will assure us that our practices can be reframed to avoid the allegedly indefensible belief that the dead have inter-

3. Poll v. Kemp (In re Estate of Kemp), 2014 Iowa App. LEXIS 482 (2014).

4. See for instance *Will v. Northwestern Univ.,* 378 Ill. App. 3d 280, 292 (2007).

5. Robertson v. Robertson, 2014 Cal. App. Unpub. LEXIS 5007 (Jul. 17, 2014).

6. Carrellas v. Carrellas, 2001 R.I. Super. LEXIS 153 (2001).

7. Estate of Anderson, 149 Cal. App. 3d 336 (1983).

ests and rightful claims on us. On the hard version, more charming in its bellicose way, our practices are indefensible and need to be scrapped. We've encountered both kinds of skepticism along the way, but let me draw out the contrast.

The soft skeptic's target isn't anything we actually do or any particular legal doctrine. Fine by him, he cheerfully concedes, if we painstakingly enforce the terms of wills, shrink from invading the privacy of the dead, and so on. These first-order practices don't concern him. His target instead is the thesis that we can justify such practices by appealing to the interests of the dead. *That,* he insists, makes no sense. But he thinks we can replace that thesis with ones he has no objection to, and that the replacements will leave our practices standing more or less as they were. So for instance: "The real reason to be so assiduous about respecting the terms of wills is to encourage the living to provide for those who will outlive them[8] or to assure the living that their own wishes will be respected. For all I know or care, the living are irrational in turn for worrying about that: I needn't adopt any view about that. It's enough that they do worry and they do want to be able to bequeath their property after they die. We console *them* when we respect the terms laid down in wills."

This isn't what we think we're doing. "But so what?" demands the skeptic. "I can give you a suitably hardheaded reason

---

8. Again, see Ernest Partridge, "Posthumous Interests and Posthumous Respect," *Ethics* (January 1981): 260–61. More generally, consider the thesis that utilitarians and their opponents have no first-order moral disagreements: Derek Parfit, *On What Matters,* ed. Samuel Scheffler, 2 vols. (Oxford: Oxford University Press, 2011), chaps. 17, 23. And notice the cursory treatment of first-order moral issues in Stephen Darwall, Allan Gibbard, and Peter Railton, "Toward *Fin de siècle* Ethics: Some Trends," *Philosophical Review* (January 1992).

for continuing to do just as you do. All my disagreements here
are what we might call second-order: how best to make sense
of what we do." We might counter that one thing we do is talk
about why we're doing what we're doing. But the skeptic needn't
be fazed. He can argue that our insisting that we care for the
dead is the best kind of assurance we can offer those anxious
living property holders. "After all," he can add mischievously,
"if we said we were doing it for the living, that would redouble
their anxiety, at least if they were alert: each one would fret,
'but when it comes time to enforce *my* will, I'll be dead, and
my interests won't count at all. My security would be thinking
that respecting my will still will be required to reassure the
living. But maybe people will figure out a clever way of distinguishing my will from the kind others write, or for that matter
distinguishing me from people alive, or just a credible way of
distinguishing the world up to the moment I died from the
world after that.' So it's best, all things considered, for us to
think and say things that really are nonsensical. All I insist on
is that when we retreat from everyday life to do theory, we talk
straight. I do suppose that we can wall off that discussion from
what we say and do once we return to the world."[9] Or perhaps
instead of conjuring up a separation in social space, where we
permit ourselves deep insight in one setting but blithely ignore
or forget it elsewhere, he will invoke a separation among the
population. Sophisticated theorists will understand the full
story about the putative interests of the dead, so they'll condescendingly see through the nonsense spouted by the hoi
polloi. (Yes, my language betrays irritation with the venerable

---

9. On that last, compare, canonically, David Hume, *A Treatise of Human
Nature*, bk. 1, pt. 4, sec. 7.

conservative lineage of such views.)[10] Either way, philosophy "leaves everything as it is," he might conclude.[11] Well, not quite everything—not the status of what we'd imagined the real justifications were—but pretty close.

Whatever you make of soft skepticism, notice that it undercuts any ground the skeptic has to oppose making it tortious to defame the dead. All he could say was that in the hidden preserves of theory, we couldn't justify such a cause of action by saying the dead have reputational interests. But provided that we came up with some other justification—an obvious one would be protecting survivors from poignant emotional distress—he'd have no objection. Indeed he wouldn't object to people and lawyers in everyday life talking about the reputational interests of the dead.

The hard skeptic's target is our actual social practices, in and out of law. He might think it lily-livered of the soft skeptic to be so intent on framing replacement justifications, to want to leave those practices standing. Regardless, he will say that he is happy to take us at our word: we do these things for the dead. And *that,* he insists, makes no sense. So we have to stop. However he thinks about the reliance interests people—the living? the dead?—have in current legal arrangements and about the best transition rule for a saner legal regime, he will be adamant that the last thing we should do is *extend* the law's irrational reverence for the dead.

10. For more, see my *Poisoning the Minds of the Lower Orders* (Princeton, NJ: Princeton University Press, 1998). In contemporary legal scholarship, compare Meir Dan-Cohen, "Decision Rules and Conduct Rules: Acoustic Separation in Criminal Law," *Harvard Law Review* (January 1984).

11. Ludwig Wittgenstein, *Philosophical Investigations,* trans. G. E. M. Anscombe, 3rd ed. (Malden, MA: Blackwell Publishing, 2001), § 124, p. 42^e.

A skeptic needn't be hard or soft across the board. A skeptic might think for instance that we should go on enforcing wills, even if what we say we're doing is indefensible, but that we should stop worrying about corpse desecration and doing the other nutty things we do on behalf of dead persons. So too both soft and hard skepticism can be elaborated or refined in various ways. But the bald or stylized distinction I've offered will suffice.

So far as my purpose is to propose tort reform, then, I've nothing to fear from soft skepticism. But the hard skeptic offers what he takes to be a fatal objection: he too sees no way to make sense of the claim that a dead person still has interests, but he's not willing to entertain the thought that somehow the real parties in interest would be the living. The skeptic thinks Epicurus had it right: when we are, death is not; when death is, we are not.[12] There are more or less fancy ways of buttressing this objection.[13] The view is often styled a metaphysical one, but I have to confess I don't grasp what that means.[14] (That's not an arch way of objecting to it.) What should we make of it?

12. Epicurus to Menoeceus, in Diogenes Laertius, *Lives of Eminent Philosophers,* bk. 10.

13. For a helpful exploration, see Stephen E. Rosenbaum, "How to Be Dead and Not Care: A Defense of Epicurus," *American Philosophical Quarterly* (April 1986).

14. "It is not easy to say what metaphysics is," begins the *Stanford Encyclopedia of Philosophy* entry. None of the topics canvassed there under the rubric "modern metaphysics" comes close to the oblivion thesis. See http:// plato.stanford.edu/entries/metaphysics/ (last visited 17 November 2014). Put differently, it is an unfathomably long way from the likes of Saul A. Kripke, *Naming and Necessity* (Cambridge, MA: Harvard University Press, 1980), to questions about whether we can make sense of posthumous interests and whether or in what respects the law ought to safeguard them.

In my more-philistine-than-thou pragmatist mood, which I lapse into more than occasionally, I'm inclined to shrug it off. On one side, we have ongoing social practices, centuries of legal doctrine, and endless writing by countless thoughtful figures approving of at least some claims of the dead. On the other, we have a metaphysical objection. Why believe that the latter is enough to make us renounce the former? What sort of leverage is this sort of philosophical argument supposed to have? Why not be nonchalant and dismissive?

Or one might turn the tables instead of shrugging. If there's a mismatch between a theory about death and our social practices, you might think the sensible inference is that there's likely something wrong with the theory. Okay, but then it would be nice to explain just what is wrong with it. Instead of thinking the skeptic has a fatal objection, think of him as stating a puzzle: how could it be that dead people have interests or claims? Having interests, he can plausibly think, depends on your life still being under way. And he can think that without thinking that all that matters is desirable consciousness. So why *doesn't* death commit us to the oblivion thesis?

Let's start here. What is a person? And what is personal identity, anyway? I don't propose to turn now and suggest we are incorporeal souls somehow communing with our bodies, maybe via the pineal gland, and that those souls outlast the bodies. I'll take any such dualism, even if put in secular terms, to be the sort of view I disavowed when I promised not to depend on any religious belief.

It might help to recur to John Locke. The view he outlines in the *Essay Concerning Human Understanding* has remained powerfully influential, whatever its difficulties; and it is more promising as a launching pad for thinking about post-

humous wrongs than you might imagine.[15] I want my account
of posthumous harm not to hang on any contentious account
of the self. "Well, they're *all* contentious." In a way, sure. But
then it's a good idea to choose a widely adopted account often
thought most at home with the sort of consequentialist views
I oppose. Kant explicitly affirms that it is wrong to defame the
dead (and explicitly denies that this claim has anything to do
with souls or the afterlife).[16] But I'd hate you to think that my
view rests on any commitment to transcendental metaphysics,
not only but not least because I'd hate you to believe that our
moral, political, and legal views need to be secured by any
philosophical foundations at all.

Locke begins by distinguishing *man, soul,* and *person.*[17]
Let's ignore *soul.* "I know," Locke offers, "that in the ordinary
way of speaking, the same Person, and the same Man, stand
for one and the same thing." Well, not always. The referent of
first-person talk—what you refer to when you say "I" or "me"
or "my" or "mine"—varies in interesting ways. It's idiomatic to

15. See Locke's *Essay,* bk. 2, chap. 27; for typography I've followed John
Locke, *An Essay Concerning Human Understanding,* ed. Peter H. Nidditch
(Oxford: Clarendon Press, 1979). See too the characteristically illuminating
treatment in J. L. Mackie, *Problems from Locke* (Oxford: Clarendon Press,
1976), chap. 6.

16. Immanuel Kant, *The Metaphysics of Morals,* trans. Mary Gregor
(Cambridge: Cambridge University Press, 1991), 110–11. Thanks to Arthur
Ripstein for reminding me of this.

17. Commentators have been puzzled by Locke's claims about self-
ownership in the *Second Treatise,* where he seems to vacillate between saying that God owns us and that we own ourselves. But he's fully consistent. He
claims God owns us as men. So, however eccentrically, that's why suicide is
wrong: it would violate God's property right in our bodies. We have property
in our own persons: we are responsible for our actions. See my *Without
Foundations: Justification in Political Theory* (Ithaca, NY: Cornell University
Press, 1985), 70–72.

say, "I am six feet tall," where *I* is what we can also call *my body*, though it would take an odd context to make "My body is six feet tall" a sensible thing to say. It's also idiomatic to say, "I hate opera," but it would be hard to construe that as a claim about your body.[18] Still, the distinction between *man* and *person* is helpful. "For I presume 'tis not the *Idea* of a thinking or rational Being alone, that makes the *Idea* of a *Man* in most Peoples Sense: but of a Body so and so shaped joined to it; and if that be the *Idea* of a *Man*, the same successive Body not shifted all at once, must as well as the same immaterial Spirit go to the making of the same *Man*." (This will entail that someone in a state of persistent vegetative unconsciousness is only a body, not a man or human being at all. That might be a reformist proposal, not an account of ordinary meaning, for both today's English and that of the seventeenth century. But it's not wacky.)

Locke's gloss on *person* is closer to Kant than some fables about the empiricist tradition would suggest: "a thinking intelligent Being, that has reason and reflection, and can consider it self as it self, the same thinking thing, in different times and places; which it does only by that consciousness, which is inseparable from thinking, and as it seems to me essential to it . . . " (This gives you not only something like deliberative capacity and responsiveness to reasons, but also something vaguely gesturing toward the unity of apperception, even if Locke's presentation of both is utterly skeletal.) *Personal identity*, though, is just the same consciousness, with a more or less

18. On this sort of thing, see Eric T. Olson, "The Person and the Corpse," in *The Oxford Handbook of the Philosophy of Death*, ed. Ben Bradley, Fred Feldman, and Jens Johannson (Oxford: Oxford University Press, 2013), 84–85. Olson adds that he doubts such linguistic points "offer any metaphysical insight": again, count me as completely unsure what that might mean.

continuous chain of memories over time. Locke notices that forgetfulness is a problem for his view, though he probably underplays how severe a problem it is.

Regardless, the distinction between *man* and *person* is immediately helpful in focusing one issue at stake in making sense of defaming the dead. If I break your arm, I have committed the tort of battery against you. But defamation is a harm to your reputation, which is not part of your body. So we needn't try to figure out if your corpse is you,[19] or the closest continuer of you,[20] or what if anything would count as an injury to a corpse, or anything like that. Those problems might arise in making sense of corpse desecration as an injury to the dead person. (Remember, here the law adopts the *Gugliuzza* solution and counts it an injury to close survivors.) But even if I'm right in conjecturing that defaming the dead and desecrating their corpses are both dignitary harms, they are importantly different in this way.

Nor is your reputation part of your mind or person. Again, it is public, objective, sociological; it's what the community thinks of you, or, to recur to the doctrinal structure of the tort, what at least some respectable segment of the community thinks of you. So whether we are thinking of *man* or *person,* in even roughly Lockean ways, there is no reason to think that making it tortious to defame the dead would founder on some inability of the dead to make out some constitutive element of

19. Fred Feldman, *Confrontations with the Reaper: A Philosophical Study of the Nature and Value of Death* (New York: Oxford University Press, 1992), chap. 6.

20. For the argument that identity is being the closest continuer—and close enough—see Robert Nozick, *Philosophical Explanations* (Cambridge, MA: Belknap Press at Harvard University Press, 1981), 29–37.

the tort. Remember that living plaintiffs can collect damages for emotional harm or pain and suffering. Those, obviously, would be unavailable to the dead, because they have no mental states at all. But remember too that emotional harm is no element of the tort, even if learned authorities sometimes miss the point: in 2011, Scottish authorities balked at making defaming the dead tortious because they couldn't reconcile "the traditional notion of the hurt feelings of the defamed person being at the heart of a defamation action with the idea of creating a cause of action for a person who is no longer alive."[21] I want to be blunt: there is no such tradition.

Whatever startling puzzle cases we can construct (and Locke is already constructing them, wondering for instance what we'd make of putting the soul and consciousness of a prince into a cobbler's body, or again presenting a case in which your body is occupied by one continuous consciousness every day and another every night), as a matter of contingent fact it looks like personal identity depends on having the same central nervous system. Brain death doesn't look anything like what we mean by death of a person—we can imagine you magically taking up residence in someone else's brain and body, or, if you're as optimistic or credulous about the future of comput-

21. *Death of a Good Name: Defamation and the Deceased; A Consultation Paper* (Edinburgh: Scottish Government, 2011), 15, available at www.gov .scot/Resource/Doc/337251/0110660.pdf (last visited 1 May 2015). The Law Reform Commission of Western Australia endorsed a cause of action in 1979: see www.lrc.justice.wa.gov.au/_files/P08-II-R.pdf, chap. 9 (last visited 23 November 2014). For a survey of various legal regimes stretching back to ancient Rome, but mostly common law and American sources, see "Libel— Defamation of Dead Person—Injury to Reputations of Surviving Relatives," *Columbia Law Review* (November 1940).

ing as some, uploading your consciousness[22]—but it looks
contingently like the best bet for a criterion.

So let's take the skeptical objection this way. You're dead.
Your once spiky brain waves are now serenely, distressingly flat.
Your consciousness is snuffed out, never to return. How can
you be wronged? (I wonder how the skeptic wants to handle
the case in which you're permanently comatose, but your body
will survive for years. Can *that* entity be wronged? Should it be
allowed to file a tort claim if it's battered?)

Recall the garden-variety case of having a project thwarted,
an interest set back, while you're still alive. Long devoted to
bicycling, you decide to bike all the way across the country.
You adopt a prudent workout regimen and negotiate a seven-
week leave from your job and buy a sturdy bike and learn a ton
about bike maintenance and get a little hand-crank charger for
your iPhone and—and then a drunk driver runs you over and
shatters your left leg. You are harmed, wronged too, and your
damages could include what tort law calls loss of enjoyment:
you can no longer take the bike ride. You might wonder how a
jury could assign a dollar value to that, but plenty of damage
awards depend on an intuitive assessment of what the law calls
nonpecuniary damages.

Now some of your projects may be thwarted by your
death. You've decided to explore the Galápagos Islands. You've
purchased the plane tickets, bought a fancy new camera, and
made sure your camping gear is in great shape. But you have
a massive heart attack and die a week before you're supposed

22. Ray Kurzweil, *The Singularity Is Near: When Humans Transcend Biol-
ogy* (New York: Viking Press, 2005), 199–200. See too http://mindclones
.blogspot.com (last visited 20 February 2015); thanks to Jill Horwitz for the
reference.

to leave. Your survivors will shake their heads sadly and say, "Such a shame she didn't get to take that trip, she was so looking forward to it." On their view, anyway, your death sets back your interest: not just your general interest in living, but your specific interest in taking this trip. In that way it's no different from the shattered leg. This example qualifies as harm but not wrong, misfortune but not injury, barring some further story about the heart attack. But we could provide such a story: it was triggered by medical malpractice, say the overdose of an anesthetic during routine surgery.

Can your projects be thwarted *after* your death? Not, surely, any project that involves your still doing something, because you're no longer around to do it. But people adopt plenty of projects that don't involve such continuing action. You set up an organization to renew the city's sadly neglected public parks. You donate money and work hard at securing donations from others. Your plan is to set everything in motion and then stand back: you're no good at the physical work involved. You round up volunteers to rip out old play structures and install snazzy, safe new ones; to design and install new landscaping; and so on. The actual work has begun when you die, but then a court order freezes the work—with giant holes in the ground and some of the parks now closed. You invested endless hours, money too, and your project will not be realized. Your project was not to set up the organization. It was to renovate the park. Why not say that here too your interest has been set back, that you've been harmed?

"Well, because you don't exist." That can't be enough. You can be harmed by things that happen before you're born. Your mother drinks heavily and you're born with fetal alcohol syndrome. (If you think you exist once you're a zygote, suppose instead your mother takes drugs and suffers genetic damage, some of which you'll inherit, before you're conceived.) A nasty corporation fouls the water supply of the community you'll be born into or leaves toxic waste in the municipal dump. Diethylstilbestrol (DES), once prescribed to pregnant women, is alleged to injure not just their children but also their grandchildren. Tort law wrestled with whether the grandchildren should be able to prevail in claims against the drug manufacturers.[23] Regardless of the answer, if the allegation is true, surely the unborn grandchildren are harmed by their grandmother's taking the drug. "Well, you *will* exist. But I think the asymmetry about time makes all the difference. Once your life is over, everything is different. Before you're born, you can be harmed but you can't harm. After you're dead, maybe you can harm, but you can't be harmed."

Let me put more pressure on that gambit. Why think that you still have to exist to have your interests set back? "Because your interests go poof! when you do." All of them? Let's revisit a sentiment I voiced in the first chapter, about how you might now think about the well-being of your loved ones after you die: "*They'll* still have interests and I *now* care about whether they'll flourish or not, even though I won't be around to see it." Suppose you do what you can to help ensure that they will be well positioned to succeed, by their lights, after you die. You help pay for appropriate schooling; you bequeath them money; you encourage them to tackle some chronic health problems. And now suppose that after you die their lives go badly. No one will dispute that this is bad for them. No one will dispute that while alive you took an interest in its not happening: you made it a project of yours to help secure good lives for them.

---

23. See for instance *Grover v. Eli Lilly & Co.*, 63 Ohio St. 3d 756 (1992); *Reeves v. Eli Lilly & Co.*, 368 F. Supp. 2d 11 (D.D.C. 2005).

So again why not think that their failure is also bad for you?
"Well, I don't exist anymore."

I take it that this too is not in dispute: if you were alive to
see it, it would be bad for you. Not merely bad for them, though
of course it's that. And not merely distressing to you: that distress registers that something bad has happened, though not
necessarily to you; it isn't solely what that bad thing consists in.
But there is more here than their foundering plus your distress
at their foundering. There is the failure of your own (financial
and emotional) investments in their success. So why isn't it bad
for you even if it happens while you're dead? Is it that you don't
know about it? But again while you're alive all kinds of bad
things can happen to you that you don't know about: someone
steals your money, you get pancreatic cancer, you're raped while
you're unconscious, and so on. "But you *could* know about
those." But you could know that your loved ones' lives were
going badly: you would know, had you only lived longer. So
yes, there's a counterfactual that takes care of harms you don't
notice while you're still alive. But there's also a counterfactual
that takes care of harms occurring after you're dead. It's glib to
assert that the latter counterfactual is too far away from the
actual world. It might not be: it might be the merest happen-
stance that you died when you did. (If only they'd gotten you
to the hospital sixty seconds sooner, you'd have survived.) And
it could be that everything would have had to be very different
for you to discover the pancreatic cancer. (Without symptoms,
you'd never ask for the relevant tests and no doctor would run
them anyway.) Maybe there is some way to finesse the two
counterfactuals to redeem the intuition that death means that
you have no interests. But I doubt that the stubborn embrace
of the oblivion thesis depends on a finicky construction of the
difference between two counterfactuals.

Person, Locke also claims, is "a Forensick Term appropriating Actions and their Merit."[24] To be a person is to be an agent, responsible for some deeds, and so to be the proper object of praise and blame, reward and punishment. Locke doesn't offer this as an alternative account of *person:* he wants to defend the view that it makes sense to treat (the bearers of) unified chains of consciousness in this way. He offers a motivational principle: because you care about your future pleasure and pain, you can guide your conduct by thinking about the prospect of reward and punishment. That might sound consequentialist, but Locke also thinks it would be unfair to punish you for something that some other person did. He grants that we punish sober people for things they did while they're drunk, even when they can't remember, and likewise that we punish people for things they did while ostensibly sleepwalking. But he thinks this is epistemic: we doubt our ability to tell when such a story is a lie. God at judgment day, he suggests, will take a different view.

You might well not wish to subscribe to even the outlines of this account. You might for instance demur that we hold people responsible for their drunken deeds in part because while sober they choose to drink, and they know or should know what might follow. But let's pursue the intuition that to be a person is to be the proper object of praise and blame, reward and punishment; and let's again turn to the law for illumination. Consider the case of delayed murder. Hannah stabs Marguerite. Rushed to the hospital, Marguerite is in critical condition. Hannah's arrested; eventually the prosecutor charges

24. This strand of Locke's treatment is emphasized in [Edmund Law], *A Defence of Mr. Locke's Opinion Concerning Personal Identity* (Cambridge, 1769).

her with aggravated assault as Marguerite continues to languish in a hospital bed. If Marguerite dies as a result of the stab wound, weeks or months or years later,[25] the prosecutor will promptly upgrade the charge against Hannah to murder. (I leave aside whether it's some version of homicide or of manslaughter.) For that is what she now becomes guilty of. She wasn't yet guilty of murder when she stabbed Marguerite; after all, Marguerite could have gotten better.

But suppose Hannah happens to die before Marguerite. I want to say that Hannah is still guilty of murder and she still becomes guilty of murder when Marguerite dies. (I touched on this point earlier, with the example of poisoned Tylenol.) While alive, Hannah set in motion a causal ripple that led to Marguerite's death. Again, she wasn't guilty of murder when she stabbed Marguerite, because Marguerite was still alive. And it seems contrived, even absurd, to say that just because Hannah is dead, she can't be guilty of murder. Why ever not? If you're worried that mere contingency is determining the severity of Hannah's guilt, notice that that's just a standard problem of moral luck. Whether Hannah's alive or dead has nothing to do with it.[26]

It's a further question whether it would make sense to

25. For a stab wound that turned into murder some fifty-five years later, see J. David Goodman, "A Twist in the Murder of a 97-Year-Old Man: He Was Knifed 5 Decades Ago," *New York Times* (24 January 2015).

26. Compare *McKee v. State,* 200 Ga. 563, 565 (1946) ("ownership of property stolen may be properly laid in the owner as of the date of the offense, and notwithstanding the fact that the owner may have died after the theft and before the return of indictment"); *Lee v. State,* 270 Ga. 798, 802 (1999) (citing *McKee* to approve of trial court's rejecting criminal defendant's proposed instruction that "if Ms. Chancey was dead when her rings were removed, there was no taking from a person, and therefore no armed robbery").

prosecute Hannah. Criminal prosecution of the dead might seem perverse, but I think mostly for pragmatic reasons: we can't punish them. Civil law countries are happier with trials *in absentia* than are common law countries—for us they would raise constitutional difficulties about the right to confront one's accusers—but that can't be an absolute bar either. Anyway it's been done. Pope Formosus died in April 896. In January 897 Pope Stephen VII decided to try Formosus for various crimes. Formosus's body was exhumed, dressed in papal vestments, and propped up in court to, um, hear the charges. A deacon stood behind the body and responded. Formosus was found guilty. The fingers of his right hand that he once dispensed blessings with were chopped off, his body dumped into the Tiber River.[27] Now that's grotesque, risible too: but agreeing that Hannah becomes guilty of murder after her own death doesn't entail any commitment to dig up Hannah's body and put it on trial.

If I'm right, Hannah doesn't need to be alive to become a murderer. Locke's helpful thought, that *person* is a forensic term, seems right even when tweaked to cover the case when the person is no longer alive: that person can still properly be the object of praise and blame, reward and punishment. The deaths of Stalin, Mao, Pol Pot and their loathsome likes do not absolve them of responsibility for ongoing human suffering. That thought neatly parallels the law's use of the estate: the

27. Peter Heather, *The Restoration of Rome: Barbarian Popes and Imperial Pretenders* (London: Macmillan, 2013), 361–62. Recently, Russia prosecuted Sergei Magnitsky four years after he died. See David Herszenhorn, "Dead Lawyer, a Kremlin Critic, Is Found Guilty of Tax Evasion," *New York Times* (11 July 2013).

bundle of rights and obligations, centered on property, that will survive your death. That estate, remember, can sue and be sued. Those claims don't disappear when you do. Death is the end of conscious experience. But your life leaves causal ripples that survive you—and plenty of those causal ripples have normative implications, for better or worse. To emphasize the point: on your death bed, you ignite a well-hidden slow-burning fuse. Two days after you die, it sets off a bomb that destroys an apartment building and kills everyone in it. You're not responsible? Really?

Try this:[28] you spend twelve years on a scholarly book of great ambition. It will make a big splash, you confide in your closest friends. You finish the manuscript. The referees for the press love it. You eagerly await its appearance and reception. Now imagine four possible paths forward:

(1) It's instantly celebrated. "Better than I dared hope!" you tell people—and you mean it. It's promptly installed on reading lists all over the country. Published reviews in scholarly journals and popular media alike are highly congratulatory. And they're right: the book is a gem.

(2) It's a flop. Reviewers press devastating objections. You wonder how none of those commenting on the manuscript alerted you to these problems. But you don't imagine that it's their

---

28. George Pitcher, "The Misfortunes of the Dead," *American Philosophical Quarterly* (April 1984): 185; and Steven Luper, "Retroactive Harms and Wrongs," in *Oxford Handbook*, ed. Bradley, Feldman, and Johannson, 322, deploy similar examples.

fault. It's yours. Twelve years of your life, wasted. Worse than wasted: you've labored mightily so that you can be pelted with contempt.

(3) The book disappears on publication. Not literally, but no one seems to be reading it, no journal ever gets around to reviewing it. It slinks its forlorn way to the remainder tables in record time. You gave copies to friends and colleagues. They muttered the usual polite phrases, but they didn't glance at it.

(4) It's a flop—but that's wholly unfair, and you're not just being defensive when you think so. Though you can't prove it or find even a scrap of evidence, your paranoid suspicions are exactly right: your enemies are plotting against you. At the leading journals, the fix is in to ensure the first reviews are negative. And because they are, pointedly and nastily so, most people don't bother picking up the book to read and assess it for themselves. (The few who do quite like it, but they sheepishly submit to the consensus.) You could try glumly consoling yourself with the thought that posterity will rediscover your work, but you know better.

I assume it's uncontroversially true that (1) is good for you, (2) and (3) are bad for you, and (4) is not only bad for you but is also a wrong against you. And again, the goodness of (1) is not exhausted by your experiencing praise and beaming, or getting a prize, or anything like that. That sort of thing is triggered by confirmation, by reliable judges, that your work is good. The confirmation is itself a good thing. But that too doesn't exhaust matters. Everything finally hangs on the underlying fact that the work is awfully good. That's not the evaluatively neutral ground on which good things happen: it is itself of great value.

To relax the omniscience or certainty built into the way I framed these paths, suppose you believe the work is awfully good, and so do the reviewers and prize committees, but you're all wrong. I wouldn't say that *nothing* good happens to you when the work is well received. But I would insist that that's a much less valuable state of affairs than the one in which the reception is sound and the work is in fact good. Deserved success is better than undeserved success, even if you can't tell the difference. I suspect resistance to that thought hangs again on the claim that all the matters in life is subjective experience, or perhaps on the claim that judgments of quality are subjective folderol. I commented earlier on what's deficient in the first view and shan't dignify the second with a response.

Likewise, what's bad in (2) is not just the dismay you suffer on reading those reviews. And it's not just learning the fact that your alleged masterwork is junk, speeding its crestfallen way to the remainder tables. It's the fact itself and what it means: that you did indeed waste twelve years of your life. Not that *nothing* you did in those years was valuable. But those endless hours of work? They might have been engaging, which is worth something, but had you known then what you know now, you'd never have tackled the project. Sometimes we can tell a story about nobility in majestic failure, but not here.

The badness of (3) is different. You've suffered a misfortune. You properly want the book to have some uptake. You want it to find its way to the relevant readers and you want them to wrestle with it and embrace it, or at least to make reasonable efforts and judgments. (Imagine the perversity of writ-

ing a really good book and then burning it without showing it
to a soul.)

In (4), you're wronged. You've suffered an injury, not a
misfortune. Now the book is still awfully good, and I've said
that that, finally, is what you want. But once again the book has
no uptake. So your conspiratorial enemies have also injured
those readers. But it's also true that in injuring them, they have
injured you: they haven't given you what you deserve and they
have deprived your twelve years' work of its proper uptake.
And surely this chorus of negative reviews is going to shake
your confidence and cause you pain. You'll have to squirm in
the nauseating fear that your book stinks and you wasted years
of your life.

Now—you saw this coming, right?—suppose you die
while the book is in press. Let's rehearse the same four paths.
Now (1) no longer has the pleasure you experience at reading
the reviews and winning the prizes. Nor do you experience the
confirmation that you've written a good book. But you have.
We could get fussy over the senses in which the public confirmation is and isn't good for you. But in one way it seems to me
indisputably true that it's good for you: it's what makes readers
read your work. That's the uptake you rightly wanted. Then
(2) means you died in blissful ignorance. The best thing would
have been for that omniscient futurologist to persuade you
twelve years before not to get started, but once again he forgot
to show up. Would it be better for you to have learned the
truth before you died? Maybe. People might well say that at
least you died without having to confront the awful news. That
that dismay would indeed be bad, though, doesn't entail that
the underlying fact—the book's badness—is irrelevant if you
don't know about it. Regardless, I'm more confident that these
negative reviews don't wrong you. You got just what you de-

serve. It's still bad in (3) that the book has no uptake, but at least you don't have to squirm or writhe about it.

The chips are down for us in (4). You suffer no emotional turmoil, so that can't count as harming you. But the malicious conspiracy does prevent readers from grappling with your work. That, I suggest, is still bad for you. Not that you find it disappointing: you don't. Not that you would bask in fair reviews: you wouldn't. Instead, here's one way to think of why it matters: you should be known as the guy who wrote that great book that made such a dent in the field. Instead, if anyone bothers noticing, you'll be labeled as that clown who wasted all that time at the end of his career—and life. This way of putting the point leans hard on the concept of reputation, but we needn't think of that as the exclusive injury, either. Part of your interest in writing, again, is in finding readers. That interest is frustrated or set back by your enemies. Nothing about that depends on your knowing about it—or on your being alive to notice it.[29]

Driven by the putative weirdness of interests that survive one's death, some authors have suggested that we shift the temporal location of the harm. When is he harmed? Here's Joel Feinberg: "I think the best answer is: 'at the point, well before his death, when the person had invested so much in some postdated outcome that it became one of his interests.' From that point on (we now know) he was playing a losing game, betting a substantial component of his own good on a doomed

29. Here I have found useful J. David Velleman, "Well-Being and Time," *Pacific Philosophical Quarterly* (1991), reprinted in his *The Possibility of Practical Reason* (Oxford: Clarendon Press, 2000); free online at *Scholarly Monograph Series*, http://dx.doi.org/10.3998/spobooks.6782337.0001.001 (last visited 26 May 2016).

cause."[30] I think this answer is mistaken, even extravagant. *Doomed* suggests some fatal necessity, the inexorable grinding gears of causal determinism. But the bad outcome here is utterly contingent, just like Marguerite's death. Feinberg's suggestion seems to me far weirder than embracing the view that some of your interests linger on after your death. If and when they're set back, that is when you're harmed. So too on the question of prenatal injury: I'd say you're harmed when your future mother takes the drugs that damage her chromosomes— and later yours—or when the corporation fouls the water supply. It's tempting to think you're injured when you're conceived or born. But it matters whether we frame the injury as "your mother having you, given her chromosomal problems," or "your having chromosomal problems." Put differently, it matters whether your complaint is: "I should never have been brought into being, given my mother's chromosomes," or "I shouldn't have this chromosomal damage."

Back to Hannah and Marguerite. Suppose Hannah is wrongly accused of stabbing Marguerite. Another woman did the deed and rushed off. Eyewitnesses were confused; Hannah's fingerprints were on the weapon only because she scrambled over to help. Surely it would be gravely unjust to convict Hannah of murder were she still alive. Why would that change if she died before Marguerite? The claim that Hannah was a

---

30. Joel Feinberg, *Harm to Others* (New York: Oxford University Press, 1984), 92. See too Pitcher, "Misfortunes." I prefer the contours of Feinberg's earlier treatment of posthumous interests in his "Harm and Self-Interest," in *Law, Morality, and Society: Essays in Honour of H. L. A. Hart,* ed. P. M. S. Hacker and J. Raz (Oxford: Clarendon Press, 1977), 304–6. For more sustained pressure on the view of Feinberg quoted in my text, see Daniel Sperling, *Posthumous Interests: Legal and Ethical Perspectives* (Cambridge: Cambridge University Press, 2008), 21–25.

murderer would still be unjust. In fact, it would be a particular kind of injustice. It would be a false defamatory statement of fact: defamation *per se*, in fact, because murder is the quintessential serious crime. Doctrinally, we don't call false conviction defamation. But its structure is identical.

No wonder some are offended by the Mormon practice of proxy baptism, used to convert the dead. Official church policy is that one may convert only one's own relatives, and that their souls are free to decline the conversion. But zealous church members have converted the likes of Anne Frank and Daniel Pearl.[31] No wonder descendants of the unjustly convicted sometimes struggle to have those convictions overturned. So President Clinton pardoned the first black graduate of West Point:

> "I welcome you all to an event that is 117 years overdue," Mr. Clinton said today at a White House ceremony attended by several dozen people, including military officers and Lieutenant Flipper's descendants. . . . "This good man now has completely recovered his good name."
>
> A number of Lieutenant Flipper's descendants applauded. "Like the rest of the family, I'm relieved that this has come full circle," said Dr. William King, a great-nephew of Lieutenant Flipper. Dr. King's mother, Irsle Flipper King, had been pushing for a pardon for some 40 years.[32]

---

31. Mark Oppenheimer, "A Twist on Posthumous Baptisms Leaves Jews Miffed at Mormon Rite," *New York Times* (2 March 2012).

32. David Stout, "First Black from West Point Gains Pardon," *New York Times* (20 February 1999).

You needn't be a religious believer to object to Anne Frank's conversion. You needn't be crassly self-interested and think that your dead great-uncle's conviction is somehow bad for you to want to clear his name. It's enough to think that these dead individuals have been insulted. Here again the link between defamation and dignitary harm is very tight.

Let's step back. The skeptic wielded the oblivion thesis—the thought that once you're dead, you have no interests—to urge that it's nonsensical to think that defaming the dead injures them. (Even a soft skeptic will assent to that formulation.) I've treated that as a legitimate explanatory query and tried to respond. Now the skeptic also appealed to the hangover thesis, the claim that our lingering regard for the dead is best regarded as a remnant of religious beliefs about the afterlife, on which the dead are aware of what we're up to, possibly vengeful about it. We could take that as a paratheory, an explanation of why we're so misguided that would kick in only after the oblivion thesis did its destructive work. But we could also take it as itself an effort to undercut or corrode our commitments to respecting the dead. Here I want to turn the tables on the skeptic. My diagnosis is that the hangover thesis depends on the view that all that matters is conscious experience, or all that's valuable is Sidgwick's desirable consciousness: only if your soul notices what's going on, the thought is, could it qualify as an injury. That allegedly commonsense view is deeply defective. It often stands behind the hangover thesis and the oblivion thesis alike. If there is to be talk of the furtive appeal of illicit views, then, I propose that we stop worrying about religious hangovers and start worrying about the seductive fantasy that only experience matters. So I'll reverse the skeptic's challenge. Cast that seductive fantasy aside: what else might properly motivate the skeptical view? Why *not* embrace the view that the dead have interests that we need to consider?[33]

Reputation of the Dead

To say the dead have interests is not to say that they have reputational interests coextensive with those of the living, or even any reputational interests at all. If we set aside the wholesale objection that there are no posthumous interests, we still have to deal with the retail worry that it wouldn't make any sense to recognize a cause of action in tort for defaming the dead, because whatever wrongs we might do the dead, invading their reputational interests isn't among them.

Let's start by considering what interests the living have in their reputation. And let's stick to the contours of the tort of defamation. What injury do you suffer if someone publishes a false, defamatory factual claim about you? Say he claims you've embezzled, diddled, and popped. Let's distinguish three kinds of injury at stake in defamation:

(1) Defamation is upsetting. It's awful knowing that this charge is spreading. Remember that plaintiffs in defamation actions can recover for pain and suffering. But remember too that emotional harm is no constitutive element of the tort, so

---

33. Sperling, *Posthumous Interests,* chap. 1 (esp. 40) suggests that we distinguish a person, who "has" interests, from a Human Subject, which (who?) "holds" them; and that we ascribe symbolic existence to the latter. This seems to me fussier than we need to make sense of posthumous interests, less apt too.

they need not allege such injury to prevail in a lawsuit.

(2) If you're defamed, others are far less likely to cooperate with you, in the relevant community or a respectable part of it. They might think you unreliable. Or they might think you something like ritually unclean and contagious: better to steer clear. Your reputation is then an instrumental good. I'm no Rawlsian, but if you unpack the social bases of self-respect, which is one of Rawls's primary goods, "things that every rational man is presumed to want," I think legal protection from defamation should be in the mix.[34]

(3) Defamation is intrinsically bad for you. This language might sound like a worrisome way of refusing to provide a reason. But the point is that the reason needn't take the form of instrumental rationality, on which the defamation is a means to a bad end, or causes some further outcome that is the real problem. You can reason-

---

34. John Rawls, *A Theory of Justice*, rev. ed. (Cambridge, MA: Belknap Press at Harvard University Press, 1999), 54. Rawls thinks of primary goods as all-purpose means, "things that men generally want in order to achieve their ends whatever they are," 288. But the language I quote in the text could also be glossed as making primary goods intrinsic, and the way would then be clear to defending the role especially of the social bases of self-respect as marking one's status as a dignified equal. In "The Basic Liberties and Their Priority," Rawls excepts defamation from a general commitment to free speech in part because it is "a private wrong," but he doesn't explore a potential link to the social bases of self-respect: John Rawls, *Political Liberalism* (New York: Columbia University Press, 1993), 336. For connected themes about dignity, see Jeremy Waldron, *The Harm in Hate Speech* (Cambridge, MA: Harvard University Press, 2012).

ably care that others not traffic in such nasty charges about you. At stake is something like dignified personhood, understood not as something you just plain have no matter what, but as having face, or the kind of self-presentation you can credibly offer—and yourself believe in—in public.[35] It's not (only) that defamation causally undercuts that stance, so that an explanation of why you no longer enjoy it as securely will recur to the independent fact of a prior defamation. It's (also) that defamation already constitutes a depredation of it. It's pernicious to imagine that all that matters is how you carry yourself or what you believe. A clown pretending to be a noble lord doesn't redeem his status. He redoubles the contempt he's held in.

All three surface routinely in defamation actions. Consider a grotesque case. Over a century ago, Augustus M. Flood of Charleston, South Carolina, sued the *News and Courier* for libel.[36] The newspaper had published a story about "Augustus M. Flood, colored," suing after a street car hit him. Flood complained that he was "a white man of pure Caucasian blood," and he had "always enjoyed the respect and confidence of his white fellow-citizens, the same having been of value to plaintiff in his business, and a source of pride and pleasure to

35. Compare Stephen L. Darwall, "Two Kinds of Respect," *Ethics* (October 1977).

36. Flood v. News & Courier Co., 71 S.C. 112 (1905). For contemporary comment and survey of caselaw on point, see *The American and English Annotated Cases*, ed. William M. McKinley et al., 53 vols. (Northport, NY: Edward Thompson, 1906–18), 4:689.

him in his social life." He urged that it was libel *per se* for the newspaper to publish the claim that he was colored: that is, without any evidence of special damages he'd suffered, he was entitled to legal relief. If you're imagining that no one could mistake a white man for a colored man, dwell for a second on the racist one-drop rule and its attendant anxieties.

The trial court had granted the newspaper a demurrer, approving their argument that the Reconstruction amendments barred a court from taking any such claim as defamatory. The appeals court made short work of overturning the trial court's verdict. "To call a white man a negro, affects the social status of the white man so referred to." Or again, "When we think of the radical distinction subsisting between the white man and the black man, it must be apparent that to impute the condition of the negro to a white man would affect his, the white man's, social status, and in case any one publish a white man to be a negro, it would not only be galling to his pride, but would tend to interfere seriously with the social relation of the white man with his fellow white men." They also brushed aside the constitutional objections, the merits of which needn't concern us here.[37] Like it or not, as a matter of social fact the newspaper's claim threatened Flood's livelihood and social life. No wonder he sued.

Flood complains that the newspaper story has lowered his social status. It has robbed him of the pleasure he took in being a first-rate member of the community: so he wants emotional damages. His reputation, he adds, had been of value to

---

37. For a more general analysis of how the law deals with illicit third-party preferences, see my "The *Kerr* Principle, State Action, and Legal Rights," *Michigan Law Review* (October 2006).

him in his business: there's an instrumental interest. Finally, he claims he had enjoyed the confidence and respect of his fellow citizens, and that's been shredded. His added reference to pride might be another kind of emotional injury or it might underline his eroded social status: either way the language of confidence and respect points to the intrinsic injury he alleges. The court endorses all three.

On (2), what sort of instrumental concerns matter? Coke didn't only prosecute the hapless likes of Lewis Pickering, that Puritan student hauled before Star Chamber for his poetaster's defamation of Archbishop Whitgift. Coke himself sued one Thomas Baxter for defamation. Baxter, he complained, had said, "Master Coke, at the last assizes in Norfolk, was of counsel with both the plaintiff and defendant, and took fees and was retained by them both." The allegation that he had so grossly travestied legal ethics, Coke went on, had led prospective clients not to hire him, so he had "lost many gains, profits and fees."[38] Loss of employment or work opportunities is just one instrumental interest, though it surfaces frequently in defamation actions. But one could also allege other instrumental harms. Consider a much-quoted gloss from a 1933 New York opinion: "Reputation is said in a general way to be injured by words which tend to expose one to public hatred, shame, obloquy, contumely, odium, contempt, ridicule, aversion, ostracism, degradation or disgrace, or to induce an evil opinion of one in the minds of right-thinking persons, and to deprive one of their confidence and friendly intercourse in society."[39] Suppose

38. Coke v. Baxter (KB 1585), in *Select Cases on Defamation to 1600*, ed. R. H. Helmholz (London: Selden Society, 1985), 67.
39. Kimmerle v. New York Evening Journal, Inc., 262 N.Y. 99, 102 (1933).

Flood has been courting a young white woman. Imagine what she does—and what her parents do—the next time he knocks on the door.

Which community matters? On (2), consider a whimsical case. In a small village in Bhutan, people despise you. They believe you've embezzled, diddled, and popped. They vociferously abuse life-size posters of you and they teach their children to regard you as a bogeyman. You don't know anything about this. Neither does anyone you know and deal with, nor anyone you will ever know and deal with. Suppose no wandering traveler or the internet will bring the story home, as it were, to people and places on your mattering map. Then I think the mere fact that these Bhutanese believe these defamatory things about you is irrelevant—as far as (2) goes. They might as well be on another planet. It's too narrow to say the relevant community is the one you actually deal with. But it can't be anyone, anywhere, anytime either.

So these are the sorts of injuries a living person can suffer when defamed. What about a dead person? Once again, I've no interest in making out a case for emotional injury: the dead have no emotions. Any instrumental injuries? Once dead, you're in no position to adopt new projects. But some of your old projects might well outlive you; this is of course contingent on what particular projects you've adopted and where they stand at your death. Return to the case where you're spearheading a drive to renovate the city parks. You die when work is just getting underway—and someone at your funeral whispers that you've embezzled, diddled, and popped. The story gets around. Who wants to keep working on what's mordantly dubbed the Child Molester Park Project? Your one-time associates withdraw. Just as if you were still alive, the defamation corrodes your reputation and makes others unwilling to cooperate with you. Even though dead, you have the same instrumental interest you'd have if you were still alive.

It seems contrived to insist that your real interest is in their working on it only as long as you're around to see it. Dismiss the zany image of your corpse suddenly speaking out and think instead about what you would say while still alive about work on the park being disrupted by your death. Imagine happily conceding, "Oh, I don't care if the thing actually gets done. I just want to know that it's in progress up until my death. After that do as you will." Those pitching in would find that baffling, not shrewd or tough-minded. Defamation aside, they will feel like they're letting *you* down if they fail to see the project through after you die, or at least if they fail to take reasonable steps to do so; just as they will happily name the park for you if they complete the work and they will not fantasize that they do so to incentivize sick or elderly others to take on such projects.

So too, I suggest, for the intrinsic interest. Suppose that within days of your funeral no one remembers you. Not literally, as if they all contracted a curiously selective case of amnesia. Rather they never think about you, fondly or otherwise. That's sad, arguably bad for you too—was your life that weightless?—but it isn't a wrong. It's not as though you're entitled to have people remember you. But suppose again that the story spreads that you've embezzled, diddled, and popped. Absent any further instrumental interest, this is bad for you. You may not be entitled to have anyone keep score, but if people are thinking about your life, they wrong you if they attribute to you crimes or other wrongs you haven't committed: if they offer a false, defamatory statement of fact about you. Again, we are vanishingly close to the case where we wrongly blame dead Hannah for Marguerite's murder.

As far as you're concerned, people in the more distant future might as well be people in Bhutan. You might properly feel differently about your own descendants, but even then, I suppose, not infinitely, not even indefinitely. I doubt we take any interest in what our great-great- . . . -great-grandchildren think of us; if we do happen to take such an interest, I doubt it's one that we or the law will think worth protecting. (Solon tells Croesus that Tellus the Athenian was the most fortunate of men, in part because his children were noble and all his grandchildren survived.[40] The sentiment is already pressing on transforming the traditional "call no man happy till he is dead" into something like "call no man happy till some time after he is dead and we can see how things turned out,"[41] but also suggesting a limit to the time horizon which can still affect his well-being, even when his descendants are involved.) But your actual community, and those reasonably nearby in (social) space and time: you can properly care whether someone publishes to them the claim that you've embezzled, diddled, and popped. It would not be irrational to swap tasty French fries for mediocre ones to make sure that that not happen. It would not be irrational to surrender a good deal more. Not only for the benefit of your surviving loved ones, but also for your own benefit. But you shouldn't have to surrender anything.

So posthumous harm is possible, even straightforward. The dead can claim some of the same interests as the living in their reputations. Whatever metaphysical queasiness you might suffer, the law is already heavily invested in respecting the in-

40. Herotodus, *Histories* 1:30.
41. Here's where I've hidden the inevitable citation: Aristotle, *Nicomachean Ethics* 1:10.

terests of the dead and claims on their behalf. Why treat reputation differently?

New York, Rhode Island, and the Case for Tort Reform

Marilyn Hioki's son, Kevin Aissa, was murdered in Queens, New York, in 1979. She was then confronted with a newspaper story claiming that Kevin was a member of Carmine Galante's Mafia crime family and had been murdered in an ongoing gang war.[42] This claim, insisted Hioki, was blatantly false. It meant that witnesses who feared the Mafia refused to help the police. "She and her family suffered the embarrassment of gawkers stopping to watch and photograph her house. . . . Her children were bothered at school."[43]

This sort of thing inspired Manny Gold of the state senate to introduce legislation providing a cause of action for defaming the dead. Indefatigable, Gold introduced versions of this measure session after session. In 1986, the senate unanimously passed the measure.[44] But apparently Governor Mario Cuomo was considering a veto and civil liberties groups were out in force against the bill.[45] Gold and the sponsor of the measure in

---

42. Sam Rosensohn, "2 Galante Men Beaten to Death," *New York Post* (27 July 1979).

43. Paul Grondahl, "Libel Bill Debated: Media Square off with Victims' Kin," *Times Union* (26 March 1987).

44. Jeffrey Schmalz, "Bill on Libeling of Dead People Makes Progress," *New York Times* (28 June 1986).

45. Jeffrey Schmalz, "Sponsor in Senate Withdraws a Bill on Libeling Dead," *New York Times* (1 July 1986).

the assembly, Alan Hevesi, withdrew it.[46] But Gold continued to introduce the measure session after session. "You have to tell people that they cannot spit on the graves of our children," pleaded another aggrieved survivor at a 1987 hearing. "You've got to give us this law. You've got to let us set the facts right."[47]

Later in 1987, fifteen-year-old Tawana Brawley was found beaten in Wappingers Falls, New York. Not just beaten, but in a plastic bag, with shit smeared over her body, "Nigger" and "KKK" scrawled on it for good measure. The story became even more explosive when Brawley alleged that she'd been kidnapped and raped by six white men, one with a police badge.[48] Al Sharpton, Louis Farrakhan, and others got involved. The authorities could find no evidence supporting Brawley's story; in October 1988, after considering the case for some seven months, a special grand jury rejected it wholesale. None of the evidence, they decided, was inconsistent with Brawley smearing and marking herself and crawling into the bag. All the preparatory materials were in a nearby apartment she had access to.[49] That grand jury had only two black members and

46. Bennett Roth, "Intense Media Lobby Kills 'Libel from Grave,'" *Times Union* (1 July 1986).

47. Mark A. Uhlig, "Debate Resumes on Libel Protection for Dead," *New York Times* (29 March 1987).

48. Esther Iverem, "Bias Cases Fuel Anger of Blacks," *New York Times* (14 December 1987).

49. "'We, the Grand Jury': Text of Its Conclusions in the Tawana Brawley Case," *New York Times* (7 October 1988), is a summary of the grand jury's 170-page report. For the full text, see *Report of the Grand Jury and Related Documents Concerning the Tawana Brawley Investigation* ([New York]: State of New York, Department of Law, 1988). See too Robert D. McFadden, "Brawley Made up Story of Assault, Grand Jury Finds," *New York Times* (7 October 1988).

Brawley refused to appear before it.[50] No wonder controversy continued—and, at least in brackish recesses of the internet, continues—to simmer along.

In March 1988, though, Brawley's advisors fingered Dutchess County assistant prosecutor Steven Pagones as one of her attackers. That same day, Pagones announced he'd sue.[51] He sought $395m from Brawley, Sharpton, and two other advisers. Brawley never responded to the suit. In 1998—the mills of civil justice grind slowly—Pagones won a total of $530,000 from the four. (Johnnie Cochran, who later became famous defending O. J. Simpson, helped pay Sharpton's damages.)[52] Pagones was still collecting damages from Brawley's advisers in 2001.[53] In 2012, the *New York Post* found Brawley living under an assumed name in Virginia,[54] and a court ordered that her wages be garnished to pay Pagones. With interest, she now owes Pagones over $400,000. Pagones says that he'd forgive the debt were she to admit that she was lying. She's not budging:

50. E. R. Shipp, "The Case without Brawley: A Grand Jury's Rare Role," *New York Times* (16 March 1988).

51. Robert D. McFadden, "A Dutchess County Prosecutor Vows Brawley Case Slander Suit," *New York Times* (14 March 1988).

52. Laura Italiano, "Now Pay up, Tawana," *New York Post* (25 December 2012). In 2009, Sharpton said he still believed Brawley's story: www.youtube .com/watch?v=IJFAyt5MN4E (last visited 21 November 2014).

53. Alan Feuer, "Adviser in Tawana Brawley Case Pays off Defamation Award," *New York Times* (7 November 2001). Pagones won a summary judgment motion that one adviser's debt to him couldn't be discharged in bankruptcy: *Pagones v. Mason (In re Mason)*, 1999 Bankr. LEXIS 90 (Bankr. S.D.N.Y. Jan. 28, 1999).

54. Michael Gartland, "25 Years after Her Rape Claims Sparked a Firestorm, Tawana Brawley Avoids the Spotlight," *New York Post* (23 December 2012).

the checks have started rolling in.[55] In 2013 the *Post* covered a fundraiser for her: "Infamous rape hoaxster and court deadbeat Tawana Brawley got rock-star treatment in New Jersey yesterday, posing for photos with dozens of supporters honoring her as a courageous victim of injustice—as they stuffed envelopes full of cash for her."[56]

I wouldn't call Pagones lucky. Not by a long shot. But at least tort law afforded him a way to clear his name and be compensated for his injury. Less lucky yet was Harry Crist, Jr., a part-time policeman in the area. Crist committed suicide four days after Brawley was found in the plastic bag. Authorities took his suicide note and later explained that Crist "was despondent over failed efforts to become a state trooper and that the suicide had no connection to the Brawley case."[57] Brawley's advisers disagreed. They fingered Crist as another of her attackers and surmised that he'd been murdered in a coverup.[58] Indeed they went after Pagones only after Pagones offered an alibi for Crist.[59]

The grand jury specifically cleared both Pagones and Crist of any wrongdoing.[60] Crist's girlfriend, it turned out, had broken up with him just before he killed himself. A decade later his mother, "Cornelia Crist, sitting with her husband in the

55. Michael Gartland, "Pay-up Time for Brawley: '87 Rape-Hoaxer Finally Shells out for Slander," *New York Post* (4 August 2013).

56. Rebecca Rosenberg, "Hoaxer Tawana Brawley Celebrated in New Jersey Fund-Raiser," *New York Post* (13 May 2013).

57. Ralph Blumenthal, "Questions and Answers in the Brawley Inquiry," *New York Times* (24 February 1988).

58. Frank Bruni, "Mourning a Son Tied to the Brawley Case," *New York Times* (5 April 1988).

59. Italiano, "Now Pay up."

60. *Report of the Grand Jury,* 76–82.

living room of their home . . . recalled the prophecy of a lawyer they spoke to after the accusations against her son surfaced. 'He told us, for the next 100 years, Tawana's name will live on,' Mrs. Crist, 68, said, adding that the lawyer also said that her son's name would be linked to Ms. Brawley's. 'This will always be there. He told us that.'" The same grand jury recommended amending New York state law to give survivors in such situations standing to file slander suits.[61]

If Governor Cuomo had had reservations about that legal change before, he had none after the grand jury report. In his annual Message to the Legislature of 1989, Cuomo cautiously demurred, "We may never know the full story about Tawana Brawley." But he went on to declare forthrightly, "Current law does not permit the survivors of a deceased person to bring an action for civil damages against a person who defames the deceased. Such defamation can impose tremendous pain and suffering on survivors at any time, but especially if it occurs soon after death." He promised to introduce legislation offering "such a cause of action where the defamation is intentional, malicious and follows immediately upon the decease of its object."[62]

I don't know if Cuomo followed through. Manny Gold retired in 1998; others in the New York legislature have continued to sponsor and introduce such bills.[63] The current version gives the spouse, parent, or child of a dead person the right to bring an action if the defamation occurs within five years of death. The remedy on offer is a declaratory judgment—that is,

---

61. Bruni, "Mourning." Compare to Mrs. Crist's language Veritas to Mr. Urban, 6 June 1800, *Gentleman's Magazine* (June 1800).

62. *New York State Legislative Annual 1989*, 42–43.

63. Most recently, S01332 (12 January 2015), at https://legiscan.com/NY/bill/S01332/2015 (last visited 30 April 2015).

a ruling that indeed the person was defamed—but no monetary compensation. (Initially Gold had wanted to offer monetary compensation, too. When he withdrew the version that
received unanimous support in the senate, he shifted to declaratory judgment. But that didn't satisfy opponents in the news
media.)[64] Apparently the proposed measure has the form of
the *Gugliuzza* solution. The party suing would argue, "when
you defamed my dead loved one, you wronged me." But when
sixty-eight-year-old Cornelia Crist sadly contemplates her dead
son being linked to Tawana Brawley for a century, she's not
thinking of her own pain and suffering. She's thinking that this
is bad for her dead son.

The Rhode Island statute with which I began this book
with is different. It was adopted in 1974. Here's the text:[65]

§ 10-7.1-1. LIABILITY FOR DAMAGES FOR LIBEL OF
A DECEASED PERSON
      Whenever a deceased person shall have been
slandered or libelled in an obituary or similar account in any newspaper or on any radio or television station within three (3) months of his or her
date of death, and the account would, if death had
not ensued, have entitled the party injured to maintain an action and recover damages in respect to the
libel, the person who or corporation which would
have been liable if death had not ensued shall be
liable to an action for damages, notwithstanding
the death of the person.

64. Roth, "Intense Media Lobby."
65. R.I. Gen. Laws § 10–7.1.

§ 10-7.1–2. ACTION BY EXECUTOR OR ADMINIS-
TRATOR—PERSONS BENEFITED—LIMITATION OF
ACTION

Every action under this chapter shall be
brought by and in the name of the executor or administrator of the deceased person, whether ap-
pointed or qualified within or without the state,
and of the amount recovered in every action under
this chapter one-half (1/2) shall go to the husband
or widow, and one-half (1/2) shall go to the children of the deceased, and if there are no children
the whole shall go to the husband or widow, and,
if there is no husband or widow, to the next of kin,
in the proportion provided by law in relation to the
distribution of personal property left by persons
dying intestate. Provided, that every action under
this chapter shall be commenced within one year
after the death of the person.

It's a tight time window and only defamation in an obituary
counts, though it also makes it possible to win cash damages,
not simply a declaratory judgment. I don't know why Rhode
Island passed this law. Apparently there's no surviving press
coverage and the state librarian reports that the legislature then
kept no records of committee or floor debates.[66] Nor is the law

---

66. Email from Thomas Evans, 6 October 2014. Thanks to Ross Cheit for
conjecturing that the law was a response to *Barrett v. Barrett*, 108 R.I. 15
(1970), in which a widow sued over a *Providence Journal* obituary labeling
her estranged husband a bachelor. But she claimed that this defamed *her*, by
implying that she was guilty of fornication. And thanks to Sharon Krause for
turning my plaintive e-query into a productive email chain.

well known. The reporter who covered law for the *Providence Journal* for forty years had never heard of it.[67] And when New York was considering its measure years later, First Amendment expert Floyd Abrams "said no other state had enacted such a law."[68]

Only if there is no executor or administrator of the estate, the Rhode Island law continues, or if that person declines to bring an action within six months, may the estate's beneficiaries bring an action. And it's the beneficiaries, not some specified list of close family members: here too the dead person's intentions are controlling.

Rhode Island, then, believes that defaming the dead is a legal injury—to the dead, not to the survivors. So what? There are all too many screwy laws on the books. I don't think the existence of the law goes to show its desirability. Nor do I think it should assuage any suspicion that I am baying at the moon. I introduce it only to show that it is possible for a legislature to offer legal relief in tort for defaming the dead. The best evidence that something is possible is that it's actual.

There is a reasonable case against extending tort liability this way. It's not the oblivion thesis. Again that's a wholesale attack on settled law in different domains, and it's decidedly wrongheaded anyway. Nor is it the thesis that the dead have no reputational interests: they do. Instead the reasonable case is more retail or local yet. Start here: on my account, the dead do have reputational interests. But theirs are a proper subset of the interests the living can claim. They can't claim emotional damages. And their instrumental interests are limited to projects they'd adopted before dying that could continue after their

---

67. Email from Tracy Breton, 21 November 2014.
68. Schmalz, "Bill on Libeling."

deaths. On the other side, the defense would lose one powerful strategy they currently have: putting plaintiff on the stand and trying to show that the putative defamation is actually true. The ongoing cultural force of *de mortuis* makes it less likely anyway that people will criticize the dead, let alone defame them: many are inclined to let sleeping dogs lie.

More pressing, perhaps, are worries about free speech. As the Supreme Court put it, "Whatever is added to the field of libel is taken from the field of free debate."[69] That's not yet an argument: it just reminds us of a logical relationship. (It's the same, that is, as saying, "Whatever is added to the field of free debate is taken from the field of libel.") It's tempting to respond that the social practice of free speech works better without defamation, just as it ordinarily works better without deliberate falsehoods, intemperate abuse, and the like.[70] But this evades the real point. If the law provides a cause of action here, defendants will have to respond to meritorious and unmeritorious claims alike—at least claims plausible enough to pass the well-pleaded complaint rule.[71] Those costs and the attendant chilling effect on free speech are worth considering. Compare a familiar debate about antidiscrimination law.[72] Some opponents of that law think that employers, as holders of private property, should enjoy the right to discriminate at will. Other oppo-

---

69. New York Times Co. v. Sullivan, 376 U.S. 254, 272 (1964), quoting from *Sweeney v. Patterson*, 128 F.2d 457, 458 (D.C. Cir. 1942).

70. But see my "Romantic Anarchism and Pedestrian Liberalism," *Political Theory* (June 2007).

71. Bell Atl. Corp. v. Twombly, 550 U.S. 544 (2007); Ashcroft v. Iqbal, 556 U.S. 662 (2009).

72. Richard A. Epstein, *Forbidden Grounds: The Case against Employment Discrimination Laws* (Cambridge, MA: Harvard University Press, 1992) is cheerfully on both sides of this debate.

nents think that the problem is that whenever an employer fires someone who happens to be a member of a protected class, she'll face the risk of litigation, even if she fired the employee for, say, simple incompetence or excessive absenteeism, and would herself never act against someone on the basis of their race or sex or. . . .

Who should have standing to bring such actions? While the estate still has an executor, she's the likely candidate. But barring protracted disputes in probate, estates don't linger long. So-called civil recourse theorists might think that here lies the fatal objection to making it tortious to defame the dead.[73] If the point of tort is to allow wronged parties a forum to redress their wrongs, but those wronged parties no longer exist, it seems like a nonstarter for tort law. But such a stance will produce confounding paradoxes: batter someone and break her arm and she can sue you; batter her and leave her comatose and there's no one to sue you. In fact, the law gives agents standing to assert the interests of others incompetent or unable to assert them for themselves. A "next friend" can represent a minor, a mentally disabled party, a party (think Gitmo in its earlier years) squirreled away without access to a lawyer.[74] I'm inclined to think that in the ordinary run of cases, members of the dead person's immediate family should be granted the right to bring such actions. But—recall the *Gugliuzza* solution—that's not to say they should vindicate their own putative interests in

73. See for instance John C. P. Goldberg and Benjamin C. Zipursky, "Civil Recourse Revisited," *Florida State University Law Review* (Fall 2011). I wouldn't have read civil recourse theory this way myself, but Goldberg tells me he would.

74. Consider too *In re Quinlan*, 70 N.J. 10 (1976).

the matter. They should have a fiduciary duty to represent the dead person and the compensation they seek should be for the injuries suffered by that person.

Whoever represents the dead defamed person might face an intriguing conflict. The fiduciary duties here run both to respecting the wishes of the dead and to the welfare of his beneficiaries. The representative might rightly think that the dead person wouldn't have sued even if he were still alive, even if he knew he might win substantial damages, even if he knew he would pass those on to his beneficiaries. But is it because he disapproves of lawsuits or because he wouldn't want to plunge into the agony of litigation himself? Or the representative might rightly think that the dead person might not want to sue because he feared that the byzantine and glacial legal proceedings would distress his beneficiaries—and the beneficiaries might assure the representative that that's just wrong, and they'd rather see the dead person's reputation vindicated.

However we sort out such conflicts, weighing a potential action for defaming the dead suggests this balance: fewer interests to muster on behalf of the pool of plaintiffs coupled with the usual worries about the costs, broadly conceived, of tort law. This framing does seem a reasonable basis on which to oppose extending defamation law to defaming the dead. But I'm not persuaded. Representatives of the dead considering launching defamation actions face the same caution that living people do: the one sure thing is that suing will bring more attention to the alleged defamation. That we continue to resonate to *de mortuis* just as easily cuts the other way: it means, not just fewer likely instances of defamation, but also fewer likely plaintiffs. An injury can be worth guarding against even if it seldom occurs. And as we saw in canvassing figures who de-

plore speaking ill of the dead, the dead can't speak up to defend
themselves against defamation. Look at one justification the
Supreme Court offered for thinking that the First Amendment
inverts the structure of *scandalum magnatum* (no, they didn't
put it that way) and makes it harder for public figures to win a
defamation action: "The first remedy of any victim of defamation is self-help—using available opportunities to contradict
the lie or correct the error and thereby to minimize its adverse
impact on reputation. Public officials and public figures usually enjoy significantly greater access to the channels of effec-
tive communication and hence have a more realistic opportunity to counteract false statements than private individuals
normally enjoy. Private individuals are therefore more vulnerable to injury, and the state interest in protecting them is cor-
respondingly greater."[75] Dead individuals have no opportunity
for self-help. I presume the state interest in protecting them is
greater yet.

But here's the consideration that finally pushes me toward
embracing tort reform. Yes, the dead's reputational interests
are a proper subset of those of the living. But we want to do
more than count how many sorts of interests qualify. We want
to think about how weighty they are. Surely the dead's intrinsic
interest in reputation is especially poignant. Your reputation
after death is a final settling of accounts, unlike your reputation while alive, ordinarily in flux as you continue to act. When
that account is damaged by defamation, it's all too likely to stay
that way. "This will always be there." Ordinarily, that's the most
pressing injury to reputation a dead person can suffer. It isn't
illusory. Offering a legal remedy for it isn't a mask behind which

75. Gertz v. Robert Welch, 418 U.S. 323, 344 (1974).

we find the face of incentives to the living or good consequences or the public interest or anything like that. Like any
other cause of action in tort, it provides a remedy for one party
wronged by another. Sometimes what you see is what you get.

I have no model statute up my sleeve. Framing one would
require answering a host of difficult questions. Among them:
how long after death should defamation be actionable? (And
that's both how long after death is the actual defamation, and
how long after that does the estate have to file an action?)
Should tort law notice the possibility that celebrities' reputational interests last longer than those of the rest of us? For
most of us, anyway, people in the more distant future are like
the people I imagine in Bhutan. They're not part of any social
world that we have reason to care about. Our reputational interests survive our deaths, but not forever. Even if Julian or
Nathaniel Hawthorne defamed Margaret Fuller, I don't think I
should be liable for republication for dredging up the episode
here, and not only because Fuller was a public figure.

Many questions remain. What sort of relief should be
available? What evidentiary rules make sense when the plaintiff can't be deposed and can't appear on the stand? And so on,
and on, and on. I'm not inclined to underestimate how intricate or important such problems are. But such bromides as *actio
personalis* and the oblivion thesis, however soothing, supply
no reason to dismiss the task of solving them.

The skeptic, soft or hard, wants us to be clear-sighted
about death. But the skeptic is confused about life: about how
some of our interests linger past our deaths and about how
central that fact is in our lives. I don't see any demand of rationality requiring us to blinker our vision or shrink our hori-
zons. If you properly don't want your will ignored, and if you

properly don't want your corpse desecrated, why resist the claims that you properly don't want to be defamed after you die, either? and that you're injured when you are? and that the law should provide succor?

Index

TE
VI

TERMINAL VIBRATO

and Other Stories

STANFORD PRITCHARD

Beaufort Books
New York

ACKNOWLEDGMENT

The author would like to thank Tony Outhwaite of the JCA Literary Agency for his encouragement, perseverance, and cheerful bonhomie.

Copyright © 2007 by Stanford Pritchard

FIRST EDITION

Library of Congress Cataloging-in-Publication Data

Pritchard, Stanford.
  Terminal vibrato and other stories / Stanford Pritchard. –
1st ed.
    p. cm.
  ISBN 978-0-8253-0513-9 (alk. paper)
  I. Title.
  PS3618.R576T47 2007
  813'.6–dc22

                                                2007027390

"Player in the Symphony" originally appeared in *The New England Review*, and "Reginald Used the Subjunctive Today" in *The Wisconsin Review*.

Published in the United States by Beaufort Books, New York
www.beaufortbooks.com
Distributed by Midpoint Trade Books, New York
www.midpointtradebooks.com

10 9 8 7 6 5 4 3 2 1

PRINTED IN THE UNITED STATES OF AMERICA

For Elona Lanigan

CONTENTS

TERMINAL VIBRATO

Terminal Vibrato: A technique invented on the jazz cornet by Louis Armstrong, where a note is held initially with no or only very little vibrato before being given steadily increasing amounts of audible oscillation.

— Dolmetsch Music Dictionary

ONE

N ow the thing you have to remember," said Nelson, "is that history is first and foremost a record of what elites have accomplished, whether as thinkers and artists or politicians and generals, and while things like labor struggles and trade issues must be taken into account – I concede that – a person who concerns himself too much with the so-called masses and the fleeting ephemera of day-to-day living may well consign himself to needless obscurity." Nelson had his mouth close to my ear as he spoke, which was natural in the circumstances, and his message was punctuated with considerable urgency. "We see this most clearly in pogroms and genocide," he went on. "We see the almost instantaneous disappearance of millions and millions of stories from the record – and I'm talking human stories – and are left with the tragic difficulty of trying to account for those whose lives have no memorial."

"Yeah," I said breathlessly, "yeah. I got it."

"So finally it's not a question of a willed and chosen exclusivism, but of embracing and consolidating the tradition of moral and spiritual values that has been handed down through the generations."

"Yeah," I said. "Yeah. Okay."

"Now another thing we're going to have to think about —"

And then the bell rang. Clang!

Nelson put some salve on the bruise over my right eye and said, "go get 'em, tiger" — or some such — and almost before I stood up, dragged the stool out from under me.

But Jerome Keady, I'm sorry to say, was in good form that night, and working his left jab to good advantage. I had practiced defending against it, of course, with my sparring partners, but Keady was in better condition than any of us expected; although I was dancing pretty well and working the right hook for which I'm known, he kept getting through my gloves with that quick jab. At one point we got tangled up in the corner and he hit me with it before the referee could wrench us apart.

By the time I went to the corner at the end of the third round, I was tired. Damned tired.

Manny, my second, put the stool out and I sat down.

Nelson was right in my ear again, his breath hot against my face.

"Now Freudianism must be seen as an aspect of the doubleness that began seeping into the culture toward the end of the nineteenth century," he said. "The drive inward, the attempt to discover the true nature of the human psyche, has correspondences in the phenomenological work of Husserl and von Hartmann." Then — without any change of tone — "you've got to stay away from that left hand of his, you've got to feint, you've got to parry and deflect. He's hurting you, he's hurting you."

"Tell me about it," I said.

"I'm telling you, man, he's hurting you. But if you keep moving to your left and stepping backward, it'll keep him from being able to reach you with that jab. Then you can work your right hook while his momentum carries him forward. Are we clear about that?"

"I think so," I said, gasping for air.

"You want more water?" Manny said, quietly.

I opened my mouth and Manny squirted. I spit in the bucket, then he worked a towel over my face and back.

"But there're other things you're not taking into consideration!" I whispered. "Doesn't Freudianism imply a weakening of moral certainty, of the moral center? How can one know and do what is right if his actions are generated by hidden or unconscious factors? How can one have any, you know, autonomy?"

"That's something we'll have to talk about," Nelson said. "But now remember what I told you. Stay away from that jab. Let him work you backward, then use your hook as he comes forward."

Again the bell clanged. It was a sound which, I confess, I had not been looking forward to. The sweat on my forehead was making my left eye sting — I would have liked to have had another go-round with the towel — and I could feel the cut above my right eye beginning to open up. I tried to remember what Nelson had told me, however, and in Rounds 4 and 5 I surprised Keady with some solid right crosses, then two devastating uppercuts. Unfortunately, I could feel him beginning to make his own adjustments, and before Round 5 was over he had opened up that cut some more. By the time I sat down I was hardly sitting, but slumping back on the stool, exhausted. I stretched my arms out along the ropes.

"You're doing okay, kid, you're doing okay," Nelson said, despite the palpable evidence to the contrary. "You're hanging in there."

"I'm trying," I said, breathing heavily. "On the other hand, what about someone like Henry Ward Beecher? We never finished our conversation about *him*. Doesn't it seem interesting to you that a person could have so much leftover energy – and we all know what kind of energy it was – that he would spend his evenings sweeping a pile of dirt back and forth in his basement? These things interest me. And what about the man who was taking Walt Whitman's brain to be weighed, after his autopsy, and dropped it? What ever happened to him?"

"Those are good questions," said Nelson, "those are things we have to talk about. But now, just remember what I told you."

My chest was heaving, rising and falling like a fireplace bellows, and the crowd noise was making me almost dizzy. "Do you realize," I panted, "that there exists a visual likeness – a daguerreotype, I believe – of Paul Revere's son? That's how young this country is!"

"I know, I know," said Nelson. "I think he was killed during the Civil War. We'll talk about that later."

He dabbed my cut with talcum and smeared liniment on my face.

"And the Civil War – speaking of the Civil War. Do you know at roughly that time James Marsh had a plan to breed camels in the southwest as a form of transportation? Can you believe it?" I was really heaving now. Manny squirted water in my mouth. "Think how different this country would be if we had camels wandering around Texas, Arizona, and New Mexico!"

"Yeah, you're right," said Nelson. "That's something to think about." Manny, too, agreed.

And then there was the bell: clang!

But perhaps I should explain.

Nelson McKendrick, my old buddy from college days, was at my house having lunch one afternoon, several years ago, when – while I was in the middle of a sentence – he interrupted and rather peremptorily announced that I was thinking too much. *You're thinking too much:* I can still hear the italics his tone gave the phrase. Furthermore, I can still hear the note of ridicule it implied. We had been talking about automobiles, and I casually asked him if he ever did what I sometimes do, tried to visualize the inner workings of an automobile engine, I mean visualize them while it's running. In fact, I asked him, had he ever thought about what goes on inside the engines of all the cars on the highway?

"Think of all those pistons going up and down," I said, "and all the sparks shooting out of spark plugs, all the gas gurgling through the lines! Think of the pressures, the heat and grease, the grinding of gears, the noise and racket, the chaos and confusion!"

Nelson slouched in his chair looking grumpy and uncomfortable. At the end of the lunch, when I was making coffee and knocked the pot against the counter top and mumbled "oops" – and later knocked the creamer against the refrigerator door and said "sorry" – he suddenly got feisty.

"Do you realize you're apologizing to the kitchen counter?" he said. "Do you realize you're apologizing to your refrigerator? Does it ever occur to you that you're spending a lot of time thinking about things that shouldn't be thought about, worrying about things that shouldn't be worried about? Why don't you try getting out of your own goddamn head for a while? Why don't you consider coming out here in the world and joining the rest of us?"

Nonplussed, in fact feeling a bit defensive, I asked him what he meant. He said he believed my thought processes and perceptions would be clearer, and I would personally be a whole lot happier, if I got involved in some kind of physical activity, in his words *gave your brain a rest.* Specifically, he suggested that I join a health club – perhaps the one where he worked out – and swim, or jump rope, or use the body-building equipment. "In fact," he said, "if you really want to develop your body, your coordination and muscle tone – if you really want to be in a position to defend yourself in this world – I'll teach you to box. Think how much better you'll feel when you learn to tattoo the speed bag instead of the refrigerator."

That, to make a long story short, is how, three years later, I found myself fighting in the junior lightweight quarterfinals at Gaston Park. Nelson had been a mainstay of the wrestling team in college and later served as assistant coach, and unbeknownst to me, afterward had had a career as a boxer. Now he was sitting across from me at my kitchen table and browbeating me; he finally extracted a promise that I would get involved in some kind of physical activity. Well, I'm not one to do things halfway. By going to the gym every day, by doing sit-ups and push-ups and using the weight-lifting machines, I really got my endorphins – which previously I had thought were some kind of marine animal – working. When I saw some young men sparring in a ring in the corner, I decided to give it a try. Before long I developed a real facility in the sport, and was competing on the amateur circuit. Nelson agreed to serve as my trainer and corner man, and Manny Lewis, a gentle black man with a sweet round face, eventually signed on as my second. Not that I have an enormous amount of power behind my punches. Rather, it's the quickness and stamina I developed through roadwork and rope jumping – my ability to stay on my feet and wear my opponent down over the course of a fight – that have gotten me where I am. Along with Nelson's help, it's my agility and careful preparation that have enabled me to hold my own with fighters of greater experience and firepower.

As I said, however, Jerome Keady was in better physical condition than we expected that night, and seemed to have hidden reserves of stamina and adrenalin I did not possess. (Did he think all the cheering, the crowd noise was for him?) In the sixth round of this, my ninth pro fight, he opened up the cut over my eye, and I knew if I had any hope of taking him before the referee stopped the fight, I was going to have to reach deep into my bag of tricks. Everything was on the line now, everything. I think it was my excitement and fatigue – the pressure of the crowd, the months of preparation, the memory of all those days in sweaty gyms, the endless nights studying the films Nelson supplied – that made my mind work faster than ever.

"Did you know that the influenza epidemic of nineteen-eighteen-twenty took nearly twenty million lives?" I said to

Nelson in the corner, while Manny swabbed my forehead. "And Venturi's Principle, what about Venturi's Principle? The principle that says that increasing the speed of a fluid over an aperture decreases the pressure at that point? Along with Bernoulli's Theorem, it explains not only why airplanes rise — the curve on the top of the wing makes the air go faster than under the bottom, therefore decreases the pressure — but why gas gets sucked into the carburetor of an automobile. It also explains why, in an automobile, cigarette smoke drifts out the window."

"That's interesting," said Nelson, leaning close and dabbing my cuts, "very interesting. But maybe we should talk about it later."

But he was wrong if he thought that the pressure of the fight was going to stop me now.

"And the Battle of Lepanto!" I went on. "Up until that time it was the largest naval battle in history! Did you know that nearly a hundred and seventy-five thousand men and over four hundred and fifty galleys took part in the Battle of Lepanto?"

"No, but I heard about it," said Nelson. "But listen, listen to me. I can keep this cut from bleeding openly for maybe *one* more round. Then it's gonna bleed so bad it's gonna blind you and the ref's gonna call the fight. Do you think you can go one more round? Now here's what I want you to do...."

"But wait!" I said, panting. "What about blimps! Contrary to popular opinion, the word does not come from type B, limp! They were earlier called 'dirigibles' because their movement could be directed. 'Dirigible' is French for directable, steerable. Did you know that people used to walk on top of those things while they were in flight? And Winchester's widow, the Winchester who invented the rifle! She was so haunted by the ghosts of the people his rifle had killed that she built a house with hundreds of rooms, then constantly rearranged them to trick their ghosts! No, no, wait! There's more!" (This when Manny tried to interrupt.) "Do you know it takes a ton of paint to paint a 727 airplane? Are you aware that Franz Liszt was such a superstar that society ladies would gather up his discarded cigar butts, stuff them in their bosoms, save them as souvenirs, cherish them forever? Do you know why the windows of airport control towers slant inward? So the controllers won't see their own reflections!"

"Now calm down," Manny said, quietly. "Calm down."

But I couldn't. I began to talk about the Prussian general staff, especially General Schlieffen, whose obsession with the Roman defeat at Cannae was one of the things that precipitated World War I. I began to talk about the Roman emperor Elagabalus, who was partial to the tongues of peacocks and nightingales, and once had the heads of six hundred ostriches brought to him so that their brains could be eaten. I began to talk about how members of the Jesse James gang would often hide in the very posses that were looking for them, and how Anton Mesmer, of mesmerization fame, became proficient on the glass harp Benjamin Franklin perfected. "And what about the balance of payments problem?" I said. "We have to think of that, too! And how come nobody ever talks about the varnish industry, or the sidewalk chalk that children use?"

Well, the last thing I remember is the sound of the bell. At least that's the last thing I remember clearly. I got up from the stool and went into the seventh round knowing it was do-or-die, that I had to give it everything I had, that if I let Keady hurt me any more, if I let him get to that cut over my eye — which looked worse than it was but was clearly drawing the attention of the ref — my shot at the semifinals was over. Fortunately, I hit Keady with a couple of jabs and then an uppercut, then we drifted into a corner, arms around one another's waists, loose and rubbery, and again the ref pulled us apart. I raised my gloves and danced out of the way of two near-misses, Keady and I traded body punches, I hit him with a left to the ribs, and another left, then a right to the chin, and then....

Then the lights went out. I was sprawled flat on my back on the canvas. I was lying there spread-eagled, arms and legs akimbo, in the middle of the ring, staring up at Nelson and Manny and the ref, staring up at those intense lights in the ceiling. And I remember thinking: what, exactly, is a halogen lamp? And how do halogens differ from holograms? In a sports arena as large as this, how do they change the bulbs? Do they use tall ladders? Scaffolding? I looked at the ref's bow tie, which suddenly seemed about five feet long and a foot wide, and the chin whiskers above it. And I asked myself, if you placed all the whiskers a man shaves in his lifetime end to end, how far would they reach?

Then I blacked out again. The next thing I remember, I was on a stretcher and being loaded into an ambulance. There were two EMTs in the rig, a man and a woman, and I believe it was the latter who several times used the word oxygen. Lying there, I thought for some reason of apples, and in retrospect the reason is clear. In an environment where the atmosphere is carefully controlled — the control being the almost complete removal of normal air — apples can be stored for considerable lengths of time, a year when the air contains only three percent oxygen, three years when it contains only one percent. The wax applied to apples to keep them shiny is made by the same companies that make floor wax.

Well, here I am. In the hospital. Flat on my back with both my right arm and left leg in traction. The concussion I suffered was apparently a mild one, and fortunately has had little effect on my thinking. But Nelson said that after Keady decked me, I got my leg and arm caught under me as I fell, and that my falling was not a pretty thing to watch. Anyway, here I am. Other than a very pretty nurse named Valerie, the main item of interest in my limited perceptual field is the bumpy cast on my raised leg which, beginning at my toes, descends toward me like a ski slope full of tiny ridges, moguls. The bandage over my eye, of course, I can't see. Although I am not enjoying being here, as who would, at least the people at the hospital have gone out of their way to make me comfortable.

But about apples. Apples have very sensitive skins. How do apple pickers load them into the primary collection bins without bruising them? Simple. They place their sacks in the bins and unhitch them from the bottom, and let them slide out slowly. At the warehouse, similarly, they don't simply turn the bins upside down so that the apples dump out onto a hard surface. No, the bins are lowered into great tanks of water, and the apples float slowly to the top.

TWO

The hallway outside my door has been unusually busy this morning. Doctors and nurses and orderlies have been bustling up and down, and in a sort of controlled cacophony the PA system has been crackling with messages and codes. It seems like everyone but me is doing something, going somewhere. One of the volunteers just brought in my lunch (we eat so early here), with a shiny red apple for dessert, and I found myself musing on what would have happened if Eve had given Adam a banana. Can you imagine two thousand years of art showing a very seductive Eve teasingly holding out a half-peeled banana? ("Why was Eve a good carpenter?" I asked the volunteer. She thought about it for a moment. "Because she made Adam's banana stand!" She frowned and quickly left the room.) But no, it had to be an apple. The apple tree is part of the genus *Malus*, and *malus*, in Latin, means evil. Anyway, a banana doesn't have quite the style and panache that a small, round, shiny red object does. Red is your color if you're depicting what went on in the Garden of Eden, yes, red is the color you want. On the other hand, the Bible doesn't even specify what kind of fruit it was, so why do I mention it?

Why do I mention it? Because I have to think of something as I lie here, I have to keep rummaging through my mind to keep from going stir-crazy. Who cares about the anonymous man in Room 416? Who, in the neighborhood of this giant white-brick hospital, with its twenty-seven floors and ten thousand ugly air conditioners, can imagine that a certain individual, in a certain room on a certain floor, is lying in this bed? I've become nothing more than a bee in a beehive, one among the stacks in a three-dimensional grid, a Lego toy, a Rubik's Cube without solution, one among a stack of people who for the moment no longer function. This is where they put us, I suppose, those who can no longer play our parts in society. It's a sort of zone, a state of mind (for it's not me, it's my body that's the problem) where fallen warriors may be kept out of public view and not distract those who are still fighting. After all, who among the functioning wants to be reminded of fallibility, of fallen comrades? When you pass a broken-down car by the side of the road, doesn't the knowledge that you could be the driver bring a twinge of apprehension? You look, and pretend you're not looking, you think about it and pretend you're not thinking about it. You race on. But sooner or later, a tiny voice says, sooner or later you know it will be your turn. I think if I were a poet, I would write an "Ode to the Fallen Auto," or if a sculptor create a memorial dedicated "To Those Fallen by the Side of the Highway."

For the moment, then, I'm one of the invisible ones, stuck away on a shelf. I'm one of those citizens you see in tableaus depicting revolutionaries fighting at the barricades, one of those fallen comrades at the edge of the scene whose death pangs make everyone else look larger than life and more heroic. Ah, poor bastard, the viewer thinks. But let's get on with it, the museum closes at five. On to the next painting, the next room, the next wing.

Not that I'm alone in the room. I do have company, if you can call it that. There is a man in the bed next to me whose legs I can see sticking out behind a partially drawn curtain. I would have preferred a private room, of course, but Nelson and Manny said that, owing to the circumstances in which I was admitted, a double was the best they could arrange. Anyway, for the first few days I tried to make conversation with the man, and when I finally commented to one of the nurses on how taciturn and unresponsive he is, she got a bit teary-eyed and explained that he is in a coma. I guess that explains why he hasn't said anything, much less moved, since I've been here. No, the gentleman just lies there with the lower part of his torso, and legs, showing. I suppose there is oxygen going in, and a food tube, and equipment taking care of his bodily functions, but they're beyond the curtain; I can't see them. In any case, it makes for a hell of a social hour, a very peppy social life, I can tell you. But I try not to let it bother me, I try to be stoical and good-natured about it. In fact, I've decided it's refreshing, for a change, to talk to someone who can't talk back. It allows me a certain, how would you phrase it, freedom of expression. "Good morning to you, sir!" I say, when I wake up. "How are you today? Lovely morning, isn't it? Aren't we lucky to be in such a pleasant, well-staffed hospital?" And then, when there is no reply, I take it as agreement and go right on. "I feel better myself today, thanks for asking. My leg itches owing to the cast, and I do get tired of having my arm frozen in this awkward position, as if I were shielding myself from attackers. I'll be glad when all these splints and traction wires are removed. Other than that, I'm feeling reasonably well, thank you. It's heartening, is it not, to think we're both on the mend?"

As I said, I have to do *something* to keep myself from going stir-crazy. In any case, one thing led to another and for the last few days, I confess, I've been having a little fun with the man. What else have I to do? "You didn't eat your Jello!" I just said, as the volunteer took my lunch away. "Usually you enjoy your Jello! Come on, Mr. Jones! If you have any hope of getting out of here, you have to eat your Jello!" (Mr. Jones. Until a better name comes along, I've decided to call him Mr. Jones.) "You must eat your entire lunch, Mr. Jones! And you didn't eat your pepper steak, last night! You can't fool me! And you didn't eat your scrambled eggs this morning! You must work at getting your strength back, Mr. Jones! Come on, Mr. Jones, you've got to hold up your end! You've got to keep up the side!"

Oh, we have a good time, Mr. Jones and I, we really do. It's rather pleasant, as I said, to be able to carry on a conversation with someone who can't talk back. And sometimes, when I run out of things to talk about and find myself getting irritated by the silence from the other side, I mimic Mr. Jones's flat, utterly lifeless position by lying low in my bed and staring at the ceiling. I pretend we're two people in canoes, two peas in a pod, two old soldiers standing at attention, two — perish the thought — cadavers lying on slabs. "Just the two of us," I mumble across the space separating us, "lying here completely still. Twins, blood brothers. Pretend we're field mice, Mr. Jones. If we don't move, they can't see us. So let's just lie here and wait for time to pass, wait for the whole damn thing to blow over. I'd go down to the lounge and get you some magazines – but for two little details. One, you can't read. And two, I can't move. Ha-ha, ha-ha-ha!"

And then, having become bored with this charade, I hike myself up again. "Hey, Mr. Jones!" I say, "what'd you think of that pretty nurse who just left the room? Did you see those va-va-vooms?" (Is it sexist to make cracks about pretty nurses? And in Mr. Jones's case, is it sexist to make cracks about pretty nurses when you, the cracker, have been stripped of mobility and bodily functions, when, indeed, you are comatose?)

I'd be less than candid if I didn't admit that I've developed a fondness for Mr. Jones. He's not so stodgy, when you think about it. Cleaving to one's silences, after all, is not the worst form of behavior I can think of – I've met people with far worse faults – and a certain, well, reticence on the other side of the curtain has meant that I've been able to delve into matters of increasing delicacy and intimacy. What a pleasure it is to be able to speak one's mind, in this day and age! To speak one's mind truly and without fear of censorship, without fear of antagonizing or infuriating people! Just now, for example, after casting about for the best way to put the matter, I explained to Mr. Jones the circumstances that led me to my career as a boxer.

"You may find this hard to believe, Mr. Jones," I said, "but it was the professors. Those damned professors I had in college. They got me thinking so much that I could hardly tie my shoes anymore, could hardly take a breath without contemplating the chemical and atomic makeup of the air. What right had they to fill me with so much book learning, then set me loose on the world ill-equipped to deal with it? To fill my mind with schemes and fantasies, quandaries and conundrums, then send me out into a world whose single most important feature is its resistance to such schemes? You see, Mr. Jones," I said (gradually working myself up into righteous indignation), "college teaching is one of the few activities that adults engage in where no other adult sees you do it. You're always and forever the oldest and smartest person in the room, you know more than anyone else, and you're expected to impart that knowledge. But no other adult sees you do it! Oh, the professors struggle to maintain the *appearance* of patient, tolerant discourse, to maintain the illusion that the classroom is a community of scholars dispassionately seeking truth. But the fact is, the professors are dealing with people who just three or four years previously were in high school! And what happens to people who spend their lives talking to people recently out of high school? Why, they become incapable of talking to adults! They lose their capacity to listen! They're used to being the cynosure of all eyes, and gradually fall in love with the sound of their own voices! Their chosen mode of discourse – the pattern of interaction with which they're most comfortable – is not the conversation, but the lecture!"

Well, the afternoon I said this, although I was doing my best to maintain my composure, I had evidently begun to scream and shout, and two nurses rushed into the room thinking I was hemorrhaging, if not dying.

"Is everything all right in here?" asked one.

"There, there," said the other, thinking I was hallucinating, or losing my mind. And then, nervously: "Can I get you some water? How's your pitcher? Is there anything I can bring you?"

"Just some magazines for Mr. Jones," I said, pointing to my right.

"Some magazines for – Oh, now come on. You're joshing. Cut it out."

"You're not very happy here, are you?" said the first.

"Oh, I'm *very* happy," I replied. "I just want to get back in the ring and punch somebody."

They took my blood pressure and gave me a sedative, and I fell asleep for the rest of the afternoon. But the next morning, I engaged Mr. Jones in a conversation about another of my obsessions.

"The psychoanalytic world view says the work of art embodies the artist's unconscious themes," I explained, patiently, "but I'm aware of everything I'm doing. It is precisely my unconscious themes, the very themes I have had plenty of time to think about and consider, that I wallow in, yes, wallow in. And speaking of unconsciousness, I have *been* unconscious, quite literally knocked out in the ring at Gaston Park. So I know whereof I speak. In fact, I've known about invisible, inscrutable things my entire life, ever since I was a baby. I knew very well what was going on in the so-called preverbal and pre-oedipal stages of my life. Yes, I knew what was going on, though of course I couldn't say it. It would have scared them, Mr. Jones, scared them to see me standing up in my crib – a four-month-old child in necktie and bifocals – discoursing on the themes that were already on my mind. But I remember quite clearly, Mr. Jones, standing in my crib and dropping things over the

[21]

side. I knew all about gravity, of course, even then I already understood about gravity. I wanted only to see what would happen, I wanted only to see how far I could throw things. I was working on my *arm*, Mr. Jones, my muscular coordination, and I already knew that I was destined for a career involving physical strength. And then, about peek-a-boo. They say a child plays peek-a-boo as a way of rehearsing the disappearance of its mother. Naturally it doesn't take very kindly to the thought that its primary source of security and gratification is going to be removed. But I knew all along this was going to happen, I knew it all along! I was just having fun! I was just trying to keep my family – a rather depressed bunch, when you think about it– amused! I suppose it was the ham in me, Mr. Jones, the part of me that had to be the center of attention, the part which, as an adult, brought me before the bright lights. And those lights at Gaston Park are awfully bright, I can tell you, Mr. Jones.

"Now. About those little toy trains that go in and out of tunnels." (I was warming to my subject.) "What about those little toy trains? There comes a point in a child's development, Mr. Jones, when he can anticipate the reemergence of the train from the tunnel, and adjusts his eyes accordingly. But I knew from the beginning when the train was going to come out of the tunnel! And while I watched for it, I deliberately made up stories about the people on the train, and what they were doing! As a matter of fact, it was all those folks standing around in lab jackets – the people conducting the tests – that really unnerved me! If Heisenberg was right, that the observation of atomic particles affects their behavior, then I have to ask: what effect did those child psychologists have on me when, cameras and clipboards in hand, they watched me playing peek-a-boo with my mother? Or stood around on the edge of the train set while I tried to anticipate the train's coming out of the tunnel? It almost made me hate trains.

"But I'm tired of talking to you, Mr. Jones."

There's no reason I can't go on talking to myself, however. It's not the so-called latent content, it's not deep, dark, unconscious drives that propel and emerge from these, my musings. (Hmm. The Drives. Sounds like a suburban subdivision.) No, the contents and the outward manifestations are precisely my subject. It is precisely the flotsam that has risen to the surface – forget jetsam, that's stuff other people have thrown overboard – that I wallow in, play in. And if you say, ha, but there are sharks, weird forms, nightmarish shapes swimming around beneath you, then I say, but that's me in my diving helmet. I'm swimming around beneath the sharks and weird forms. And if you say, yes, but beneath you in your diving gear there's a submarine down there, I say, look again. I'm that crab you see digging into the ocean floor. I'm a fish on the bottom of the sea, glancing idly up at the submarine.

Do you know what I should have told them, Mr. Jones, those nurses who rushed in here yesterday afternoon? I should have told them about the time I went to a physical fitness trainer, and he asked me what part of my body I was interested in building up. I replied, my mind.

Damn. This bed sure is uncomfortable.

THREE

Mummies, Dr. Jones. That's what we are, mummies. Two ancient, dignified kings lying in state, getting ready for our trip through eternity. You've apparently been embalmed (or is it pickled?) and I'm wrapped around with strips of gauze and staring uphill at a long plaster tube. What with the casts on my right arm and left leg, and this turban on my head, I feel like the object of a children's game, a craft project, something that's been constructed from papier-mâché. Ah, but that's us, isn't it. Two ancient pharaohs lying in state, in Room 416. Sometimes I'm surprised there aren't lines of people coming through to view us.

But let me tell you more about my own pickle, Dr. Jones. (No, not that one! It's unseemly for a fellow in your condition, or noncondition, to be having such thoughts!) Let me tell you about the pickle I've gotten myself into. You're an affable fellow,

Dr. Jones, and you have good insights into these things, perhaps you'd enjoy hearing about it. Perhaps, indeed, you'll have some advice for me. Are you listening, Dr. Jones? Are you aware that I've elevated you in rank? That I'm calling you Dr. Jones now, out of respect, a demented but somehow appropriate filial piety? Okay, let me put the problem succinctly.

Imagine that you've gone to a restaurant for dinner, and there's a boisterous party at the table next to you, four or five people whooping and hollering and having a good time. Now imagine that someone comes into the restaurant whom these four or five know, but haven't seen for a long time. Suddenly there's a great outpouring of surprise, pleasure, and happiness, everyone begins jumping up and shaking hands and kissing. Well, you know what my problem is, Dr. Jones? If I happen to be sitting nearby, *I* start smiling! I don't even know these people, and I start smiling, too! Although I try to *keep* from smiling. I stare at my dinner, I try to concentrate on my food, but despite myself, I'm smiling! I've unconsciously made myself part of their scene, I've let myself be drawn into a scene in which I don't even belong! No, that's not quite accurate, Dr. Jones. (Are you listening, Dr. Jones?) To put it accurately, some magnetic field, some inscrutable fluid or medium has enveloped me, enveloped us all, and I have become a participant in spite of myself! I know exactly what it's like to experience such reunions – don't we all? – I've been part of such situations – haven't we all? – and now I've insinuated myself into this one – and I'm smiling!

Now I want you to tell me what it is, Dr. Jones. I want you to tell me, what is the force in the room?

Don't hold back now.

Don't be shy.

Cat got your tongue, Dr. Jones?

Well, since you're having so much trouble remembering, let me give you some help. I'll tell you what it is. It's consciousness, Dr. Jones! Sticky, gooey, gummy consciousness! It's consciousness that keeps me from attending to my dinner, a viscous web of consciousness that's stronger than any thought in my head, stronger than the lure of the food in front of me, stronger even than my own attempts at self-composure! It's quicksand, Dr. Jones, the quicksand – the ant trap, the siren song – of consciousness, some generalized alertness and vitality in the world that appeals to my own alertness and vitality! Some secret password or tribal call that has priority over every other thing, and will not resist being answered! And you know what, Dr. Jones? Suddenly I'm blushing! Blushing for the simple reason that a few anonymous people at the table next to me are having a reunion! The phenomenon – and the attempt to resist it – figure as aspects of a single thing. Suddenly my face grows red. I'm blushing! I glance at the table where the cheerful five- or sixsome is talking excitedly, trading news and gossip, and – I cannot too strongly say this, Dr. Jones – I'm blushing! Naturally I hope that no one has *noticed* me blushing, and that only makes me blush the more!

You know what, Dr. Jones? (Are you listening, Dr. Jones? Can you hear me? Can you understand what I'm saying?) You know what I'm doing? I'm blushing at existence! I'm blushing at the mere fact of being alive! Or is it that I'm blushing at consciousness? Or is *consciousness* blushing at consciousness? Or alertness and vitality blushing at –

Now calm down. Calm down, Dr. Jones. There's no reason

for you to get upset. I suppose you're thinking I haven't reasoned this out correctly, that my problem is heightened and excessive *self*-consciousness. But it's not that, Lenny, it's not self-consciousness, I'm not, at the moment of blushing, conscious of *myself*. No, I'm conscious of the people at the table next to me. Or rather, there's some subtle mixture of the two, a consciousness of how these other people would feel if they were conscious of *my* consciousness. There is something that fills the room, Lenny, something that fills the world, something of which I'm only a tiny part, some overarching, all-pervasive thing, which is nothing more than—

Lenny. I called you Lenny. Is that your first name? And is it all right if I call you by your first name? Or is your first name Roland? Roland sounds better. Anyway, Roland, you interrupt. You say it's all my problem. Is that what you said? Come on, Roland—or Irving is it?—speak up! And don't give me that pseudoscientific language of separation-individuation, don't give me object relations, don't argue with me, you old fart! Because the cat is out of the bag, Irving! And there is nothing that you or I—two hoary, ancient, dignified kings lying in state—can do about it! For no matter what consciousness is and where it comes from, and whether you call it maladjustment, neurosis, or anything else, it's still there. Consciousness! The lifelong tingle, the eternal *frisson*, the irrepressible blush of consciousness!

Okay, calm down. There's no need for our getting into an argument about this. But listen, Irving, check this out. So you finally get the color out of your cheeks, and finish your dinner and pay your bill, and still secretly ruminating on, indeed monumentally pleased, with this reunion in which you had absolutely no part, you make your way out of the restaurant. And as you are making your way out, you step around a good-looking couple in the foyer who have their arms around one another. For some reason you slacken your pace, or maybe it's only time that slackens. In any case, the man steps closer to the woman, they wrap their arms more tightly around one another, and they sink into a long, impassioned kiss. Head for the water pumps, Irving, they're smooching! They've stepped right out of the world, right out of time, they've stepped into the place where you wish you were – and they've taken you with them! Your face, and the inside of your brain reddens, flares and skyrockets go off, searchlights illuminate the night sky, and you see your life, in one foolish, all-encompassing image – everything you ever were or will be – passing in front of you! You feel happy, envious, small, excluded, and hopeful all at once, and it's enough to make existence itself, all the experience since the beginning of time, all the hope and joy, sorrow and pain, pass in front of you! Something has cut to the quick, threatened you, undermined you, mocked and annihilated you, robbed you of – what? – of consciousness! And do you know what it is? (Are you listening, Irving?) Do you know what it is? It's animal heat, George! Animal heat!

Sorry. Donald.

Donald, was it?

Now calm down, Donald. Still, these two people in their moment of bliss have taken you out of yourself, taken you with them, they've taken you to a place of abandonment where everyone wants to be, and when, once there, no one wants to leave. And they've left you with what? Consciousness! For paradoxically, the momentary loss of consciousness is itself consciousness! Ah yes, you know how it is. Don't pretend you don't. You try not to look at the couple smooching in the foyer, you try not to intrude on the shared animal heat, but the bus is leaving, Donald, the bus they're on is leaving, and secretly you've joined them. You've already left. Now tell me, please. Who has stayed behind? Who has stayed home to mind the store? Who is walking out of the restaurant with you? Consciousness, George! Poor, beleaguered consciousness!

Uh, George.

George? Are you there?

You don't seem impressed.

Say something, George. Don't leave me alone like this.

Okay, you need time to mull it over. I understand that. But I know what you're thinking. You're thinking I've gotten myself into this, I have to get myself out, that this little pickle I've gotten myself into is of my own making, so it's up to me to get myself out. I'll tell you, it's not going to be easy. Because consciousness is not going to go away, Dave, not unless we sedate it with drugs or narcotics, not unless we get involved in something that really gets our adrenalin flowing, like jogging or tennis or boxing. No, we're stuck with it, Dave, I say we're stuck with it. Damn. It's like that advertisement that shows a gallon of house paint being poured over the Earth from above the North Pole. Do you happen to know that advertisement, Ray? Are you aware of anything, Ray? Do you know that image of the red or green paint – I forget which – dripping down over the entire globe? We Cover the Earth, says the slogan. And that's consciousness for you, Ray. That dripping liquid, covering everything, is consciousness.

So I say count your blessings. Because as difficult as it is to go through what you're going through just now, in some ways you're a lucky guy.

Still, I wish you were listening. Are you listening, Al? Can you hear me?

Don't leave me alone like this!

Say something!

FOUR

The Hardy Boys, Dave, that's what we are. A couple of fear-less crime-stoppers or intrepid explorers. We're just two travel-ers telling tales, travelers on the way to Canterbury, so to speak, two people sliding down the river of life in comfortable canoes, coursing down the slopes in bobsleds, a couple of reg-ular sit-wallahs. Well, at least one of us is going downhill. Noth-ing personal, Dave.

Anyway, it's funny. I was just sitting – I mean lying – here imagining that you had asked me about that night at Gaston Park, asked me what it was like to be out cold in a boxing ring. Had you asked, I would have been tempted to reply that I've always been out cold. I would have been tempted, but I wouldn't have said it because when I consider the situation you're in, my circumstances seem like a cakewalk, a walk in the park.

(Is that what we agreed to call you? Dave? It seems to me it was. Anyway, I was growing tired of those other names, and in the circumstances Dave will do.)

In any case, suppose I had told you that those minutes when I was out cold were actually quite pleasant. You probably would have thought it was because I was unconscious, unaware of myself or the world around me, in a state, as it were, of dreamless sleep. But the fact is (Dave, are you listening?), even then I was dimly aware of my head on the sweat-soaked canvas, dimly aware of the ref's shiny black shoes next to me. I was even conscious of Jerome Keady's monstrous shoes jerking up and down as he pranced around triumphantly. Mostly, however, I was aware of the commotion at the apron of the ring, the photographers lurching forward taking pictures, the fans staring open-mouthed and wide-eyed in horror or jubilation. But there was one person I noticed most of all, and that was the ring girl, the perky young lady who made a circuit of the ring, that night, with cards announcing the numbers of the rounds. In the state I was in, she appeared to me less a person than a vision, a benevolent angel. At the edge of the ring, as though she'd never witnessed such a sight, she was leaning forward, and out of the corner of my eye I caught a glimpse of her fulsome chest. And that made me remember the way her skirt puffed out over her hips, and how it barely reached her knees. Believe it or not, Dave, although I had completely exhausted my supply of adrenalin I had not run out of testosterone. But what is testosterone, Dave? (Are you listening, Dave? You know, I really like talking to you. I feel you're someone I can communicate with, someone with whom I can have a free and open exchange of ideas. When they initially brought me here, it never occurred to me that it would lead to such a lasting friendship.) Anyway, what is testosterone, Dave? A chemical, that's what. A chemical that somehow acts on the cells of the brain. But how exactly does a chemical that acts on the cells of the brain — or rather, how did it that night — continue to make me, *in extremis* as I was, obsessed with a beautiful chest and the way a skirt dangles above the knees of beautiful legs? If we lived in a different time — I'll put it this way for the sake of argument — how would a crystalline androgenic hydroxy steroid ketone, $C_{19}H_{28}O_2$, to be exact, make me obsessed with the nape of a woman's neck, or her thin, delicate ankles? How in one age would it make me interested in a skinny, emaciated figure, and in another, a fully rounded, even corpulent one? Is testosterone so versatile, Dave? So fickle? So polymorphously perverse?

Well, they say the unconscious remembers everything, and I suppose there were other things I thought about as I lay there. By the way, Dave, I've always had trouble with that one, the notion that the unconscious remembers everything. I remember the time I flunked out of a spelling bee in junior high school; my mortification at missing an easy word will never let me forget that. I even remember the word. But do I remember what I wore to school that day? Do I remember what I had for breakfast? Do I remember what I said to my parents at breakfast, or whether I walked to school or took the bus or got a ride? And if I got a ride, do I remember whether I slammed the car door, or closed it quietly? Is consciousness really just a bit of flotsam afloat on a vast sea of memory?

But it's not just the things I thought about as I lay there, that night, that changed my life. No, it's the revelation I had.

Suddenly it seemed I had crossed a magic boundary, and had come to know the unknowable. At that moment, Dave, I came into possession of my own unconscious. Oh, they think it was a defeat I suffered – indeed, the press reported a knockout – but for me the knockout was only technical. For that night, as a result of an uppercut from Jerry Keady, my unconscious suddenly became completely and totally open to me.

Think of it, Dave.

Dave, are you listening to me?

Think of what I'm saying! Consider the new territory I had opened up! Suddenly I was the squatter *par excellence,* suddenly I was in possession of horizonless vistas, I was sitting on a gold mine – or was it a powder keg – I had a new and secret weapon. Why had no one told me about this before? Such a feeling of freedom it gave me! My very own unconscious! My new companion and plaything, my new self! Everything, I reasoned, was going to be easier now. I was no longer alone in the world, but going forward at the head of a vast army with a vast supply of arms and materiel, a vast resource. In one instantaneous accumulation, I suddenly had four things at my disposal: the unconscious (we all know about that), the subconscious (whatever that is), the preconscious (however that relates), and the co-conscious (useful, I was sure, in a great variety of situations). I was no longer just the tip of the iceberg, Dave, I was the entire iceberg! The vast swarm of unruly, mutinous energies, the burial ground where people put their disposable memories – the Dispose-All, the trash bin where people shelve and hide what they've repressed – were all, suddenly, available to me! I had found the secret password required to unlock the files! Imagine it. Suddenly I could say to a beautiful woman – and I am thinking of the ring girl now:

"My unconscious is totally infatuated with your eyes and lips, your curvaceous chest, and has asked me to invite you to dinner. My unconscious, being totally open and candid in all its deliberations, has also asked me to announce that it would like to take you home afterward, turn the lights down, put on some music, and while getting to know you better, gently, delicately, inch by inch, slide the zipper down the back of your...."

Of course, if the young lady had arrived at the same level of self-awareness I had, she might be tempted to reply:

"Thank you, that is indeed a very kind offer. I meet a lot of sleazebags in this business, and it's not often that a gentle, soft-spoken person like yourself invites me to dinner. Unfortunately, however, my unconscious has asked me to tell you that it knows damn well you're asking me out only on the pretext of taking me home and plying me with liquor, then attempting to get your hands on my...."

Of course that would be the problem, wouldn't it? A radio announcer, committing a slip of the tongue, could catch himself:

"I didn't say that. My unconscious did."

And a person at a dinner party, having committed a faux pas, could say:

"I didn't do that. My unconscious did."

Two people having a fight could stop and rationally summarize their motivations:

"I didn't call you a jerk, you jerk, my unconscious did."

A sample reply might be:

"It wasn't me who said you are one of the most loathsome people I've ever met. It was my unconscious."

And then:

"Okay, I accept that! But you should know that it's my unconscious that has thrown you against this wall!"

Then:

"Well let me go, because it was only my unconscious that grabbed you by the throat and knocked you to the ground!"

At the conclusion of a war, two generals from opposing armies could write to one another:

"You know, it was my unconscious that made me send an entire battalion through the Vischer Gap just when your troops were assembling in the mountains."

And in reply:

"It was my unconscious that made me deploy a thousand men to Schönwachen just when you were completing your encirclement of the area. As a child I had some toys that came from Schönwachen, and my unconscious was secretly, irrationally obsessed with reclaiming the town."

Two dictators, writing to one another about the legions of people they had killed or imprisoned. . . .

And so on, Dave, so on *ad infinitum.*

Anyway, there you have it, Dave. The real story of what happened that night, when I was sprawled on the mat after being decked by Jerome Keady. That is the secret realization, the secret triumph which beyond the purview of floodlights and flashbulbs, wire stories and news reports, I wrested from the jaws of defeat. One small step for an unconscious, one giant leap for the collective unconscious.

Or something like that.

Are you paying attention, Dave? Because I should tell you that this is my unconscious talking now. Although I can't move, at least move enough to get out of this bed, it doesn't mean that both my conscious and unconscious can't go on conversing with you. And since you're unconscious – a bit of irony there, I'll admit – my unconscious can talk to your unconscious. Isn't it wonderful, Dave? During our time here, neither of us has to give a hoot about rationality, neither of us has to be responsible for anything! I can let my unconscious do the talking, and therefore have complete psychic mobility; I can pretend that yours is talking to mine, and therefore have companionship. It's a perfect arrangement, is it not? Well, almost perfect. Because I continue to appreciate the sight of normal, functioning human beings, I do relish it when one of the nurses comes in. When I see one of the nurses, especially the slinky, silky Amber or the very buxom Valerie, my unconscious goes to the circus, it goes on holiday, it sinks into its pleasures and is content for the rest of the afternoon. Then, if I have nothing else to think about, I can dip into it – as I've said, it's become totally available to me – and become a warm and enthusiastic spectator of its enjoyment, the passive audience of its, um, show. It's wonderful to have such entertainment in-house, so to speak, to have a nearly bottomless well of amusement so close to home. Ah, the bubbly cauldron, Dave! The bubbly cauldron!

Now where was I? I know I sound lost just at the moment, but if I wait a bit, my unconscious will tell me exactly where I was. Oh yes, there. You see? What I – or rather it – was saying is, doesn't it seem curious to you that the unconscious is treated like something people didn't discover themselves, but

was discovered *for* them? Wouldn't discovering the unconscious be sort of like discovering happiness or aggression, or
like discovering the ego or the psyche? When someone discovered electrons or Pluto or the North Pole, it wasn't like they
hadn't been there all along. And the same with the unconscious. You don't really believe men sat around for ten thousand years and thought about things, but didn't realize there
were parts of themselves that were dark, mysterious, and unknown. I would suggest, Dave, that it was a case of giving a
new name to a very old thing. The old gods and spirits (Dave,
are you paying attention?), the old tricksters and merry prank-
sters on whom people formerly blamed things or looked to for
an accounting, were disappearing, and suddenly it seemed as
though man were playing tricks on *himself.* But where were the
tricks coming from? Since the modern world has no place for
such tricks and pranks — which interfere with the smooth functioning of society — it invented a dumping ground, a holding
tank in an obscure region of the psyche, to hold them. They
say that the mind and the world grow up together, Dave, and
that's how it happened. The modern world needed something
called the unconscious, so it invented it. And the result? For
one thing, evil got swept under the rug, it no longer seems a
feature of the world, at least not of our world. Since one can
no longer know himself, really know himself, and thus take full
responsibility for his actions, as a consequence there have to
be dependencies, and places of dependency, to which everyone can have recourse.

Ah, so many hospitals, so little time.

But speaking of time, Dave, these are new times. And what

happens when we become totally conscious of the unconscious, as I have? What happens when we expose it, illuminate it, flood it with light, smother it with attention, when we kick it, stomp on it, ridicule it, write books about it, open the doors and fill the room with people — or other unconsciousnesses — who watch it? What happens when we haul it out of the house, drag it into court, exhibit it, force it to answer questions, allow others to interrogate it, make it account for itself — where it was on a certain day, what it was doing, who it was with? What happens when we unfold it, race about the world with it, dip into it, give away pieces of it, talk about it?

Oh, I know what you're saying. I'm not a psychotherapist but I play one in real life. Or I'm not a human being but I play one in real life.

Well, speak for yourself, Dave.

Because I'll tell you what happens.

We begin to *be.*

Even you, Dave. Do you understand what I'm saying? You begin to be! You tear away your covers and your life-support equipment — the oxygen, those tubes and wires, the monitor — and jump up out of bed and begin to dance! You do the polka, the jitterbug, the tango, the mad fandango!

You're a hell of a dancer, Dave. But I'm telling you, if you don't want to be a creature with a soul more elusive than a cat's, if you don't want to be a creature with a soul made up of air or smoke or boron or quicksilver, you have to think more about the unconscious.

Hell, Dave, you sure are the talkative one.

Dave? Dave, I just thought of something. Who ever said that

dreamless sleep is such a desirable thing? Personally, I always feel a lot better when I dream. Even when the dreams are terrible, scary and disconcerting.

Speaking of which, I think it's time for a nap. Do you think you can do without my company for a while?

I'm taking your silence for assent, Dave.

So it's 'nighty-night. Talk to you in a little while.

Dave?

Dave! Answer me!

FIVE

M y god! I've just been dealt another knockout punch! This is unbelievable!

A small army of doctors and interns, making their rounds, just trooped in, and one of them, while evaluating the condition of my roommate, absent-mindedly pulled the curtain back. Naturally I was curious to see who I'd been talking to for so long, so I looked over.

Holy mother of Jesus! It's not some anonymous gentleman, some poor amorphous blob dependent on me for conversation and amusement – it's Dr. Harry Pierson! The same Harry Pierson I had as a psychology professor in college! While the doctors and interns conducted their evaluation and made adjustments to his life-support equipment, I stared at him and tried to sink lower in the bed, tried, in effect, to disappear. I lay here horrified, and pretended I wasn't even in the room.

Imagine my embarrassment at the way I had talked to him! Imagine my embarrassment at the way I had razzed and ridiculed him, this man who had once had such godlike power over me, this man before whom I had cowered! I lay there, stunned. Finally, as the doctors and interns were completing their deliberations, I drew one of them aside.

"Uh, you can leave the curtain open if you want to," I said.

"No, I think we had better return it to the way it was," he replied, in an I'll-just-pat-the-poor-devil-on-the-head-and-get-the-hell-out-of-here tone. He looked at me as though I were morbid and weird.

Around midday lunch came, a lunch I had a hard time dealing with. It was as though a scrim, an inscrutable veil, had been removed between — I can't think of any other way to say it — unconsciousness and consciousness. When the volunteer finally took my tray away, I glanced at the curtain that separated me from my former teacher. I stared at it for a long while and then, gathering up my nerve but feeling rather like a person who is disturbing another's sleep, said:

"I know you can't hear me, Professor Pierson, and I'm sorry for that. Very sorry. It kills me to see you in, uh, the condition you're in. It saddens me to think that life has brought you to this, uh, bend in the road. All of us who are still alive" (and then, catching myself), "I mean, all of us who are not in quite such dire straits as you, hope that your problem is only temporary." (What else could I say?) "But since we're both going to be lying here for a while, perhaps you won't mind if I take advantage of this bit of serendipity by continuing our conversation. Who knows? Perhaps the sound of my voice will have a calming effect on you. Although you can't actually comprehend what I'm saying, perhaps my voice will have a soothing effect on your soul, some inner part of you. Perhaps it will console you to know that there is someone in the room talking to you, and caring about you. You always were a very verbal person, Professor Pierson, at least when you had gotten warmed up" (here, I admit, I chuckled), "and your present indisposition is no reason for our conversation to stop. Indeed, wouldn't it be comforting to think that eternity were a situation like this, and consisted of good friends whiling away the time engaged in pleasant conversation? And if eternity is where we're headed (you, from all appearances, a bit sooner than me), perhaps the sound of my voice will ease the, uh, transition. But it's quite a turnabout, is it not? Given that I was once your student, it's quite a turnabout that you're now the only person I can talk to, or talk at, indeed, lecture. Well, perhaps you're still talking right now in your mind, lecturing to your classes, lecturing *me*, and enjoying the illusion that I can hear you. I hope so."

I sank back in my bed, exhausted. It was not easy trying to say such delicate things... delicately. Then, I confess, I chuckled again. "Just so you don't grade me, Professor Pierson," I said, "just so you don't grade me! You always were a stern grader, you know, and while you may think I've come to class one more time unprepared, I'm not here to pass another test! I'm not a student anymore, Professor Pierson! I'm not wet behind the ears! I'm not just an anonymous person sitting through one of your interminable lectures! So don't grade me!"

There was silence from the other side, of course, but I swear, it seemed to me I could hear Dr. Pierson mulling all this over.

In any case, I again summoned up my nerve.

"I'm going to take the liberty of pretending you can hear

[45]

me," I said. "I'm going to pretend that you're enjoying all this, and smiling inwardly. If it isn't presumptuous, I'm going to treat that hint of a smile I thought I detected on your face this morning, when the doctors were here, as a sign that you might be interested in what I have to say."

Then I stopped. After all, I had no wish to insult the man, I mean insult him further. On the other hand, I knew this life-long seeker after truth would not have wanted me to speak any less than directly and honestly. The problem was, where to begin?

"Where to begin, Professor Pierson?" I said. "I used to think if only I could find the right place to begin, I would at last know how to, well, begin. It seemed to me, even back in college, that if I could only describe, faithfully describe what I saw simply walking around campus – if I did nothing more than start with the trees and the squirrels, the students slouching on lawn chairs during warm weather – the rest, everything I needed, would come to me. At least I would have had a beginning, and although a job begun is only a job half done, I'd at least have had a start."

Was I making any sense? Would he have understood the point I was making... if he could have understood?

"So where to begin? I could tell you a story, I suppose. I could pretend we're two tired and weary pilgrims making our way to Canterbury, or a couple of Italian noblemen riding out the plague in their country villas – you see, I haven't forgotten, Professor Pierson – and tell a diverting story. But do I know any stories?"

It was strange. Now that I had someone to talk to, now that I knew I was in the presence, at least the residual presence, of another intelligent person, I seemed to have become tongue-tied. All my usual verbosity seemed stifled and undermined. Determined, I nevertheless pushed on.

"If I told you a story, would it interest you or bore you? You never did have much patience for chitchat, for jokes and gossip, and in any case, maybe another story is not what you or I — indeed, the world — needs. The world is awash in stories, Professor Pierson. Who cares anymore whether the boy gets the girl, or to be up-to-date about it, whether the girl gets the girl? Or the girl gets the boy? Who cares whether the cops catch the robbers, or whether the terrorists sneak through customs? Or whether one lonely hero, with the assistance of one beautiful woman, saves the entire planet? Or whether.... Well, you see what I mean. Who cares about *individuals* anymore, Professor Pierson? Who wants yet another story about an individual, another sniveling little miniature, another precious little cameo? Sometimes I think someone should write a story without any people in it. A story that contains only furniture. Or empty rooms. That would go over pretty well in *this* room, wouldn't it?

I paused to consider what should come next.

"You see," I went on, "everything is so transitive now, so goal-directed, so set on proving a point. There's nothing like the patient, disinterested dialogue we engaged in back in college" (here, I was trying to atone for my earlier sarcasm), "the inquiry we used to engage in purely for the pleasure of inquiry. Conversation is a lost art nowadays, Professor Pierson, it's more like push and pull, I-think-you-think, it's more like voting. No one asks, anymore, why there is something rather than nothing, everyone just assumes the world and places his particular story in it. Oh, I suppose our cousins across the pond still get down to business, but on this side we're almost congenitally unable to do it. And with all due respect, Professor Pierson, I wish you had told me that. You don't know how much time it would have saved me, and how many blind alleys I might have avoided. We're just too hopeful and idealistic in this country, Professor Pierson, too full of peace and light, too energetic, too much in a rush to get things done. We're no longer comfortable with the undertow, the pull from beneath the surface, we're no longer comfortable with nuance, subtlety, chiaroscuro. And I wish you had told me that. It would have saved me so much time."

I glanced over at the scrim, the funereal veil that separated me from the professor. Was he in agreement with what I was saying, or at least impressed by my attempt to say something at all? Was he pleased that I could still, so to speak, pull rabbits out of the hat, that I could fashion coherent sentences? What was he thinking? That is, what would he have been thinking if he had been thinking?

A nurse came in. She would not have understood that I was engaged in productive conversation, so I did not say anything while she was in the room. But after she left:

"A nurse just came in and changed your dialysis bag," I said. "Like the doctors and interns who were here this morning, she seemed satisfied with your progress. On the other hand, perhaps you knew that. You always *were* more cagey than us students gave you credit for. Just chock-a-block full of things you knew but didn't say.

"But now. A story. A tale. You know, Professor Pierson, sometimes I feel like writing a story that consists of nothing but blahs. 'Blah-blah. Blah-blah-blah. Blahdee-blahdee-blah.'

You know, forty, fifty, sixty pages of 'blahs.' Do you think that would get their attention? No, I suppose no one would pay attention to that, either. Even though my story were so spare and economical, so smooth and predictable, I doubt it would get their attention.

"Ah, but you're a stern critic, Professor Pierson. I know what you're saying. You're saying I'm too caught up in my own mental world, my own cerebrations. I remember you once told me that if I didn't want to get caught in the ant trap, as you called it, of consciousness, I should read history, factual things. But there are too *many* facts now, we're drowning in facts. It's not like the old days. Nowadays the little devils seem to spawn and multiply by themselves, they reproduce faster than rabbits. And my trouble is that I keep absorbing more and more of them, and remembering fewer and fewer. That's what put me in this bed in the first place, that's what got me into trouble the night I fought Jerome Keady. *Facts* are what distracted me." (I paused, and took a breath.) "So maybe someone should teach a course in forgetting, Professor Pierson. Perhaps, working together, you and I could devise a course list. Let's start with, oh let's see, 'Forgetting the Middle Ages.' After that we'll have 'Forgetting the Renaissance.' And after that, 'Forgetting Chemistry.' And for sure, 'Forgetting Psychology.' Oh don't take that personally, Professor Pierson, but didn't you always say our real pursuit is not the world of facts, but the fact of the world?"

There was a noise in the hallway and I was quiet for a minute. Then:

"There's a commotion going on in the hall, Professor Pierson. Shouting, screaming. I think some folks, perhaps an entire family, are having a showdown with their doctor. It's settling down now, but damn, where was I? Oh yes. So I struggle on alone, Professor Pierson, just as you would have wanted me to. And but for my momentary lapse of attention in the seventh round against Jerry Keady, you would have been proud of me. Because what with the assault of the news, all the noise and confusion, the relentless babble, it's not easy nowadays. Sure, there's a clamor of voices that seems almost deafening, but it's hard to pick out of it what matters, what matters most. So much hustle and bustle, Professor Pierson, so much chaos and confusion. Damn! Now they're screaming again in the hallway! If I could only get out of this bed – if only I could move – I'd go out there and take charge of things, settle the score! Still, it's like you used to say. No one seems able to concentrate on one thing at a time anymore, no one seems able to concentrate on the one true thing. Because the truly important thing, you used to say, the most important thing, and the only thing that matters –"

At that instant, as though taking refuge from the argument in the hall, two nurses came in and closed the door behind them. They gave me that suspicious look they always get when they hear me talking. They took my blood pressure and changed my bedpan, not that it needed changing. I think they did it to show their power over me. On the other hand, maybe they were just trying to absent themselves from the commotion in the hall.

"Two nurses just came in," I resumed, when they left. "And do you know what they were talking about? They were talking about two things: what they're going to serve their guests at the Superbowl party they're throwing on Sunday – one was saying she once went to a Superbowl party where the host and hostess left the sound off on the television, can you believe that? – and about their problems with men. Given how distant and aloof you used to be, Professor Pierson, I don't think their conversation would have much interested you. Still, in a curious way you've gotten your wish, haven't you? Because as distant and aloof as you used to be, you can't be much more distant and aloof than you are now!"

For some reason I now found myself growing irritated with Professor Pierson. Here I was doing my best to entertain him, and I was getting no cooperation, no appreciation whatsoever. I know there are a lot of cool cats out there, but I'm not one of them. I'm more like a hungry dog. And when I do my tricks, when I jump through hoops or carry someone's newspaper, I like to be acknowledged, stroked, petted.

"For pete's sake, Professor Pierson!" I burst out. "Loosen up! Relax! Get with it! This is life, after all, and you can't hide from it! You can't control it! People are people! You can't shut them up! If you ask me, when people try to amuse you – as I did with all those papers I wrote in college – the least you could do is respond!"

Eventually I realized I was growing abusive, and regained control of myself.

"Still, there is all that noise to contend with, that noise I referred to. When this great bustling country of ours finally goes to sleep every night, doesn't it provoke in you – even in your condition – a sigh of relief? Don't take this wrong, Professor Pierson, but sometimes I think you're lucky not to have to listen to the noise all day long, you're lucky to have it out of your head, to be oblivious to all the hubbub and confusion."

Were those gunshots I heard? Are they shooting at one another in the hall? Tempers out there are definitely heating up!

"Well, I might as well tell you, Professor Pierson, I might as well say what's on my mind. I have nowhere to go. No place to be. I have no appointments, no schedule. Nelson and Manny haven't come to see me recently — I can't tell if they're playing a game, or what — so I hope you won't mind if I take advantage of our time together, and rattle on. Once I leave this place, after all, I will be back on the streets. *Really* out in the cold. Oh, I neglected to tell you. The injuries I sustained in the ring have effectively put an end to my career as a boxer. Effectively, hell, they have. And while I agree it's no great fun being here, at least we've established a firm bond of friendship, at least it's given us an occasion for fruitful conversation."

Then, while musing about all the things Professor Pierson could have told me in college and didn't, and becoming increasingly annoyed by the racket in the hall, I got really feisty.

"Do you realize I'm having an affair with your wife, Professor Pierson? Do you realize that? If I could get out of this bed, I'd be in *her* bed right now! Furthermore, if I could get out of this bed, I might just hurry over there and give your fact-filled, scholarly body a shake! Rattle your bones! I'd let you *know* what I think about how you sent me into the world ill-equipped and unprepared! In fact, Professor Pierson, if you continue to provoke me, I'm going to pull your plug! I'm going to pull all the tubes and throw all the switches on your machinery!"

Although some kind of fracas involving the police or security guards was developing outside, I willed myself to ignore it and gradually calmed down again.

"Oh, just kidding, Professor Pierson. You know I would never do a thing like that. Because who knows, maybe there'll come a point when they'll have to put an oxygen mask on *me*. Then we can lie here like two astronauts inside glass bubbles, two astronauts studying the switches and meters and knobs around us and sailing into space, merrily flying our spacecraft to...."

"To where, Professor Pierson?"

SIX

Wandering in space, Professor Pierson. We're out here with bubbles, or bell jars over our heads, in a tiny cocoon, a match box with windows and a zillion pinpricks of light shining in. We're sailing through a cold, forbidding vacuum at thirty thousand miles an hour. Lonely out here, isn't it, Professor Pierson? Well, cheer up. At least we have each other. We know how the spacecraft works, we have partial control over its movements, and if we thought about it we might even remember why we signed on for the mission in the first place. If we did that, we might get some inkling of where we're headed.

So here we are, sailing along in a hermetic bullet train, a couple of flyboys on our way to . . . I wish I knew. I play a game in my mind sometimes, Professor Pierson, in which I place myself on the most distant object in the universe. I start on the most obscure and indeterminate object known to man, and work my way back to Earth. At a speed consistent with the magical power I've accorded myself, I make my way inward from the furthermost rim, and back toward objects in the universe that can be identified by our telescopes. When I reach them I pass them and keep on going, always speeding inward. I can see everything as I sail along, it's as though I have a movie camera with me and can film the universe as it comes toward me. I sail through gas clusters and nebulae, sweep past quasars, take the long way — the very long way — around black holes, observe blue giants and white dwarfs — these are not particularly hospitable places so I swerve to avoid them — and eventually I spot our own Milky Way. See it out there? See it twinkling like silver dust, or Christmas tinsel, or a beautiful, delicate necklace? I pause for a moment to savor the sight, then resume my progress inward. Eventually, even though it seems at first no more than a footnote in this whole glittering panorama, I spot our sun, our very own sun. I speed toward it, camera in hand, and eventually discover the few insignificant stones revolving around it: our planets. Some are bigger than others, some have an orange hue, some are blue, some have no color at all. But there is a particular stone that interests me and which, all along, has been my destination. You guessed it, Professor Pierson. I zoom toward it until it gets larger and larger and begins to fill the entire lens of my camera, then, like a streaking meteor, I zoom into its atmosphere. I make a quick appraisal of the continents and land masses I see, I choose the one that particularly interests me, I sweep down through the atmosphere, I choose the city I'm looking for and find the very street I want, I identify the house which, all along, has been my true destination, I swoop into the yard, I fly in through a window, and —

I'm just in time to catch the expression on the face of a little boy whose older brother has spitefully wrenched a toy out of his hand. Do you know that look, Professor Pierson? That incredulous, devastated look that comes just before a five-year-old, realizing the horror and magnitude of what has happened, begins to cry? Well, that feeling, that moment – which will probably remain with the child forever – that moment, for me, began at the outer edge of the universe, and I believe we would have to go that far before we could ever understand it. For what does that look mean, Professor Pierson? In a universe that's billions and billions of light years across, and with all that's going on in it, why did that anonymous child, on an obscure planet near a second-rate star, have to suffer that hurt? Couldn't it have been avoided, Professor Pierson? Couldn't things somehow have been worked out better? Couldn't it have been part of the intrinsic design of toys that they are never wrenched from the hands of those holding them? Indeed, of the nature of brothers and sisters that they never have arguments and disagreements? Tell me, would it really have been so hard to arrange things differently?

I trust you're thinking of an answer for me, Professor Pierson. Well, take your time. I'm in no rush.

Of course, I could have chosen a different house to enter – many different houses. It might have been a case where the mother has just scolded the child, it could have been the look on the face of a teenager whose boy friend has told her he no longer loves her, it could have been the expression on a farm hand who, entering a bank for the first time, realizes that he has no idea how to conduct himself, how to approach the tellers, how to conduct a transaction.

Are you wearing such an expression just now, Professor Pierson? I hope not.

But let's go back to the place where I started out, and again approach the Earth for the first time. I go through the journey I described before, I find the particular city which, since the beginning of time, has been my destination. Attracted by the lights, I veer off toward the sports arena near its center. Miraculously, I sail through the domed ceiling, push my feet forward and skid to a halt, and hover there.

And I'm just in time to see, in the brightly lighted ring below me, a man in shiny red boxing trunks going down before the massive uppercut of a man in black trunks.

Why did it have to be, Professor Pierson? Tell me, if you can, precisely what was the sense of that in this whole far-flung universe? What was the point of a thousand spectators lurching forward, throwing down their cigars, screaming, bellowing, slapping their companions on the back, waving their arms in triumph or frustration? What was the point of their later filing out of the arena, gratified or disappointed, and going home and telling their friends or spouses what they had witnessed, even pontificating about it at the local bar?

We would have to go out to the very edge of the universe, Professor Pierson, to find the answer. We would have to start at the farthest remove, formulate the question there, and slowly, very slowly, come back in. There is no other way, nothing else would be sufficient to give the true meaning of that scene.

But we've learned something, haven't we, dear Professor? We've acquired a feeling for the way the universe revolves around its mysterious center, some point from which every known thing is constantly fleeing. We've gotten a feeling for the way stars gather into nebulae, the way galaxies organize themselves in majestic pinwheels, the way planets circle stars, the way moons revolve around planets. But that's exactly what the so-called experts, our shamans of the moment, discovered: the stuff that comprises the universe – at least our home-grown stuff, the stuff with which we're familiar – organizes itself on a similar model. At the center, they say, is a proton, perhaps coupled with a few neutrons, and swirling around them at dizzying speeds are what they choose to call electrons. But our souls, Professor Pierson, follow the same model. They consist of protons and electrons and neutrons. The proton is the stuff at the center (the ego, they call it), electrons are the stuff that swirls around it (the confusing buzz of consciousness), and neutrons are lumps of the unknown and inscrutable (the unconscious, with its obscure relation to the id). You see, Professor Pierson? Souls are just like matter! We're constructed on the same model as galaxies and solar systems – or silicone or barium or tree trunks. And there you have it, the long-sought, the true unified field theory.

But where does unconsciousness end and consciousness begin? How much of what we call consciousness is secretly unconscious, functioning, how much of the unconscious can, in an instant, be brought into consciousness? Let's play a game. Let's divide up the territory. You be the unconscious and I'll be consciousness. Given the present state of things, that doesn't seem unreasonable, does it? Now, having divided the territory along those lines, how much of my talking about you is really a talking about me? And how much of my talking about me is really a talking about you? I don't want all this to get masturbatory — hell, I couldn't reach it even if I wanted to — but I will say that it's quite pleasant, for a change, to think that you, the erstwhile judge and authority figure, are presently *hors de combat,* and *in flagrante delicto.* It creates so much psychic room, it creates so much room... in the room. The air, suddenly, is clear and transparent. Look at that sunlight flooding in the window! There's nothing here but the two of us, and clear air, propitious — delicious — clean air!

I paused, at this point, to collect my thoughts. Then:

I have another idea. You be the id, and I'll be the ego. No, you be ego and I'll be the *super*ego. After all, you're a mysterious little proton lying there, and I'm a batch of teeming, restless electrons swirling around you. And I have the *privilege* of electrons, Professor Pierson. When I reach a new excitation level, I can make a quantum leap into the next orbit. Zmm-zmm-zmm! Here I am, going faster and faster! I'm orbiting faster and faster, I'm going round and round, I'm revolving!

Oh hell.

What's the use?

All I can think of is that little boy on the verge of tears, that young woman whose lover has told her he doesn't love her anymore, that man who didn't see the gloved hand coming up beneath his chin, and had to retreat to the farthest reaches of the universe to try to understand it.

Professor Pierson? Are you listening to me?

I've hypnotized you, haven't I?

You haven't said anything for the longest time.

I never realized I had so much power.

But honestly, it was never my intention to hypnotize you. I

don't wish to control you, I wish only to be able to say what's on my mind, and have you agree or disagree.

Uh-oh, perhaps I've reasoned it out wrong. Perhaps you've hypnotized *me*. Because I'm the one who's babbling on, I'm the one who's spilling out my guts, and lying here chatting up a storm. Perhaps I've forgotten what drove me to such a state of loquaciousness and verbosity, maybe I'm in a hypnotic trance and don't know it. Indeed, maybe I've lost all contact with the world and am only imagining that you – the actual hypnotist – are unconscious. Scary thought is it not, Professor Pierson? To know that you are cut off from the world, but in your own cut-offness can't even be sure of that? To hear your own voice and wonder where it's coming from? Echoes, maybe it's only echoes I hear. But then, where are the echoes coming from? And all along I thought it was you who were stripped, denuded, and defenseless. Well, perhaps I ought to take a nap. But if I took a nap, I might dream. Is it possible that this *is* the dream, Professor Pierson?

I remember the lecture on dreams you gave, back when. You referred to an experiment in which rats were placed on a wire drum that was slowly being rotated in cold water. The rats couldn't get more than fitful sleep, you explained, because they had to keep scurrying from the part of the drum that was sinking into the water to the part that was emerging from it. The experimenters discovered that young rats learned to sleep in periods of seconds, to sleep even while appearing to be awake, but older rats were too trapped in their patterns to do it. Young rats could go nearly a month before they became disoriented and toppled into the water and drowned, but older rats fell off after two or three days.

Then there was that experiment with cats. Do you remember that, Professor? The experimenters kept prodding the cats just as they were about to drift into sleep and the consolation of dreams. They did this for about two months until the cats became tense, frightened, and paranoid. A year later, the researchers claimed, they could still tell which cats had been included in the experiment, and which hadn't.

The lecture was ostensibly about dreams, Professor Pierson, but all I took away from it was an image of the poor cats. The poor rats. Imagine having to wake up every ten seconds and run to the dry side of a rotating wheel to keep from getting dumped in the drink! Oh, I learned something about dreams, all right, because I dreamt of those cats, and those rats, for days afterward. In fact, I still dream about them. Maybe you should have told us at the beginning of your lecture that its subject was, in fact, nightmares.

Furthermore, did it ever occur to you that the animals might be gods, and humans merely their servants? That we're their subjects, their playthings, *their* pets? Did it ever occur to you that they know and remember who has done what to which of them, who has used them for scientific experiments, who has rendered which of them extinct? When I see a person walking a dog, I sometimes think that the dog is walking the person, that the dog is secretly in league with the other animals, and together they have a clear record of who has been humiliated or maltreated, killed or slaughtered. When a dog struggles over to a tree to take a piss, perhaps it's just a ritual in which he's testing his servant in leash management. When animals, in what they consider an ancient symbolic ritual, run in front of cars, perhaps it's a premeditated, self-conscious act, a willed act of suicide, hara-kiri. When a groundhog runs across your lawn, knowing very well that you have a rifle.... The point, Professor Pierson, is that the animals are just awaiting their moment for revenge. One day they will join forces and gang up on us. I think that with their premeditated façades of docility they're just trifling with us, they're having us on with their so-called instinctual natures. Suppose they're the gods in this whole business! How many gods can you kill? How many gods can you eat?

True, you didn't eat your pepper steak, two weeks ago.

But you see the tricks consciousness plays, Professor Pierson?

Now, getting back to hypnosis. Given that you can quite easily hypnotize a chicken — I grew up on a farm and spent many hours doing it — is it any wonder that there is some confusion about where consciousness begins and where it ends? When you're trying to start your car on a cold morning and the motor won't catch, and you hear the battery beginning to tire from its exertions, don't you try to put a spell on it? Don't you talk to that battery in your mind, pray to it as though it had a life of its own, as though it, too, were conscious and could hear you? Or when you're dismantling something, say a piece of machinery, and you sense that it's going to break rather than come apart cleanly, don't you talk to it, talk to the screws and nuts and bolts that hold it together? Don't you plead with them, curse them, coddle them, address them as though they were dear friends or threatening enemies? And food — my gosh — food! When you're about to cut into a juicy thick steak, don't you enter into a dialogue with it? Apologize to it, say a little prayer over it, give thanks to it — consciously or unconsciously thank the birds or pigs or cows that have sacrificed their lives for you? Finally, can anyone in his right mind look up at the stars on a cold winter night without engaging in a dialogue with them? Is not the sky, on an icy winter night, filled with voices, or at least echoes that one can almost, but not quite hear? So I ask you, where does consciousness end and the world begin?

But it's not you and I who have hypnotized one another, Professor, it's that awful thing up there on the wall. It's creatures from another world who have us under hypnosis, television is only the means by which they do it. (I try to play it quietly so as not to disturb you. Or perhaps, along with the sound of my voice, you appreciate the sound of television, too?) Oh, we think the networks have their headquarters in great, sleek, glass-and-steel skyscrapers, but in fact they're headquartered on other planets, other galaxies, other worlds. The CEOs and station managers, the scriptwriters and program directors, are just stand-ins, proxies, agents of weird, otherworldly powers.

Well, I certainly have gone on today, haven't I, Professor Pierson? Perhaps it's time *I* should lighten up, relax, get a life. So here's a little rhyme for you. I just made this up.

I don't mind the pratfalls and the catcalls, but must you be so deadpan with the bedpan?

Damn.

Where is that bedpan? Will they ever bring the bedpan around?

SEVEN

T hat's all very interesting. So that's what you think, is it?"

The words exploded like a bombshell. Where on earth were they coming from?

I looked up to see if the television was on.

It wasn't.

I looked to see whether someone were at the door.

There wasn't.

And then I stared at the curtain.

"So you've had fantasies about my wife, have you? And you think you can explode the unconscious, do you? Kick it, stomp on it, ridicule it, drag it out of the house, haul it into court, force it to answer questions?"

"Dr. Pierson! What the — !"

I could hardly get the words out.

"Dr. Pierson! Is that you? Are you — ?"

"Am I what?" said the voice, obviously annoyed.

"Are you awake? Is that you ... *talking?*"

"Who'd you think it was, Santa Claus?"

"But I thought you were" — I didn't want to commit yet another blunder — "I thought you were" — I stammered and fumbled — "I thought you were ... on vacation!"

"You call this a vacation? Hell of a vacation."

There was a moment's pause, then he said:

"Would you do me a favor and call the nurse? I'm having a helluva time here."

Stunned, completely nonplussed, I reached down for the nurse-call cord that was draped over the guard rail of my bed, and pushed the button.

A voice on the other side of the curtain mumbled:

"Jesus, I'm hungry."

Eventually a nurse came, and approached me with a what-is-it-this-time look.

"It's not me!" I blurted, pointing at the curtain. "It's him!"

"Ah, another of your little jokes," she said. She looked at me judgmentally, and turned toward the door.

"No! Really!"

"Uh, nurse, could you help me with some of these damned needles and tubes?" Dr. Pierson said.

She caught herself, swung around, and glowered at me. "Look, I don't have time for this. I have patients with serious problems."

Then, betraying a hint of confusion coupled with curiosity, she went to the other side of the curtain.

"And the dialysis machine. And this tube in my nose. I don't think I'm going to be needing them anymore."

I heard her gasp—no, it was more like the shriek of a person in a movie who discovers a dead body. In a flurry of motion, she hurried out of the room and quickly returned with another nurse and two doctors. I heard expressions of surprise, amazement, relief, and eventually the room filled with more doctors and nurses. At first it felt like a funeral gathering—except that this instance the subject was alive and alert.

"I guess I've had enough of this particular dispensation for a while," said the object of all the attention.

Although people came in for the rest of the afternoon to monitor his vital signs, Dr. Pierson—especially after he was given a substantial meal—remained conscious, stable, and even talkative.

Needless to say, I had a lot of backing and filling to do.

"So you were going to pull the plugs on my life-support equipment, were you?" the new, still-unfamiliar voice said after the speaker had had his lunch.

That was the first zinger I had to contend with.

"No, no, Professor Pierson!" I said. "That was just a joke! If you remember I said that, you can also remember I said, 'just kidding'!"

"'Just kidding.' Harrumph."

"And although you can't see it, my leg is in a cast and my arm still has pins in it! I couldn't get out of this bed if I wanted to!"

"You don't have to tell me what condition you're in. I've heard you and the doctors talking about it."

"You heard us talking? You heard...everything?"

"I heard enough. Believe me, I heard enough."

"But you have to realize, Dr. Pierson, that I was just making up stories to entertain myself! I was just trying to keep myself amused! And you *will* remember the charitable things I said, you know, about how perhaps the sound of my voice would soothe you, have a calming effect? Really, I was just trying to keep us both amused!"

"You thought I would be amused by the reference to my 'interminable lectures'?"

"But you have to understand! I was just a college student back then! I was young, naive, and impatient! I'm sure every word of your lectures would interest me – make sense to me – today! Now that I'm grown up, I'm sure I would take from them all the knowledge and wisdom you were trying to impart!"

I felt like I was down on my hands and knees – until I remembered the condition I was in. I was more than backing and filling, I was abjectly apologizing.

"Please, Professor Pierson, have a little sympathy for a young man's immaturity! You know how college kids are! Besides" (here, I was really reaching), "didn't I refer with satisfaction to the 'firm bond of friendship' we had formed? When they pulled the curtain back and I realized who you were, didn't I make it clear that I was genuinely consoled by your presence?"

There was a thoughtful silence, during which I had an inspiration. Instead of trying to duck out of the situation, instead of futilely going on trying to vindicate myself, I would alter my tone and change course. I would try a distraction maneuver. I would throw up a flurry of tinsel and confetti, and try to distract the man.

"Well, for better or worse we're still in this together, Professor. And I'm honestly pleased that from here on, it's going to be a genuine, two-way conversation. I will listen avidly to anything you wish to tell me, or condescend to tell me, and I will try to profit from what you say." (Okay, so I was fawning: still I had a plan.) "But to clear the air, perhaps you'll allow me to tell a story that's a favorite of mine. I think you'll find it relevant to our present circumstances."

There was silence from the other side, which I took to signify assent. I hurried on.

"I once met a man who, to attend the funeral of a relative, made a hasty trip across the country with his wife, in a Winnebago camper. They drove nonstop, each taking turns at the wheel while the other slept. Eventually the routine became automatic. He would climb in behind the wheel while she retreated to the rear and slept, then she would come forward and take the wheel, and he would retreat to the rear. One day – I'm not making this up, Professor Pierson, this is exactly what the man told me – they both found themselves in bed while the camper was zooming down the highway. She turned to him and said: 'Honey, who's driving?'"

There was a pointed silence. I felt like I was still being graded. Or was it *de*graded?

"Don't you understand?" I resumed. "We're in bed together" (catching myself), "we're in *adjacent* beds in an anonymous hospital room, and at the mercy of unknown forces, a huge medical bureaucracy. And although it appears you're going to be released sooner than I am, for the moment, at least, we have to make the best of it."

There was a long pause, then the voice said:

"I suppose you're right."

Sensing that I was on the right course, I tried to consolidate my gains with another tale.

"You're a student of human nature, Professor. Here's another anecdote you may find amusing. In my late lamented career as a boxer, I had an assistant handler named Manny —"

"I know who Manny is."

"You do?"

"Yes. And I can't understand why he and your corner man haven't come to see you. Considering the circumstances that put you here, it seems the least they could do."

(Good. I was gaining the man's sympathy!)

"Well, Manny and I were having dinner one night," I went on, "at a time when I was feeling lousy about myself, and dubious about my prospects as a boxer. Suddenly he pipes up: 'I'll bet you twenty dollars you're going to feel better soon!' Considering the mood I was in and thinking I had nothing to lose, I took the bet. Well, Manny bought my dinner, and I had to confess, I *did* feel better. I forked over the twenty bucks. Now here's the kicker, Professor Pierson. Later I remembered that my dinner had cost him ten."

"Ah, a sucker born every minute."

"Isn't that the truth, Professor Pierson? I was taken in by that one! I was a real sucker!"

"Perhaps, if you weren't so enamored of your so-called 'School of Forgetting,' you would have seen it coming."

(Oh-oh, was I losing ground again?)

"Oh, that was just a little conceit, Professor Pierson. A little fantasy. We both know that schools of forgetting would be impractical, I mean impossible. Believe it or not, I respect knowledge as much as you do. I'm just as much a seeker after truth as you are."

"Well, I'm thankful for that. That does make me feel better."

(Whew! I quickly went on.)

"Furthermore, I can give you a very graphic example of what happens when people don't train their minds, don't keep them exercised and alert. For one thing, their attention spans get shorter and shorter. In fact, yesterday I had the following exchange with one of the nurses' aides."

"I heard it."

"You did?"

"Yes."

"But can you believe it? I said to her, 'does it seem to you nowadays that people's attention spans are getting shorter?' And she said, 'what?' I repeated the question. 'Does it seem to you that people's attention –' 'What?' she interrupted. I tried one more time: 'Are people's attention spans shorter?' And she said – you heard it yourself – 'no. Who won the Giants game?'"

"I agree, it was embarrassing. I'm familiar with the problem, and think I can go you one better. I once went to a lecture at the local library – not the college's rich and lavish library – but the one in town. And this pundit, some sort of self-styled 'alternative therapist,' got up and purported to give a talk on, quote, 'Why No One Can Remember Anything Anymore.' His talk went something like this. 'Why no one can remember anything anymore. That is the subject of my lecture this evening.' He paused and said, 'now where was I?' There was another pause. 'Oh yes,' he said. 'I remember, the building of the Great Pyramid at Giza. The building of the Great Pyramid at Giza began in the year....' Pause. 'No, that's not right.' Pause. 'Oh yes, my subject. Why no one can remember anything anymore.' It was pathetic. As I recall, the poor fellow never did quite find his way to his subject."

I was breathing easier now. The professor and I chatted and reminisced for the rest of the afternoon, and when one of the nurses came in late in the day, he asked her to open the curtain and leave it open.

EIGHT

I wanted to tell him about the parrot, but as he had been all evening, Professor Pierson was musing on the academic life. It was now midnight and the lights were off. We lay there in the darkness like two kids chatting and kibitzing long past their bedtimes. I should report that over several days of conversation during which I continued to make amends and show respect, Dr. Pierson had opened up to the point where we both could say precisely what was on our minds, we had arrived at a salutary state where no subject seemed off limits. Still, I had something that I wanted to talk about, so out of mild frustration I decided to challenge him.

"What is it about the academic life?" I said, drawing on my memories of my college years. "Why, outside the classroom at least, do professors seem so beleaguered, so downtrodden? It would seem that they have everything going for them. They have a secure, if not cushy, environment in which to work, they have institutional protection in the form of a nourishing mother, alma mater, they have time in the summer to pursue their scholarly interests. What's their problem? Why do they seem so unhappy?"

I knew instantly that I had put myself on very thin ice. Fortunately, Professor Pierson seemed not to take it personally.

"Why do they seem so unhappy?" he repeated. "Because in college teaching, no one knows what the rules are, the underlying, bedrock rules, therefore no one is absolutely sure what constitutes success. If you're in business, for example, you can be as high-handed as you want to be, a real son of a bitch, but if the bottom line is profits and you're showing them, you're successful. If a chemist comes up with a new formula, or a scientist invents twelve new procedures and has nine patents to his credit, he's successful. But in the academic world, now that you provoke me to think about it, no one has any great desire to see anyone else succeed. Each can only slog on, do his best, and hope he's getting through to the students. Despite appearances, there's little real power in academia. Unless you're one of the leading lights in your field, a ground-breaker or trendsetter whose example others follow, the only real power you have is over your students. For professors to be in the company of their colleagues is uncomfortable precisely because it reminds them of that fact."

"Still," I asked, "is that any reason why, when they got together, professors always seemed to exude such a hangdog, defeated aura? In the entire recorded history of mankind, has there ever been anything more cheerless than a potluck supper hosted by and for professors? I remember being invited to one as a guest, and they all hunched over their meals as though they thought they didn't deserve them, as though the food might be yanked out from in front of them. There seemed to be an unwritten rule that no one should talk very much. But a party is supposed to be fun! You talk, you laugh, you dance! But no, the professors I knew in college seemed to feel that dancing was somehow unprofessional and beneath their dignity, too much a letting down of their guards. Is there anything more awkward than a professor dancing?" (Careful here, I told myself.) "Oh, the wives and secretaries would dance, they wanted nothing more than to dance. But I used to watch them looking around sadly and forlornly: no one to dance with. Could it have something to do with the fact that professors go from grade school to junior high school to high school to college to graduate school — then turn around and go right back in the classroom? With the result that they spend their entire lives eating institutional food, smelling institutional smells, having institutional conversations?"

(How had I gotten out on such thin ice!)

"Oh, I'll admit those functions are rather gloomy," Dr. Pierson confessed, "but perhaps it's as you said in one of your ramblings. If you're used to lecturing others younger than yourself, the free flow of ideas, the free give-and-take with adults, becomes increasingly difficult to achieve. But I'm not an egghead, I'm certainly not the egghead you made me out to be, so kindly don't tar me with that brush. I can understand your allusions to glass bubbles and spacecraft and the like (by the way, did you notice the amount of womb imagery you used?), but I am not a hard-boiled egg perched in an egg cup. And while I'll agree that, by and large, teaching is one of the few occupations

where no other adult sees you do it – unless you consider
strapping, six-foot-six basketball, and two-hundred-and-eighty-
pound football players adults – it may surprise you to know
that I'm still able to talk to people over the age of twenty-one.
Are you and I not talking? Are we not having a free and open
exchange of ideas? Besides, my research on social stratifica-
tion has given me some insights that have proven personally
useful."

"Such as what, may I ask?"

"For one thing, I've developed a keen nose for the hidden
agenda with which Dr. Clear is running the college."

"Carl Clear – 'Crystal' Clear, we used to call him? Is he still
president?"

"Yes he is, I'm sorry to say. A lot of us on the faculty think
he should have retired years ago, but unfortunately he has
support from certain powerful members of the board of trus-
tees, members who want the college to remain exactly as it was
when they were students. So year after dreary year, he soldiers on."

(I was amazed at how things were going. I rushed to fill the
void.)

"And does he still make those speeches that sound like he's
appearing before privileged subjects, or confronting the world
through a magnifying glass, worse, a monocle? Does he still refer to you as the 'fuckulty'?"

"You remember that, do you? Yes he still does it. He still
calls us the 'fuckulty.'"

"And is Professor Hilbert still teaching in the English Department?"

"Yes he is. He, too, soldiers on."

"I once had dinner with Professor Hilbert at his home – I had somehow tricked him into liking me – and because his wife was away, he took occasion to tell me the most personal, the most intimate things about his life, his gripes and grievances, his frustrations with his work, his secret fears and fantasies. When I passed him on the street two days later, he looked right through me."

"Well, he looks right through me too, though I must say he's become a little less distant lately. Poor fellow. He recently came out on stage at the end of the intermission of some kind of avant-garde play – he's been running the Arts Series – and fumbling, falling all over himself, had to announce that there *wasn't* any intermission, there had been a mistake, the play was over. The audience, apparently not liking what they were hearing, began to hoot and howl. 'You provide the second act, Professor Hilbert! We don't want to go home yet! You do something!' So he started doing a soft-shoe, a cakewalk, an imitation of a music-hall dance. He pretended to have a cane and top hat, at first, then jabbed his forefingers at the ceiling and smiled like Al Jolson. His wife, sitting in the third or fourth row, was trying to get his attention, trying to signal him to stop and get offstage, then began pleading with the professors on either side of her to do something. Finally the kids in the lighting booth took pity on him, and turned the lights down."

"My god, that's unbelievable. And very sad."

"Anyway, it's in the students that I find – or at least used to find – my reward. When they move about in groups, students become something more than the sum of individuals, professors, I'm sorry to say, something less. Students seem eager to know one another and to find out who's who, professors

are always vaguely embarrassed, if not threatened, by one another. Let me tell you, there's nothing more depressing than a
faculty synod. When professors gather in one place, it makes
them feel like the thing they fear being most. Students."

I started to say something about what had happened to me
that afternoon, but Professor Pierson interrupted.

"But even that's changing. The students are so cheeky nowadays. It's not like it used to be. They have no fear, and no respect for their teachers. It's bad enough when they raise their
hands and say things like: 'Professor Pierson, why do we have
to know this?' It makes me want to strangle them, I want to get
a running start, hurl myself into their midst, and strangle them.
I feel like saying: 'Because your parents are spending umpteen
million dollars a year to send you here, and when we're here in
this learning environment, this is what we do. Learn.' Or I
want to mimic them and say: 'Why do we have to listen to
Beethoven?' 'Why do we have to look at Rembrandt?' But no, I
maintain my composure, and try patiently to explain that what
they're learning is part of a liberal, humane education, that education is good for the soul and if the soul feels good it just
might enable them to live better lives. In addition, that people
have studied such things — when they were lucky enough to
have books, and people to teach them — for five thousand
years. Or I want to say: 'Why do you need to know these
things? So that when you're fifty-five and getting paunchy, and
have curly black hairs on your shoulders and back — when
your legs are lined with blue veins and your bathing suit is sagging around your hips — you will still be able to climb the ladder to the high-dive at the local swimming pool and, while
others are watching, walk out to the end, raise your arms

gracefully, and dive with equanimity. Also, so that when you walk through life's swinging doors, for example when you walk into a crowded room, you will be able to do so with complete self-composure.' And if I did say these things, still the little pipsqueaks would sit there and stare at me sullenly so I'd know I hadn't convinced them."

"If what you're saying is true, it sure isn't like the old days. I used to be terrified of my professors."

"Worse than that, my friend, are the ones who try to blackmail you. I had a kid to whom I had given a bad grade approach me the other day, with a twisted smile, and ask when my teaching methods had last been reviewed by the Faculty Review Committee. I told him it had been about ten years and that they seemed pleased with my performance, but that he was welcome to write them a letter if he wished. Another kid, glowering at me, grade in hand, reminded me of the time I got slightly over-served at one of the local pubs, and began acting rather silly; he intimated he was going to tell the administration about it. Hell, the kids can drink themselves into oblivion, if they want, but if a professor loses control, even slightly, it's a mortal sin. And the little tricks and ploys they use. I had one kid who asked if he could delay turning in a paper because his grandmother had died. Later that semester, by coincidence, his other grandmother died. But he forgot to cover his tracks, I guess, because he pulled the same stunt the following year. I asked him, 'is there yet another? Do you have a *fourth* grandmother?' And you'd be surprised at the number of airplanes that develop mechanical problems right at the end of spring break."

I was about to interject something, but:

"It used to be that we could guide the students, run our courses the way we wanted to, run our own shows. Now the students have control over *us*. It's some state of affairs we've arrived at when, in order to fail a kid, you have to get the dean's permission, and when, if you do fail him, he's as likely as not to sue you. Sometimes it seems like I don't deal with students anymore, but corrals full of wild, unruly animals."

Professor Pierson sighed, and I inferred he had reached the end of his reflections.

"Well, that might be a good subject for a psychology paper," I said, with no intent to be funny.

(Oh. I forgot to mention that the cast on my leg has been removed. I can get about now on crutches, although the hospital seems to think I need help in other areas. I haven't been told when I'm to be discharged.)

"I went to my psychotherapist this afternoon," I said. "And if you can believe it, he has a talking parrot."

There was a silence while Professor Pierson seemed to disengage himself from his thoughts. "Well, therapists are people, too," he said finally. "They have private lives. They have a right to their hobbies and personal interests."

"I guess I didn't make myself clear. My therapist has a talking parrot that lives in his office. Sometimes the damn thing even sits on his shoulder during the sessions!"

"Are you kidding?"

"No, I'm not. It sits there on his shoulder and talks. It sat there the whole time, today, and mimicked me. 'My brother, my brother!' it said, at one point. 'My brother got all the attention!'"

"You're joking."

"I tell you, I'm not. 'Oh, don't mind him,' Dr. Huberson said, with an embarrassed laugh, 'he does that all the time.' And he turned to the bird. 'Paradise' – his name's Paradise – 'Paradise, you be a good boy and don't interrupt.' I resumed talking and a few minutes later it shrieked, 'depressed, depressed! I feel so depressed!' I was describing what happened to me the night I fought Jerry Keady, and again the thing began mimicking me. Once again, Dr. Huberson turned to it with a look of disdain, and the goddamn bird leaned over and began nibbling his ear! I waited while the doctor cooed and giggled and said things like, 'you bad boy, you, you're such a ham, you never know when to shut up.' Then, after I had resumed describing my troubles, the parrot began crowing away, putting up a real stink. 'Heard it all before, heard it all before!' it screeched. 'Last line same as the first!' Maybe it thought I was somebody else – apparently it listens to *everyone's* problems – but suddenly it began taking a role in the session, an active role! 'Time to prescribe drugs, doctor, time to prescribe drugs!' it screamed. All the while, Dr. Huberson was turning to the thing and trying to calm it down, literally smoothing its feathers, then turning back to me with an embarrassed laugh and – trying to downplay the interruptions – saying, 'you've really got to hand it to him. Paradise is a very special bird. Sometimes I think he knows more than I do, and I ought to let *him* conduct my sessions. Then I could play hookey, and stay home and clean house, or play golf with my colleagues. But that would be unethical, wouldn't it. And besides, I have no intention of billing this hospital for services I don't provide. Now, where were we?' By the time I got out of there, the parrot was staring at me like it pitied me and hated me at the same time."

"Perhaps you would feel more comfortable if Paradise sat on *your* shoulder."

"Hey, wait a minute, Dr. Pierson! Whose side are you on? I've taken enough abuse in my life, my body is already covered with bumps and scars! I don't need a goddamn bird to sit on my shoulder and put nicks in my ears!"

"Well, at least you're getting your money's worth. You *are* getting two opinions."

"Professor Pierson, I can't believe you're saying this! Really, whose side are you on?"

"Oh, just kidding, as you would say. Just trying to keep it light, just trying to offer a little comic relief during your time of crisis."

NINE

Incredulous, and still irritated by what had transpired at the therapist's office, I thanked Professor Pierson for his conversation, and we fell asleep. I know I fell asleep because I woke up just a little while ago. And I know Professor Pierson fell asleep because I spent much of the night listening to him talking in it.

Because I'm usually a sound sleeper, I don't know whether this is something he has been doing all along or whether last night was an aberration. I only know that I was awakened in the middle of the night and can remember – have the misfortune to remember – some of the things he said. One feels embarrassed when one overhears a person talking in his sleep, one feels like a voyeur, one fears that the talker will embarrass himself. But there I was, wide awake, and I had no choice. Although I'm sure I've scrambled the order, I remember some of the things he said.

"Evil, no place in present scheme of things for evil. Medical model rules it out, psychological model not interested. Finally removed tubes and constraints. Feeling better, breathing better. Yes, finally able to breathe. Classes. Hoping to return to classes soon. In a room with one of my former students. Good-natured, well meaning. But finally a rather silly man. Patent goofball." (Thanks a lot!) "Don't know what his problem is. Tired of talking to him, tired of listening. Theory of cognitive dissonance. Students, do you remember the theory of cognitive dissonance? Studies in schizophrenia. Schizophrenia, by god. Roses are red, violets are blue, I am schizophrenic and so am I. Former student in next bed. For some reason obsessed with Jerome Keady. Right about some things, but unfortunately, in areas where there is no right. Good news is that he's not a guilty character, bad news is that he's not a character." (What the hell did he mean by that?) "Goes every day to therapy, says therapist is his mother." (My mother!) "Says he doesn't put his head on her bosom or anything, that she doesn't hold him, cradle him, that there's no physical contact, she never oversteps the boundaries, maintains propriety at all times. Says nothing like going to the heart of the problem. Kills two birds with one stone." (Oh sure!) "Says doesn't have to do a lot of explaining, doesn't have to go into personal background, she knew what the problem was all along. Pretty new secretary in English Department. Maybe I should learn to dance." (At least he had taken that part of our conversation seriously.) "Put your left foot forward, put your left foot back, do-si-do your partner, do the hootchy-kootchy. Rock of ages, cleft for me, is there any cleavage for me to see. Evil, evil, what to do about evil?"

And so on.

There was a fair amount of twisting and turning while the professor mumbled, but I was able clearly to make out his words. And who should be more irritated, more embarrassed, Professor Pierson for what he revealed about himself, or me for what he said about me? Fortunately, when I woke up this morning – I don't know how much more of this demented speech I missed, but I finally went back to sleep – Dr. Pierson was as genial and talkative as ever, and I decided not to take his rantings personally. If the mind is fundamentally a mess, I reasoned, a swamp full of confused shadows and twisted vegetation, it shouldn't be surprising that some lurid forms should occasionally emerge from the swamp. No, I decided not to take his comments personally. In fact, I was fascinated by some of the subjects he alluded to during his nocturnal ruminations, and when the occasion seemed right, I brought up the subject of evil.

Professor Pierson looked at me, startled, he looked at me as though I had peered into his mind – which, in a sense, I had.

"Evil?" he said. "Oh, until recently I've never given it much thought. It doesn't seem to play much part in our present-day world views, does it? A person with my cast of mind, who likes to codify and order things, and study what is measurable, has a difficult time with concepts like evil. It seems to me, nowadays, that when we think about evil, we know vaguely what we're referring to, but we tend to think it's something that existed in the past; we are aware only of its murky, unpleasant echoes. Nowadays, we treat it as something that can be reduced to, and treated by psychological, therapeutic, or even pharmaceutical processes. And while I'm a professor of psychology, I would admit that that's not always a good thing. In a sense, I suppose, we've reduced all the great moral problems to psychological ones. We think that beneath so-called moral problems there's always a parent, a sibling, or a situation to blame; moral problems get reduced to circumstantial ones, financial ones, prudential ones. Nowadays, it seems, even war is just a political, procedural difficulty. Beneath the grand notions, the notions that guided men for thousands of years, there simply isn't the bedrock there used to be."

I was musing on these thoughts when, out of the corner of my eye, I noticed an image of a boxing ring on the television set, mounted on the wall. The sound was very low and, apologizing for the interruption, I asked Professor Pierson if it would be all right if I turned it up.

"Sure. Go ahead," he said, a little surprised that I wasn't responding to his comments.

I reached for the remote on the bed stand at my side, and pressed the volume button. I couldn't tell what was going on, at first. In the boxing ring, limbering and loosening up in opposite corners, were two well-dressed, slightly overweight ladies. One was wearing a print dress and holding a red purse, the other was decked out in a formal evening gown. Although her ostentatious necklace sparkled under the bright lights, the fact that she was wearing flats, not high heels, compromised the aura of refinement she apparently intended. The two women looked fidgety, anxious, and querulous.

Then came the announcer's voice.

"Good afternoon, ladies and gentlemen! Welcome to this world-championship fight, this world-championship . . . kvetch-off!" (Did he really say that?) "We're here at Taunton's Grand Arena to determine who will be the world's greatest kvetch! We'll get under way with this verbal battle, this sally of criticism and complaint, in just a moment, but first — No! Wait! I can't believe it, ladies and gentlemen! The lady in the print dress apparently doesn't like the lights! She's complaining about the overhead lights! She's talking to the master of ceremonies, and pointing at them, gesticulating! She doesn't like the lighting arrangements! I tell you, ladies and gentlemen, I've never seen anything like this! Now she's going after the referee! She's pointing at the referee, she's saying she's not satisfied with the referee! Can you believe it? She's fought all the way to this championship kvetch-off, and now she doesn't like the set-up! The fans are booing, and I don't blame them! In all my years at ringside, I've never seen anything like this! What? Now she seems determined that the match not even get started! And now — this is incredible — she's going after the referee in person! She's swinging her purse at him! Well, she had better not hit him with it, because there's no physical abuse allowed in this sport! But she's criticizing him to his face, she's telling him what she thinks of him! I wish the master of ceremonies would hold that microphone closer so we could hear what she's saying, because she's really letting the referee have it! Can you believe this? I certainly don't! But now — I swear, I've never seen anything like it — the referee's pronouncing her... the winner! Before the match has even begun, ladies and gentlemen, he's pronouncing her the winner! He's trying to hold up her arm — but she's not having it! He's trying to declare her the winner, and she's *still* complaining! I don't know what the official judges are going to say about this! Oh no, now she's leaning over the ropes and talking to *them*! She's already won the match, and even that's not good enough for her! She's complaining to the judges! Naturally her opponent is upset, and now she's —"

"Do we really have to watch this?" said Professor Pierson. "This is sickening, disgusting. Could I ask you kindly to change the station, or at least turn the sound down?"

Obligingly, I went him one better. I turned the television off.

"My therapist says I have to get my aggressive instincts under control, but something like that really brings them out," I said. "I probably shouldn't tell you this, but there was a point, early in my career, when I went to a sports psychologist to try to figure out why I wasn't making better progress as a boxer."

"That sounds like a reasonable thing to do. What was the result of your visit?"

"He made me really angry. I beat him up."

There was a silence that strongly connoted disapproval. Then:

"It sounds to me like you need help in more ways than one."

"Oh, but I would never do that now," I said, hastening to explain. "You have to understand that in boxing, as in the military, they train you to be aggressive. The trouble is, too many people, when they get out of the military, never get, so to speak, debriefed. I'm happy to say that my time here in the hospital is finally giving me a chance to get debriefed."

Dr. Pierson glanced at me approvingly, as though he hoped I meant it.

"Obviously, we can't take out our aggression on everyone around us," he said. "Society simply can't function that way.

Some, even many things have to be stifled, stymied, reined in, that's the only way people can get along with one another. And when you have two good-looking women brawling in a ring, you know things are out of control. On that note, I have a little fantasy about something I call 'The President's Council on Rage and Repression.' Would you like to hear it?"

"Of course I would."

"In my fantasy, the Council would give an award each year. The announcement would go something like this. 'The President's Citation for Repressing Rage goes, this year, to Bob Mulligan' — we'll call him — 'a steel worker from Pittsburgh, Pennsylvania. Bob lost his job in February and had his car repossessed in June. He found out that his wife was having an affair with a bisexual hairdresser, and that his youngest son was stealing drugs from the local pharmacy. A project Bob had worked on for some years, an intricate three-masted sailing vessel constructed inside a glass bottle, fell off his workbench and was destroyed.'"

I looked at Professor Pierson in amazement. Where was all this coming from?

"'But Bob did not get angry,'" he went on, "'Bob repressed it, held it in. Through all these misfortunes Bob remained a committed family man and faithful churchgoer. Furthermore, he retained his reputation in the community as a man with a ready smile and a natural willingness to do a person a favor. At six-foot-three, two hundred and seventy-five pounds, Bob is well-equipped to take out on the world any hostility he might feel. But Bob Mulligan is not that kind of man. Bob has continued to be what he always was, a decent, quiet American, and he stands before us today as an example that the President's

Council on Rage and Repression can commend to all Americans. And so, Bob, congratulations!'

"There would be a burst of applause, then Bob would step forward to the microphone.

"'Thank you, thank you very much, ladies and gentlemen. It's true I been dealt a pretty lousy hand lately, and I know I could get kind a' angry. I know that. I could be bitter, 'ril bitter. But that's not my way. Like that fella that's been foolin' with my wife. I could a' gotten my huntin' rifle and wasted him, I'm tellin' you wasted him. 'Cause I know who the motherfuck is. Uh, excuse my language. But damn straight, I know who the motherfuck is. I'm no goddamn fool, I know what's goin' on. I could a' gotten my rifle and blasted his fuckin' face to smithereens. But I didn't 'cause that's not my way. And then, about my son. I could easily have taken 'im down in the basement and fed 'im to the alligators. That's a phrase we use around the house, heh-heh. Or I could a' smashed up that car I bought 'im, smashed it up good. In fact, when I think about what's happened to me in the past coupla years, I could wrench this microphone right outta this wooden stand and crush it between my two hands. But that's not my way. On the other hand, I'm tellin' ya, don't any of y'all be messin' with me. So, in conclusion....' Well, as you would say, I think you get the picture."

What a ham Professor Pierson had turned out to be! Was he mimicking me, showing me he could give tit for tat, and proving once and for all that he was not just a stodgy professor? Or after what he had been through, had he simply decided there was no use keeping up egghead pretenses anymore? In any case, what a long way we had come in our relationship!

"That's quite a sketch, Professor Pierson," I said, laughing. "That's something you should take into the classroom."

Then I remembered it was time for my therapy. Hauling myself out of bed, I grasped my crutches. Although I was walking much better now, I took them as a precaution. I could never tell when the pain and muscle weakness might return.

"Well, ta-ta," the professor said, as I banged my way out of the room. "Have a good session."

When I returned an hour and a half later, I was not exactly in the most tranquil state of mind.

"So how did it go?" the professor asked, putting down the book he was reading. He seemed genuinely interested.

"This time I went in there armed," I said. "I've been working on countermeasures. I tried mimicking the parrot. I decided I simply wasn't going to stand for it anymore. Every time the parrot opened its mouth to say something, I interrupted with my personal version of parrot-speak. 'Neurosis, neurosis, even birds suffer from neurosis!' I squealed, in a carping, high-pitched voice. 'Birds should know their places! Birds should know when to be quiet! All birds do is poop and peck at themselves!' The bird, I must say — I'm pleased to say — looked totally confused; it was practically cross-eyed. It scrabbled down Dr. Huberson's arm, perched on his wrist, and squinted up at him as though trying to decide whether *it* needed therapy. I sat there in triumphant silence for a long while, and finally Dr. Huberson looked at me like I was fucking up his bird, messing with his brain. 'Now if you'll *both* be quiet,' he said, 'perhaps we can continue.' For the rest of the session, that bird glared at me like I was one tough customer; I think it realized it had finally met its match. The problem was, it took me a long time to regain my normal speaking voice. For the rest of the session, I talked in a sort of carping, high-pitched squeal. I hate to say it, but I seem to have developed a desire to talk like a parrot."

"Well, you seem to be talking in a normal voice now."

"Yes, that's because I've finally come to my senses. My little triumph has made me feel better about things, myself, the world. Still, I'm a bit put out by Dr. Huberson's saying that, next session, he's going to bring me birdseed."

"Oh, he can't have meant it. Don't you think he was being facetious?"

"I certainly hope so, because I would much prefer that things get back on an even keel."

TEN

Then one day, I don't know how long afterward—the days had begun to blur and melt into one another—he was gone.

I woke up, one morning, to find the bed next to me empty. I was alone in the room.

When had he left? During the night? Early in the morning, while I was still asleep? Had he purposely timed his exit so that I would not notice it?

He never even said goodbye, I thought, sadly.

I felt abandoned, deserted, I felt like a child who has been left alone for the first time at summer camp.

Curiously, I also felt like a new person.

Then, for the first time, I heard — really heard — my name.

"Good morning, Professor Pierson! How are you today?"

Cheerful as ever, one of the nurses — the beautiful Valerie — burst into the room.

"Would you like me to open the blinds?" she said. "It's a beautiful sunny day."

"Yes, that would be nice," I replied. "I'd like that."

"Dr. Fried says you've been making excellent progress with your therapy."

I was never told why, but one day it was announced that Dr. Huberson had left the hospital, and that my case was being taken over by a Dr. Mary Fried. When I showed up at the usual office, one afternoon, there she was, a pretty, pert, and incisive woman sitting in the chair. I got along very well with Dr. Fried, and credit her for getting me through the mental breakdown I had suffered.

"She's a very compassionate woman," Valerie continued, bustling about and arranging things on my bedside table. "She understands when people are going through a bad patch in their lives, and need a little re-tuning."

"Yes, she's helped me immensely," I said. "I was in a heck of a condition when I arrived here, I can tell you. Not only that, but the numbness has gone out of both my arm and leg."

"Well, you can be pleased with yourself. You've done the work, and now you're to be discharged."

"I am?"

"Yes. Didn't Dr. Fried tell you? You can go home today."

"Gee, I was beginning to like it here."

"Now don't start."

"Oh, I'm just kidding. I'll be glad to get back to the normal, workaday world, and be with, uh, normal workaday people. You can't imagine the hell I've been through."

"You think I can't? You think you're the first person with

mental issues I've cared for on this ward? Of course I can imagine it! Just be thankful you've made a good recovery! But Dr. Fried wants you to continue to take your medication, and she wants to see you again in two months."

I was being released. I could go home.

I was in shock.

"To think," I said, "the day we've all been waiting for. I guess you're happy I'll no longer be a thorn in your side."

"Oh, you haven't been a thorn in my side, Professor Pierson! In fact, you're one of the few patients on the ward with a sense of humor."

"Still, I'm afraid I haven't been very cooperative, and I know I haven't been very appreciative. I thank you and the other nurses for your good care, and especially for all the days you escorted me around the grounds."

"You weren't in any *condition* to be cooperative, or appreciative. That's why they brought you here. Anyway, you don't have to thank me. It's my job."

"Still, I thank you."

"Okay, I accept."

"And will you tell the other nurses?"

"Yes."

After a few more pleasantries, Valerie bustled out of the room.

As I lay there with my last meal, my last hospital meal in front of me, I thought about my many sessions with Dr. Fried, and how, together with the medications she prescribed, she raised me out of the depths of despair. It was the phrase she gave me – she called it a mantra – that helped as much as anything.

"Take a cue from your name," she said. "Pierson. I. Person. I. Person, I *am* a person. I have great inner resources, great inner strengths. My wholeness comes from deep within.' Above all, make this your mantra: 'I am a person.'"

While in bed, or walking around the hospital grounds, I did say that to myself. And it helped a lot. Yes, I give Dr. Fried a lot of credit. She was incisive, all right, and never let me get away with anything.

"You've got to stop calling your mother the 'ring girl'!" she said, at one point.

"Is it all right if I call my *wife* the 'ring – ?'"

"No! No! Stop! Wait a minute! Women were not put on Earth to encircle, surround, and engulf men! Isn't it time you became a little more mature in your attitudes toward women?"

"But marriage does require a ring."

"Fine, I understand that. But stop using that expression. It's unbecoming for a man of your stature. Anyway, this has nothing to do with the crisis that brought you here. You should be looking to your wife for support, at a time like this. She was with you the night of the party, wasn't she?"

"Yes."

"So tell me again. What happened?"

It was the most awful night of my life, and what I did was the most foolish thing I've ever done. But in order to get me to "face up to my feelings, confront my emotions," Dr. Fried insisted that I recount the experience one more time.

"Well, we were at a dinner for a group of professors," I explained. "Actually, it was just a potluck. And Jerome Keady was there."

"The infamous Jerome Keady? The Jerome Keady who denied you tenure?"

"Yes, the Dr. Keady who heads the Tenure Review Committee. I swear, that man is positively evil. He took a dislike to me from the day I arrived at the college, and did everything he could to block my advancement. Then, as head of the Tenure Review Committee, he used his power to see that I was denied tenure."

"How do you know that?"

"I heard it through the academic grapevine. One of the other professors, a man who actually likes me, told me how the procedure had played out. He told me he voted for me, but the other people on the committee had had their arms twisted by Dr. Keady."

"Okay, so you're at this potluck supper. What happened?"

"Well, needless to say, I had been very upset — more than upset, at wits' end — ever since I got news of the decision. I went over and confronted Keady in a corner — I think we both had plates in our hands — and we began to have, as they say, words. The next thing I knew, I had put my plate down, he was doing likewise, and I began poking him in the chest."

"And then?"

"He began jabbing back. We didn't get into a fistfight or anything, but we were about to. The full magnitude of the humiliation I had suffered suddenly welled up, hit me all at once, and overwhelmed me. I hauled back — I was all set to take a swing at him, I was actually hoping for a knockout punch — the ladies in the room started screaming, the men came over and tried to restrain me, and then...."

"And then?"

I had come to the most difficult, the most humiliating part of my story.

"Well, I lost it. I completely lost it. I began talking incoherently, babbling. I was shaking my fists at the ceiling, at the world I suppose, and babbling on, making no sense at all. They tried to calm me down, but it was no use. I felt I had been dishonored and disgraced, that I was through, finished, washed up. And at that moment, even though incoherent, I knew what I had to do, I knew there was no way out, no recourse. My wife apologized to everyone and we left. I instructed her to bring me...here."

"And do you still think the punch was laced with something other than alcohol? Isn't that what you said before, that you thought somebody had put drugs, or something, in the punch?"

"They must have, or why would I have flipped out?"

"Because of the traumatic nature of the news you had received! Don't you think that was a serious enough blow to your ego—your entire being—to make you, as you say, 'flip out'? I've known people who've 'flipped out' over far less important things."

"But you have to understand, I've always prided myself on my self-control. I'm a psychology professor, after all. I have a fair understanding of human motivation, and the way the mind works."

"Yes, but even you, Dr. Pierson, are human. And it is precisely the things we think we have most control over that are likely to fester and bubble beneath the surface, to roil and churn with their own agenda, their own imperatives, and then, when we least expect it, erupt like a volcano."

"That describes what happened to me, all right."

I suppose I didn't have to say what I said next, but I did. I suppose it was a measure of the trust I placed in her.

"Dr. Fried, you've been forthright and honest with me, so I'm going to be completely forthright and honest with you. Do you remember when I said that Professor Hilbert came out on stage during what he thought was an intermission, and had to announce that it *wasn't* an intermission, the play was over, and proceeded to make a fool of himself?"

"Of course I remember."

It pained me to say it, but I had committed myself.

"Well, it wasn't Dr. Hilbert from the English Department. It was me. It was I who came out on the stage that night and, fumbling, falling all over myself, announced that the play was over. So I'm not the greatest public speaker in the world: I thought I was making a contribution to the college by running the Arts Series, I thought it would provide a foil for my scholarly pursuits and make me more likable to the students, more accessible, less stuffy. So I goofed up. I was busy taking care of things backstage, and never even had a chance to look at the program."

"I see."

"But tell me, Dr. Fried, did that justify my faux pas being reported on the front page of the campus newspaper, so that for the next six weeks I was the laughingstock of the entire college? I can assure you it didn't do much for the level of attention in my classes — not to mention the enrollment level in succeeding semesters."

"Oh, I doubt you were the 'laughingstock of the entire college.' As usual, you're being too sensitive. The kids probably just thought it was funny, and I bet it endeared you to more of them than it offended. They saw a side of you they hadn't seen before, a playful, funny side. Anyway, people forgive. And time passes. I think you should get over it, you should stop worrying about it."

"Okay," I said, with a sigh of relief. "If you say so."

"I do say so. And it's one less thing for you to talk about. I understand you've finally stopped talking to yourself."

"You couldn't prove it by me," I said, with a laugh. "But if that's what you've heard, I guess it must be true."

As I lay in bed and thought about all this, it seemed that my recovery had had an element of prayer about it, that in Dr. Fried's efforts to return me to wholeness there had been not only love, but prayer. Prayerful love. Loveful prayer. Then I caught myself. Prayer to what? Science? Psychology? Hardly. Our prayers, nowadays, hardly seem to reach to the rooftops, much less the tops of skyscrapers; it's hard to believe they penetrate the clouds. The canopy is so low that we can hardly raise our voices, hardly talk in more than whispers. Instead, we sit and converse horizontally with trained professionals, as helpful as they are. But could it be that all our speaking, all our thinking, constitutes prayer? Whether or not there's anything or anyone to pray to, maybe prayer is essential to us in and of itself. If only we could let down our guards and admit that, consciously or unconsciously, we're constantly praying, think how much better we'd feel. We could admit to our insatiable, unquenchable desire to know the meaning of the world and of our lives, our indomitable hope that things will get better, our refusal to give up hope. We could admit that whatever horizontally conducted conversation can do for us, we also have the option of living vertically. We could perhaps, at last, stand up.

I set the remains of my meal on the tray table and began gathering up my belongings. I went to the pay phone in the hall and called my wife and surprised her with the good news. As the hospital is situated in a busy cul-de-sac, she agreed to pick me up on a nearby corner. I said goodbye to the other nurses who were on duty, and thanked them, and still in a bit of a daze walked to the elevator. Feeling like a new person, someone markedly healthier and better than my old self, I ambled across the lobby and pushed through the revolving door. When I reached the sidewalk, I paused and rejoiced for a moment at being back in the world again. Was I humbled? Yes I was humbled. But I knew, knew beyond doubt, that I would return to teaching. Teaching is my first love, after all, and Jerome Keady notwithstanding, what I'm good at. Furthermore, when one is in the actual process of teaching, the question of tenure, job stability, is totally irrelevant.

Carrying my belongings in the bag the hospital provided, I loped up the street toward the corner. As I did so, I passed a sidewalk fruit stand.

Sometimes an apple is just an apple, I thought.

When, after a few minutes, my wife arrived, she could not imagine why I was laughing.

STORIES

PREFACE TO SOMETHING IMPORTANT

If you were searching for a metaphor, you could describe it as two armies approaching one another on a vast plain, two cumbersome, unwieldy armies plodding slowly, blindly, forward toward one another with all their wagons and weapons, shields and rams, supplies and provisions. The gradual convergence of the two armies would be discernible, at first, only in a vague shimmering, a hazy trembling in the air; then a muffled rustle and clamor would produce two billowing clouds of dust. Presently you would hear the clinking of armaments and gear, the rumble and squeak of iron-clad wheels on wooden axles, the creak of stirrups and cinches, the snapping of whips and reins, after that the sound of horses and wagons bumping and jostling through the pits and gullies, rocks and stones. Eventually you would hear the lumbering sighs of the soldiers themselves, the whinnying of the horses and swishing of their tails, the exhortations of their commanders, fierce and defiant on their mounts, giving orders, shouting encouragement. Were you to elaborate your metaphor, you might describe the expressions on the faces of those commanders, their excitement over the impending battle, their pride in their training and experience, their obvious relish for the pursuit of glory.

As the two armies caught sight of one another and began adjusting their movements accordingly, you might want to pause and consider the factors that led to the engagement, the factors that produced this tragic (or depending on your point of view, heroic) joining of forces. You might want to describe the negotiations that had been carried out during the preceding months, or describe how secret agendas had determined the outcome of those negotiations; you might want to show how, in the end, words had proven insufficient to reconciling the differences between the two sides. If you were to do this, you would want not only to describe the declarations and pronouncements made publicly, but the unconscious motivations which, unbeknownst to the protagonists themselves, had influenced their arguments and strategies. This digression (which would not in fact be a digression, because so pertinent to the events at hand) might lead you to investigate the opposing leaders' personal backgrounds, the manner in which they had been raised, their parents' attitudes and influence, the presence or absence of siblings. If you were to pursue this inquiry, you might uncover many dark, irrational factors which, quite beyond the conscious realization of the opposing commanders, had led to the present impasse; indeed, you might be able to show that the entire battle originated in trivial instances of blindness and illusion, stubbornness and willfulness, ignorance and jealousy. You might even be forced to admit that the protagonists, had their attention been called to these factors, would have used their powers of fiat to proceed in spite of them.

If pursued to its logical conclusion, this examination of the opposing commanders' personal histories would entail a description of the cultures from which they derived, in which, *in vitro*, as it were, they had been nurtured and sustained. It would include background investigation of class and race, family structure and social position, political belief and private superstition, above all, of religion. For it is likely that religion would play a major part in the clash of world views that specific soldiers, with specific weapons and armaments, were about to undertake. In the end it would be all these things — personal, familial, societal, and religious — that would form the background and *causa belli* of the impending engagement.

Having been so attentive to backgrounds and antecedents, you might want to pause, at this point, and reflect on the tragedy and heartbreak you know, know assuredly, is coming, on the other hand you might consider such a task beyond you or consider it, by virtue of your role as historian and disinterested observer, unnecessary. In any case, were you to describe the moments of anguish and brutality, pain and misery, you would also be obliged to describe the moments of ingenuity and inventiveness, tenderness and heroism, of dashing elegance and proud nobility.

Having traced to its origins the entire record of misunderstanding — the thwarted expectations, the misappraisals of the other side's intentions, the overestimation of factors later found to be trivial, the blindness to factors later found to be crucial —

having described the failures of the past to be requited, the honor waiting to be avenged, the hidden agendas of which only the opposing commanders were aware — you might want to admit that the battle you were about to describe was not tragic, but sweet: sweet because inevitable. You might be forced to admit that the protagonists, as they contemplated the impending siege, would not have countermanded or aborted it even if they could, indeed, would not have had it any other way. Finally, you might be forced to admit that the armies of the two sides considered the battle not a battle in the true sense of the word, but only what humans do.

You *could* say or do all these things, but you need not.

It was only, after all, a man and woman meeting and deciding to fall in love.

VOYAGE TO A NEW WORLD

T he first thing I sensed, as we approached the new world, was that it was going to be very much as I expected it to be, and at the same time very different. Nothing more exhilarating has ever happened to me than standing at the rail of that great ship and watching it ease slowly into the harbor of my destination; I was nearing the long-awaited moment of truth, and soon the truth would be revealed. But would the old part of the city be as beautiful as the travel books depicted it? Would the people be as friendly, the city itself as dangerous, as the travel guides suggested? Would the capital, and the country of which it was a part, be as saturated with history, and *reveal* their history, as readily as my information indicated? Would the food, the wine be as memorable?

I am the kind of person who likes to derive maximum benefit from his travels, so I had done a considerable amount of background reading before setting out on my journey; having plenty of time on the passage over, I had continued to read on the ship. On the ship, however, I was still surrounded by my own countrymen, at least mainly my own countrymen, so there was not yet anything truly new and foreign to experience, there was as yet little to surprise me. I found that vaguely irritating, because as hungry as I was for new experience, while I was on the ship it was almost as though I had never left home. It was as though the owners and employees of the cruise line wanted to *ensure* that the passenger feel like he had never left home. The entertainments and diversions were so wholesome, so generic, as to be almost irritating, and the food, although good, was talked about so incessantly that dining seemed almost a fetish, not the routine act of providing sustenance for one's body but a keenly awaited, pseudo-sacred ritual. And the folks who dressed up for the evening meal: I am astounded at the number of men who brought tuxedos on the voyage. Of what earthly good were tuxedos going to be in the country to which we were headed? And the women who brought evening gowns: were they doing anything more than showing the rest of us that they were people of substance, worldly people or, to put it accurately, people with money? Some, perhaps, had acquaintances in the new country with whom they could store their finery, but when we disembarked, weren't the great majority of us going to be reduced to improvising, thinking on our feet, looking over our shoulders as we tried to get the hang of things? To living with sharply focused, heightened senses as we navigated cities, roads, and crowds that were new, foreign, and unfamiliar? Of what earthly good were tuxedos and evening gowns going to be, when simply managing the necessities of life would be a constant struggle and the last thing one would want to do would be to stand out?

The willfully innocent atmosphere in which our passage took place was epitomized by the movies that were shown every night, and the lavish extravaganzas that were staged. The latter, great charivaris of noise, glitter, and confusion, aspired to the grand effects of Las Vegas floor shows, but there was something disheartening, even depressing, about the way they inevitably fell short. It's not that the singers and dancers weren't talented, rather that the themes of the shows (the thrill of being in love, the importance of friendship, the excitement of traveling to new worlds) were so predictable, noncontroversial, and middle-of-the-road that they invariably came off as Pyrrhic victories. I suppose it was necessary to present shows that were suitable to children as well as to adults but, if truth be told, that meant they were geared for, and directed at twelve- and fourteen-year-olds.

Speaking of which, there was a shuffleboard court and Ping-Pong table for the kids, though owing to the boat's motion the kids seemed to spend a lot more time ball-chasing than ball-*pinging*. At least someone had the foresight not to install pool tables. There was also a tennis court, and a workout room and massage parlor: anything to keep the passengers busy, busy, busy, anything to keep them distracted.

One evening I went to a magic show in the main auditorium. Unfortunately the magician had all but lost his voice, and didn't have the stage presence with which to make something of the fact, or exploit it as an element of his act. And when he got someone up on stage who inadvertently kept giving him straight lines, he had no capacity whatsoever for capitalizing on them. Worse, he had succumbed to a fatal flaw that can sabotage any magic act: he was *too* good. When he had a blindfolded passenger open a book at random, place her finger on a phrase, remove the blindfold and read it to the audience – then turned a blackboard around to show that the identical phrase was inscribed upon it – he fell into the trap of what magicians call the Too Perfect Syndrome. Any person with a sound mind over the age of twelve would have realized that without some sort of skullduggery, flim-flam, there was absolutely no way he could have produced this so-called bit of magic. The blackboard, mounted on a stand, had originally been turned away from the audience and, contemporary magic effects being tremendously sophisticated, a backstage confederate would only have had to listen as the woman pronounced her phrase, write it on a pressure-sensitive tablet, and transfer it to the blackboard via the wire that ostensibly supplied power to its clip-on light. I can think of other ways the effect could have been accomplished, but it does not bode well for magic when audiences aren't giving themselves over to surprise and amazement, but ruminating on the ways an impossible effect has been achieved. If that weren't sufficient to rob one of pleasure in the act, seeing the magician lumbering around the deck, every day, without a shirt, and in short pants and flip-flops – or splashing and cavorting in the swimming pool – destroyed the mystique once and for all.

If the stage shows weren't enough to give the passenger the feeling he had never left home, the movies that were shown were the *coup de grâce*. What sadness I felt at being at sea, five hundred, then a thousand, then two thousand miles from home, and watching small-time cops chasing small-time criminals around this or that innocuous city, or watching lovers talking quietly in bed while the boat swayed and rolled and the motors rumbled beneath me. The movies were time out of time, a mesmerizing distraction from the real adventure I was taking part in, an element in an overarching philosophy that said that at all costs, the passenger must be shielded from boredom. Boredom! Here, I was on one of the greatest ocean liners in the world, a technological marvel of which I would have given anything to have had a complete tour – and without which, my curiosity and fantasies only increased – and I was being routinely seduced into a tumbling, rolling Plato's Cave, and massaged with dream images. After sitting through one of these mass-consumption dreams, it was always a relief to go up on deck and smell the air and water, to observe the stars or distant lightning, or see the moon laying down its glistening triangle in the water, its twinkling, cheerful fan.

But the greatest affront to my sense of adventure, during the passage, was the casino. Here, amidst a steady drone of electronic noise (designed, I suppose, to make the gamblers feel something very exciting were happening, or were about to happen), people stared with dull, glazed eyes at screens filled with dancing fruit and, robot-like, pushed buttons or pulled levers in hopes that if not the last or the one before, the next push or pull would cause a torrent of nickels to rain down. Then, instead of talking about the excitement of voyaging to a new world, they could spend the rest of the trip telling their friends how they had won perhaps half a day's expense in that new world. If anything could, the people at the craps, roulette, and blackjack tables seemed sadder. I imagine that each of these folks kidded himself into thinking he had a measure of control over his destiny, but with stone-faced impassivity, night after night, the dealers and croupiers, sweeping the real profits into slots in their tables, faithfully perpetuated the reality that the house always wins. It amazes me how little gamblers want to believe, or admit, that the house, even if it's a boat – a boathouse – always wins.

So it was primarily in the bars and lounges of the ship – and there were many – that I kept my sense of adventure alive. Here I met people who were as curious about our destination as I was, and people who were interesting in their own right. (The most interesting people, I've found, are always night owls.) Here I heard stories and pieces of autobiography that fascinated me, and shared both my knowledge and my ignorance about the country to which we were headed. One of the reasons I found the experience so refreshing was that I didn't have to hold back, as it were, because I didn't have to drive home. The bars and lounges became an intimate part of my world, my house – or rather, I became an intimate part of theirs. At the end of the evening – I enjoy bars so much that I invariably stay till they close – I had only to find the elevator that provided the most direct route, then navigate the endless hallway – it always seemed endless, no matter which elevator I chose – to my cabin. Navigate is perhaps too fancy a word: in my case, there were no twists or turns, I could go only forward or backward, forward or aft, in a corridor that seemed as long as a football field and in which I could see, from one end to the other, lines of anonymous doors. If one isn't traveling first class, with a cabin on the upper decks, and I wasn't, having to trudge past an endless line of doors, while knowing one's own is no different from all the others, is quite dispiriting. One has spent the day being pampered and catered to, wined, dined, and entertained; now the return to one's cabin, like a cold, damp rag on the face, is a stark reminder that one is indistinguishable from a thousand other passengers, one is only the temporary inhabitant of a small room with a single porthole, one is, in effect, just cargo. One night as I was trudging down the corridor, I remembered a cartoon I had seen showing a man standing in the doorway to his apartment, on a bleak hallway lined with doors as far as one could see. I'd invite you in, Peterson, he was saying to a friend in the hall, but this is my own private hell. No, there's nothing glamorous about the economy-class doors that line the hallways of huge ocean liners.

Mercifully, the hall seemed less dreary and monotonous after I had spent several hours in the ship's bars and lounges, when my eyes were bleary and I had much to think about. Although I was in no condition to read by this time, I enjoyed reliving the experiences, and rethinking the conversations, I had had during the day; with the aid of a nightcap or two, I enjoyed reconstructing the day's dream of newness and adventure. Although bringing alcohol onto most ocean liners is prohibited, I carried with me a bottle of scotch. (Cruise ships and ocean liners want you to buy your alcohol from them, but why are so-called duty-free shops, which are supposed to be inexpensive, so expensive?) With the help of a hefty glass of scotch, I would sink into, and savor my dream, I would rekindle and nurse the sense of adventure I was experiencing as I journeyed to a new world, and, temporarily at least, a new life.

But the moment always comes too soon, which is why I consider the sound of alarm clocks the most hateful sound there is. (I patronize a pizza shop that has an electronic timer that sounds like an alarm clock, and every time I hear it, I cringe.) Finally it was borne in upon me that I could put it off no longer. Cursing daylight, subtly cursing life, if truth be told, struggling to excise confused dreams of gambling and magic and long hallways lined with anonymous doors, I rubbed the sleep out of my eyes, winced with pain at my headache, threw the covers back, and got up.

CONTACT

M*ay the gods have mercy.*

Tomorrow I will go to the temple. I'll make sacrifices.

But will the gods understand that these people were making fun of us? Will they understand that they've been making fun of us all along, right from the time we retrieved them at the airport? Because whether or not the gods understand, these people deserved this. They deserved to place — what is their phrase? — they deserved to place the other shoe on the foot.

If this isn't the damndest thing! Okay, go ahead and talk, you two. Sit up there and talk all afternoon, for all I care. But I'm not going to get off this bus. No sir. You couldn't pry me out of this seat with a ten-foot barge pole.

I could tell from the moment we retrieved them at the airport that they were going to be a mean, unruly crowd. I've been a tour guide long enough to know how to spot the difficult ones, and I know that we sometimes get visitors to our country who are interested in what we are showing them, and other times we have people who are difficult and unruly. But these people here, they deserved this.

If this isn't the damndest thing I ever saw! She's sitting up there on her crossbar, and he's slumped down over the wheel and — I swear — I think they're just trying to keep from laughing! But it's clear to me now, clear as the ass of a goat. That's why I told her I wasn't going to get off the bus. She came back here and stared at me, and I explained: I feel a little sick to my stomach, don't take it personally if I don't get out and help the others. Well, she went back up to the front and spoke to her driver — Mr. Stoneface — and I could hear them laughing, and mimicking me: The gentleman feels too sick to get off the bus! The gentleman feels too sick to get off the bus!

Olahpiti! Look at Chien-Shi! He doesn't know whether to laugh or cry! How long should we wait before we call the people back? He doesn't know, and neither do I.

Now I'll admit it wasn't her fault, that the group was doing everything it could to provoke her. On the other hand, there was no reason we couldn't have gone to the Temple of Mishnahati. We had plenty of time, I know it. But she kept saying: You want to see the ruins at Asnayah, don't you? I don't see how we can possibly visit the Temple of Mishnahati and still see the ruins at Asnayah. Then she turned to her driver — Mr. Stoneface — and smiled. And he grunted and kept on driving. And we were supposed to think that if the tour guide said there wasn't time to visit the Temple of Mishnahati — and Mr. Stoneface grunted — it was god's honest truth.

We are doing the very best we can in our country. I realize we

*don't have the most modern baggage-handling equipment, and I'm
sorry that so many of their baggages got lost in transport. But that
gave them no right to laugh and make fun of our people, to say they
all look like children and that the policemen's pants are too short.
And that big lady with the sun hat, she had to have a – what do they
call them? – a soft beverage the minute she arrived on land. Welcome! I said. There will be tea and refreshments for you at the hotel!
Please follow me! But no. She had to have a soft beverage right then
and there. So I tried to be polite. Your airplane was two and a half
hours late making its arrival, I said. I'm sorry but we must now proceed to the hotel. Everyone, please, follow me.*

So why wouldn't she let us off the damn bus? Here we've
come halfway around the world to get to know the people and
their culture, and we pass one glorious shrine or temple after
another that everyone wants to photograph – or we pass pro-
cessions of priests in their colorful ceremonial robes – and
everyone is shouting: Stop! Stop! We want to take pictures! We
want to get off the bus! And what happens? The bus keeps
rolling along, as if the driver had no idea where the brakes
were, or couldn't for the life of him imagine what it was we
wanted to see. So we're all pointing our cameras out the window, and the bus is bumping and thumping down these
kidney-piercing roads, and I know damn well there are going
to be a lot of blurred photographs – and unhappy photographers – when we get home.

*So why did everyone take so long at the Friendship Store?
Everyone kept acting like the number one thing for all their happiness was to shop for souvenirs and trinkets, and if we had to wait for
stragglers it is not my fault. Futhermore, they could have used the*

toilets when I gave them the opportunity. I said: The Friendship Store is one of the few places you're going to find the kind of toilets you like, so please take this opportunity. But no. They didn't. And I am forbidden by the Tourist Authority to stop in any but authorized places.

Now I don't mind some of those little jokes she was making, some of those jokes were actually quite cute. Palace of Chow Ping, she kept saying at the Friendship Store. Palace of Chow Ping. Oh, and The Temple of the Two Joys. But you'd think there'd be more than one *Temple of the Two Joys* in the whole damn province. There was absolutely no need to go bouncing along these kidney-wrecking roads all the way to Asnayah before stopping. Some of the ladies, well, and some of the men too. . . . I don't think I've seen Mr. Gruber run so fast this entire trip. There might as well be a sign up there that says: Once This Bus is in Motion There Will Be Absolutely No Stopping. Don't Even Ask!

Will you look at Chien-Shi? He doesn't know whether to laugh or cry! All he can do is hunch down over his wheel, and stare out the window. How long should I let them go on looking? When should I call them back? He doesn't know. And I don't either.

So it was on and on, up hill and down dale all the way to Asnayah. No Temple of the Two Joys, and not a happy tourist — or satisfied photographer — in the lot. I hope the folks back home don't hold *me* responsible for this.

And that lady in the flaming red — what do they call them — hot pants. I'm sorry she didn't enjoy her lunch, I'm sorry the spices and hot peppers made her sick. I tried to warn her, I tried to warn all the people. But just because she got sick didn't give her the right to be obnoxious, and to ask me about sex and sexual practices among our people. To ask whether I had a boy friend, and was he a good lover, and was I a good lover, and how old was I when I first did it? We were coming up Tishmani Gorge then, coming up the side of Honoragha Mountain, and I tried to point out some of the features I thought would interest them. So I made up a few things, they weren't listening anyway. No, they were laughing and joking, and asking me how I stay so — what is their word? — petite. I tried to explain why Tishmani Gorge is sacred to our people, and why we never laugh and joke in this area. But all they wanted to do was tease me, and talk about how petite our women are and how small their breasts are. And then — olahpiti! — they began to clap and sing! To clap and sing on Honoragha Mountain! During Penitence Week, the most holy time of the year! Chien-Shi — realizing how uncomfortable I was — said he was going to stop the bus and go back and punch some of them in the face. But I told him no, he must not, if he did that we would surely lose our licenses.

I should have known something was wrong, and should have said something earlier. But I've grown pretty rusty in their language, and for a while, I admit, I was enjoying the spectacle. The men were acting foolish and silly and letting off steam, and I thought it would be good for them, I thought it would help relieve some of the tension that's been building. But then when it started to get ugly, well, by then it was too late. I stood up and gave my little speech about the need for good will and understanding, the need for us to act as good-will ambassadors when visiting foreign countries, but instead of calming them down, it only got them more excited, more riled up. The women began to squeal and goad their husbands, and I thought one of the latter was going to come back here and punch me. They were hellbent on satisfaction, at this point, they were going to have satisfaction come hell or high water. Well, I may be the official leader of the group, but I can't control everything that goes on.

That man in the—what do they call them?—pitch helmet. I'm sorry he paid too much for his ceremonial mask. I told the people not to buy from the vendors that come to the side of the bus, I told them to wait until we got to the next Friendship Store. The masks these people sell are fakes, I know that. I know how they hold them over hot coals, and singe and burn them, to make them look ancient. Masks they claim are five hundred years old were probably made yesterday. But no, no one would listen to me. And when we are up in the mountains like this, and especially here at Tishmani Gorge, I cannot always control what goes on. Anyway, after the way that man behaved, I am not so sorry. He stood up in the aisle and began shouting: I've been ripped over! I've been ripped over! I want my money back! Can't you turn this bus around? Stop, stop! Turn this bus around! So I explained to him: Sir, the person who sold you that mask will have disappeared into the jungle long before Chien-Shi can get this bus turned around. But now all the people began shouting, he was ripped over! He wants his money back! Turn this bus around! Why can't you turn this bus around! Well, my friends, there is no way Chien-Shi can turn this bus around. Not here. Not on this mountain road one thousand two hundred and twelve feet above Tishmani Gorge.

Do I think the people were so agitated they would have stormed up out of their seats and gang-tackled Mr. Stoneface? Do I think they would have dragged him *and* our guide to the edge of the cliff, and thrown them over? No, they weren't quite

HOMAGE TO SWEGA TAGABODU

When my work takes me out of town and I have to fly, I make it a point to arrive at the airport well in advance of the flight. After disembarking from my cab or limousine, the first thing I do is to bless the skycaps who are waiting for business on the sidewalk. These people so much remind me of the Meneschi of my own religion, the porters who carry one's earthly goods on the celestial flight to Noruba, and while I do not consider myself more than ordinarily religious, it is difficult for me not to note the resemblance.

My first real act of observance, however, comes after I have checked my bags and received my seating assignment. In the old days, before the airports became so crowded, it was easy to find a secluded, out-of-the-way spot for this ritual. I would kneel down behind a trash receptacle in some little-traveled corridor and, placing a picture of the god Wunja on some date palms (which I carry with me for this purpose), I would make a fire from scraps pillaged from the can, or from scrap paper from my briefcase. It is not necessary that this be a large or ostentatious fire, which in any case would attract the attention of the security personnel, only that there be a moment of actual flame. Once I felt that Wunja had taken note of my observance, I would quickly extinguish it. Nowadays, however, when airports are so congested, I am obliged to carry out this ritual in the men's room. I locate a restroom at some distance from the main concourse, wait until I have privacy, and conduct my offering there: sometimes on the tile floor, other times on the sink counter. Some practitioners of my religion burn incense, at this point, or recite verses from the Haja-Luna, but being of a more modern temperament I usually dispense with this formality.

Having allowed plenty of time for the following observance, I next bless the aircraft in which I am to fly. Standing at the windows that overlook the runways (but not rocking back and forth, in keeping with the pure form of the observance), I say a prayer to Wilkud, and follow it with one to Grudrugen. The first, of course, concerns the winged chariot of Levrahum, the second the great triple-winged bird, Wuni-Argossa. In addition, I say a prayer for my luggage, for in my religion one's earthly possessions, too, have spirits, and it is not unnatural to think that the jostling they suffer as they are loaded onto the plane, then tossed onto the baggage carousel at the end of the flight, disturbs them considerably. I should say that over the years the gods have looked favorably on my punctiliousness; aside from a snowstorm a few years ago, and what last year was officially described as a mechanical failure, I have never endured a significant delay or cancellation. In the former case, I believe it was my propitiation of the spirits of darkness, Telforness and Mulqamanida, that enabled me to find a motel near the airport, and rest comfortably.

Of course there are many other things for which one could – and in strict observance, should – say a blessing or prayer. These include the concessionaires and shopkeepers in the concourses and the owners of newsstands and gift shops, but also the escalators and moving sidewalks, the TV monitors providing schedule information, and the beeping carts ferrying people to and fro. Most of the time, however, it is not until I have boarded the plane that I resume my observances. Having found my seat and gotten my carry-on luggage stowed away, I sit quietly for a few minutes and, as it is written in the Haja-Luna, say a prayer for the pilot. If there happen to be passengers around me who are incapacitated, walking with crutches or wearing braces for example, I say a prayer for them, too. Naturally I say a special Huerlina for the stewards and stewardesses, or flight attendants as they're called nowadays; in my religion one blesses not only the food one receives, but the people who bring it. In the Haja-Luna, these are called Euphimes, food-deliverers or food-bringers.

I know there are people in this country who think such observances are nothing more than superstition, the by-product of a primitive or atavistic religion, but as I glance at the passengers around me I am certain that if more people understood the reality of Haja-Luna-Laka, they would feel much less anxious about air travel. Especially as the aircraft ascends into the heavens, coincidentally imitating Wunja's ascent to the celestial sphere, I think back on the faceless crowds coursing through the concourses and waiting areas, and realize it is only a *façade* of insouciance and impassivity they present. For I consider it one of the prices of Americans' secular way of living, especially the way their technology makes it possible for so many people to be in motion at once, that people must retreat into faceless anonymity and pretend to lack concern, that they must act like mere cogs in a vast machine, items to be moved around, and cannot cry out with the fear and apprehension they actually feel.

This suppression of psychic reality – psychic truth – is nowhere more evident than when the plane is in flight. At this stage, a scientifically devised pressurization system, so necessary to flight at high altitudes, also serves to suppress, at least render invisible, the true expression of human emotion. So-called moderns should not have any illusions about this. The pressurization system of an airplane not only affects the body's breathing and circulation, but the mind's incipient recklessness, in normal circumstances what would be its fantasy-abandonment to the realm of Meguddik. Does not an aircraft's ascent, and eventual descent, perfectly mirror Wunja's dramatic, danger-fraught ascent to the celestial sphere, his later purified descent? In my religion we are encouraged to contemplate – in the orthodox version, to recite – the dangers Wunja confronts during his journey, the trials and tribulations he must undergo, the detours and side journeys he must make. But your modern, secular ways keep you not only from true religious thinking in general, but from such purifying flights of the imagination in particular.

I would concede that modern air travel, with its regimentation and cramped conditions, is not conducive to contemplating the religious aspects of flight. Still, by remaining alert while in flight I am able to overcome the natural tendency to day-dream, and to say prayers in passing to the gods of the air, the gods who actually hold the plane up. I should say, also, that in keeping with Wunja's initial longing for home, his initial reluctance and fearful glancing over his shoulder, it is important to bless the ground over which the airplane passes. If I have been able to secure a window seat, which I invariably try to do, I say a prayer to the god of fields and farms, Adehi, and if I chance to see such geographical features, to Mannu the god of mountains, and Adelina the goddess of rivers. But it is my first glimpse of the landing field, especially at night when the twinkling lights of the city around it resemble the fires of Batsann navigated by Wunja on his journey to Noruba, that provokes me to special propitiation, as it is written in the Haja-Luna.

At last, when the plane has come to a stop at the gate and I am walking up the ramp toward the brightness and commotion of the new airport — that is, when I realize the trip has indeed been uneventful and the gods have kept us from falling out of the sky — this is when I say a final prayer, a prayer of thanks to Swega Tagabodu. It is Swega Tagabodu, after all, who is the supreme god of love and devotion, and at the same time the god of chance, accident, mystery, and fate. Although I do not burn incense at this point, in keeping with strict tradition, I pause and give thanks for the indulgence of all the gods, and go on my way refreshed.

THE IMMIGRANT

The air, the air! Feel the air! Finally! A chance to be who I am! A chance to be myself!

Dammit, if only anyone had ever asked me who I am. If only they had asked, I could have *told* them. I could have told them who I am, and where I come from.

But no. No one ever asked.

And now it's too late.

What would I have told them if they had asked? I would have described the day I arrived in this great country, that unforgettable day when I got my first glimpse of these shores. I was feeling pretty low by then, I can tell you, I was feeling like a stowaway who ought properly to have been in the bowels of the ship. Although I had been a longshoreman in my own country and was familiar with the vacant looks of seamen who idle away their time in port, staring at the water or at nothing,

appearing and disappearing in dark doors and companion-
ways, the crew of that ship gave me no respect, no respect
whatsoever. And because I could not yet speak English, and
especially as I was seasick most of the way over, they treated
me derisively, condescendingly, treated me almost as though I
were invisible. It was only an accident that I happened to stare
out my grimy porthole as we were coming into the harbor. My
heart pounding, I jumped out of my bunk and ran up the com-
panionway and stood by the rail. I sensed that even now they
wanted me to remain below and keep out of sight, but this was
a view I had dreamed about for years, and I was determined
not to miss it. I stood by the rail and watched the ship ease
silently past the Statue of Liberty and into the harbor, and with
mounting exhilaration watched as she was maneuvered into
the dock and tied up.

Unfortunately, that was the last time I was able to view this
great country with unclouded and unobstructed vision; until
this very moment, that was the last time I was able to see the
world, so to speak, from above. For the fact is, the minute I got
off the boat, my troubles began. First there was the question-
ing by the immigration authorities; they wanted to know who
I was and where I came from, what my intentions were in entering this country, what diseases I might be carrying, who I
proposed to live with, and what political, even subversive purpose I might be serving. Oh, the interrogation went on and on!
And because I couldn't speak English, and the interpreter they
provided spoke a different dialect than mine, I behaved rather
foolishly. I stammered, fumbled, and tripped over myself, and
at one point actually feared they were going to put me back on
the ship and send me home. Fortunately, I was carrying a piece

of paper with the name of a family whose last name is the same as mine, and fortunately I was able to convince the immigration people that this family was going to take me in. Then, after they had searched, or rather ransacked my luggage, they stamped my passport, signed off on a handful of forms, and waved me toward the street.

If anyone had asked me what happened next, I would gladly have told them. I would have told them how I found my way to that roach-infested hotel, hotel, perhaps, being too polite a word: it was more like a stack of chicken-wire cages in which men slept without privacy, one man's coughing or spitting disturbing all the others. Many were the nights, those first three months, when I awoke to find bedbugs and roaches, even rats, scurrying across my face and chest. But I was here, wasn't I? I was here in this great country, and free to do what I always dreamed of doing and could never have done in the Old Country. I was free to begin climbing the ladder to prosperity and success.

If anyone had ever asked me, I would have told them how, at first, that ladder led directly to a basement. Because the first job I got was as a dishwasher in the basement of a greasy, all-night diner. It was not very pleasant down there, I would have told them. The only break I got was when the manager ordered me upstairs to clean up the mess someone had made, or when I was told to raise the trapdoor to the street and put out the garbage. I remember lingering on the sidewalk in my soiled kitchen whites, and watching the rich people, especially the beautiful women, strolling by. I also remember the way they looked right through me. That's something I'll never ever forget.

But I showed up for work on time, and did what I was told to do, and when they realized what a good worker I was — and when I realized what a good worker I was — I took a chance, and quit. I got a job as a busboy in a more upscale restaurant. And it was while I was working at this restaurant that I met Harold Wedwaldt. I'll never forget Harold Wedwaldt, as long as I live I'll never forget that man. I was bringing a flat of glasses out to the bar one night, when Mr. Wedwaldt cracked a joke which I initially thought was at my expense. I carried a pocket dictionary with me at all times, in those days, and when I consulted it I realized he wasn't teasing me, only making a comment about restaurants. On a subsequent evening — at least until the manager came out and ordered me back to work — we got to talking. He gave me his name and I gave him mine. Mr. Wedwaldt came to that restaurant quite frequently, and several weeks later, to my surprise, asked me if I was interested in a job in the shipping and receiving department of a factory he owned. I said yes, of course, then, when I returned to the kitchen, looked up *shipping* and *receiving.* And that's how I got out of steamy restaurants and noisy kitchens, that's how I got to be a shipping and receiving clerk — in my case, a fancy name for an opener and packer of boxes — in the Garment District. And that's how, with some presentable clothes, I was eventually able to go to the post office and apply for a job.

It was Harold Wedwaldt who supplied the clothes, of course, and Harold Wedwaldt who helped me get my green card. It was Harold Wedwaldt who suggested I go to night school and learn English while working as a custodian at the post office, and Harold Wedwaldt who took me under his wing and guided me through the immigration and naturalization process. It was he who came to the ceremony in which I took the oath of citizenship, he who invited me to his home and introduced me to his wife and family, and he who arranged a job for me in his brother's pharmaceutical firm, a firm in which I eventually became personnel director.

I won't relate everything that happened after that; suffice it to say that this country, if only because of people like Harold Wedwaldt, is very special to me. I just wish he were alive today and could meet *my* family, and see the wonderful house I live in. I so much wish he could have known how his brother continued in his spirit of kindness and generosity by helping me establish my own company.

Yes, that is my story — or at least that is the story I would have told them. But they never asked and now it's too late. Standing here with my face to the wind — feel the air, the air, the absolute freedom! — I know it's too late. For I am *not* that immigrant, and never was. I am — as I have been my entire pathetic, miserable life — Jack Willoughby's son. The famous, the one and only Jack Willoughby who founded, and parlayed into international success, Willoughby Communications, Incorporated. I am neither more nor less than the son of the President and CEO, I have *always* been the son of the President and CEO — that and nothing more. While there isn't actually a *Junior* after my name, there might as well be, because that's the way they've always treated me. Jack *Junior*. And half the time that's what they called me: Jack Willoughby, Junior. Dammit, I was born into, and have lived my entire life in a world that was already made! Did I grow up in a luxurious house in the suburbs? Of course I did. Did I have the best schooling money can buy? Of course. The Shelton School. Where else? Who in my parents' circle would have sent their children anywhere *but* to the Shelton School? And college? Harvard, of course – where else? Oh, I don't know that my grades actually qualified me for admission to Harvard, but Father – the old man, dear old Dad – was an alumnus, and an important one at that. He had given millions of dollars to Harvard, hadn't he? So there was never any question of my being admitted there. And after Harvard? Anna-Marie Carlton. Was there any doubt that the beautiful Anna-Marie Carlton would marry me? Not one iota. I don't know that she ever actually loved me – to this day I'm not sure she loves me – but we had grown up together, and moved in the same social circles – hell, I was often her partner at cotillion and her escort at her coming-out party – so it was naturally *assumed* we would marry. And then the clubs. The Crockett. The Salisbury. The Polo. I don't even remember applying! It was as if admission were a hereditary right and guaranteed before I was even born, it was as though they couldn't wait to have me as a member! Of course that meant endless parties, charity balls, and holiday dances. The Polo Club – who were they kidding? I don't even like horses! But it was as though the Willoughbys were royalty, and we were expected to go through the motions. But if we were royalty, what was the kingdom we ruled? The kingdom of money. Old money. New money. Inherited money. Money, money, money. It was the kingdom of appearances, the kingdom of talk, the kingdom of air!

And then one day, dear old Dad retired. And was there any doubt who would take over the company, was there any doubt who would succeed to the throne? Well, I did the best I could, didn't I? I did what was asked of me, I did what everyone expected of me. But the business has changed considerably since

Dad founded the company. The market is much more competitive now, and Jack Willoughby Junior hasn't had quite the success his father had, Jack Willoughby *Junior* doesn't have the magic touch his father had. That's what they say. I hear it all the time, in the hallways, in the mail room, in the men's room. But what none of them realize is that in his mind, dear old Dad still comes to work every morning, he thinks he still gets out of his limousine and struts through the lobby and takes his private elevator to his ornate office, he still thinks he runs the show. They don't understand that dear old Dad still exercises veto power over everything I do.

So, my little boy — my little failure — Jack *Junior*, is there anything you've done successfully? Done completely by, and for yourself? Is there anything you've done without direction from your family, done entirely on your own initiative? Yes, you can be proud to say there is. If there's one thing you've done without interference or guidance from above, it's figuring out how to remove this window in your forty-eighth floor office. Oh, it wasn't easy, Jack Junior, you're not very mechanical. Everyone knows that. It's just another of your failings. But by bringing the right tools to work — a screwdriver, a pair of pliers, a pizza knife, a crowbar — by staying late after work, then covering up your progress until the next day — you've managed to pry the window out.

So here you are, Jack Junior, forty-eight stories above the street. Feel the air, the clean refreshing air! Finally you're on top again! And look at the tiny people down there, those restless, squirming little ants! Look at the cars, the taxis, the buses squeezing around one another, jockeying for an inch here, a foot there, jockeying for position, each trying to be first! But most of all, feel the freedom, the release! Now you have an opening, Jack Junior, now you have a way forward! Finally you can do something completely, entirely on your own! Finally you, John Earl Willoughby — without the *Junior*, damn it — are in a position to do something on your own!

So.

One foot up.

Then the other.

Now.

JUST TELL WHAT HAPPENED

Okay, why don't you go ahead and, uh, just tell what happened.

Well, I was coming home from work, last night, from Simmondsville –

Push that thing closer to you. Good. That's better.

I was coming home from work last night, from Simmondsville – I work at the Simmonds Paint and Varnish Company – and as I was passing the rest area near the cut-off to Chelmsford, I looked over –

Damn. Hold on a second. The little red light isn't on. The light should be on to let us know we're recording. Is the mike turned on? Jiggle the wire. That's right. Now, please, start over.

Okay. Well, I was coming home from Simmondsville last night, where I work the late shift at the Simmonds Paint and

Varnish Company, and as I was passing the rest area near the cut-off to Chelmsford —

That would be Route 127?

Yes.

Good. Try to be specific.

The rest area near the cut-off to Route 127, I happened to glance to the right, and I saw a car that looked like my girl friend's car. It seemed pretty strange to see her car sitting in an otherwise deserted rest area on a rainy night, so I slowed down —

What time would this have been?

It was about twelve-twenty, maybe twelve-thirty. My shift ended at midnight, and I was happy to get out of there, so — especially as it was raining — I made a dash for my car. But I wasn't wearing a watch, and the clock on my dashboard is broken —

Damn. This thing *still* isn't working. The red light ought to be on, you know, to tell us we're recording? Let me push the plug in. Ah, that's the problem. You'd think they'd give us better equipment to work with, being as how we're the only police department in town, but there've been some pretty hefty budget cuts lately. I think Mrs. Clauson on the Board of Selectmen — and this is strictly off the record — has a problem with the Chief. But don't quote me. Do *not* quote me, okay? There's no need to put you through that again. I'll just summarize. The witness says he was driving home last night from his job at the Simmonds Paint and Varnish Company, and at about twelve-twenty or twelve-thirty, as he was passing the rest area near the Route 127 cut-off to Chelmsford, he glanced over and saw what looked like his girl friend's car. Now, please, go on.

[142]

It seemed pretty weird to see Kathy's car, or what *looked* like Kathy's car, sitting out there in a deserted rest area, so when I got to the ramp at the end of the area, I slowed down and turned back in.

You backed in?

No, I made a U turn and drove in front-ways.

Good. What happened then?

I drove in real slowly, trying to stay away from the overhead lights so as not to attract attention. It was pouring by that time, which made it hard for me to see clearly, but the closer I got to the car, the more I was convinced it was Kathy's. For one thing, there was a bumper sticker that I recognized, and a parking sticker from the community college she attends.

What kind of car would this be?

A '99 Chevrolet. White.

Do you happen to know the model?

A Celebrity, I think.

Good. What happened then?

There was nobody in the car, at least not that I could see. I came up behind it real slowly; I was keeping my distance, you know, keeping it in front of me. When I was about twenty feet away, I grabbed my umbrella and a pipe wrench I happened to have on the back seat, and got out. I began walking cautiously toward this other car. At first I thought I saw something moving behind it, that is, moving in the *woods* behind it. So I stopped and stood completely still, waited for my eyes to adjust. Then when I was more or less convinced I *hadn't* seen anything, I continued forward.

Hi there, Frank.

Hi, Bill. How's it going?

Real good. I'm getting some really useful information here. Frank, this is Travis Keyton. Mr. Keyton, this is my partner, Frank. Uh, you don't have to worry about the interruption. I pushed the pause button.

Kinnon.

What?

My name is Travis Kinnon.

Oh yeah. Of course. Sorry about that. But now, let's continue. So you're walking slowly toward this other car, carrying an umbrella and a pipe wrench. What happened then?

Well, again I thought I saw something moving in the woods. I stopped, squinted, and waited. Then I approached the car very slowly. I went over and peered in the front window, and there on the front seat –

The pause button.

What?

The pause button, Bill. You forgot to release the pause button.

Oh damn, you're right. Sorry. Repeat that, will you Mr. Kinnon?

I approached the car very slowly, keeping one eye on the woods behind it. I held the umbrella up and peered in the driver's-side window. And there on the front seat, I saw what looked like –

Hi ya, guys.

Not now, Dolores. Please. We're busy.

This'll only take a second. Carrie wants to know if –

Not now, Dolores! Can't you see we're busy? Close the door, Frank.

Hey, don't get all bent outta shape! I'm going, I'm going! But I need to talk to you later.

holding them up. ...Yes, I know. I realize that. How do you think it makes us feel? ...Well, they're *all* after your you-know-what. ...Mrs. Clauson especially, I know that. Mrs. Clauson.... Yeah, okay. Yeah, I will. Sure, Chief. Thanks. 'Bye.

So I made my way over to this darkened phone booth, and finally got my umbrella to collapse – it's one of those cheap ones, you know, that pops up when you least expect it – and what I discovered was –

So what the hell is his beef?

He says the D.A. isn't too pleased with the way we're handling the Stevens case. Says the Breathalyzer results weren't in the file we sent over, and he's afraid the defense is going to try to get the kid off on a technicality. When we're through with this, we'd better go back and check on it. If you'd heard what I heard in the Chief's voice –

Jesus H. Christ.

Okay, sorry, Mr. Kinnon. You stepped into this darkened phone booth, and –

I was trying to be as quiet as I could be, because I didn't want to call attention to myself. I figured that if whoever was hiding in the woods hadn't noticed me so far, there was no point in calling attention to myself *now*. But the door squeaked, and the damn wrench banged against the glass, and that stupid umbrella wouldn't collapse – in fact it got wedged in the door. Finally I got the umbrella flattened down, and the wrench stuffed inside my belt, and what I discovered was that though the phone was working –

Bill. This time you're out, you're definitely out of tape.

Damn, you're right.

I think you forgot to hit the pause button while you were talking to the Chief.

So why didn't you say something! You know what it's like dealing with the Chief nowadays!

Hey, this isn't my gig, this is *your* investigation!

Yeah, but if you saw that the tape was running out, why didn't you say something? This won't take but a minute, Mr. Keyton. Your account of what happened last night is extremely important to us. When this case goes to trial, your account of what you witnessed is going to be absolutely crucial. Let me turn the tape over. ...Okay. That does it. Now go on.

Kinnon.

What?

My name is Kinnon, Travis *Kinnon*.

Okay, okay! Kinnon! Go on, please!

I didn't have any change.

You what?

I said. I didn't have any *change*.

Of clothes? Or what? Were you really *that* soaked?

No, no! Change for the phone!

Oh yeah, of course. Change for the phone. So what did you do?

Well, I remembered later that there was some money under the floormat in my car, but at the time I was too keyed up to think of that. So I held the umbrella between my legs, and adjusted the wrench so it wouldn't bang against the glass, and with my hands shaking so badly I could hardly hold the phone, I dialed the operator.

Uh, Bill. I just thought of something.

What, for chrissake?

Carrie and Ray Dolman are cousins.

So?

So Carrie brings her cousin's wife in here as back-up dispatcher.

So?

Sounds like nepotism to me. Doesn't it to you?

Maybe, but let's talk about it later. So, Mr. Kinnon, you dialed the operator. What happened?

Well, there I was, standing in this pitch-black phone booth on a rainy night with my umbrella between my legs and a wrench that kept banging against the glass, and leaning out the door, every so often, and listening for footsteps, then stepping back in and trying to close the door so it wouldn't squeak — that was the hard part, trying to keep the door from squeaking — and finally I got an operator. I explained who I was and why I was calling, and whispered the name of the Beatons to her.

Frank, excuse me. Tell me something. How the hell do you know so much?

Like what?

Like, that Carrie and Ray Dolman are cousins.

Hey, I'm a detective. I get paid to know things!

And you think it's just good-old-fashioned nepotism?

Sure sounds like it to me.

Okay, okay, sorry, Mr. Keyton. But tell us. Was your girl friend home, or not?

The line was busy.

Oh no. So what did you do?

I waited a few minutes and called again. I explained to the next operator I got that it was an emergency, and asked her to cut in on the Beatons.

And did she?

She didn't have to. This time the line wasn't busy. Mrs. Beaton answered. Hello?

Damn, I think that's how I got them confused.

Got what confused?

Your names. Beaton. Keyton. They sound alike.

Well, anyway, at last I was talking to Mrs. Beaton. Hello?

I think you said that. It's not necessary to quote every single word.

No, that was *Mr.* Beaton. He had picked up a second phone. I whispered my name again, and apologized for calling so late —

And meanwhile, had you seen anything suspicious, either in the woods or in the area around the phone booth?

You don't need to scream.

I am *not* screaming. I am merely asking you whether you had seen anything suspicious in the woods, or in the area around the phone booth.

I wasn't accusing *you* of screaming, I was mimicking Mrs. Beaton. She kept telling Mr. Beaton not to scream. So I whispered, is Kathy home? Because her car's out here in the rest area near the Chelmsford cut-off, and I think something very suspicious is going on. No one has seen her all evening.

If you were at work, how did you *know* no one had seen her?

No, that was Mr. Beaton. No one has seen her all evening? he said. You don't need to scream.

I am not screaming, Mr. Keyton! I'm just trying to get a lead on your girl friend's whereabouts!

I'm not accusing *you* of screaming, sergeant! I was just mimicking Mrs. Beaton! She kept telling *Mr.* Beaton — on the other phone — not to scream! This is important, you see, because the Beatons were so upset they were having trouble making sense of what I was telling them. And I in turn couldn't find out what I needed to know. Now calm down, Malcolm, calm down. We don't know the details, give him a chance to tell us the details. Excuse me, but if this is a long-distance call —

Now who the hell was that?

That was the operator. At this point the operator broke in. If this is an emergency, she said, that's one thing, but if you're going to chitchat and pass the time of day, I'm going to have to charge you for the call.

Uh, Bill, about that other business. Do you think we can get that other business cleared up this afternoon?

What other business?

The Stevens case. Do you think we can get it cleared up so I can be out of here by five? I have a date, and I'd really like not to be late for it.

Sure, sure. But let's concentrate on the business at hand. So, Mr. McKinnon. The operator has broken in.

Give us a goddamn minute! Mr. Beaton said. If you knew how much money I've plunked into your goddamn phones, over the years, only to get no dial tone or some god-awful squawking — and then not have my money returned — you wouldn't jump in on us like this!

Frank —

Malcolm, you're screaming! Now just calm down!

Frank, it seems to me that since the Stevens case is your responsibility —

I'm going to have to ask both of you not to interrupt.

We're not interrupting, Mr. McKinnon! But we do have other business to take care of! If we don't get the Breathalyzer report over to the D.A.'s office by five —

No, that was Mrs. Beaton —

We're going to be in really deep yogurt! And Frank, here, has a date —

Shouting at the operator *and* her husband. I'm going to ask both of you not to interrupt! she said. Then Mr. Beaton had an inspiration. Give us the number you're calling from! he said.

And meanwhile, you still didn't know whether Kelly —

Kathy.

Kathy was at home, or even whether she was alive or dead, is that right?

That's right. And I didn't know how long it would be before someone came crawling out of the woods with a knife or gun. I leaned down in the darkness to try to make out the number on the phone, and the wind blew the door open, making a horrible squeak, and I dropped the damn pipe wrench, and the umbrella popped open —

The tape, Bill.

And I was absolutely *terrified* by this time. I held the door open and kicked the umbrella out of the way, and the rain swept in, then, in the shadows at the edge of the woods —

Bill, the tape. You're out of tape again.

No!

Yeah. Look.

I saw them.

Well, get another one! There're some more in the drawer, there!

No there aren't. I used the last one yesterday.

There aren't any more tapes? We're on the last one?

Afraid so.

Then look in the other drawers! Look in all those drawers!

I will, but I don't think I'm going to find anything.

Well, why didn't you tell me? You know, Frank, you're going to have to start taking some responsibility for a change! Start planning ahead!

The feet.

Hey, like I said, this isn't my case! This is *your* gig! You saw what the problem was, you could have taken care of it just as easily as I could!

Look, Mr. Keyton. I feel bad about this, but I should have some new tapes by tomorrow. Could I, uh, ask you to come back tomorrow? Say around one o'clock? Is one o'clock okay with you, Frank?

No, it isn't. I have to be in court in the morning, then I was hoping to get a birthday present for my son and drop it off at his mother's house — that is, if she'll even come to the door. I just hope Carrie doesn't give me that look she's been giving me, lately. For some reason she seems to think I'm slacking off, not doing my job.

Gimme a break, Frank, what is it with you and that girl? Ever since Carrie stopped going out with you, you've done nothing but badmouth her! Like all that talk about her and Ray Dolman being cousins! What the hell difference does it make? I mean, gimme a break! What *is* it with you and that girl?

INDEPENDENCE

M arion.

A marionette.

A person whose strings have been cut. A puppet whose knees have crumpled, whose joints have collapsed, who's slumping forward in the dirt.

Is that me?

No. No!

But ask yourself this, old girl. Would you rather be waitressing, or working in some dreary office somewhere? Is there enough going on at church to keep you busy?

No.

Still, do you have any business being out here in the hot sun like this, crawling around on your hands and knees? Looking for musket balls, pieces of glass, flintstones? And finding chert? Chert, for pete's sake!

But you have to do something. You can't just sit at home and wait for time to pass; you'll spend half the fall waiting for Leonard to come and fix the furnace, as it is. No, no use starting now. You have to keep busy, stay active, get out here and work with these young people. But crawling around in the dirt, in the hot sun? Next they'll be asking you to do the digging with pins and needles. Paintbrushes, whisk brooms aren't fine enough, they're going to ask you to go back over the entire field with pins and needles. I can still hear Stevie screaming at those youngsters. *Don't dig it up! Remove the earth from around it! And that trowel, that trowel's too big! Use the paintbrush we issued you!* Next I suppose, it'll be: *You all have pins and needles around the house, don't you? Please bring your pins and needles to work on Monday!*

Well, just because Stevie's the crew chief doesn't give him any right to scream at me. Not at my age. I resent that.

Pick, pick, pick. Scrape, scrape, scrape. I guess if that bunch of Revolutionary War soldiers had known that an overweight, middle-aged lady were going to be crawling around on her hands and knees in the hot sun, searching for what they dropped, discarded, or forgot, they would have taken more *care* with their possessions. On the other hand, we wouldn't have wanted them to have been *too* careful, would we. If they had been, I wouldn't have found my lovely glass inkwell.

Damn, it sure is hot out here. I can still hear Stevie. *This is rule one, folks. When you're not working, get out of the sun.*

But I'm working, I'm working!

Anyway, how careful was a motley group of Revolutionary War soldiers supposed to have been? They were so busy fighting for independence, and founding this great big wonderful country of ours – where you can't get your furnace fixed if your estranged husband doesn't want to do it – that they just let the chips fall.

Gosh. That's exactly what Leonard did, isn't it. Let the chips fall where they would. He and Deenie tore up a perfectly good marriage, and just let the chips fall. Trusted that someone – me, to be exact – would come along and pick up the pieces. Well, surprise. I *am* picking up pieces.

Slowly, Marion, slowly. Or you'll have someone standing over you, screaming at you again. I sure am thirsty. I should never have drunk all my juice so soon, after lunch.

But hold on. That's about as far as Leonard's understanding ever went, wasn't it. *Love is a tacit agreement between two unhappy people to overestimate one another.* That's what he used to say. But you'd think a marriage that lasted twenty-five years amounted to something more than an agreement of two people to overestimate one another. I wonder if that's what he's telling Deenie, now that they're off on the boat together. I wonder if they're sitting back there in the cockpit having drinks and staring into the sunset, and talking about their tacit agreement to overestimate one another.

Slowly, there, Marion, slowly. Don't dig it up, remove the earth from around it. And your trowel's too big, don't use a trowel, use the paintbrush they issued you. Well, Stevie can scream at the kids, if he wants to, but he had better not scream at *me.*

Is this anything? No. Just a damn root. Oh, it's so hot out here.

But Deenie doesn't know Leonard like I do, she hasn't lived with him long enough. Why, when he chose to be, Leonard was the most willful and stubborn man alive. So tell me, why did they have to move in right down the street? Now, I suppose, I'll have the supreme pleasure of seeing them out walking together. Holding hands, laughing and cuddling.

Careful. Careful here, Marion. Use your paintbrush, the way they told you to. Have you found something? No, just more rocks. Darn.

Rule Two, they said. If you don't like your pit partner, ask for a change right at the start. Well, I don't *have* a partner! Not here and not in life! I was the odd man – the odd woman – out. And to think. It was I who introduced them. I got him going to church again, and he eventually became so enthusiastic about church that he joined the choir. And met her at choir practice.

Oh-oh, my sweat is making the trowel slippery. I'll wipe it off with my handkerchief. I'm sure not finding much here.

I don't believe in messes. That's what he always said. *I don't believe in messes.* Well, for pete's sake, who does? Certainly not men. Not when they think there's a woman who'll clean it up! Men treat life like a great big kitchen. After they've cooked a big meal, and dirtied every pot and pan in the place, they walk away and expect a *woman* to clean it up. But if Leonard had had to clean this one up by himself, for a change, without Deenie to help him, maybe he'd –

Is this anything? Chert. Just some more damn chert. Marion, this time you have yourself a sterile pit. But it's not for me to reason why, lah-di-dah-di-dah-di-dah, so I'll just pick, pick, pick, scrape, scrape, scrape.

Now they're off on the boat for the summer, having a high old time. And I'm out here crawling around on my hands and knees in the hot sun, my blouse hiked up and my underwear probably showing. I bet my whole *behind* is covered with red dirt; the elastic in these pants isn't any good anymore. I guess if I'm going to get out here and work with the kids, I'm going to have to get some pants that'll stay up.

Watch it. Don't dig it up, remove the dirt from around it. And what have you got for me today, my little square pit, my little square meter of ground? What are you going to present me with this afternoon? A horseshoe? A belt buckle? Another beautiful glass inkwell — a glass inkwell that they'll probably catalogue and store in the basement of a building somewhere, so that someone else can come along in another two hundred years and dig it up again?

No, just more rocks. And roots. More of that damn chert.

Hmm, these sloppy old clothes didn't discourage Stevie in the beginning. I saw the way he was looking at me, I knew what was going on. And I'm *glad* they didn't discourage him. I was enjoying his attention. It's more attention than I've received from anyone in a long time.

No! What am I talking about? I'm much too old for him! True, I have beautiful blue eyes and lovely auburn hair. Lovely hair. At least when it's not covered with red dirt. This very historical, and *important* red dirt.

Oh-oh, the corners of the pit are crumbling. They don't like it when their corner balks crumble.

But tell me, why did Leonard and Deenie have to move in right down the street? Did they really think I could ignore them? Did they think I would simply crawl away on my hands and knees and bury my head in the sand? Did he think, just because our boys are working for him, that the only time I'd see them was when he sent them over to change the furnace filter, or fix a spigot or something? Doesn't he understand that what happens between parents shouldn't alter their love for their children? Didn't he understand anything about love? *Love. The beast with two backs,* he used to say. And all that talk about relationships. You'd think a marriage that lasted twenty-five years was something more than just another relationship! He must have gotten the word off television.

Oh no, is *that* what I'm doing? Crawling away on my hands and knees and burying my head in the sand? No. I'm trying to make a new life for myself. I'm trying to meet new people, develop new interests.

I just wish it weren't so hot out here.

Pick pick pick. Scrape scrape scrape.

Relationships. Let's see, there used to be trysts. Dalliances, elopements. Affairs, assignations. Marriages of convenience. Now? Now there are only relationships. I remember how I tried to get him to open up and talk about his feelings. Doesn't *love* enter into it? I said. You'd have thought I was talking about in-line water heaters or solar heating panels, or something. Love? he answered, getting that willful, perverse look. *Love is complementary neuroses.* Just like that. Love is complementary neuroses! I wonder if that's what he's telling Deenie right now, now that they're on the boat together. I wonder if they're sitting back there in the cockpit with their feet up on the gunnels, and talking about *complementary neuroses.*

When *will* the sun let up? I shouldn't have drunk all my juice so soon, after lunch. I sure hope they'll come around with the water bucket. Darn it, my trowel's slippery again. I tell you, if those Revolutionary War soldiers had known that some middle-aged woman, wearing pants that won't stay up, were going to be crawling around on her hands and knees looking for what they dropped or forgot or left behind, I bet they wouldn't have been so cavalier with their possessions. Still, this is better than playing bridge with the ladies, isn't it? It's certainly more interesting than doing make-ready, and digging shovel-test pits. I was getting pretty tired of that.

Not holes, Mrs. Watson! Archeologists never dig holes! They always dig pits!

Okay, Stevie. Pits. They still look like holes to me.

But you can't tell me he wasn't impressed when I found that inkwell. Most of the kids have found nothing but buttons and arrowheads, and a few musket balls. Most of them have had nothing but sterile pits.

Not empty, Mrs. Watson! Pits are never empty! They're always sterile!

Ah, I see the soil is changing color. I wonder if it's time to record a Munsell number, show that I've reached a new soil layer. I'll ask Stevie about it. That is, if he'll deign to talk to me.

I bet this is what happened. Sure enough. Some Revolutionary War soldier – an officer perhaps, possibly even a general – was sitting over there writing a letter home, or sending out orders, or asking for more troops – that's more like it, asking for more troops – and over *there*, the British were getting set to attack. The Indians, meanwhile, behind those hills, were deciding who to help, who to fight. All of a sudden this officer found he had to abandon the fort and make a run for it, he had to fight a rearguard action all the way down to the river. And this rearguard action, so they say, is what bought time for the Revolution, and enabled the struggle for independence to succeed. But in his haste, the poor general forgot to take his inkwell, the lovely glass inkwell some woman, somewhere, had probably given him.

Well, Leonard, is it independence you want? You wish to fight a *War for Independence?* Then I'll *give* you a war. Because my lawyer's guns are just as big as your lawyer's, and my cause is just as honorable as your cause. And while I may not be as young and pretty as I used to be – while my pants may be sagging and my behind covered with red dirt – I still have my hair, my beautiful eyes.

Now keep your mind on what you're doing, Marion. Have you found something here? Have you found another priceless artifact that must be handled very carefully? Or is it just another rock? Darn. Just another rock. When *will* they come around with the water bucket?

He hoped we'd still be friends. He as much as said he hoped I'd be friends with Deenie, too. That I'd walk up the street from time to time and observe their connubial bliss, watch them sitting by the fire, I suppose, drinking sherry, staring into one another's eyes. I told him I'd do no such thing, that I had no intention of remaining friends with Deenie, that if I hadn't raised a family, and made a life on that street, I'd pack up everything and move away in an instant. Which only made him laugh. Move away where? he said. With whom? He said I reminded him of a secretary he had once had, who out of loneliness took to cooking onions and garlic to make her house smell homey. Sent herself telegrams, CandyGrams or something, so she could pretend someone was thinking of her. Well, I'm not going to do it. I'm not going to start cooking garlic and onions to make my house smell homey, I'm not going to send myself CandyGrams! No, I'm going to get out here where there are people – if only Stevie's age – who will *look* at me.

Uh-oh, the soil is definitely changing color. Am I reaching a new soil layer? Or is it only clay? I'll ask Stevie what he thinks. I'll ask him, at least, if he doesn't scream at me.

What is it about men? They find a woman who wants nothing more than to take care of them, and make a home for them, a woman who – when they go on a picnic and it starts to rain – says, Oh honey, I'm so sorry, it's raining! Well, *she* didn't cause the rain. It's not *her* fault. She can't control the weather! Furthermore, she does these things for twenty-five years, and meanwhile, what is *he* doing? He's slowly starting to withdraw. He's developing his own agenda. Here she's devoting her life to the marriage, and he's secretly directing his attention elsewhere. He has his Work. His Duty. His Mission to Perform. Plumbing and heating – why, Leonard wouldn't consider himself worth speaking to if he didn't own the biggest plumbing and heating outfit in the county!

Now calm down, calm down, Marion. There's no need to get upset. Not out here in the middle of a dusty field, on a scorching hot day like this. But I tell you, Stevie had better not scream at me again. He may be the crew chief – he may be cute as a button, and the hottest thing on this dig – but he had better not scream at me.

Not arrowheads, Mrs. Watson! Projectile points! We don't know whether they came from arrows or spears!

Okay Stevie, okay. Projectile points.

And then, when the wife – no, when I, Marion B. Watson – sitting at a kitchen table night after night trying to be civil, trying to converse in an adult manner, finally tell him what I really think—that if I hadn't been so sympathetic to his needs and aspirations right from the beginning, I could have married *better* than him — when I sit there night after night and listen to his arguments and excuses, and finally, reaching my boiling point, say, This is all so boring, Leonard, this is all just so boring! — what does he say? *Women. Women. They never let themselves get really angry, they never let themselves get really pissed off. They just say, this is all so boring, that's all just so boring.*

Well Leonard, I am. I'm reaching my boiling point. I'm beginning to get really pissed off.

Okay, calm down. Keep your mind on your business.

Pick, pick, pick. Scrape, scrape, scrape.

I wonder what would happen if I brought a young man like Stevie home? A young man not much older than the boys? No, my lawyer wouldn't stand for it. Not while we're in litigation. It would throw a monkey wrench in the whole business, I'd probably end up losing the house along with everything else. And I know what Leonard would say. *Your furnace is broken? You've got a young man around the house! Get him to fix it!* So be honest, Marion. It's too late to play the *femme fatale,* too late to play Helen of Troy. Me, Helen of Troy in a sterile pit. Helen of Troy in pants that won't stay up. Whose whole behind is covered with red dirt.

Finally. I see they're bringing the water bucket around. But look, the soil has definitely changed color. I'll ask Stevie if he wants to record a Munsell number. Or is this as far as I should go? We're not looking for prehistoric relics here, we're not trying to dig a hole all the way to China. For pete's sake, maybe I shouldn't even be out here, crawling around on my hands and knees, looking for what other people dropped, or discarded, or forgot.

And doing it, the whole time, on pins and needles.

A marionette.

Is that what I am? A marionette whose strings have been cut?

Here's Stevie. I hope he's calmed down. I *realize* it was the best thing anyone's found so far, and I didn't *mean* to do it — really I didn't. I reached up to hand it to him, and the way he was looking at me — those beautiful eyes, that seamless tan, that silky blond hair flowing over his shoulders —

Mrs. Watson, Mrs. Watson! We spend a lot of time setting up these excavations, and a lot of time trying to preserve the artifacts once we've found them! If you can't hand me a glass inkwell without dropping it on a rock — and breaking it in smithereens — then why don't you just go off to the beach, somewhere, and play in the sand! We have plenty of other volunteers out here! Why don't you just take your summer vacation someplace else!

CRYING

As I was leaving the office last Friday afternoon, I noticed, to my surprise, that Bob Thiele was crying.

"Bob!" I said, catching up with him in the hall and, frankly, nonplussed at the sight. "What's the matter?"

The market had taken a dive that day, and I don't think any of us had had a good quarter, but that hardly seemed reason enough for Bob – whom I'd always thought of as the rugged, stoical type – to be crying.

"It's – it's Crissie," he said, raising his shirtsleeve to his cheek, then attempting to disguise the gesture by leaning over the water fountain.

"Crissie? Your cat?"

"Yeah, dear, sweet little Crissie. We had to put her down yesterday."

Pretending that he was drying his lips, Bob pulled a handkerchief out of his pocket, and dabbed his eyes.

I should say that Bob's family and mine are pretty close, and I've been to his house many times, over the years. And I would be the first to admit that Crissie is – or was – a cute and lovable little cat. Still, it surprised me to see Bob crying over the loss of a cat during office hours at a brokerage firm.

"She was so gentle," he said, fighting back new tears, "so affectionate. And so frail at the end, vulnerable. She never *was* anything but a little bundle of desire for affection, you know that. We've decided to have a service for her tomorrow, and bury her in the back yard, perhaps pile up some stones as a marker. Is there any chance you'd come?"

"Sure, sure Bob," I said, trying not to show how nonplussed I was. "You've stood by me all these years, and if this is something that's important to you, well, you can count on me to be there. What time is the ceremony?"

"Around four. We'll do it around four o'clock."

I gave Bob a friendly pat on the shoulder and, leaving him standing by the water fountain looking downcast and brokenhearted, headed down the hall. I had an appointment with my dentist, and didn't want to be late for it.

I'm very fond of my dentist. Malcolm Schneider has a good sense of humor, and likes to joke and kibitz as he works. But on Friday, Malcolm was hardly in a joking mood; in fact he kept turning his head to the side, and rubbing his cheek on his shoulder. At first I thought chemicals or something in the air were irritating his eyes, then I decided he had a cold and was sniffling. Finally I realized he was crying.

"What's the matter, Malcolm?" I said, after I had raised my-self in the chair several times to spit. "Is there something wrong?" And then (trying to put him at ease), "Come on, you can tell me! In my other life I'm a doctor!"

Shelley, Malcolm's assistant, looked at me encouragingly, but the good doctor continued to act as though he were a mil-lion miles away. He went on scraping and poking around in my mouth like a man who had lost all sense of where he was and what he was doing. When he wheeled around to make a note on my chart, I said, more emphatically this time, "Come on, Malcolm. I mean it. You can tell *me*."

"Well, it's Susan," he said finally, inserting a bit in his drill and staring at it. "Sexy, sweet, beautiful Susan. I've been thinking about her all day. I just can't seem to get her out of my mind."

He stopped and lowered his face to his shoulder.

"Susan?" I answered. "Oh yeah. I remember her." (In fact I had not the slightest idea who Susan was, but in my effort to be of help my memory somehow rose to the occasion.) "Wasn't she the lovely young woman you told me you went out with in medical school?"

"Dental school," he corrected, as I opened wide. "That's right. God, she was a beautiful woman."

He turned and stared out the window for a moment before resuming work.

"But Malcolm," I said, "that was a long time ago!"

"I'm afraid I wasn't very kind to her," he said quietly, staring out over his utensil tray to the window beyond. "I'm afraid I treated her quite badly, and now I'm ashamed of it. I keep asking myself what might have been, you know, if I hadn't been so damn full of myself and if I'd taken the time to really get to know her. All day long I've been asking myself what might have been."

Malcolm swiped his cheek across his shoulder and stuck the drill in my mouth. It squealed for a few minutes, and then I heard him mutter, "After all these years, I still wonder who she's with. God, she was a beautiful woman."

He reached for another of his little torture implements, and raised his arm to allow a quick swipe across his shoulder. For some reason I was beginning to feel vaguely put upon.

"Oh, come on, Malcolm! That was a long time ago! That was, what, twenty, twenty-five years ago! You've been married to Melissa, for, what, twenty years? You've got a grown son and two grown daughters!"

"I know I do," he said defensively, dabbing his eyes. "And I love Melissa, I really do. It's just that sometimes, well, quite often if you want to know the truth, I find my thoughts returning to Susan, and to what might have been."

I was never able to get anything more than this out of Dr. Schneider, and he seemed distracted and far away for the rest of my visit.

I returned to the office and an uneventful Friday afternoon, but – I swear – when I wandered out to the parking lot at five-thirty, there was Wally Solomon sitting in his car, crying. I was getting in my own car when I noticed him. He was hunched over his steering wheel with his face in his hands. I closed my door and wandered over.

"Wally, Wally," I said. "What's the matter? Are you all right?"

"Yeah, yeah, sure," he replied. "Never been better. I've just been sitting here thinking about my beautiful daughter. My firstborn. My first *baby.*"

"Oh no," I said, recoiling. "Is something wrong? Has something happened to her?"

"No, no, she's fine. It's just that she was, well, *such* a beautiful baby. You should have been there when she came out. You should have been in the delivery room and seen that little face when it was coming out! What a sight it was!"

"But what's happened?" I repeated. "I mean, she's all right, isn't she?"

"Absolutely. She's fine. It's just that she was *such* a beautiful baby. And how does one ever get over the birth of one's first child? It's so special, you know."

Wally leaned over to the glove compartment and took out some Kleenex.

"Okay," I said wearily. "Just so she's all right."

Leaving Wally sitting there with his face buried in tissue, I turned and went back to my car.

On Saturday, to my amazement, it happened again. Before going out to Bob Thiele's for the interment of his cat, I drove into town to pick up some Scotch and to stop at the hardware store, and the florist's. I thought that since Bob was so broken up over the death of his cat, I would take flowers. Would you believe it? Buster McLellan, as he rang up my rake and work gloves, was crying!

"Bad news in your family?" I said, in my best good-neighborly tone. "Hope it's nothing serious."

"My mother," he replied, in a kind of is-that-serious-enough-for-you tone.

"Your mother, your mother...."

I stared at Buster over the cash register.

"Well, I know she can't be sick, because you told me she died ten or twelve years ago."

"Yes, she did," he said defensively, "but that doesn't mean I don't still love her, that doesn't mean that I don't *think* about her all the time. That doesn't mean she wasn't the only mother I ever had — or will have."

Lowering his head to disguise what was now outright sobbing, Buster turned away from the cash register, as he did so calling to an assistant to finish ringing up my purchases.

For pete's sake, what was it? Unhappiness over his recent divorce? Regret for what his parents had suffered in the old country? Some sentimental insight about the irremediable loss of the past? What? Why was Officer Grabowski crying? When I came out of the hardware store, I saw Nolan Grabowski standing next to a car he had pulled over, and writing a ticket, and *wiping his eyes on his shirtsleeve*. Nolan eventually got the ticket written, but not before he had raised his arm several more times, then pulled a handkerchief out of his back pocket and dabbed his cheeks. I wandered over to the curb to try to see what was going on — Nolan was absorbed in his work and didn't notice me — then turned back to the arcade of shops where, along with the lawn rake and work gloves, I had purchased a bottle of Scotch and some flowers.

In the flower shop I could see Ray Salvador fiddling with some poinsettias — and wiping his eyes. In the liquor store Sherman Daley was standing with his foot on a pile of liquor boxes — and weeping. I thought of my next door neighbor, Allan McKeown, who, when I stopped to say hello that morning, had mumbled something about *the pipes, the pipes are call-ing*—and had turned away in tears.

Bob Thiele was crying and Malcolm Schneider was crying. Wally Solomon and Buster McLellan were crying. Nolan Grabowski, Sherman Daley, Ray Salvador, and Allan McKeown were crying. I crossed the street and looked in the window of the pharmacy, then moved to my left and glanced in the gift shop next door. Finally I walked down the block and peered in the window of the supermarket.

All the men were crying.

I returned to my car, placed the rake and work gloves on the back seat, and with the Scotch and flowers got in the front.

I sat there for a moment and thought about it, and suddenly I was crying, too.

REUNION

Well, I guess one has to take one's friends where one finds them. I suppose I ought to be thankful for these, my new friends – for I continue to think of them as new – and I am. I just wish that when we got together for these reunions, we didn't have to sit in the front window. I've grown accustomed to their talk and laughter of course, and to the pleasure they derive from one another's company, I've even gotten used to their telling how they met. That telling and retelling seems to be the thing that holds them, well, holds us all, together.

But I wish we didn't always have to sit in the front window. It's not so hard to understand how it makes me feel, after all. And I know that they choose to sit here, because someone phones ahead every year and makes a reservation. As long as I've been coming to these things – what, six, seven years now? – this is where we've always sat.

Can't say the food wasn't good. Always is. Can't complain about that. There's something reassuring about the way the restaurant has kept up its standards, all these years. At a time when so many restaurants have had to make concessions of one sort or another, how many have been able to maintain their quality the way this one has? More expensive than it used to be, but then what isn't? Anyway, I didn't have to pay for my dinner. I never do.

Well, there they go, dancing off down the street, happy as larks, full of kisses, handshakes, and fond farewells. Soon they'll return to their everyday lives, at least the ones that aren't going on to their vacations; I know some of them plan their vacations, every year, to make attendance at these re-unions possible. And I get a kick out of these reunions too, at least I think I do; it's really been fun getting to know these folks. I'm sure they wouldn't begrudge my coming back – me of all people – to stand here at the front window. There wasn't time when I arrived to stop and admire the flowers in the box. And I suppose it would have looked silly in any case, my run-ning over and making a big fuss over the flowers in the win-dow box. I'm glad they still have flowers. I remember them so well from that first summer night. Let's see. Geraniums, marigolds, petunias, roses. They brighten up not only the front of the restaurant but the whole street. And look, the roses have gone positively iridescent under the street lights!

Still it makes me sad to see our table sitting empty, I wish someone would come along and take that table. I'd rather a new party were under way, and new friendships were being formed around that table, than see it looking so abandoned and for-lorn. But the waitresses haven't finished clearing it yet, and they'll have to do that before they can push the other tables back, the tables that were bunched together for our reunion.

Uh-oh, one of the waitresses is staring at me. She must think it strange that I — I of all people — should come back and peer in the window. Maybe she thinks I've forgotten something, or am trying to remember whether I've forgotten something. At least she knows I'm not a bum. Or does she? Does she see it's only me, and not a bum? Perhaps I wouldn't feel so strange, standing here, if I *were* a bum. Well, don't mind me, ma'am. I just came back to admire the flowers. Just admiring the flowers.

I don't suppose she was here, that first summer night. No, it's been too long, what, six, seven years? A few years ago there was still a familiar face or two, but even that may have been my imagination. I remember how I used to plead with everyone not to tell other people our story; it's not so hard to understand how it made me feel, after all. But it must have been someone who resembled this waitress who served us, that night, and it must have been someone who looked like that hostess in the back who seated us. Luckily, the restaurant still has the same owner. I'm glad for that, at least I think I am. I remember how he came over, that night, and made a big fuss over us, and poured the first glass of champagne. And winked at us, kept *winking* at us. It must have been he who told the others, that's the only thing that makes sense. Mr. Duclos must have told the waiters and waitresses, and they in turn told the people they were serving.

Oh-oh, she's staring at me again. Well, don't mind me, ma'am! Just came back to admire the flowers! Just admiring the flowers!

I remember how fortunate I felt, when I was making the arrangements, that I could deal with Mr. Duclos personally. I was still awfully sure of myself at the time, and I knew exactly what I wanted. I wanted the ceremony to take place in *this* restaurant, at *this* table in the window. I knew I wanted flowers on the table, and I wanted the best champagne – oh, I had it all worked out, right down to a tee. And because Mr. Duclos helped me plan it all, he knew exactly what I had in mind. He knew I was going to propose to Jeannie over dinner, at this flower-filled table in the window.

But the best-laid plans of mice and men.... What's that old phrase? I guess if we'd gotten here on time, things would have been different. But I was late getting out of work, then I had to pick up Jeannie, and the traffic coming out of the city was horrible that night. So what happened? We were an hour and a half late getting here. Little did I realize, when we walked in the door, that we were already so well known. Oh, no one stared at us or anything, no one giggled – at least not that I was aware of. Or maybe they did, and I was just too keyed up, too much in a tizzy, to realize it. Still, how could I have known – how could either of us have known – that the people around us knew exactly why we were there? How could I have known they were glancing over one another's shoulders, peeking around one another's backs, and trying to follow the course of our deliberations? I can still hear them.

This must be the couple! Shsssh! Here they are! The hostess is showing them to their table! And the owner is bringing them an ice bucket, they're going to have champagne! Pouf, there goes the cork! Look, the owner is pouring the first glass! Have they raised their glasses yet? Is this the proposal, do you think? Or will he wait until after dinner? Looks like he's going to wait until after dinner! Look, now he's holding her hand! Has he reached in his pocket, has he taken out the ring? No, the waitress is bringing them menus, they're going to wait until after dinner! Gosh, they're so busy staring at one another that they don't seem to realize they have their menus in front of them!

How could I have known that everyone in the restaurant *knew* why our table had been sitting empty for so long, *knew* for whom and for precisely what purpose it was waiting? How could I have known that such a sense of excitement had been building that people at adjacent tables had struck up conversations, deliberated on what they were about to witness, had even traded names, addresses, phone numbers?

Well, I don't begrudge them their happiness. I never did. One has to take one's friends where one finds them, after all. And I love each of them dearly, at least I think I do. Maybe their striking up new friendships was the best thing to come out of the marriage. Not that I like to admit it.

But it was a shock at first, a real shock. I had no idea that that evening I came back out here was the exact anniversary of the night I proposed. Maybe I came out because I was feeling sorry for myself, maybe I thought if I revisited the scene of the crime, so to speak, I could erase the memories and make a fresh start. But when I walked in the front door, what a welcome I received! What a welcome! I don't remember who was the first to recognize me, I just thought I had stumbled into a private party and was being accused of stealing a coat or umbrella, or something. Then I heard someone say: It's him! It's him! And the whole place went up. I swear, I've never been so surprised in my life. People started clapping and cheering, and some of the women practically wept. It's our reunion! they kept saying, it's our reunion! And while I know that some of the attention they lavished on me that night was an attempt to cover up their awkwardness and embarrassment, I also know I've never had so much attention, at any one time, in my life. But when they started inquiring about my *beautiful bride,* my *beautiful young bride,* I nearly broke down. Even that didn't deter them, no. It's our reunion! they kept saying, it's our reunion!

As I gathered myself together, I knew I was hooked. I knew that as long as their reunions went on, I had to attend, that I would feel stranger if I were absent than if I were present.

I just wish things had worked out better between Jeannie and me. No use going back over it now, I'm tired of the recriminations and arguments, the bickering and fingerpointing.

Damn, that reminds me. And I have to do it the minute I get home. But how am I going to remember? I *have* to do something to keep from forgetting.

Ah, the waitresses have their backs to me. I don't think they, I don't think anyone can see me. I'll take one of these petunias, just one pretty little yellow petunia, and stick it in my buttonhole as a reminder.

Because I know Jeannie. And she can get pretty unpleasant when her check is late.

THE VISITOR

Oh. There's the phone.

I *told* her I would run up for it, there was no need for her to stop what she's doing just because the phone is ringing. But she said she had to go up anyway, she wanted to get some mosquito repellent, and a sun hat. And I believe her when she says the mosquitoes are really bad this year; I've only been out here ten minutes and they're eating me alive. I'd hate to be out here and have to deal with them all afternoon.

So I'll bide my time on the fence. She ought to be able to finish giving me the tour, after all, what she calls the tour. She works hard to keep the place looking beautiful, and the results are, well, everywhere you look. Tulips, daffodils, peonies, and now impatience — is that what they're called? — hanging from the eaves of the house. And look over there. The string beans are coming up, the eat-all peas are doing fine, and over in the corner there're some tiny new sprouts. I wonder what they are.

What's in a name? I guess it was only natural that Rosie would enjoy planting flowers and maintaining a vegetable garden, it was only natural that she would have a green thumb. Still, it all makes me nervous. I mean, those mountains. Those mountains make me nervous.

Damn! There's one now.

Got 'im.

I could go round to the other side of the garden, closer to the treeline, but then I'd have to look at the mountains. Those mountains have made me nervous ever since we moved here, though I doubt I could make Rosie understand that. I remember the afternoon we closed on the house. Secretly I was hoping those folks wouldn't come down in the price, because secretly I had the feeling this wasn't quite the right house for us. But they were anxious to sell, and every time Rosie dragged me out in the hall and said, *maybe we could offer them a thousand dollars less, maybe we could offer them five hundred dollars less,* damned if they didn't take it. And all the time I knew something about this house was making me nervous.

And it was those mountains.

Damn, there's another one!

Gotcha!

But how could I ever have made her understand that? How could I have stood in her way, when she had her heart set on this house – and especially when those old folks kept coming down in the price? I should have tried to explain it to her the way I explained it to Denise. Denny, I said, I need plenty of room, I need plenty of air. I need space around me. I can't stand to be cooped up. I'm sorry, it's just the way I am. There we were, trying to make a life together back when I was in the office supply business. We had an apartment whose walls were so thin you could hear the people on the other side arguing and shouting and carrying on. If you were very quiet, you could actually hear them making love. It nearly drove me crazy. I couldn't wait to get out of there. If we'd had to raise our children there, I don't know what I'd have done. And that's what I tried to tell her. I know it sounds silly, I said, but I have this little problem with space. I have to have a table in a restaurant that feels right, I can't stand to be wedged into a corner where I can't see who's coming in and who's going out, I have to keep people in front of me. And I definitely can't stand to sit facing the kitchen. So what are you? she said, a cowboy sitting at the back of a saloon waiting for the posse to arrive, waiting for a shootout? But it wasn't that. It wasn't that at all.

Got 'im!

Pesky little creatures. Damn things'll eat you alive.

No, it wasn't that at all. It's just something about me, I told her, something I can't explain. Like on airplanes. I have to have a seat on the aisle so I don't feel cramped, boxed in, so I can get up and move around if I want to. And when I'm driving through little nondescript, down-at-the-heels towns where people keep their Christmas lights up all year, I actually get claustrophobic. You know these down-at-the-heels towns that anybody in his right mind would want to get out of? Well, I can't wait to get out, too. Get back out on the open road. Get out where there's air to breathe.

Oh no you don't, you little bastard! Damn, Rosie's right! They're really awful this year!

Oh-oh, blood. Guess he got me.

At heart, I guess I'm just a visitor. Always was, always will be. I'm never so happy as when I'm in a strange city and don't know where I am, and everything has a sheen of mystery and excitement. And I guess that's why living out here among these mountains, like this, makes me nervous. But how could I make Rosie understand that? She works hard to keep the garden planted, the lawn neat and clean, the house festooned with flowers. And she takes pride in showing me what's she's accomplished, in giving me what she calls the tour. But sometimes — sometimes — I find myself thinking, are we going to have to stay home and take care of all this? Are we going to have to spend the rest of our lives maintaining what we've built? Will we never again sail down the highway like we used to — just the two of us — in love, visiting new places, seeing new things?

That's what I tried to tell Midge, Midget I called her. I'm never exactly anywhere, I used to say. I'm never exactly in one place, I'm always everywhere at once, and thinking about everything. Oh, a sort of philosophical promiscuity, she shot back. But it wasn't that, it wasn't that at all. I wasn't thinking about other *women.* And at the time, I loved Midge, I really did. It was just that, well, I was hungry for more, I was hungry for life. And I *gave* her a good life, didn't I? Raised a couple of beautiful kids with her? But by the time I left that brokerage firm every night, I was hungry for more, all I could think about was more. And I knew I couldn't go on, knowing there were vast unexplored vistas out there, but something was keeping me from them, keeping me from seeing and experiencing them. Let's go, I used to tell her, let's go to the coast for a while! Let's get down close to the water where we can breathe!

Damn. Got that one. Sure 'nuff, the mosquitoes are really terrible this year.

I guess when I decided to go around for the third time, I should have known better. Because if anything could have whet my appetite for travel, it was that job at the sporting goods store. And that's the way I put it to Amanda, Demanda I called her. Everybody comes in and buys skis, backpacks, and jogging suits, I said. Tents and canoes and camping gear. They're all going somewhere. We have this lovely condo, sure, but wouldn't you like to be going somewhere, too? The payments on this place are taking up both our incomes, and with all the work we've put into it, I'm not sure whether we've made it ours or it's made us *its*. Let's be honest, I said. With all the money we're sinking into this thing, we could be on a boat somewhere, sailing around in the tropics. But of course we had the baby by then, and I felt it was my duty, my obligation to stay home and help raise her.

Damn! They're almost as thick as gnats! I *see* why Rosie went up to get some bug repellent!

I guess it was inevitable that the fourth marriage didn't work out. Lasted just long enough to have the twins, but not much longer. I should have realized by then – especially since, as a sales rep, I could work out of my car – that I just wasn't the type to stay put. Luckily, I got that job with the airline and the work began taking me around the world. And that's when I met Rosie. Meeting Rosie on one of those international flights was the best thing that ever happened to me. In Rosie I finally had someone who shared my sense of adventure, my love of travel, my pleasure in just being able to kick up your heels and *go*.

Gotcha! There's one for my side!

But of course Rosie had never played at homemaking, had never had a house to call her own, and who was I to deny her that privilege? One needs a place to call home, doesn't one? A base of operations, a place to store one's things? Who wants to live without an address?

Well, a lot of good it did, crossing my fingers at the real estate office, that afternoon we closed on the property. I knew something was wrong with this house but I couldn't quite put my finger on it. And all the while it was those mountains. Those mountains that loom like a fence, and make it impossible for us to extricate ourselves, go anywhere. If only I had known then what I know now. But those folks kept coming down in the price, and every time Rosie dragged me out in the hall and we discussed it – Rosie the little businesswoman, Rosie the wheeler-dealer – I knew it would be unfair for me to stand in her way. Still, I'm convinced we could have found something more spacious. Something with bigger windows, more air around it, something with views in all four directions. I hate feeling like I'm backed up against these mountains, I need plenty of room. I need to see who's coming in and going out the door.

Damn! They're positively frightful! I'll scrape this little one off my wrist. But damnit, there's blood again! He got *me*.

Those little sprouts in the corner. I wonder what they're going to be when they grow up.

* * *

From the top of the terrace now, he heard the screen door slam. He turned to see his young wife emerging from the house with a hoe and bandana in one hand, and a sun hat and can of mosquito repellent in the other. At the top of the wooden steps she paused, and surveyed her creation. He let himself down off the fence and leaned against it, arms folded. As she descended the stairs, he contemplated her lovingly, adoringly, and finally, inquisitively; he was eager for news of the caller.

But she did not call out to him, in fact she seemed determined not to raise her voice. It was as though she did not want the neighbors, the surrounding hills, the sky itself to hear what she had to say. She gingerly descended the stairs, her demeanor at once resigned and cheerful. Once in the lower part of the yard, she went to the garden fence and leaned her hoe against it, then carefully placed the bandana around her hat, and began stuffing the ends through the holes in either side. She placed the whole cheerful contraption on her head and adjusted it, and finally, as she was gathering the ends of the bandana beneath her chin, paused and stared up at him.

George, she said quietly, squinting up into the sun as she tied the knot, *your mother's on the phone.*

DAYLILIES

Remember the good times! Don't be too hasty! they're saying. Remember how it all began! Remember what a good friendship you had!

And what am I going to tell them?

I know one thing. I'll never forget how it all began.

There we were, sitting by the side of the road in the one spot we could find that was out of the scorching sun, sitting there with the perspiration dripping down our faces, watching the traffic rushing by. He was picking up strands of grass and chewing on them, and throwing them down again and picking up more, and things had gotten pretty tense by then, I can tell you. We hardly dared to look at one another, and I was afraid if I said anything – if I so much as opened my mouth – he would start chewing on me, chewing *me* out. So we just sat there about three feet apart and pawed around in the grass for want of anything more to say to one another.

Finally, staring straight ahead, he said:

At least we got some pretty flowers to keep us company.

I give him credit for trying to make conversation, but the fact was, even at that moment I felt like someone whose toes had been stepped on. Here I was, sitting by the side of the road on what must have been the hottest day of the summer, sweat pouring down my face, my handkerchief soaked, my car all banged up – and feeling like an absolute fool if you want to know the truth – and this guy stumbles right onto the one subject on which I'm an expert, he tramps right into my garden, so to speak. At the time, I remember, I gave him pretty short shrift.

Daylilies, I said.

Well, of course they were! I saw them the minute I got out of the car. How could I not see them? In fact, after we'd stood around for a while and studied our little problem, it was I who suggested we walk up the hill and sit in the shade. A stand of daylilies was about as much consolation as I was going to get, and if we had to bide our time by the side of the highway, I figured we might as well surround ourselves with some beauty. But hell, we all make mistakes, everyone makes mistakes once in a while, and I didn't want this guy to think that I was a complete ignoramus.

Hemerocallis fulva, I said. Daylily enthusiasts refer to them as road-ditch lilies, and sometimes they're called the poor man's orchid, or the lazy man's flower. That's because they seem to thrive on neglect.

He stared straight ahead, seemed to think about it.

Sort of like me, he said.

Okay, okay! So maybe I didn't like feeling I was on the defensive. Anyway, I decided to enlighten him further.

They're really quite common, I told him. After all, all plants are just weeds until they've been domesticated. Weeds are just plants that grow where people don't *want* them to grow.

At this a hint of amusement came into his face:

Are you telling me you know something about daylilies? he asked.

Do I know something about daylilies? Of course I do.

And for some reason it was the first time since the whole thing began that I felt quite right in the head.

I don't suppose you subscribe to *Daylily Journal,* he asked.

Sure do, I replied. (Who did he think he was talking to?)

Then you belong to the American Hemerocallis Society?

Now, at first I couldn't figure out how this guy knew so much about me. We both were silent for a while, and when I finally turned and glanced at him . . . he was beaming.

Which region? he asked.

Suddenly – no, no use not admitting it – suddenly I was beaming, too.

Well, we were off and running. It was as if we had completely forgotten why we were sitting there. We started calling up the names of our favorite cultivars, and trading notes on the new catalogue offerings, and talking about who we liked to order from, and which of our favorites had made it through the winter and which hadn't. We talked about the activities going on in our region – I don't know why we'd never met before – and the shakeup that was going on in the national society – oh, we got right into it. Tets, diploids, cross-pollination, working with the newest and latest as compared to working with the tried-and-trues, going for variety as compared to going for a pleasing, overall design — we got right into it. We even had a laugh over the way people are constantly driving by our houses and slamming on their brakes, and stopping to look.

And why do people do that? Well, look around *this* yard. Front, sides, back — everywhere you look — the yard is aflame, practically bursting with color. And when I'm out here pruning and deadheading and tending to my beauties, and people slow down to gawk, I just putter along like I don't know what I'm doing. I just go about my business and let them have all the pleasure out of it they want. Because that's the beauty of daylilies, that's what makes them so endlessly fascinating. There are hundreds and hundreds, even thousands of varieties, and they come in every color, crimp and twist, every ruffle and flute, stripe and striation, you could imagine. But while I often get five, ten, fifteen buds on a scape, and have been lucky with reblooming — god, we even talked about that — the blooms themselves, each little bloom, lasts only a day. A yard full of daylilies may have a thousand flowers all blooming at once, but each little treasure lasts only a day. Oh, it was amazing, suddenly, how much we had to talk about.

Now I admit it was my fault. I never tried to deny it, I never tried to duck out of it. My mind must have been on something else, that day, and the heat and noise didn't help any. I pulled out to pass and — wham — I slammed right into him, got him by his rear fender. But that wasn't the half of it, no, that's when the real trouble started. He swerved to his left and we cut back into one another — and locked bumpers. God, it was awful. We started fishtailing down the highway, and I could hear my headlight crunching, and our bumpers locking tighter. He slowed down – I was pushing, he was pulling – then one of those big eighteen-wheelers got behind us and I thought we were both going to be killed. He waved his arm and motioned to the right, and I don't know how we managed it, but somehow we got ourselves slowing down at the same speed and heading off the road in the same direction. Finally, *finally,* we began rolling to a halt – I still thought that eighteen-wheeler was going to get us both – and coasted onto the shoulder and onto a patch of dry grass. Five more feet and we would have sunk into a big concrete drainage ditch. Then, like two old horses that couldn't go another step farther, we sputtered to a halt.

I thought my car was going to explode when I got out of there, or that *I* was going to explode; I couldn't believe I was still alive. But right from the beginning, Harry was cool about it, much more cool, calm, and collected than I. Not that there wasn't plenty of fury in his eyes – and maybe I should have taken my cue right then – but outwardly at least, Harry was completely unruffled. He didn't say anything, at first, he just came over and looked me up and down, and went over and studied the problem. He walked to the back of my car, then up front again, and had a look at it from that angle.

Your fault, friend, he said. *Well, we won't know whether we're gonna be able to go our separate ways unless we try to pull our cars apart.*

I was all for sitting down and trying to catch our breath, but Harry was determined to see if we couldn't get our cars separated. I think he felt there was something vaguely embarrassing about having the two cars twisted up with one another like that, one horse sort of sniffing the rear of the other. I think he felt that if the police and the wrecker were going to come, the least we could do was not look like we had played a game of kootchy-koo right in the middle of the highway. In any case, I made it clear to him that it was my fault. As angry and keyed up as I was, I didn't try to duck out of it.

But wouldn't you know it, the two cars wouldn't come apart. I don't know how we'd gotten our vehicles so tangled up in one another, but even with him revving his engine and trying to back up, and me revving mine and trying to go forward, the damn things wouldn't come apart. In fact, we only made matters worse. I could hear his tail light cracking, and see the lid of his trunk being pried up, and it began to feel like we were two rams who had locked horns on the side of a mountain and couldn't get them unstuck, two rams who were going to die right there on the spot from exposure and starvation. In the end all we succeeded in doing was rolling ourselves farther along the shoulder toward that damn drainage ditch.

So there we were, two fish out of water, biding our time by the side of the road: he, a tall good-looking black man in a business suit, and I – I, wouldn't you know it – in my worst-looking old gardening clothes. Well, it was a hell of a way to form a friendship. And it might never have *become* a friendship if Harry hadn't kept his head in the beginning, if he hadn't shown so much self-control. Who knows what kind of shenanigans a black man – even a tall good-looking black man in a business suit – might have pulled, standing out there by the side of an anonymous highway? Yes, I'll admit, it was Harry's restraint that enabled our interest in daylilies to transcend this little mess I'd gotten us into. And when the police and the wrecker finally came, and with much prying and wrenching they got us pulled apart – wouldn't you know it, it was Harry who had to be towed: quarter panel wedged against his rear tire – even then, as we were getting ready to go our separate ways, there was a hint of friendliness, even forgiveness in his eyes.

I mean go our separate ways for the moment, because it was pretty well understood that once this other little matter had been taken care of, we would get together again. *We met by accident.* That's what Harry's said to this day, when people ask how our friendship got started. And it *has* been a good friendship, no question about it. There have been the fans we've exchanged, the cross-pollinations we've attempted, the types we've tried to hybridize. And socially, well, socially it's been pretty good, too. In fact, lately it's come to seem like Harry was part of the family. I don't know how many times I've heard Betty call, Harry's on the phone! Oh honey, it's Harry! Or heard Jessica thumping down the basement stairs to pry me out from under the plant lights and tell me, Harry's here, Harry's at the front door!

Recently, however, I've also begun to have second thoughts, I've begun to wonder whether I should have been so damn big-hearted and generous, from the start. I've begun to wonder whether I should have been in such a big rush to take all the blame. He *was* over in my lane, if you want to know the truth. And if I'd chosen to make an issue out of it, I could have proven it. Yeah, maybe I shouldn't have bent over backwards to be nice, easy-going, friendly because lately something's gotten into Harry, something's been *bugging* Mr. Harry L.

Jefferson. I first noticed it a couple of months ago, when we were discussing that new commuter line the state wants to build. I suppose it was inevitable we'd come down on opposite sides of that issue, but my position was: good for the city, bad for the suburbs. Gimme a break. It would not only take people into town, but bring them out *here*. We tried to leave the issue alone, and focus on daylilies, but then there was the question of the municipal bond, all the money they wanted to raise to convert those riverfront factories to public housing. Well, I'm all for that – up to a point. Why, it'd cost millions to convert those buildings, and it's common knowledge that whatever the county spends, the little towns eventually get taxed for, too. After that, it was the little things. How I was handling my registration data. How much fertilizer I was using. Whether a hundred and fifty, two hundred dollars wasn't too much to pay, in this day and age, for somebody's exotic new hybrid. Well, I'll buy the fans I want to buy, thank you very much, and I'll buy 'em from the people I want to buy 'em from. Oh, lots of things come back to me, now that I think about it – things he's said or done over the years, things I chose not to notice, or glossed over in an attempt to be friendly, easy-going, nice. The little hugs and kisses with my wife, that's one thing. From someone who's practically a member of the family, you'd expect that. And after I had a little talk with her about it, I got over any misgivings on that score. But now that I think about it, I believe he would like to have had something going with Jessica the whole time. Just waiting for her to grow up, I suppose, just waiting to pounce. Oh, there are lots of things I could point to, now that I think about it.

But tonight, tonight was the last straw. Tonight he showed his true colors. He just wouldn't let up, he wouldn't get off my case, he kept having to butt in, kept having to have it his way. Okay, so the grill wouldn't light up. That happens. Maybe the charcoal was damp, or had been sitting out in the garage too long. Then, being called away to the phone, that didn't help any either. But it's not so very complicated. You just squirt a little starter fluid on the bricks, and they'll light right up. But no, Harry has to put his two cents in. He says I don't have the bricks *arranged* correctly, that the charcoal has to have more *air circulation* around it. Oh, he has a million ways to help me run my own show! And finally, when I have a nice little fire going and have the chicken all laid out, he starts telling me I should *push the thickest pieces toward the center.* Well, I've done enough barbecuing in my life to know jolly well what I'm doing! Hell, he was driving recklessly himself that day, if you want to know the truth. And the starter fluid does not — repeat, does not — give a bad taste to the food. But the wife and kids were getting restless — Christ, I saw the fireflies, I knew what time it was! — and then what does he do? He starts making suggestions about my sauce! He dips his finger oh-so-scientifically in my sauce, like he's some kind of fancy chemist or four-star chef, and dabs it on his lips! And says it needs Tabasco! That *adding a touch of Tabasco* would give it just the flavor it needs!

And then? Oh, I've had it, I've really had it! Then there was that little wisecrack of his. That was the last straw! He turns to me and smiles that supercilious little smile of his, and says:

Frank, you know something, when you get right down to it, you don't barbecue chicken any better than you drive a car.

Well, it's the Fourth of July, isn't it? We invited *him*, we invited him to *our* house. And I wasn't going to stand for it. No sir. Not after all I've done for him over the years.

I turned and looked him straight in the eye, and said:

You know, Harry, ever since the day I ran into you, you've been nothing but a goddamn freeloader.

Well, look who couldn't take the heat. He didn't say a word. He turned on his heel and walked off, stormed up the terrace, here, and marched across the driveway and got in his car. I knew something was up. I could hear it in the way he slammed his door, I could hear it in the way he squealed his wheels – I think he did it just to be infuriating. Then I heard what I think was the most sickening sound I've ever heard in my life.

And just look at this, will you? This car isn't a year old – and look at it! A foot-wide scratch all the way down the length of it! He sideswiped it! He sideswiped it, goddamn it! I ran out to the street – you can bet I ran out to the street – but he had already turned the corner and was gone.

Now here are the wife and kids telling me to calm down, telling me not to be too hasty, telling me to remember the good times, and how it all began.

And what am I going to answer?

I'll tell you what I'm going to answer. Damn right I will. This was hit-and-run. And this, my home, is private property. This was wanton, willful, and malicious destruction on *private property*. Well, there are laws that cover such things, and fair is fair, right is right. I don't know whether he did it on purpose, I don't know that for sure. But I know damn well he did it. And I'm not going to stand for it. I'm not going to take this with just another smile and a shrug.

You wanna to know what I'm going to do? I'll *tell* you what I'm going to do.

On Monday – no, Tuesday, when this long holiday weekend is over – I'm gonna get in touch with a lawyer. Damn straight I am. I'm gonna get in touch with a lawyer.

I'm gonna sue that sonofabitch.

REGINALD USED THE SUBJUNCTIVE TODAY

R eginald used the subjunctive today...."

Father O'Mallon looked up at Father Wilson, standing in his doorway, and like generals in a bunker receiving good news from the front, their eyes met with tired and weary satisfaction. But the battle was too monumental, their glance also said, and its outcome too uncertain, to allow more than brief rejoicing.

After the significance of the statement had sunk in, Father Wilson wandered off, and O'Mallon was left alone in his dreary, dimly lighted office. He picked a bit of fluff from the frayed cushion of his swivel chair, and swung around to the window behind him. Through the skewed and twisted slats of the blinds (which he parted with his fingers), he could see the flickering images of the movie being played high on the side of the building across the street and, to his right, the motley crowd of people standing on the corner watching it. For several minutes he followed the stream of images which, at a height of four stories or more, was lighting up the neighborhood and competing with the gradual descent of darkness. A woman with garish blue hair and lurid makeup was singing, or perhaps mouthing, the words to a song. Her manner was dreamily distant, as if she were in some other movie or on some other wall, indeed in some other city. A tumbling mist came up behind her and she receded into it, then a horse's head emerged from the mist, and its eyes sparkled and burned brightly. When the sparkles disappeared, worms crawled out of the now-hollow sockets and metamorphosed into tears; the tears trickled down the horse's face. Presently the horse tilted its head back and bared its teeth and, by some trick of cinematography, smiled. The swirling mist returned and the horse, now with fire in its eyes, faded from the side of the building; the singing, or mock-singing woman appeared again. This time, however, her face was full of strength and intensity. She turned to a chandelier high above her, and piece by piece its facets shattered; then she turned to a wine goblet on a table nearby, and it too cracked, a red liquid oozing from its fissures. The fragments of the goblet, exploding like shrapnel across the side of the building, gradually transmuted into snowflakes, which swirled and floated down dreamily. Now the woman stared at a dark, ill-defined window behind her, and its panes shattered and toppled forward in a deranged kaleidoscope; the window filled with iridescent mist, which slowly cleared to reveal a horrifying masked creature with dark, crooked teeth.

Father O'Mallon removed his fingers and let the slats close, and his thoughts returned to Reginald. Indeed, it was miraculous, the progress the boy was making, for Reginald had been one of those they had picked up off the street, a tramp, a street urchin, a tiny beggar who had been abandoned by parents who could no longer take care of him or simply had gotten bored with the task. There had been a number of boys who had come to them this way (*yes, start with the boys,* he had thought in the beginning, *Sawtooth and Willy and Q-Bruiser*), but it had been Reginald who had shown the greatest enthusiasm for the work, Reginald who had most quickly forsaken his old ways as he recognized the benefits of the new. (*Yes, start with the boys. Boys could be more easily regimented and disciplined than girls. Add girls as occasions arose, but keep the sexes segregated at first; try to reduce the distractions of sex.*) Of course there had been parents who had brought their children, for security reasons appearing at the door in the middle of the night, and occasionally a child had shown up on the doorstep eager to be taken in anywhere, eager to have anything to do but wander the streets and beg. (*Had the time come to establish a second conventicle? Ought they to limit the enrollment, in that one, to girls?*)

Father O'Mallon's thoughts were interrupted by a horrendous squealing and scraping noise; again he split the blinds with his fingers. "Jobs Promised in Febuary" said the sign on a tram-jitney that was passing. It was the first such vehicle he had seen in a week, and what was this one running on, he wondered? The crowd on the corner moved aside to let it pass, and with much shouting and hooting between the crowd and the passengers — one man going over and angrily kicking the thing — it squealed and clattered down the tracks. Except for the monotonous pounding of drums in the distance, the funereal, gray street returned to silence.

No, no, out of the question, he thought, recalling his morning interview with Spike the Knife. *Perhaps he would encourage the boy to use a more friendly nickname, perhaps he would encourage all the boys to use their real names. That is, if they remembered them.* Spike the Knife had insisted that he was working hard and making good progress, and ought therefore to be allowed to leave the conventicle and return as he pleased. *No no, absolutely not,* he had replied. Spike the Knife knew as well as anyone the risk of being apprehended by the authorities, or lured back into a gang, indeed, of having the work of the conventicle pried out of him. And he had accepted the terms of admission when he had arrived there. No, the retreat, and the work it was engaged in, were still on too fragile a footing to allow the boys access to the outside. Such a policy might encourage investigation by the authorities, and that in turn could lead to their being closed down.

There was a shriek of breaking glass from outside. Irritably, Father O'Mallon peered through the blinds again. Though he could not detect the source of the sound, he spied several men on the corner engaged in a transaction involving a plastic pouch. In the distance the monotonous pounding of drums went on. A pallid, ashen light filled the street.

But what were they going to do for books? If their effort to establish a second retreat proved successful, where would they find enough books – printed matter of any kind – to be able to go on with the instruction? They had only a few editions of old romance novels to work with as it was, a few gothic thrillers and advertising pamphlets, and if the Fathers could not find a way to reproduce them, or at least pages of them, they would have to circulate the material between the two retreats. And how could they do that without being found out? They could have the boys and girls copy them, of course, which would be good practice for them, but it was important to move as quickly as possible to the work of pronunciation and comprehension. Besides, couldn't they do better than copy texts that were already corrupt?

In the distance, the monotonous pounding of drums continued. Chastising himself for doing so, Father O'Mallon parted the blinds and looked out. On the corner now, oblivious to a pig nosing about in some garbage behind them, a man and woman had their hands deep in one another's clothing and were groping one another. Suddenly – lancing the air – there was an announcement from the public bullhorn across the street. As if it would contribute to blocking out the sound, Father O'Mallon let the slats drop. "In keeping with municipal information process and retrieval, food will soon be distributated by the arthorities," the voice boomed. Father O'Mallon wondered if the boys could hear it, and whether it were distracting them from their work. Beneath the street lights that weren't broken or from which electricity was not being siphoned off, a blue metallic light rained down, shimmering in the smoky air. Spying someone dragging a mattress out to the curb, and being harangued by the men with the pouch, Father O'Mallon resolved that when darkness came he would exit the conventicle and drag it inside, and place it with the mattresses they had begun using to line the walls for quiet. "Farthermore," boomed the voice from the bullhorn, "the municipal arthorities have new movies to place in context for your listening and delighting enjoyment."

He removed his hand once and for all, and let the blind drop: it was time to get washed up for supper. And would it be the same porridge again, the same mixture of cereals and grains that had constituted the evening meal for many days? Thankfully, the boys seemed satisfied with it. At least it was an improvement on what they would be getting on the outside, at least it was regular and predictable.

Get washed up for supper.... To create a sense of solidarity, and to emphasize that they were involved in a communal endeavor, he had insisted that the Fathers — as they called themselves — use the same bathrooms as the boys. But would the water be running this evening? And if it was, would it have the same dark, rusty color it had had for many days now?

There was some miscellaneous shouting and screaming, the sound of sirens and gunshots, from outside. As he contemplated the prospect of the evening meal, Father O'Mallon smiled ironically, and thought:

They don't even know we're here.

He swung around to his desk, adjusted the few papers that were on it, consoled himself once more with the news of Reginald that Father Wilson had brought, standing in his doorway, and said to himself again:

No. They don't even know we're here.

A NEW LIFE

When John Grantham pulled himself forward in the shabby, overstuffed armchair that had more or less become his home within his home, he made a sound that no one heard, a deep, resonant *aaarrrgghhh* that came less from his throat than from his stomach, and — seemingly — less from his stomach than from the chipped linoleum, the sagging floorboards, the very earth beneath him. It was the sound not only of old age and too many cigarettes, but of soul-ache and frustration, an instinctive commentary on the whole fuss and bother of being alive. If he needed something by his chair, it seemed to say, some demon had probably taken it to the other side of the room. And if he went looking for it on other side of the room, this demon that had apparently chosen to accompany him through life had moved it to the table by his chair. If someone knocked at his door, the knocking would invariably come while he was in the bathroom — where he wouldn't hear it — and if he felt his way to the door in time to greet the caller, he would inevitably forget the soup or macaroni he had on the stove, and burn the pan.

Aaarrrgghh, he said again, making the sound out of which, in a sense, his singing had originated, and to which, in a sense, it had now returned. Having made the sound for so long and without thinking about it, he did not hear it. And because he lived alone on the first floor of an anonymous row house in the city, *no one* heard it.

Or at least no one had heard it until recently, when young Nelson (Nelson, was that his name?) began to visit. Nelson (yes, that was it, Nelson) had brought a tape recorder and asked him a lot of questions about the old days. When he heard his own voice on the recording he had been both startled and saddened to remember the extent to which this bluesy, gravel-voiced growl had once been his trademark.

But where was his magnifying glass, *ahhhrrmmmm.* How could he work on the picture puzzle in front of him if he couldn't find his magnifying glass? He pulled himself forward in his chair, oblivious to the bits of foam flaking from its armrests and, squinting, directed his attention toward his bedroom. The room had originally been a dining room and, he imagined, boasted a big round table, and elegant mirrors and pictures on the walls. What a contrast with the rusty iron bedstead it contained now, the sheets gone the color of tobacco juice, the frayed blankets that some demon had probably pulled to the floor. Was his magnifying glass in the bedroom? Was it among the medicines and odds and ends on his bedside table?

What little tricks had the genie cooked up today, in order to plague him?

Deciding he didn't have the energy, just now, to get up and shuffle into the bedroom, John Grantham leaned to his left and pulled forward the cassette recorder that was on a nearby table, and placed it in his lap. After contemplating it solemnly, he settled back in his dilapidated chair. He had already listened to the tape once that morning, but now resolved to start from the beginning and listen again. He felt along the edge of the machine and pushed the rewind button. There was a quiet whirr and, eventually, a noisy thump; the button clicked up. He adjusted his hands on the machine, felt along the buttons, and pushed play. There was a pause during which the leader fed in, then some jarring clicks and bumps – the sound of the microphone being jostled about – and finally the sound of young Nelson's voice.

"I'm sitting here today talking with John Grantham, the famous, the one and only 'Bootleg' John Grantham. I wonder, John, if you could begin by telling us how old you are."

Pause.

He had a pang of remorse that felt like a hot poker being jabbed in his side, as he remembered the awkwardness he had felt, in the beginning. But there was no time to dwell on it, for here he was.

"Well, sir. I must be eighty-eight by now, *aaarrrgghhh*. I can't be 'xactly sure 'cause my mama never told me, never told me 'xactly when I was born. And I never had a real birth certif'cate. But I'm damn sure it's more than eighty-six. Damn sure a' that."

Pause.

"Well, that's the way I figured it. Or, should I say, reconstructed it. Some of the resource material I've been consulting would put you at eighty or eighty-two. But from my background reading and what scholars call 'internal evidence,' I knew you had to be older than that. Now tell me if you would, John, where did you get the nickname, 'Bootleg'?"

Pause.

He was hearing himself now, hearing a voice he had not heard for so long he had almost forgotten what it sounded like. Not like the old days, not like the old days at all!

"Well, we didn't live, back then, quite the way you young fellas do today, and I guess by the time I first started steppin' out, I already had friends who were makin' their own whiskey. Fermentin' fruit, goin' to the sukey joints. Things like that. I was a little slower with it than some a' the boys, but I suppose one of them must a' given me the nickname."

"That's interesting. You mean it wasn't something you acquired during Prohibition?"

"Nah, I don't think it was. But now it may a' been, it just may a' been. I know the old jazz and blues players would sometimes take on colorful names, or the companies that were recordin' for what was called the 'race market' would give you a name, you know, if they thought it would help sell records. But people may already a' been callin' me that. Yeah, I think they were. I'm, uh, just not too sure on that."

"I see. I had the impression that 'Bootleg' was something you picked up during the Prohibition years. Be that as it may, tell us about when you first started performing, tell me about your first guitar. Was it a Mr. Lamartine —"

"Well, now. You got to realize a lot of the fellas was makin' their own instruments back then. You know, way back in the 'teens and 'twenties. I'm not sayin' they were fancy instruments, don't get me wrong. They weren't your store-bought rigs, they was just little 'gits' or 'git-boxes,' we called 'em, that we assembled out of boxes, pieces of wood, and some wire. If we were lucky, sometimes we could get hold of some catgut, or somebody else's discarded strings. But now, as to when I first started playin'. Well, we heard the people in the fields. The work songs, the shouts, the hollers. We heard music at social functions and picnics, and at church — especially at church, we heard *good* music there. And I suppose it was only natural for us to want to play —"

"But your first guitar, your first real guitar. Wasn't it a Mr. Lamartine, a clerk at the local post office, who gave it to you?"

Pause.

"Now it may a' been, it just may a' been. I'm not too sure on that. It's been quite some time ago, now, *aaarrrgghhhh*. And to tell the truth I, uh, can't rightly remember."

"Gerald Wissler, in his four-part history of the blues, says it was a Mr. Leroy Lamartine, a clerk at the local post office, who supplied you with your first guitar."

"He does, huh?"

"Sure. Sure. But it's not critical, so let's go on."

Wincing as though he were being jabbed with a poker, and knowing already what was coming, John Grantham pushed the stop button. He felt his way along the buttons to forward, advanced the tape, and pushed play.

"Agree. But isn't it true that you spent five or six years traveling around with the band, playing off the backs of trucks at medicine shows and the like? And isn't that when you first met Deeward James, traveling around like that to the little towns?"

Pause.

"Well, I don't remember 'xactly *when* I first met Deeward. I had a cousin who I think, I *think*, was a friend a' his. On the other hand, it may be just as you say, that I met him when I was travelin' around doin' the fairs an' minstrel shows. I don't rightly recollect on that. It's been quite a few years, you know, *aaarrrgghhhh*. But sometimes I think I'd a' been better off if I'd gone to school and gotten an edjication like young boys was supposed to. If I'd a' stayed in school and gotten an edjication, maybe I wouldn't a' ended up...like this."

"But it was you, wasn't it, who first brought Deeward James into the recording studio? After you'd come up north and gotten established?"

Pause.

"Was it, *aaarrrgghhhh?* Now it may a' been, it just may a' been. I don't quite recollect on that. I thought Deeward made a record *before* him and I teamed up. I'm not, uh, too clear about that."

"Peter Stillman, in the notes he did for one of the early Delta label recordings, says it was you who, in 'twenty-seven, got Deeward James to come into the studio with you, and record."

Pause.

"He does, huh?"

"Yeah. Furthermore —"

Feeling like he was getting nowhere, John Grantham advanced the tape, lowered the volume a little, and let the sound of the conversation arise, again, from the now vaguely menacing box in his lap. As the voices emerged from the machine and filled the tiny space in which he lived, they seemed extraordinarily loud.

"You remember, don't you? Those historic sessions you did for the old Rockett label? There were labor disputes going on, at the time, and you made all the musicians in the band join the union before you would go back in the studio."

Pause.

"I did, huh?"

"Sure. Sure! You remember! You were playing a nine-string guitar at the time, and you brought in Dexter Eads for what was billed as a 'Delta Blues Reunion.' You had all the delta blues greats who were still living and still playing!"

"Oh yeah, yeah. Sure. Dexter Eads, old Dexter Eads. 'Dizzy,' we used to call him. I wonder what ever happened to old Dizzy."

"Oh, he died some years back. Down in Louisiana, I think."

"He did, huh?"

"That's right. Lived to be only seventy-two, maybe seventy-three. Never got to be a real old-timer like yourself."

"So that's what happened, huh? Died down in Loo'siana...."

"Yep. Do you remember how they used to make him put a pillow under his feet when he was recording, because he stamped so hard?"

"Hey, that's right! They did! They used to put a pillow under 'im 'cause he stamped his feet so hard! They sure did!"

Pause.

John Grantham pushed the stop button again, lifted his head, and stared idly at the vague, indistinct shapes around him. Was there *nothing* he could remember anymore? He felt along the front of the machine, pushed the fast forward button, and tried again.

"My composition, 'Needlepoint Blues.' Sure I do. I'd have to say that was one a' my favorites, too. Oh, there must a' been a hundred of 'em. But I'm glad you got that list, there, 'cause there's quite a few I don't remember anymore. These days, it seems like my forgetterer works better than my rememberer, *ahhhrrmmmm.*"

He pushed the button and advanced the tape.

"Played for a bunch a' them house-rent parties. Oh sure, I enjoyed that, I enjoyed that quite a bit. We'd be playin' way into the night and eventually into the mornin', and it'd really put you on your mettle, you know, 'cause people would come up and ask you for the darndest things, just about anything they could think up. 'Too Terrible Parties,' we used to call 'em. 'Chitlin' Rags.' 'Skittles.' But other than that, to be perfectly honest, I can't remember."

Again he pushed some buttons.

"No, I don't remember *who* finally took that guitar, whether I sold it to somebody, or what. When I got the damn arthuritis in my fingers, they wouldn't work so good anymore. Wouldn't work like they used to. But sure, sure I miss it."

And again.

"You were askin' before about those nicknames they used to give us. I remember, on the very first record I made, I don't recall the label, they called me 'Anthem.' Anthem Grantham. You see, it rhymes."

"Oh yeah, yeah, I knew that. That's something that gets mentioned in the histories. But I wanted to go back, if I could, John, and prod your memory. See if I could get you to call up anything about –"

The sound of the stop button being pushed, this time, was emphatic and definitive. John Grantham pulled himself forward and placed the tape recorder on the table next to him, then set a large ashtray in front of it so he wouldn't have to see it. With yet another groan of resignation, he slumped back in his chair. That Nelson fella (Nelson, was it? yes, Nelson) had asked him to listen to the tape with the hope that it would jog his memory on certain things. But it was no use. It was just no use. Hearing himself *forgetting* like this, hearing himself unable to remember even elemental facts, was an embarrassment, a humiliation – a trick some little genie was playing on him.

He decided to return to his picture puzzle. That is, if he could find his magnifying glass.

But where was his glass? Reminding himself to step around the faded needlepoint footstool at his feet, he braced himself against the arms of his chair. As he pushed forward, his hand slipped into the crevice next to the seat cushion, or rather, slipped against the hard object that was lodged among the crumbs and shards of foam rubber. Of course. Might have known. *Ahhhrrmmmm.* He pulled the glass out of the hiding place where some demon had decided to hide it, and set it on the little child's table at his right, then pulled the puzzle forward and groped for the first of the pieces that were still floating loose. Nelson must not have realized how blind he was, when he had brought him the puzzle. Not completely blind – they hadn't completely robbed him yet – but blind enough to make the puzzle easier to do by feel than by sight. He ran his thumbs along the tips of his fingers. His calluses had long since disappeared, and although his fingers were too stiff to control the strings of a guitar, they were still better at picking out the details, the sharp edges of things, than his eyes were. He leaned over to the child's table and felt among the gaps in the puzzle, then stroked the edges of the piece he was holding. After a moment he found the appropriate hole, and inserted it. He paused to relish the tiny click it made as it went in, and imagined the precise and perfect coherence of the fit. The next few pieces went in after several more minutes, and that reduced the choices for those that remained. Despite his desire to see the puzzle finished, he took his time, and savored the placement of each piece. Now, after another satisfying little click, the next-to-last piece went in. And that left only the last.

He had known *generally* what the puzzle represented, known all along. Like a picture feeding out of one of those fancy new cameras, he had gotten a sense of it as it was developing. But he could not fully relish and enjoy the image until every piece was in place. Now, with the final piece snapping triumphantly into place, *ahhhrrmmmm,* he reached to his side for his magnifying glass. Raising it and adjusting it to his face, he spread his knees and leaned forward, and began moving it around until he had the clearest focus he could get.

And there it — or rather, he — was. There he was, in that old photograph he hadn't seen for fifty years or more. Why, he had completely forgotten existed. There he was, standing in front of the Willow Club, the Willow was it (or the Sawyer's Favorite? no, the Willow), there he was, big as life, standing in the doorway to that fancy club the night of his first big-city engagement, standing there on the threshold of success. Just look at that fur hat. And the topcoat with the velour collar. And that tie, look at that necktie. The beautiful girl on his arm, look

at her smile. Of course. His first sweetheart, his first real sweetheart; the first woman who ever really meant anything to him.
Oh, what was her name? Stayed with him for three or four
years, went to the gigs, came to the rehearsals, everything.
Dammit, they should have gotten married, the way they always
talked about. Oh, what was her name? Abilene. Emmaline. Something like that.

Like a detective examining evidence, John Grantham
worked his magnifying glass over the puzzle – this photograph
that Nelson had had made into a puzzle for his amusement –
moving it around slowly, patiently, raising it, lowering it, in-
specting the details of his clothing, the reflections on the guitar by his side, the lettering over the nightclub door, the
painted willow tree. But he kept coming back to the beautiful
girl on his arm, kept trying to remember her name.

At last he put the glass down and twisted himself back into
his chair.

And then it came to him.

Nelson would know. He could ask *him*. Nelson had all the
facts, all the answers. Nelson would know.

How curious, he thought, with a twinge of sadness. Nelson
knows more about my life than I do.

TWO THIEVES

I t looked like it was going to be an easy job at first. The house, though not so isolated that their presence in the neighborhood would be noticeable, was set back from the houses around it on a low hill, and the property was bordered by a crumbling snake-rail fence which further suggested an air of abandonment. On the several trips they had made through the neighborhood, using not the van they would use on the night of the job, but one of their cars, they had noticed a patch of dried grass next to the house where a trailer had evidently been parked, and observed that the lights in the upstairs windows were not being changed. The woods at the rear of the yard, they reasoned, would allow them to park on a deserted lane several blocks over, and walk through.

Finally, they had resorted to a bit of subterfuge that had worked well for them in the past. Taking the owners' name off the newspaper box next to the road, they had gotten a number out of the phone book, and dialed it at random hours. Connecting to a voice on an answering machine – hearing not a human voice but a recorded message, no matter what time of day or night they called – they had become reasonably certain they were going to have an easy time of it.

In fact, they became almost cocky in this certainty. Partly to disguise their ruse, and partly to have themselves some fun – so confident had they become – they had placed several messages on the answering machine, each time covering the mouthpiece of their phone with a rag, and speaking in what they imagined were credible foreign accents. On one occasion the first had pretended to be the dispatcher of a cab company asking for a confirmation, and on another the second had purported to be soliciting donations to a charity. After promising to call back, he had done exactly that. The two had shared a chuckle, which eventually turned to outright laughter, after making these calls.

Now the first took the rock he had picked up while sneaking through the woods, and tapped it quietly against a pane of glass on the kitchen door that they had covered with masking tape. While the second cupped his hands to catch any shards that might fall, the first extracted the jagged membrane and exposed a hole. After pulling his sleeve back, he slid his hand through the opening and unlocked the locks.

"Why go in through the basement when you can get in on the ground floor?" he whispered.

"Shsssh!" replied the other.

A glow that came from the front of the house gave them light to see by without otherwise exposing them. They listened for a moment with pricked ears, then gingerly tiptoed forward.

I am not pleased at havin' people yakkin' at me in the middle of the night. That is *not* helpin'."

"Okay. In a minute I'll —"

Tuweeee!

"Mr. Seeley? You know that problem with the flying squirrel I told you about? Oh. This is Helen, Helen Inglewood. In apartment nine. I'm sorry to keep bothering you, Mr. Seeley, but the horrible creature has now found a way in *and* out of my apartment, so that it now comes and goes exactly as it pleases. But I can never tell when it's going to be in, in residence, you might say, so I can't have my breakfast cereal. And if I don't have my cereal, Mr. Seeley, I don't have the strength to go through the day. Are you still there? Have you gone away? Oh dear. Well, it's Helen. Helen Inglewood."

Click.

"You see what I'm sayin'?" said the first, taking out a drawer insert containing pins, buttons, and needles, and feeling around underneath it. "She probably drives this Dooby guy crazy. I think if I were Dooby —"

"Hurry up, Gino! Never mind them! Look under the table. See if there's anything taped on the back of it. They're here somewhere, I know they are. I can practically smell 'em."

Tuweeee!

The man at the bureau glanced at the machine despite himself.

"Mr. Seeley, this is Bill Harris, of Harris Electric. I can't remember when you said you were going away, but I find I got a free afternoon next week and I was wondering whether you'd want me to come over and look at that wiring you said's been giving you trouble. What was it, some suspicious-looking wiring in the basement? Well, I got a free afternoon, so gimme a call. That's Bill Harris, Harris Electric."

Click.

"Gino! For chrissake!"

Tuweeee!

"Mr. Seeley? It's Dave Dubie again. Well, it's starting to get real interesting around here. That old hag downstairs accused me of slipping a *squirrel* or something, into her apartment, and now she's threatening to call the police, that's right, get the police out here. I got a right to play my stereo, Mr. Seeley, and I got a right to have my friends in. But I'm tellin' you, I think you'd better come over and have a talk with her. If you don't, there's gonna be trouble."

Click.

"Will you do me a goddamn favor, Gino? And turn that fuckin' thing —"

"Hey, Dooby didn't do it!" said his partner, glancing at the machine wistfully, then going over and standing in front of it. He studied it for a moment, turned the volume down, and returned to work. "I'm tellin' you, *he* didn't put no squirrel in —"

Tuweeee!

"Mr. Seeley? This is Ralph McKay. In your apartment sixteen. I hate to complain, Mr. Seeley, because you know I like living in your building. But I'm not sure how many more nights I can take of what's going on over here. There's shouting and partying and carrying-on practically every night of the week, and I have to get up and go to work in the morning. I work, Mr. Seeley, and I'm not sure how much more of this I can stand. Can't you come over and straighten things out? Try to restore order? And soon, please? Thanks."

Click.

"You're really somethin', you really are," said the second, staring at his partner furiously. He grabbed some pantyhose and a lacy negligee off the bed, and derisively waved them at the other man. Eventually his thoughts returned to business:

"Believe me, they're here somewhere. I can almost smell 'em."

"What I want to know is, when do we get to us?" said the other, glancing inquisitively at the machine. When there were some aborted clicks and thumps, he returned to work. He took the sewing machine off the sewing table and removed its base and felt around inside it, then got down on his hands and knees and began taking the foot pedal apart.

Tuweeee!

"Carol? Hi. Susan Kelsey. Sorry not to have called you in such a long time, but it's nothing personal, believe me. Maybe I can make amends by saying that some of the ladies are going to play tennis next Friday, and we were wondering if you could join us. Call me if you can, I'm at three-eight-eight, two-eight-eight-one. Hope to see you there! 'Bye."

Click.

"Dammit, Gino. I am not –"

Tuweeee!

"Mr. Seeley? Sarah Posner. You remember, I called you about the apartment that's for rent? The apartment listed in the paper? I'm beginning to get, well, desperate, Mr. Seeley. To be perfectly frank, they won't let me out of the psychiatric treatment center where I am until I've found my own place to live.

But I don't have a phone. Well, there's a pay phone in the hall, but I don't trust the people around me. The people on this ward are filth, Mr. Seeley. Scum. So I guess I'm going to have to call you back. That's Posner, Sarah Posner."

Click.

"Dammit, I know they're here somewhere!" repeated the second. "People who don't hide their silver when they go away don't take their other valuables!"

He went to the large closet at the end of the room and began pawing about among the clothes on the hangers, then yanked some boxes off the shelf above and ripped them open, finally crouched down and fumbled with the shoes and boxes on the floor.

Tuweeee!

"Hi, this is Patty. For Kevin. Hi, Kevin. Are you home? I just thought it would be fun to talk to you. Are you coming back to school soon? I'm not supposed to tell you this, but all the kids miss you. Well, g'bye."

"Yeah, I know what you're sayin'," said the first.

Tuweeee!

"Have I reached Mr. George M. Seeley? Mr. Seeley, this is Lieutenant Harlan Samuels of the Haddonville Police Department. We received a call from one of the tenants in your building last night concerning some kind of melee, or fracas. We responded, and heard a lot of shouting and carrying-on from an apartment on the second floor. We proceeded to apartment nineteen, and found several individuals drinking and smoking marijuana. We arrested, and took into custody two men, Mr. Seeley, one of whom is your tenant, David Dubie. He contacted a bonding agency and is presently out on bail. But call me, please, I need to talk to you. That's Lieutenant Harlan Samuels, Haddonville Police Department. You can call me direct at three-eight-eight, oh-seven-one-five. Thank you."

"Uh-oh!" said the man in the closet.

The two stopped what they were doing and stared first at one another, then at the machine.

"You think the old lady called 'em?" said the first.

"Naw, I don't think she'd do a thing like that. I don't think she'd risk havin' Dooby come down and rough her up, get in her face. It could a' been that other guy, McKay or whatever his name was, the guy that was complainin' about the noise. Now please, do me a favor. Turn that fuckin' thing —"

Tuweeee!

"Mr. Seeley? It's Helen again. You remember, Helen Inglewood? In apartment nine? Well, I guess you heard about what happened last night. And I want you to know I had nothing to do with it, I had nothing to do with the pandemonium — the free-for-all, really — that got the police out here. I know nothing, absolutely nothing about it, Mr. Seeley, and had no part in it. But I feel I *should* tell you that I've had two more locks installed on my door, because I no longer trust Mr. Dubie. And I think it's only fair to ask you to pay for the locks because, after all, this is your building and these are your tenants. Oh dear. Are you back yet, Mr. Seeley? Will you ever come home? Well, it's Helen. Helen Inglewood. Apartment nine."

Click.

"Don't worry, don't worry, we'll find 'em!" said the first.

And walking over to the desk in the corner, he began yanking

out the drawers and dumping their contents on the floor, then
with a violent sweep of his arm proceeded to knock books and
bric-a-brac off the shelves behind it.

"I tell you, I think if I was Dooby I'd give that old lady a
good swift kick in the —"

"But I tell you, it wasn't her!" interrupted the first, his certainty on the subject adding new violence to the sweep of his
arm. "She may be crazy, but she's not —"

Tuweeee!

"Mr. Seeley? Sarah Posner again. You remember I called you
a couple of times about the apartment you have for rent?
Tell me, Mr. Seeley, are you avoiding me? Are you playing
games with me? I don't think it's very polite to put an ad in the
paper for an apartment, then not be home to answer the
phone. I wonder how many other people you're inconvenienc-
ing this way. But I've learned. You people are all alike. The way
you gouge the public. The way you charge exorbitant rents for
your tiny little matchboxes — oh, I've been through this plenty
of times. So maybe I'll call you back and maybe I won't. But I
have to get out of here, Mr. Seeley. I'm desperate."

Click.

The man at the desk stopped sweeping papers, files, and
bric-a-brac from the shelves, and picked up the lamp next to
the answering machine and peered down into its base. The
second was pulling clothes off the hangers in the closet and
feeling in their pockets, then throwing them into a large pile in
the middle of the room.

Tuweeee!

"Hello, George. This is Carol. Your wife. Remember me?
I've been thinking about it George, and I've made up my mind.

I'm not coming back, not until you've decided what you want to do. I'm going to stay up here in the country with the kids. You just decide what you want to do. It's simple. Either she goes, or I go. You just think it over. You can give me a call when you've decided. You have the number."

Click.

"Oh-oh, sounds like there's no joy in Mudville!"

"Poor guy. Got himself in real trouble, ain't he?"

The two thieves were at once more relaxed now, and more frustrated. The first returned to yanking books and papers off the shelves behind the desk, the other came out of the closet and stared at the second bureau, then went and eased it away from the wall and peered behind it. Eventually he went back to the closet.

Tuweeee!

"Have I reached Mr. George Seeley? Mr. Seeley, this is Chief Winslow, Haddonville Fire Department. I'm sorry to report that there was a fire in your building last night. Started in the basement, as far as we can determine. My men got there quickly and did a good job of containing it, and I can tell you that there's not much structural damage to your building. But there *is* some smoke and water damage, mainly confined to the first floor. Several of your tenants spent the night elsewhere, and one of them, a Mr. McKay, I think, intends to move out permanently. Otherwise things are pretty much back to normal, and I wanted you to know that. But call me, please, I need to finish filling out my report. That's Chief Bill Winslow, Haddonville Fire Department. Five-three-five, oh-four-nine-three."

Click.

"Pay dirt!" shouted the second.

He came out the closet waving a tissue-paper bundle tied with a bright red ribbon.

The other turned and smiled.

"Pay dirt!" repeated the second.

Tuweeee!

"Mr. Seeley? This is Helen. Helen Inglewood? In apartment nine? Well, I guess you heard about the fire, last night. Fortunately I'm *all right*, Mr. Seeley, so you don't have to *worry*. And I feel much safer now that Dooby has left the premises. But there's a sort of unpleasant odor in my apartment, Mr. Seeley, and it's not from the smoke, or the wires that burned. When you've returned from your vacation, would you come over and find out what's causing it? Oh, that's Helen, Helen Inglewood. Are you back yet, Mr. Seeley? Will you ever come *home*?"

Click.

"So, you think Dooby set it?" said the first, as his partner began unwinding the ribbon.

"Naw, naw, he's already in trouble with the police. Why would he set a fire when he's already up on a drug charge? That'd be stupid."

"But then, who called the police? I mean, the night they came out and booked him?"

"Got me."

"But look at it this way. Dooby was pissed at the old lady, right?"

"Yeah, but so was that other guy, McKay, the guy that was complainin' about the noise. He was probably pissed at Dooby *and* the old lady."

"Well, there was also the chick who was tryin' to get an

apartment. It sounded like *she* wasn't workin' with a full set a' marbles. She could a' done it."

"But you gotta remember, it could a' been just a wiring problem. A short circuit, or somethin'."

"Yeah, but look at it this way. Dooby had the best motive."

Tuweeee!

Startled, the two thieves turned and stared at the answering machine.

"Hi, George, it's Kathy. Look, George, I'm sorry to tell you this, but your wife's been calling me lately. Calling me at all hours of the day and night. I don't know how she got my number, but I'm not real happy about it. I hate to say it, but I think we should stop seeing one another, at least for the time being. We need to let it rest for a couple of months, let things cool off. Maybe after that we can go back to the way we were."

Hoping this new voice would throw light on the mysteries, the two men stood quietly and listened. When it did not, they returned their attention to the tissue-paper bundle, all the while arguing about who had called the police, and who had set the fire, and whether the flying squirrel had been real or only a figment of the old lady's imagination.

They did not stay around long enough to hear their own voices, however. Leaving the answering machine running, and as they descended the stairs already putting out of mind everything they had heard, they took the jewels and left.

PLAYER IN THE SYMPHONY

T he monumentality of the work is apparent from the very beginning. Deep, rumbling cellos and contrabasses mark the first twenty-one measures of the piece with a long, somber passage of slowly changing harmonies that suggests a gathering up out of gloom and void and darkness of the hesitant, sluggish first sunrise of creation. A brass choir comes in at measure twenty-two — sneaks in, as it were — and extrapolates the opening theme in tones that are at once funereal and full of promise. At measure forty-five, the combined strings and horns are joined by a violin, playing as a harmonic, a single high note that alternately seems sweet and angelic or portentous and full of threat; a muffled roll from the tympani is added. This chord, or tone cluster, is sustained long enough to heighten anticipation, there is a rapidly descending passage from an oboe, a series of grace notes – a glissando almost – and then the whole orchestra comes in with a fiery crash.

So begins one of the most ambitious and grandiose works of modern times, the Symphony in G Minor by Gustave Esteban Spengler. Penned when the composer was almost ninety, the work is conceived on a vast scale and exhibits the harmonic ambition and thematic daring of a much younger man. As a consequence, however, its performance requires a prodigious amount of rehearsal and preparation. Along with a greatly expanded force of strings, woodwinds, brass, and percussion, the score calls for a four-part chorus and soloists, a boys' choir, a chamber ensemble, a pipe organ, and a piano. Spengler, an exile from his native Romania, is known to have contemplated using at least one of all the major instruments in the Western tradition, and among the anomalies of the work – or inspirations, as many critics would say – are the addition of an accordion, guitar, three saxophones, celeste, chimes, and marimba. To manage such a large force two conductors are sometimes employed, and more than one scholar has suggested the desirability of three. The movements are marked *Andante sostenuto e mysterioso – Allegro risoluto; Scherzo; Allegro energico – Adagio;* and *Andante con moto – Maestoso alla marcia – Allegro con brio.*

Except in the fourth movement, the piano is limited largely to percussive bursts of accompaniment and occasional cameo passage-work, but in the final movement, before the entrance of the organ and gathering of forces for the finale, there is an interlude where the piano holds the floor alone and plays – almost as if the piece were a concerto for the instrument –

what amounts to a cadenza. It is a notoriously difficult sequence of measures, in part a recapitulation of what has gone before, in part a statement of new ideas from the composer's seemingly limitless imagination, in part an attempt to make the instrument imitate the orchestra and produce a sheet of sound so thick that individual notes lose all meaning, and it is of this passage that the pianist in the performance just beginning is thinking. Or rather, the pianist is thinking – as he has so often during the previous week – of a little brown footstool. He can see it, a little brown hardwood stool on the sidewalk of a city street, alone and abandoned in the midday sun. What a nice thing to find, he had thought. He could use it in his studio when he had extra students or, alternately, as a plant stand. He had leaned over to pick it up, then realized he was standing in front of a hotel where there was usually a doorman. Was it the doorman's stool, or someone else's associated with the hotel? He had walked to the canopy that extended from the hotel's entrance to the street, peered through the revolving door and back out among the parked cars, and had seen no one. Should he take the stool? Or should he carry it inside to the desk and ask if it belonged to someone? No, that would be silly – banging through a revolving door and across the lobby with a piece of furniture in his hand. Clearly it wasn't his, but had it indeed been abandoned? *If he didn't take it, someone else would.*

The conductor looks his way now, and he inserts the long cantabile phrase that ends in a trill on a high A flat. The situation reminded him of some grotesque toy or novelty item whose manufacturers, whether they saw that it was grotesque or not, must have known that if they didn't produce it, someone else would. Or it resembled the logic of the newest disaster movie; once a plausible sequence had become clear and the next horrifying disaster imagined, if one studio didn't produce it, another one would.

Glancing at his music, he plays a chromatic run in thirds with the clarinets, then hammers out a series of discordant tone clusters with force almost sufficient to bang through the keyboard and to his knees. Orchestra and chorus are in full swing now, and the soprano soloist is making her entry. Or real estate, he thinks. It might be a stand of woods or a vacant lot better left untouched, but each firm said, *if we don't develop it, someone else will.* And so it was destroyed. He thought of the intersection across town that used to be so vibrant and alive with shops, fruit stands, and fence railings on which people hung their paintings and handicrafts. The first bank had decided that there was substantial pedestrian traffic there, and proceeded to build a branch. After they had done so, another bank saw the wisdom of such a move and quickly occupied a second corner. Because people were now associating the intersection with banking, a third institution followed suit. Now, however, it seemed a deficiency for any other bank not to be visible in the area, and the fourth corner had quickly been bought up and converted. And so far as amenities and urban vitality were concerned, that was the end of the intersection. With the corners dead from five o'clock on, automobiles reclaimed it and the life of the neighborhood – and most of the pedestrians – went elsewhere. If only the second bank hadn't followed the first, and the third hadn't imitated the second, and the fourth hadn't followed the third – if only the whole process hadn't started. But no, *if they didn't do it, someone else would.* Fast food franchises, office towers, shopping malls, tract housing....

He plays some treble runs in unison with the altos of the chorus, hears the percussionist give a shake of the sleigh bells above him, enjoys anew the bouncy, *galop*-like interlude which, under the lead of the chorus, seems to make this part of the composition dance along in fields of snow, and turns the page of his music. The thoughts streaming through his mind that are extraneous to the performance are not really thoughts at all, but instantaneous images, feelings compacted into single pictures or, more accurately, flashes. What in words would take minutes to describe is present in his mind only for milliseconds, shooting across his unconscious like atomic particles and leaving as little trace. But they *are* extraneous. The flowers in the public garden, for example. Who would be the first to pick them? Knowing of course that everyone else would, *though no one had done so yet.* And books pilfered from the library, and shoplifting as retribution for high prices, which only contributed to higher prices, and development for the sake of tax revenues — which soon proved insufficient to cover the hidden costs of development. Up and down the keyboard he sweeps, in arpeggiated runs, while the basses hammer at the chord a tritone away and the trumpets blare as if shooting rockets into the audience. The conductor has his hands up, fingers contorted, asking for more, down in the violas music on a stand is covering up a light and someone leans forward to move it. But where did it end, this mania for the next step in bad taste, this fascination with the depth of the next hole? For that is what it was, a hole in the seat of one's pants that one could no more keep from poking a finger in than a cow could keep from chewing its cud. Chewing. Teeth. Tooth. A hole in a tooth – a crevice that the tongue could no more stay out of than a thief out of a till. It was a veritable Pandora's box, this world of temptation. The glockenspiel comes in with its cheery melodic punctuation, and he remembers the time during rehearsal when the percussionist entered a measure too early and had been scolded by the conductor. He turns the page and counts off sixteen measures of rest. Yes, a Pandora's box, a fascination with whatever was behind the next door, no matter how ugly and reprehensible it might be. No one doubted the existence of the world until the philosophers set out to prove it. Things were what they seemed until someone asked how you could be sure that things were what they seemed. He plays a melodic filler that heralds the entrance of the strings. Now everything was investigated equally, everything had its moment of exposure, everywhere people spent their energies exalting the futile and inconsequential, relishing the boring and ugly, reveling in distortion and the distortion of distortion, investing the trivial with nobility and the noble with triviality. *I only wanted to see what others were experiencing, I wasn't interested in it myself,* each said. Could a major power keep from moving into a vacuum, keep from flexing its muscles and extending its influence among developing nations? No. *If they didn't do it, someone else would.* He plays the large polytonal chords that contribute to the long, slow conclusion of the first movement. He thinks of Quig.

The coughing and scratching and shifting of players and audience bring him back to his senses for a minute, enable him to relax. Strings are quietly plucked to allow subtle adjustments in tuning, tubes of bassoons and oboes and clarinets are twisted, reeds studied, spit valves activated. In the chorus, music is shuffled, the risers creak as people shift and change positions, he can hear a quiet tap-tapping on the kettle drums. He muses on all the times he has been positioned up on a stage like this, in a setting of improvised formality among plywood risers and electric cords, and tuxedos and gowns that looked elegant from a distance but swished and shuffled and became unbuttoned up close. And he muses on the noises the audience rarely hears, the scraping on strings, the rush of air from horns, the little clicks and bumps and scrapes of hands and instruments. The conductor looks pleased with the orchestra's treatment of the first movement. He leans over and whispers to the first violinist. Now his hands are in the air. All is quiet.

The pianist comes in *fortissimo* with the rest of the orchestra, then leans back slightly as the basses and tenors go to work. Did actors ever get tempted to think of something else, anything else but their lines? he asks himself. Where did this impish, self-defeating impulse come from, this willingness of the mind to work against its own projects, to self-destruct, to abort? The White Bear Society. Only those were welcomed to join the society who could sit in a room for two hours and not think of a white bear. He had been working too hard lately. He realized that. He hadn't given enough time to Allen, his long-time companion, he had been short-tempered with him, disagreeable. Three recitals in a month plus a part in this symphony: too much. But why, tonight of all nights, was he suddenly afflicted with a failure of nerve? Why had he become seized with fear that in the fourth-movement passage – his moment of greatest exposure – he would hit a wrong note? His mind was playing tricks on him, jumping into mere potential, unrealized possibility. The phrase *nervous breakdown* enters his thoughts and he decides that if he can say the words, the thing itself must not be happening, at least not happening right then. Too much pressure from agents, reviewers, publicity bureaus. He must make some phone calls.

Still obsessed by his impending solo, as some passagework and rhythmic figures move easily under his hands and the boys' choir enters on his left, he finds himself asking the question that has haunted him ever since his days at conservatory. Is perfection a matter of grace, or just plain hard work? Are the long hours of practice sufficient to produce a perfect performance – accurate and faithful, at least, could any performance be perfect? – or is there something beyond that that one could only hope for, never demand? Furthermore, should the question be applied to things? Was an intricately constructed thing – a piano, the other instruments of the orchestra, any man-made object – ultimately just a collection of orderly processes, or at some level of ingenuity was it bathed in mystique? A Stradivarius. A collection of wood, glue, and catgut, or a unique, inimitable work of art? Workmanship. He thinks of the house painters he had noticed, high up on scaffolding, during the remodeling of the performance hall at the conservatory. A windy day, the autumn of his second year. Twenty-five feet up. Working in bluejeans and sweaters, casually dressed, spilling nothing, dropping nothing. Or the young man in the print shop where he often went to have fliers or programs printed: the white pants, white and spotless always, as if to thumb his nose at the press and the cans of ink, as if to thumb his nose at the risk, as if for him no risk existed. Or the repair shop that serviced his car, where machines were given their due, where the work was always done on time and done well. He thinks, finally, of the music building basement where, as a student, he had often gone to practice, of the cacophony of sounds filling the gloomy halls and permeating the walls of the practice rooms, of the many nights he had come upstairs and away from the tentative honks and shrieks, and found the ground unexpectedly covered with snow: quiet, beautiful, and serene. Then a fresh realization comes to him; how had he for so long overlooked this possibility? Perfection was a combination of grace and hard work, it was a *combination*. For the second time, he feels more relaxed, more in control. Nevertheless, he picks up the handkerchief he keeps at the end of the keyboard for his fingers, and mops his brow. *Please, Quig, help me now,* he thinks.

The pause between the second and third movements is not as long as the earlier one, still he has time to inspect the microphones above and among the players, and to watch a technician in the opposite wing making adjustments to the sound baffles. The performance is being recorded live, for the first time, and because it is the premier occasion on which the forces demanded by the symphony have been assembled in their entirety, great expectations are being placed in the result. He thinks of his first piano lessons at his teacher's cluttered house in the tiny town in which he grew up, and remembers the sometimes funny, often humiliating occasions on which he had learned the euphemisms for mistakes — *clinker, clam, oyster, playing in the cracks* — and his mind closes down on the subject, or tries to. The conductor taps for attention and he breathes deeply, the thought leaps up as if out of nowhere of the looming difficulties of the fourth movement, he puts it away, instruments are poised at attention, he flashes on the references to television he had overheard during rehearsal, and the third section of the piece, the *Allegro energico,* is under way. While sound with almost the force of wind pours out behind and around him, and washes over him in waves, a further needling irritation races through his mind. The thing about the show under discussion was that everyone knew it was junk from the beginning. In thoughts that are not thoughts at all, but mere traces of feeling which nevertheless keep exhibiting a strange desire to expand, he recalls how everyone had said how awful the show was, but they wanted to see what other people were watching. He plays a lilting figure in harmony with the celeste and bells. It was no different from a sports audience, a racetrack crowd, say, where people stood up to see better, so the people behind them stood up and then – naturally – the people behind *them,* and soon *no one* could see any better. But did horses ever get it in their heads that they were going to stumble going into the stretch, lose their footing, trip and fall? Become fixated on the possibility, and then for no reason other than the fixation – the possibility – do it? No. Horses were smarter than that. He contributes some percussive tenths simultaneously low in the bass and high in the treble, then the symphony begins to gather out of near-chaos for the modulation to B flat major and the long, sweet *Adagio.* But there was something about humans that could never leave well enough alone, that had to see lawns clipped and manicured, beards teased, historic sites sanitized, natural attractions spruced up. Like those Renaissance architects who had straightened out the streets of Rome, razing precious monuments to make way for horses and carriages. Or the clerics who had whitewashed the walls of ornate churches, windows and all. The phrase *nervous breakdown* enters his mind again, and somehow he cannot dissociate it from the lack of coherence and order he feels around him. I must make some phone calls, he thinks, rid myself of some obligations. Cancel some classes, postpone one or two recitals. But will that put my career in jeopardy? Wooden nickels at the county fair. They had run out of wooden nickels at the county fair he attended as a child, and had begun handing out nutmegs, and everyone had had a great laugh. The following year they had given out nutmegs, but this time when they ran out, they were forced to substitute wooden nickels. And again everyone had had a great laugh. He mops his brow and hands, thankful that the center of attention in the music has moved to the chorus, and away from him. His mind is beginning to steam up, to race, it's become two trains rushing toward one another on the same track, where composure necessitated that one or the other be dismantled piece by piece, bolt by bolt, and reassembled going the other way. All over a possibility, a situation that had not even arrived.

Why do the hands go on? Why don't they just stop, forget where they are and what they're doing, and lift themselves from the keys? The thought plagues him as he glances over the music to his solo during the third and final break. But haven't I taught generations of students that in the moment of performance you must not think, you must trust your instincts? If you study your feet while you're walking, you'll trip. But don't I often look at my hands while I'm playing? He surveys the blur of black dots, of dynamics markings and penciled notations. There is nothing unfamiliar, at least nothing that he can see.

Much of his solo he has committed to memory, and he has bent the corners of the music in such a way that there should be no problem turning pages. Still, certain measures seem new and strange to him. Has he ever really analyzed the gigantic leaps of 402-420, or completely mastered the trills of 438-448? If I am confronted with the possibility of a nervous breakdown and the world exhibits a loss of nerve, am I, then, the world? Yes, I am the world. If I grow nervous and fatigued the way civilization, at certain periods, grows nervous and fatigued, am I then civilization? Am I history? Yes. My birth was at the dawn of civilization, and everything before it – prehistory – is in me unconsciously. Childhood was that archaic period of myths and ignorance, of poems and fairy tales and bedtime stories. I came of age around the beginning of the millennium, developed through strife and turmoil just as history did, had my dark ages, my period of enlightenment, became sophisticated, knowledgeable, urbane. I fought my battles for survival, suffered my unexpected, unprepared-for periods of depression. When I was young, history was young: fresh, new, promising. When I grew old, history became old: slow, weighty, ponderous. Let me see, could I correlate specific reigns, battles, and scientific discoveries with the events of my life? Constantine. Kepler. Ludwig II. The Boer War. The invention of the lightbulb. Gregorian chant. Josquin des Prez. Beethoven. Liszt. Webern. Gustave Estaban Spengler. Ah, but that's the problem, isn't it. The world is where it is today, this minute, but my own time – my own history – has grown sluggish. I have fallen behind, I am still somewhere in the early twentieth century, even the nineteenth. The years have outdistanced me. The world and I are living at different tempi, by different clocks.

He studies the face of the conductor as the conductor scrutinizes the faces in the orchestra and chorus, and thinks, it won't do for him to know that time has outdistanced me. It is fortunate that many minutes are left before my performance, my command performance. Or is it? Would it be better if it were over and done with? He smiles inwardly: In truth I don't have any idea how old I am, each age must be examined individually. He thinks again of Quig, thinks tenderly and wistfully of Jason Quig. Of his childhood in that tiny farming town, of his father plowing the fields first with horse, then with tractor, up and back, up and back, of the bewilderment, then amazement of the neighbors when he began to play sophisticated music on a piano that was always in tune. He recalls how Mrs. Klinges, his first teacher, had arranged for Daniel Slade to come all the way from Gary, and after that how he had taken the train to Chicago twice a month to study with Serge Melmuth. But always, when he came back, there was Jason Quig, plowing the acreage bordering their own. Quig the silent, often sullen one who knew nothing but sowing, reaping, and turning over, getting the cows out, getting the cows in, tending to the calves and goats, taking in the eggs, getting the hay baled and up in the loft. Quig who was not sullen, really, just taciturn, who always had the best vegetables, the best sausage, the best predictions about the weather and the size of the crops. Quig to whose workshop one would go to have farm implements repaired, or welding done.

As the orchestra prepares for the final movement, he runs his hands over the keyboard and remembers the first time Quig, standing in their front room and looking ill at ease, had heard him play. It had probably been Chopin's *Black Key*

Etude, maybe the *Winter Wind*, or Opus 25, No. 12. When he had finished, the man had looked over his shoulder and out the window as if to confirm that the fields were still there, that no one had stolen the setting sun. Finally after a long pause, during which his parents waited hopefully, he had said simply, *Unh huh.* He could not even recall the man's face anymore, but Quig had become the ground and base and standard of reference that had always comforted him, the name for all those in any time or place who went up and back, up and back, bound to the soil and to the labor of their hands, the name for all those who lived in the shadows and darkness of history and, more often than not, were buried without memorial. Quig of the tenth century, the countryside of France, say: as he stood with a hoe and looked toward town, did he appreciate the new style of polyphonic singing called organum? Quig of seventeenth-century Japan, ankle-deep in a rice field: did he appreciate the subtle new developments in Kabuki? Quig of earliest sixth-century Greece, rattling olives off a tree: did he appreciate the reduction of the world, by Pythagoras, to number?

The fourth movement is under way now. So far there are no problems. A garden. Jason Quig in his garden, stooping, weeding in the late-afternoon sun. Coming to the fence to fill their basket with tomatoes, squash, cucumbers. Even after the family had moved into town and opened a hardware store, they would still go out to visit Quig, occasionally the young virtuoso would be asked to inspect letters Quig had written, and correct his spelling. Once it was a confusion between *think* and *thank*, the *i* and *a* being used indiscriminately. *Think* here, *thank* there, he had pointed out. Quig had contemplated him for a long time:

Well, it's pretty much the same thing, isn't it? The family's hardware store had carried the tools and materials required for the
new methods of construction, as well as some of the appliances
the five-and-ten-cent store carried. Again, seeing his father
puttering among the rows of drawers and boxes had set the
standard. There were rules, there was a procedure for buying
and stocking. In order for stove bolts and wire nails to be
where you wanted them, they had to have been ordered,
checked off on the packing lists, and placed in their appropriate bins. Eventually their new home had been equipped with
steam heat, and his parents had been so proud of it that they
had run the pipes up the chimneys and placed the radiators in
front of the fireplaces. The radiators were the new centerpieces
of the rooms.

And what would Jason Quig say now, he thinks, as orchestra and chorus gather for the climax that precedes the entrance
of the piano, *his* entrance. Quig who had faded from his life
after he had gone away to school, but Quig who was with him
always. There were radiators and automobiles and radios and
television and computers and cordless phones, and were people
any happier than they were before? Radio would bring music
such as he was playing – good music – to the world, and its civ-
ilizing influence would calm passions and mitigate war. But
did it? If only they could find a vaccine for smallpox, lives
could be lived with confidence, in health and happiness. And
were they? Or was each new invention, each new improvement, quickly taken for granted, and followed by a hankering
for something else, something more? If Quig were alive right
now, would he be addicted to television?

A tongue in a hole in a tooth.

The orchestra begins the final crescendo on an upward-moving melodic figure that will take it to a peak on an extended dominant, a plateau of expectation on which the piano will enter. But suppose I fail to enter? Suppose I just sit here and stare dumbly at the keys? All man's problems begin when he gets the freedom to do what he wants. But Quig behind a plow, or in his garden? There the rules were clear. There was no reaping without sowing, no reaping without fertilizing, no reaping without turning under. Once the process had begun, the only purpose of man's work was to have it bear fruit; he was the attendant, the supplicant, the instrument of elemental imperatives. He served. But isn't there something in that I can draw from? Doesn't music have *its* rules, isn't even improvisation based on the mastery of orderly processes? Isn't the body an extension of the instrument, the instrument dictating what the body will do? Hasn't years of playing shaped my hands, turned up the tips of my fingers, hasn't pedaling widened my ankles, determined, almost, the way I walk? In certain ways, playing the piano is no different from riding a horse; it makes out of you its own motion. It's a question, so to speak, of being in tune.

He comes in at measure 344 without consciously registering the cue of the conductor. The keys seem reassuringly familiar, his fingers warm and nimble, it's as if he were sifting potting soil through his hands, or playing in garden dirt. Muggy, yes, a little sluggish, perhaps, but precision and evenness of touch are returning quickly. He seizes the moment now, plays broadly and with plenty of wrist action, works his fingers crablike into the legato passages, leans into the keys during the first of the high runs. As the tempo and dynamics increase, he finally lets go, forgets, takes off, soars. He hammers at the notes, he thrashes, he makes sparkles, he caresses. He talks to the piano, he ignores the printed music, he sings the lines, he dreams. Single-handedly – as the composer intended – he tries to sum up nearly two hours of music, tries to exhibit the thematic structure in microcosm, as an echo, a release that will set the stage for the tremendous finale. His part is going by smoothly, masterfully, instrument and player in a single spell – it's over, he has only to run up the keyboard in a lightning-quick arpeggio and land on a high B flat – and then, and then, and then....

He awoke the next morning as if still in a dream, in a bed that seemed unfamiliar. He put on his bathrobe and slippers, hung up the tuxedo that had been thrown carelessly over a chair, retrieved the Sunday paper from the hallway, and made a cup of tea. Eventually he went into his living room and sat down on the sofa, and stared at his grand piano. He had no recollection of his playing during the rest of the performance, or of what the audience's response had been to the symphony, or of what the players had said to one another as they packed up their instruments and filed out. He could think only of the moment his finger had missed the B flat – just nicked the edge of the black note – and come down sharply, squarely on the B. Crushed, humiliated, mortified, he sat in the silent room and stared at his mute piano. He could hear both notes clearly in his mind, and the interval between them. What he could no longer tell was whether the mistake had been a routine one, normal and inevitable in a career as long as his, or whether it was the direct and obvious result of not keeping his mind in order, of not having had the right mental attitude when he sat down to play: how often had he lectured his students on just such a necessity! In the morning stillness he sat and thought, sat and listened, studying the piano, hearing the symphony move along, hearing the fourth movement begin, hearing his own entrance approaching. He heard his part commence, heard the difficult measures going by without error, heard himself approaching the final crescendo, heard the last fateful arpeggio. Then, as if to revise the matter and set the record straight once and for all, he got up slowly, walked to the piano, and at the exact moment when it should have sounded, struck the B flat sharply, once.

He had been a teacher and performer for forty years. Was not an occasional mistake, an occasional failure to live up to the ideal, inevitable? Was he going to let one performance tarnish his career, ruin his life? Would he stay away from the reception that was to be held, that afternoon, on account of temporary doubts and misgivings of which neither the conductor nor the other musicians could possibly have been aware? Close his ears to the provisional tape that would be played out of fear – impermissible in teacher and student alike – of hearing himself? A new day had begun, and slowly his mind adjusted to the fact, began even to relish it. A night's sleep had done wonders, had had a desired restorative effect. He stared thoughtfully at the B flat and at the other keys, then over the surface of the piano, and reasoned that attendance at the reception would not only be professionally appropriate, but would provide an occasion, too long postponed, to be with friends and colleagues.

He took a bath and got dressed, and left the apartment an hour before the party was to begin to allow himself time to walk. It was a gray day, monotone as if one brush had painted both buildings and sky, but one in which warm gusts – the definite harbinger of spring – provided an underlying cheeriness, a bit of hope that all could share. He listened to the varied sounds of the city, and played the game with himself that he often played: If the noises he were hearing were part of a single symphony, how would the music be scored? He remembered the time he had first played the game, how in his apartment near the conservatory he had lain on the couch and tried to integrate into one composition the banging of the steam pipes, the whine of an oil-delivery truck, the distant shouting of children, the squeaking of the sign over the store downstairs, and the music that was playing on his stereo. This, in turn, reminded him of his fantasy that on mornings when the apartment was cold, to simulate the sound of radiators starting up, the superintendent was merely going down to the basement and banging on the pipes with a wrench. Now as he walked through the streets of the city, he listened to a song some children were singing in a playground and, in the distance, the droning of congas. The ancient philosophy of the music of the spheres came to mind, and he toyed for a moment with the possibility that music, the planets – all physical things – were governed by the same mathematical proportions, moved and functioned according to principles which were, at bottom, musical. The world as an orchestral creation, a harmonium of possibility....

Suddenly there was a shriek of breaking glass on his right. From a doorway under a sign saying Agassiz Social Club, a man stumbled backwards, losing his balance and shouting in Spanish, and two others followed, grabbing him by the collar, and before he could fall hitting him again and again, punching him in the face and shoulders. When the man finally fell, his head hit the sidewalk with a loud thump. Instinctively, the pianist curled his fingers into a ball, withdrew his arms into his sleeves, and increased his pace. There was nothing he could do about it, nothing someone twice his strength could do about it. He moved quickly around the disturbance, close to the parked cars, and pretended not to see. But he heard. He heard it once and for all, and for all time: the smack of a skull hitting cement, the monstrous ear-splitting discord, the misplaced howl, the error penned – by what composer? – into the music of the spheres.

It was an inevitable part of city life, and although its echo stayed with him, he did not let it ruin his enjoyment of the reception. The event was a noisy and festive one, held in a large room at a private club, with all the soloists and many of the instrumentalists and chorus members in attendance. When he entered the hall, the conductor, the composer's daughter, and the president of the record company that had taped the performance were clustered in an animated group at the center. He accepted a glass of champagne from a waiter bearing a large tray, and before he could offer his congratulations to several cellists he passed, was complimented by them. In the background, meanwhile, he could hear a tape of the performance being played in an adjoining room. But it was an occasion on which everyone was treating everyone else as the virtuoso and star; what, he wondered, had been the conductor's reaction? When he could do so gracefully, he edged toward the cluster